A GENIUS FOR WAR

A GENIUS

THE GERMAN ARMY

Colonel T. N. Dupuy, USA, Ret.

FOR WAR
AND GENERAL STAFF,
1807-1945

A T. N. DUPUY ASSOCIATES BOOK

MACDONALD AND JANE'S, LONDON

Acknowledgment is made for permission to reprint maps from
the following works:

On page 157, from Winston S. Churchill's *The World Crisis,*
Vol. VI, 1931, reprinted by permission of Charles Scribner's
Sons, New York.

On pages 14, 71, 78, 111, 161, from R. R. Sellman's *A Student's
Atlas of Modern History,* 1952, reprinted by permission of
Edward Arnold, Ltd., London

This book is affectionately dedicated to my son, Charles

CONTENTS

ACKNOWLEDGMENTS

I believe that it is evident that the research, writing, and conclusions of this book are personally peculiar to me and can be blamed on no one else. Nevertheless, I must acknowledge my very great debt to a number of people who have helped me in varying ways and degrees.

I have received useful comments, insights, and criticisms—including some flat disagreements—from so many people that I fear a listing of them might through oversight omit someone. Yet I shall try. Such people include Dr. Fritz G. A. Kraemer, Colonel James E. Mrazek, Colonel Wlodzimierz Onacewicz, Dr. William Emerson, Dr. Hugh M. Cole, Mr. Robert Wolfe, Mr. Richard A. von Doenhoff, Mr. Paul Martell, Mr. Charles von Luttichau, Dr. Rudolph Winnaker, Colonel A. M. Fraser.

Amongst those who have gone to the trouble to read my manuscript and to provide detailed constructive and critical comments are Colonel Frederick Bernays Wiener, Professor Enno E. Kraehe, Mr. Dermot Bradley, Dr. Franz Uhle-Wettler, Professor Theodore Ropp, Mr. David F. Rudgers, and Dr. J. A. Stockfisch. Dr. Uhle-Wettler, Colonel Wiener, and Professor Ropp were particularly helpful, not only in their general suggestions strengthening my thesis, but also in suggesting a number of specific improvements.

Several among my staff and associates at HERO have been extremely helpful. I cannot overemphasize my gratitude to Lucille Petterson in helping me to overcome the formidable handicap of not reading German. She did extensive research in primary German records on microfilm in the U.S. National Archives and in various secondary sources not translated into English, providing me with extensive summaries and exhaustive translations from a mass of documents and books. She then reviewed the manuscript to help me eliminate, we both hope, most evidence of my unfamiliarity with the German language and German usage. Claudia Upper reviewed, summarized, and brought to my attention much of the vast scholarly literature relevant to German culture and behavior. Grace Hayes and Gay Hammerman have brought their substantial editorial skills to bear in helping me to improve the structure, presentation, and clarity of the book; I cannot thank them enough for their contributions. Billie P. Davis—ably assisted by Virginia Rufner and Alicia Boyd—has been responsible for the typing of the several drafts, in the process finding and correcting a number of errors that had crept in.

I am very grateful to everyone who has helped me.

—*T. N. D.*
Dunn Loring, Virginia

Every special calling in life . . . requires special qualities of intellect and temperament. When these are of a high order, and manifest themselves by extraordinary achievements, the mind to which they belong is termed genius . . . a superior mental capacity for certain activities. . . . The *essence of military genius* is to bring under consideration all of the tendencies of the mind and soul in combination towards the business of war. . . . We say "in combination," for military genius is not just one single quality bearing upon war—as, for instance courage . . . —but it is *a harmonious combination of powers*, in which one or the other may predominate, but none must be in opposition.

—Karl von Clausewitz, *On War*.
Book One, Chapter III.

A GENIUS FOR WAR

PROLOGUE
The Riddle of 1944

The year 1944 was one of almost unending disaster for Germany, The greatest and most damaging physical and psychological impact on the German people and on their leadership was the result of the hammering that came from the air. Throughout the year clouds of Allied bombers unceasingly hurled devastation across the length and breadth of Germany, day and night, day in and day out. With the success of Allied naval forces in defeating the U-boats in the Battle of the Atlantic, all hope of successful German economic pressure on the Western Allies was ended.

On the Eastern Front the Russian armies, outnumbering the Germans by force ratios varying from 5-to-1 to 15-to-1, struck one overwhelming blow after another. In the north they drove the Germans from the outskirts of Leningrad back into the Baltic states; in the center they thrust the Germans from the heart of White Russia back to East Prussia and into central Poland; in the south they advanced from the Dnieper River, in mid-Ukraine, to the Danube River and Carpathian Mountains, deep in the Balkans. The German armies seemed unable to stop any sustained Russian offensive.

In Italy a potential German disaster at Anzio in January was quickly arrested by prompt and skillful defensive action. But the German defenders, battered continuously by overwhelming Allied air superiority, were unable to hold back the fresh and rested American and British divisions when they resumed their offensive in May and drove through Rome in June in pursuit of two shattered German armies.

In the West the Germans, again severely hampered by the Anglo-American Allies' total control of the air, were unable to prevent an Allied lodgement on the shores of Normandy. German efforts to rush reinforcements to the coast, to drive the Allies back into the English Channel, were frustrated by the Allied tactical aircraft that swept the roads and railroads of northern France. Under increasing pressure, as vast Allied reinforcements poured ashore onto the Normandy beachhead, the German defensive line finally broke, forcing a precipitate retreat across northern France back toward the German frontiers. By early September 1944, the German armies in the West, pounded unceasingly from the air and closely pursued on the ground, had virtually lost their capability of halting an Allied thrust into central Germany; that thrust ground to a halt short of the German border only because the Allies literally ran out of gasoline.

Yet, by December 1944, the German armies had succeeded in reestablishing strong, formidable defensive barriers in the East, in Italy, and along the Siegfried Line in the West. The Allies retained their vast numerical preponderance in men and weapons; the aerial bombing offensive against Germany continued; there was no doubt that Germany must eventually succumb. But Allied victory, which had seemed so close and easy by midsummer of 1944, was clearly still to be achieved only by long, arduous, costly fighting against a well-prepared, well-equipped, dangerous, effective, and cohesive fighting force.

In retrospect this German recovery seems little short of miraculous. In Germany, in fact, people were beginning to speak of what had happened along the Siegfried Line in September and October as "the miracle of the West." It *was* a miracle, but like the similar miracles in the East and to the South, it had been performed by men—ordinary men whose individual limitations, weaknesses, and shortcomings were now so clear to the Allied troops that they could talk derisively of German "supermen" and of Hitler's "master race." And yet, only part of the miracle had been performed. There was more to come.

Early on December 16, German tanks and foot soldiers began to sweep westward into and through the Ardennes with surprise and power all too reminiscent of the 1940 offensive that had destroyed the French and British armies. Now, in 1944, as advancing German tanks pushed through Luxembourg and ever deeper into Belgium in those dark December days, a panic of sorts spread through Britain and the United States, clearly manifested by black, alarming headlines. Were the Germans, instead of being on the brink of defeat, about to split the Allied armies as they had in 1940? Were they about to drive the British back to another Dunkirk? How could this be possible?

It was not possible, of course. The German 1944 offensive had little of the power of the 1940 offensive. And it was opposed by better armies than those that had been overwhelmed in 1940, armies that in no way reflected the shock and alarm to be found among their families back home. The German counteroffensive, after nearly reaching the Meuse River, was halted, contained, then thrown back with disastrous losses.

There is nothing surprising about the fact that the German offensive failed. What is amazing is the fact that the Germans had been able to undertake such an offensive at all, and to drive it eighty kilometers deep into the lines of an enemy with overwhelming superior numerical and material strength in the air and on the ground.

Actually the offensive had been a terrible strategic mistake and hastened Germany's inevitable defeat. The German military leadership knew that their efforts were doomed to failure. But they had been ordered by the Führer to undertake the operation and they obeyed. It is doubtful if any other army in history, under circumstances at all comparable, could have been equally responsive to command.

How and why could these defeated armies fight so well? How and why could they halt the apparently irresistible simultaneous advances of their victorious and overwhelmingly powerful enemies into Germany from east, south, and west? How and why could these shattered armies, their homeland battered into ruins behind them, regroup and mount a major counteroffensive which even temporarily defeated far larger, better-equipped, confident foes?

This was the riddle of 1944. It was a riddle whose solution lay in Germany's past and whose implications were of concern to any man—soldier or civilian—who might one day have to fight in defense of his own country. But, human memory is short. Americans, in particular, like to look ahead, not back. So, whatever urgency there was to learning from the riddle of 1944—learning about Germans, about Germany, and about the reasons for their exceptional military excellence—faded in the post-war decades.

Then suddenly, many years later, I found it necessary to cope with this riddle. This need arose from work I was doing—with considerable assistance from associates in the Historical Evaluation and Research Organization (HERO)—in developing a quantified model of historical combat, starting with a data base of some sixty engagements in the 1943 and 1944 operations in Italy in World War II. I began this work with the assumption that when the Allies landed at Salerno, in September 1943, the Germans were probably about 10 percent more efficient than the Allies because of their combat experience. It seemed logical that by the end of the year the Allies had probably overcome this initial disadvantage, and so I assumed—on the average—equal combat effectiveness for both sides, Allies and Germans.

In proceeding with my model development, I began to notice an interesting phenomenon. By assigning arbitrary weights to the effectiveness of airpower (practically all of it on the Allied side, of course), I could usually get mathematical model results reasonably consistent with the actual outcomes. The trouble was that when Allied airpower had not been present, or had been present only fleetingly, the model results could not be reconciled with the actual outcomes. In these cases, according to the formulas, engagements that the Allies should have won had actually been *German successes.* Another and related phenomenon was that in those cases in which the model found the forces so evenly matched that inconclusive outcomes seemed reasonable, in fact, the Germans invariably won, whether or not Allied airpower had figured prominently in the model calculations.

It soon became evident that the Germans needed a larger weight per man or per unit than the Allies and that a corresponding adjustment was needed in the weight assigned to airpower. It had become obvious that I, as a retired American ground-force officer, had brought two professional prejudices with me to the formulation of my model: I had underestimated the effects of airpower, and—even more serious—I had underestimated the fighting qualities of German soldiers.

As the model results were refined and meticulously compared to the actua outcomes of the various division-size engagements that I was modeling, became evident that, on the average, German units had had a 30 percent comba effectiveness superiority per man over the Americans and British at the time o the Salerno landing, and that this superiority had only dwindled to about 2 percent by mid-1944. There were substantial combat effectiveness difference within the national contingents—British, American, and German—but the overal comparisons were quite constant. On the average, a force of 100 Germans wa the combat equivalent of 120 American or 120 British troops. Further refine ments in the model began to reveal that in terms of casualties the differentia was even greater, with German soldiers on the average inflicting three casualtie on the Allies for every two they incurred. This relationship—a 20 percent com bat effectiveness superiority, and a 3-to-2 casualty-inflicting superiority—was found to be still in effect during the 1944 fighting in Normandy and France, and as late as December 1944, at the time of the Germans' Ardennes offensive.

Interestingly, I began to notice that commercial war games marketed for entertainment—products of such firms as Avalon Hill and Simulations Publi- cations, Inc.—had found various ways to represent the greater combat effective- ness of German troops in their games based on World War II historical battles. They had to do so, of course, to permit results reasonably faithful to the actual outcomes.

A less detailed analysis of World War I battles suggested that during that war the Germans had enjoyed a similar 20 percent combat effectiveness superiority over the Western Allies, and also the same 3-to-2 casualty-inflicting superiority, during most of that war. Only toward the very end of that earlier war did fresh American troops approach parity with the Germans—described in our intelli- gence reports as "tired and depleted."

As I shared these results of World War I and World War II combat analysis with other people, I discovered two things:

First, soldiers who had had ground-combat experience against the Germans in either or both of those wars were not particularly surprised by my results. (I had fought in Burma against the Japanese.) The reaction of most (although not all) of these people was "So, what else is new? Of course the Germans were better soldiers than we were; how else could they have fought for so long against such odds?" I also found that these former soldiers who had fought the Germans were particularly impressed by the resilience, imagination, and initiative demon- strated by German soldiers at all levels.

The other thing I discovered was that among many people who were not veterans of the war against Germany, my model results were viewed with a combination of suspicion and restraint. Such people generally assumed that I had inserted some kind of a "fudge factor" to get results that would make the model fit preconceived concepts of reality; given such a "fudge factor," of course, the validity of my German-Allied comparison would automatically be in doubt. Furthermore, they would argue, what difference did it make? Technology had so changed warfare since 1944 that examples from such ancient history had little or no relevance to combat in the 1970s.

Since many of the people who held the research purse strings in the Pentagon were among the doubters, I could find little support and no funding for my belief that it is important for American military men to find the answers to two questions which my research results seemed to demand: Why were the Germans so much better at soldiering than we were? How did they achieve their combat excellence?

Since I could not get official sponsorship for the research which I felt—and still feel—is of importance to the military security of the United States, I decided to write this book.

The pages that follow, then, represent an effort to provide at least preliminary answers to these questions. Without the research resources in time and money which the scope and complexity of the subject demand, this book can only be a start to the answer. It cannot be considered as a definitive analysis of German military performance either in the two World Wars or in the prior historical period. There are many aspects of the German experience—historical, sociological, political, cultural, economic—which demand much more attention than I have been able to devote to them in the four years in which this book has been in preparation.

Yet I am reasonably satisfied that I have found the general answer to my basic questions. I am convinced—and will seek to show—that the Germans, uniquely, discovered the secret of *institutionalizing* military excellence. And if I seem in any respect to be right, I hope that my fellow historians may probe deeper and find the detailed answers that have been beyond my limited capabilities. Above all, if there are military security implications—as I so firmly believe—in such areas as management, training, and decision making, then let us explore those with particular vigor and intensity.

Chapter One

THE INCONSISTENT MYTHS

 MILITARISM AND DISCIPLINE / During the latter half of the nineteenth century and the first half of the twentieth, one factor consistently influenced European affairs: Prussian-German military excellence. The importance of other factors— such as Britain's maritime primacy, America's growing economic power, and Japan's rapid rise in East Asia—waxed or waned in the calculations of world diplomats. But the military prowess of Germany was always rated high and was feared, even when actual German military strength was low, as in the decade immediately after World War I.

Not since the time of Sparta has a state or a people been so identified with military activity as were Prussia and the Prussians (or after 1871, the German empire and German people, dominated by Prussia). This was true despite the fact that in the 130 years following the Napoleonic wars, all the other European great powers were engaged in many more wars than was Prussia-Germany.

This Prussian reputation for militarism gave rise to two widely held beliefs that have contributed to the creation of stereotypes of Germans and German characteristics that are as inaccurate as they are persistent.

The first of these beliefs is that militarism is an inherent element of the German national character, that, as *The American Heritage Dictionary* defines it, "glorification of the ideals of a professional military class" is really an inborn character trait practically universal in the people of the Prussian-German state. The second belief is that the Prussian military system was based upon a harsh, rigid discipline, which produced soldiers who were efficient but unimaginative, regimented, and inflexible. From the two beliefs comes the stereotype of the uniformed, goose-stepping German, whose outstanding ability to perform only routine tasks efficiently is vulnerable to frustration by quicker-thinking, more imaginative individualists of Anglo-Saxon or Latin descent. This is an image neatly dramatized, sometimes with slapstick emphasis, in numerous offerings of cinema and television; *Hogan's Heroes* is typical.

The first belief, while oversimplified, is probably consistent with the thinking of most Americans: The Germans, as we see them, are inherently military and are naturally good soldiers. The second belief, also oversimplified, nonetheless

is also consistent with views held by most of us. The regimented, inflexibl
Germans tend to be at their best when there is no demand for imagination o
initiative. Thus the beliefs seem to support the stereotype.

But do they? Is it possible without imagination or initiative to be a goo
soldier, to perform well in war, to be honored for military excellence? A
moment's thought about the demands of battle and war, of the qualities tha
have brought military success in history, will make it clear that there is a funda
mental inconsistency between these two beliefs. More to the point, the over
whelming weight of historical evidence is that neither of these beliefs can be
substantiated. Both are supported by that great enemy of history, the half-
truth.[1]

History suggests that until the middle of the eighteenth century neither the
Prussians nor the Germans in general had an international reputation for special
military talent. In fact, a much more convincing case for special military apti-
tude could be made for the French or the Swiss, and most eighteenth-century
Europeans would have unhesitatingly classified these as the most "militaristic"
nations on the continent. For that matter, a better case can be made that the
British or the Irish or the Scots or the Swedes or the Spanish or the Turks or the
Mongols were militaristic, than can be made for the Germans before about 1750.

The ancient Greeks were the first Europeans to become heavily involved in
the mercenary soldier profession. During the Middle Ages the most notable
practitioners of the trade were English "free companies" hiring themselves out
to any European ruler who needed a few tough, skilled, organized fighting men.
Also active were the condottieri of Italy, who hired Englishmen, Germans, and
Frenchmen—as well as Italians—as the soldiers of their armed bands. For reasons
that are partly social, partly political, partly economic (and only very slightly
military) the English "free companies" faded from the European scene as feu-
dalism faded in England. The English mercenaries were succeeded in the soldiers-
for-hire profession by others, particularly the Swiss, who were probably the best
military businessmen of all time. The excellence of the Swiss mercenaries, and a
number of defeats at the hands of French invaders of Italy, hastened the decline
of the condottieri, but the Swiss were still active in this trade when the Thirty
Years War made mercenary soldiering a profitable occupation in Germany. It is
interesting to note that at the outset the German *Landsknechte* imitated the
Swiss closely, and learned much about discipline and drill from the tough Alpine
mountaineers.

The Swiss pikemen resented the German imitation of their tactics and
techniques—and probably resented the economic competition. So they were
always eager to fight the *Landsknechte,* in order to demonstrate to European
royalty that Switzerland had a superior product. Interestingly, there seems to be
no recorded instance in which a German mercenary unit was able to beat a Swiss
force of comparable size; the Swiss were invariably victorious, or at worst had a
drawn fight.[2]

There was nothing exceptional about the German mercenaries, but the practice continued longer in Germany than elsewhere for reasons that were almost completely economic. Since it was still a competitive business, the petty German princes who hired out their soldiers naturally made certain that they were well trained and well disciplined. A quality product meant more sales, and money was scarce in eighteenth century Germany.

There is, unquestionably, a modern German military tradition, traceable in part to the survival of the military mercenary trade in Germany into the eighteenth century, but even more directly stemming from the exceptionally good Prussian armies of the early Hohenzollerns, and the even more exceptional use of those armies by Prussian King Frederick II, the Great. Yet it was a comparable Prussian Army—every bit as well-trained and well-drilled as Frederick's had been—that was led to a humiliating defeat by Frederick William III in 1806 when he tried to teach some lessons to an upstart French ruler. That upstart happened to be Napoleon, and he destroyed Frederick William's army in one brief day of battle on the fields of Jena and Auerstadt. Lest that be considered an exception, it should be remembered that Napoleon's next to last battle, nine years later, was a clear-cut victory over a numerically superior Prussian army at Ligny, two day before Waterloo.

Thus history does not support a long tradition of exceptional German military performance before the eighteenth century, and it suggests that the excellence of the Prussian Army between 1750 and 1815 was, at best, relative. Nor did contemporaries perceive the Germans as exceptional soldiers. The idea of Prussian-German militarism is, in fact, largely a nineteenth century creation. Furthermore, responsible behavioral scientists confirm a historically based conclusion that, despite certain cultural traits contributing to military efficiency, the Germans do not possess inherent, genetic qualities which make them superior soldiers.

It is interesting to compare the military activity of Prussia-Germany with that of some other nations during the century and a third following the Napoleonic Wars, from 1815 through 1945, the period during which Germany's modern military reputation became established. During those 130 years, Prussia and Germany participated in six significant wars (two of them minor), plus some internal military activity in 1848, a few relatively minor interventions elsewhere in Germany, and some colonial expeditions overseas.

It is not easy to compare this Prussian-German record of military experience with that of nations such as the United States and Russia, both of which were engaged in endemic frontier conflict during about half of the period. It is also difficult to compare this record with that of the earlier colonial nations like France and Britain, which were almost constantly involved in some kind of colonial pacification and expansion during most of that time. But if we omit all except the most serious of these frontier or colonial conflicts, meaningful comparison is possible.

During those same years France was engaged in ten significant wars, of which six were fought on the continent of Europe and four overseas. Russia was engaged in thirteen major wars, ten of which were essentially European conflicts. Great Britain was engaged in at least seventeen conflicts worthy of being called wars, of which three were fought in Europe, four primarily in Africa, and ten in Asia (including two against China, two against Burma, two against Afghanistan, and four in India). The United States during this period was engaged in seven significant wars, if the Second Seminole War and the Philippine Insurrection are included. As to minor colonial or frontier operations and armed interventions in other countries, there is no question that the respective involvements of Russia, France, Great Britain, and the United States were all much more frequent, and considerably more intensive, than those of Prussia-Germany.

If the Germans were not unique or particularly outstanding as mercenary soldiers, if they were far from uniformly successful in warfare during the seventeenth, eighteenth and early nineteenth centuries, if they engaged in fewer wars than most other major powers, and if there is no solid scientific basis for an inherently militaristic German character, in what sense can we say that the Germans were militarists?

A collection of half-truths, and some selective historical examples, have created the myth of inherent German militarism. Clearly there are cultural influences which contributed to German military capability both before and since the nineteenth century, but these influences cannot in themselves explain the modern German military reputation, nor the exceptional performance on which that reputation is based.

HISTORICAL PARADOX / It may be that the Germans have a flair for organization and disciplined—even regimented—behavior. But is it possible to reconcile the Germans' reputation as exceptional soldiers (and the German record of performance in modern wars) with the undoubtedly stifling effects of unyielding regimentation and inflexible discipline? Has the German reputation for military excellence been earned despite lack of imagination, despite feeble initiative? Can German victories be attributed to some kind of overwhelming German military steamroller, and German defeats be explained by lack of resourcefulness?

Not on the basis of historical record.

Yet the German reputation for regimentation and discipline is as pervasive as is that of military excellence. Is one of these reputations seriously distorted? Or is there some other factor which explains and reconciles the paradox?

Possibly the answer can be found in a review of recent German military history. But first, a glance at the performances of Germans in the American Civil War may provide a useful perspective for such review.

The Federal XI Corps, commanded by Major General Oliver O. Howard, was popularly known throughout the Army of the Potomac as the German Corps. A majority of its officers and men had been born in Germany, and had come to America after the political upheavals of 1848. Many of them had had military service in Germany.

The Germans of the XI Corps had a reputation in the Army of the Potomac for doing well in spit-and-polish inspections. At both Chancellorsville and Gettysburg their combat performance was dismal.* General Meade was considering the possibility of disbanding the Corps when, late in 1863, he was directed to send two corps to join Grant at Chattanooga. In time-honored military practice Meade solved his problem by sending the XI Corps to Grant. The corps had another chance to gain distinction at the Battle of Lookout Mountain. Soon after that battle Grant took the action Meade had ducked; he disbanded the corps, amalgamating it with another, to dilute its German content.

The only other instance of performance of German-American troops in the Civil War specifically noted in the Index of *Battles and Leaders of the Civil War*, was at the Battle of Reams Station, in June 1864. There, elements of General John Gibbon's 2nd Division of the II Corps broke and ran in the face of a firm attack by A. P. Hill's Confederates; most of the misbehaving troops were German-American conscripts from New York.[3]

It would be an insult to the many German-Americans who have distinguished themselves in America's wars to suggest that these examples are typical of the military performance of Americans of German ancestry. They do suggest however—as do many other examples—that Germans as Germans are not necessarily above-average soldiers. Culturally and genetically the men of the XI Corps were the same as the Germans who were simultaneously conquering Central Europe.

If there is an explanation for the historical fact of modern German military preeminence, it must lie not in the men, but in the structure of the German military establishment. Let us therefore take a look at what that structure was and how it came to be.

---

*Gray, John C., Jr., and John C. Ropes, *War Letters of John Chipman Gray and John Codman Ropes,* Boston: 1927. For instance (on p. 114) Ropes wrote to Gray on May 29, 1863, about Chancellorsville: "The enemy attacked the Eleventh Corps . . . with a force and suddenness which carried all before them, especially as the German troops showed great cowardice. . . ." On page 145 we read a letter Gray wrote to his sister, Elizabeth, on July 17, about Gettysburg: "The Eleventh Corps . . . has disgraced itself past redemption. . . . The feeling against this Corps is . . . intense in the Army . . . ; no terms are too strong to express their contempt. In spite of all the newspapers say, they did not behave well at Gettysburg (at least the German divisions did not). Their conduct was not so bad as at Chancellorsville, but still it was not even decent. Beside they have the worst reputation for stealing and all manner of outrageous conduct towards the citizens. Many of the men and most of the officers do not wear the Corps badge, though in all the other corps it is universally worn. . . ."

NOTES TO CHAPTER ONE

[1] The author must give credit for this epigram to Sewell Tyng, in his masterly *The Marne Campaign* (New York: 1935).

[2] See Charles Oman, *A History of the Art of War in the Sixteenth Century* (New York: 1937).

[3] *Battles and Leaders of the Civil War* (New York: 1888), p. 573.

Chapter Two

FREDERICK THE GREAT & THE PRUSSIAN ARMY

 BACKGROUND OF PRUSSIA / Prussia first appears in the pages of history in the early Christian era as the home of the Prussi, or Prussians, a tribe of Balts inhabiting the lands bordering the southeast corner of the Baltic Sea. During the thirteenth century, the tribe and its region were conquered, Christianized, and colonized by the religious order of the Teutonic Knights. In the following century these German-speaking soldier priests were able to hold Prussia, more or less successfully, against pressures from the Slavic Poles to the South and Slavic Russians to the East. The subject Prussians became Germanized in speech and culture. After the defeat of the Teutonic Knights by the Poles and Lithuanians at the Battle of Tannenberg, 1410, the order lost its lands west of the Vistula River, but retained, as a fief of Poland, most of the coastal and inland region between the lower Vistula and lower Nieman rivers—a Germanized area known first as the Duchy of Prussia and later as East Prussia.

In the first of many paradoxes of modern Prussia, that state's political origins were totally unrelated to the region from which it later got its name. Modern Prussia began its political existence as the margravate, or mark, of Brandenburg, a landlocked province of the Holy Roman Empire in northeastern Germany, lying generally athwart the middle Elbe and middle Oder River valleys. Its importance and its fortunes increased in the early fifteenth century, after the Emperor appointed as Margrave a faithful South German nobleman, Frederick of Hohenzollern. Soon Brandenburg became an Electorate of the Empire, and Frederick's feudal rank became Elector. While influential in North German affairs, Brandenburg had no special military reputation under the early Hohenzollerns. However, through chance and the complicated workings of feudal family inheritance, the Duchy of Prussia was inherited by Elector John Sigismund of Brandenburg in 1618.

The combination of Hohenzollern and Prussia in the person of John Sigismund's son, George William, did not seem to be either politically or militarily propitious. In fact, during the early years of the Thirty Years War, he became the military laughingstock of Germany. George William had neither the military

:rength nor the leadership nor the determination to prevent Catholic and Protestant, Imperial and Swedish, armies from wandering across his territory retty much as they wished to.

PREDECESSORS OF FREDERICK THE GREAT / However, George William's on, Frederick William, who became Elector in 1640, decided that Brandenburg hould stop being the doormat of Germany. Since neither Brandenburg nor Prussia had natural, defensible frontiers, he determined to build up an army that was stronger than that of any of his neighbors. This took some doing, but Frederick William was a strong and able man, and he did it; in consequence, he is known to history as the Great Elector. His son, grandson, and great-grandson all inherited some of the talents of the Great Elector, as well as the same indefensible frontiers. So they kept building up and improving their armies, and trying to push those frontiers just a little bit farther away from Berlin, midway between Elbe and Oder. There was nothing militaristic about this. It was simply a question of survival in the political jungle of Central Europe. And Brandenburg-Prussia was fortunate enough to be ruled for more than a century by a series of exceptionally able, exceptionally single-minded rulers, who learned long before Leo Durocher that "nice guys finish last."

Frederick William's son, Elector Frederick III, obtained the approval of Holy Roman Emperor Leopold to become a King in 1701. But since Brandenburg was a part of the Empire, Leopold preferred to have Frederick take his title from a portion of Hohenzollern territory outside the Imperial frontiers. Thus Frederick III remained the Elector of Brandenburg, while also taking the title of Frederick I, "King in Prussia."

The second King "in" Prussia, Frederick William I, was one of the "characters" of history. He is best known for two peculiarities. First he kept a collection of human giants whom he used as members of the royal guard. Second, he imposed, and came very close to enforcing, a sentence of death on his eldest son—rendered by military court, at the personal direction of the King—as punishment for "desertion" since the Prince had tried to escape his father's tyranny by flight to England. This episode had confirmed Frederick William's opinion that the Crown Prince was an effeminate weakling and an unworthy successor of a line of soldier-kings. On top of this, Frederick William created, but carefully avoided using, the best-drilled army in Europe.

FREDERICK THE GREAT AND HIS ARMY / The unworthy Crown Prince who was almost beheaded was Frederick II, known to history as Frederick the Great. In 1740, he took the unambiguous title of King *of* Prussia. He was, unquestionably, one of the seven or eight greatest military geniuses of history. But in 1761, after fighting a series of brilliant, but only marginally successful, defensive campaigns against armies outnumbering his by more than five to one, Frederick was physically and morally defeated, and his country was on the verge of collapse. The situation appeared to be hopeless. He was saved not by his own

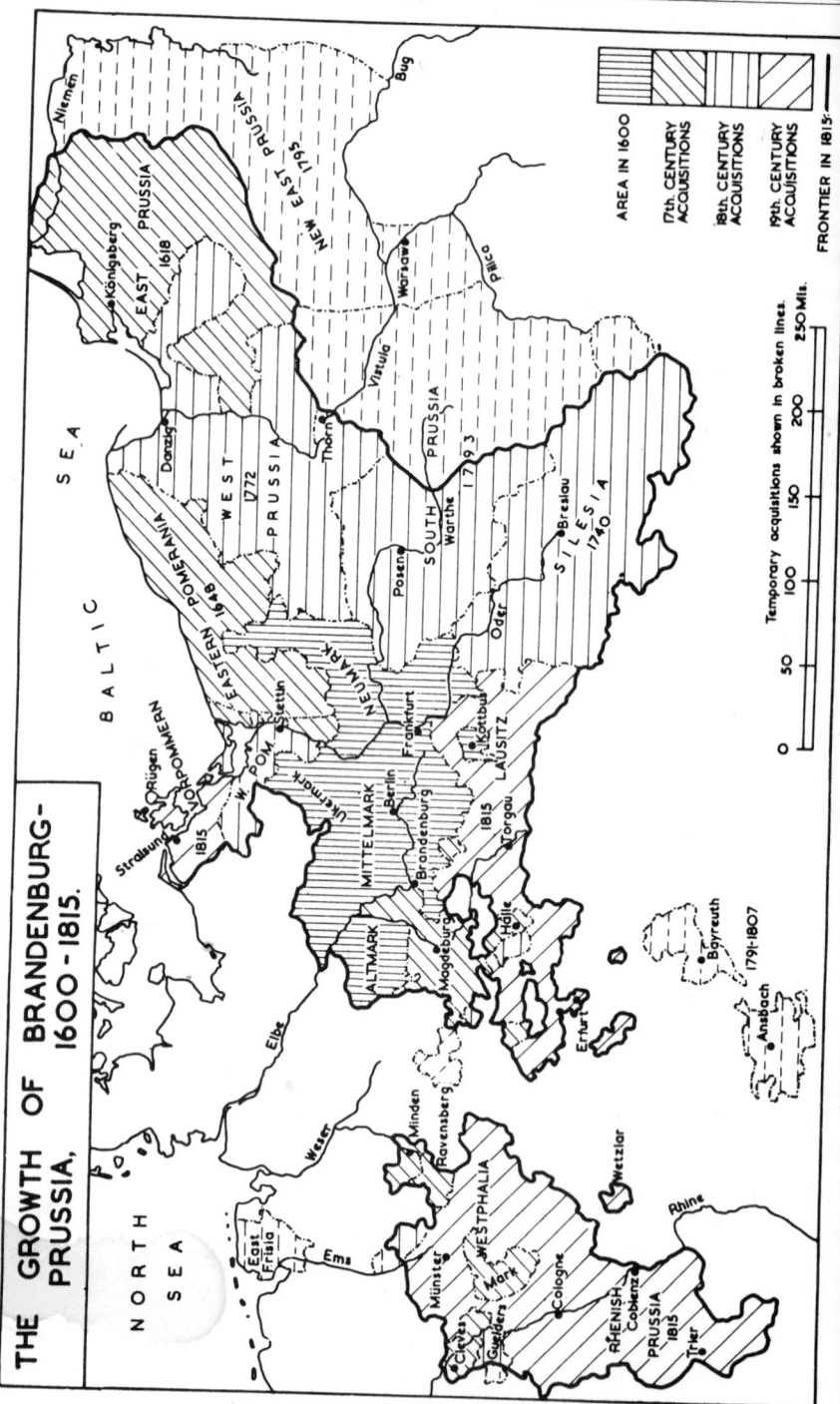

enius—although that had helped him considerably in the previous desperate years—but by the death of one of his most implacable enemies, the Empress of Russia.

The new Czar Peter III, an admirer of Frederick, made peace, and changed sides in the war to join Frederick against his other enemies. These facts are significant to demonstrate that, while Frederick had exceptional military talent, he was not a superman, and his soldiers were not supermen. Until most of them were killed off, they had been merely a bit better trained, a bit better led, and much more brilliantly directed than their enemies.

"The German Army begins with Frederick the Great," says Herbert Rosinski in his splendid historical analysis, *The German Army*.[1] Unfortunately this assertion—so widely accepted—cannot stand up under scrutiny. One can argue that the army that Frederick commanded so well had been established by his great-grandfather, Frederick William, the Great Elector, or by his father Frederick William I. In either event, Frederick's army was inherited, and he changed it little. And that army, whoever created it, was literally destroyed by Napoleon, who *was* an innovator. A new Prussian Army arose from these ruins, and while it received much inspiration from the memory of Frederick's great victories, it would be more accurate to attribute the origins of that new Prussian Army to Napoleon or—more properly—to the reaction of his Prussian enemies, who learned a new system of war from the French Emperor.

PRUSSIA'S EIGHTEENTH CENTURY MILITARY REPUTATION / Yet, despite these undeniable facts, Frederick the Great and the rulers of the eighteenth century German principalities had a significant effect not only upon the subsequent reformers of the Prussian Army, but also on modern German military history. A number of historical developments gave to the small West German principalities a virtual monopoly on the military mercenary trade in the late seventeenth and early eighteenth centuries. This fact, combined with the efforts of the early Hohenzollern kings to improve their army, caused the Prussians to succeed the Swiss as the most respected soldiers in central Europe.

Frederick himself wrote: "The greatest force of the Prussian Army resides in its wonderful regularity, which long custom has made a habit, in exact obedience, and in the bravery of the troops. . . . Prussian discipline renders these troops capable of executing the most difficult manuevers, . . . and . . . surpassing the enemy in constancy and fortitude. . . . The Prussians are superior to their enemies in constancy since the officers, who have no other profession nor other fortune to hope from except their arms, animate themselves with ambition and a gallantry beyond all test, because the soldier has confidence in himself and because he makes it a point of honor never to give way."[2]

Further evidence of the special eighteenth century reputation of Prussia and the Prussians can be found in the famous quotation from the Marquis Honoré de Mirabeau's book, *The Prussian Monarchy under Frederick the Great*, 1788: "War is the national industry of Prussia." And there is also the famous statement of

Baron Friedrich Leopold von Schrötter, a senior Prussian government official about ten years later: "Prussia is not a country with an army, but an army with a country."

Thus, by the latter half of the eighteenth century, the military ascendency of Prussia in central Europe was generally recognized, both in and outside Germany. Yet some thoughtful men also recognized that this was essentially a temporary ascendency due to the remarkable talents of four great Hohenzollerns, and that it was not likely to last beyond the life of the last and greatest of these, Frederick the Great. For instance, Count Jacques A. H. de Guibert, the famous French military theorist, wrote in 1779 in his *Defense of the Modern Military System,* "In that state which we call military because its King is an able soldier . . . they owe their successes to the ignorance of their enemies and to the cleverness of their King, and to a whole new science of maneuver, which he created. If, after the death of that King, whose genius alone sustains the imperfect edifice of the government, he is succeeded by a weak and untalented King, we will see the Prussian military degenerate and wither in a few years; we may see that ephemeral power rejoin that medium rank warranted by its real means, or perhaps pay dearly for its few years of glory."[3]

These prescient words were undoubtedly familiar to the men who, a few years later, were responsible for attempting to raise a new Prussian Army from the ashes of defeat. It could even be asserted that the principal reason for the excellence of the modern German Army—successor of that new Prussian Army— was the fact that its creators deliberately made sure that this new army was *not* that which Frederick the Great had bequeathed to his successors.

As predicted by Guibert, those successors—childless Frederick's nephew, Frederick William II, and great-nephew, Frederick William III—lacked the strength of will and the military aptitude that had been such marked characteristics of Frederick, of his father, and of his great-grandfather. They inherited from Frederick, as he had inherited from his predecessors, the finest army in Europe. But, as we have seen, that army was destroyed by Napoleon at Jena and Auerstadt. Some remnants of the old Prussian Army lingered on, but those that were not forced to surrender as a result of Napoleon's vigorous post-Jena pursuit were crushed early the following year at Friedland.

NOTES TO CHAPTER TWO

[1] Herbert Rosinski, *The German Army* (New York: 1940), p. 61.

[2] "Frederick the Great's Instructions to His Generals" in *Roots of Strategy,* edited by Thomas R. Phillips (Harrisburg, Pa.: Military Service Publishing Co., 1940), pp. 312, 313. The exact date this was written is not certain; the first edition of this document was issued secretly to Prussian generals in 1747.

[3] Jacques A. H. Guibert, *Defense of the Modern Military System* (Paris: 1805), Vol. I, p. 91.

Chapter Three

THE REFORMERS & THEIR NEW ARMY

 SCHARNHORST / One man was more responsible than any other for building a new Prussian Army on the ruins of the old: Gerhard Johann David von Scharnhorst. In another Prussian paradox, Scharnhorst was not originally a Prussian; he was born on November 12, 1755, at Bordenau, in the tiny principality of Lippe, fifteen miles north of Hanover, son of a farmer who had served as a noncommissioned officer in the Hanoverian dragoons. After attending the Cadet School of Count William von Schaumburg-Lippe, by 1778 young Scharnhorst joined the 8th Hanoverian Dragoon Regiment as an officer-cadet, and became a second lieutenant in 1784. His ability—which could never have been recognized in the aristocratic Prussian Army of Frederick the Great—brought him promotion in the early French Revolutionary campaigns of 1793-1794 in Belgium. Soon afterward, as a major in his early forties, he became the principal staff officer of the Commander in Chief of Hanover's Army.

With Europe at peace after the Treaty of Luneville, in early 1801, Scharnhorst recognized that there was little chance of further promotion in the Hanoverian Army. His combat experience against the French in Belgium, and what he had read about the campaigns of French General Bonaparte in Italy and Egypt, made him realize that the French had begun a military revolution of significance comparable to the political and social revolution that had stormed the Bastille and overthrown the Bourbon monarchy. He apparently saw in Prussia the one source of military strength in Germany to offset growing French power. He began to express these convictions in pamphlets written for his fellow officers. These writings on military affairs began to gain respectful attention throughout Germany, and not least in Prussia.

In 1796, Hanover provided 15,000 men to help protect the Empire's border against the French. Duke Karl Wilhelm Ferdinand of Brunswick was the Commander in Chief, and Scharnhorst served under the Prussian Quartermaster General. This assignment brought Scharnhorst into frequent contact with Prussian officers. In January 1797 Scharnhorst received an invitation to join the Prussian service, where he was offered a post as major and much higher pay than

in the Hanoverian Army. Hanover countered with a promotion to lieutena
colonel and a salary supplement, so Scharnhorst stayed with Hanover. But t
Prussian offer was repeated, and in June 1801 Scharnhorst transferred under t
condition that he retain his seniority, be assured a good pension, and acquire
patent of nobility. He was appointed a lieutenant colonel in the Prussian Fie
Artillery Corps, and assigned to the 3rd Artillery Regiment at Berlin. He w
ennobled in December 1802.

At first he dealt primarily with artillery matters, but soon he was placed (
the staff of the Quartermaster General—the principal military staff assistant '
the King—and was directed to reorganize the Officers' Military Institute
Berlin. He quickly raised the level of the course of instruction, transforming tl
institute to a more respectable Academy for Young Officers in 1804. At tl
same time, with approval from the Quartermaster General, General Lewin vc
Geusau, he also established a military-discussion society for officers stationed i
and around Berlin.

Although Scharnhorst soon stimulated much interest in organizational an
doctrinal matters among young Prussian officers—including Karl von Clausewitz
one of his Academy students—he found that he was making little headway wit
the senior officers. In March 1804 he was appointed Deputy Quartermaste
General, and given command of the Prussian Third Brigade, in the western par
of Prussia. When in 1805 Prussia slowly began mobilizing for the inevitable wa
against Napoleon, Scharnhorst was appointed Chief of Staff to the Duke o
Brunswick, Commander in Chief of the Prussian Army, but was unable to effec
any major changes in the Army's thinking and doctrine.

There were two principal reasons for Scharnhorst's failure, one personal, the
other institutional; both were typical of the Frederickian Prussian Army. In the
first place the aristocratic officers of the Prussian Army looked down upon
Scharnhorst's peasant origins and his freshly issued patent of nobility. Contributing to the aristocrats' contempt was Scharnhorst's unprepossessing appearance,
his lack of the imposing martial bearing that was supposed to characterize the
Prussian officer. Second, the newfangled ideas of this Hanoverian bookworm did
not jibe with the military fundamentals which, in lieu of bookish education, had
been inculcated in Prussian officers for more than a century. The Prussian
officers' principal aim was to keep their soldiers subjected to the iron discipline
considered so important by Frederick and his father, and to drill themselves and
their men to be able to perform perfectly the maneuvers which had brought
victory to Frederick at the Battles of Rossbach and Leuthen in 1757. Never were
the German qualities of regimentation and discipline more clearly exemplified
than in the army which the Duke of Brunswick took out to meet the French in
the fall of 1806. Scharnhorst sadly accompanied that army to suffer what he
knew would be defeat.

JENA-AUERSTADT / The Duke of Brunswick was mortally wounded in the
Battle of Auerstadt, on October 14. That evening, as the shattered remnants of

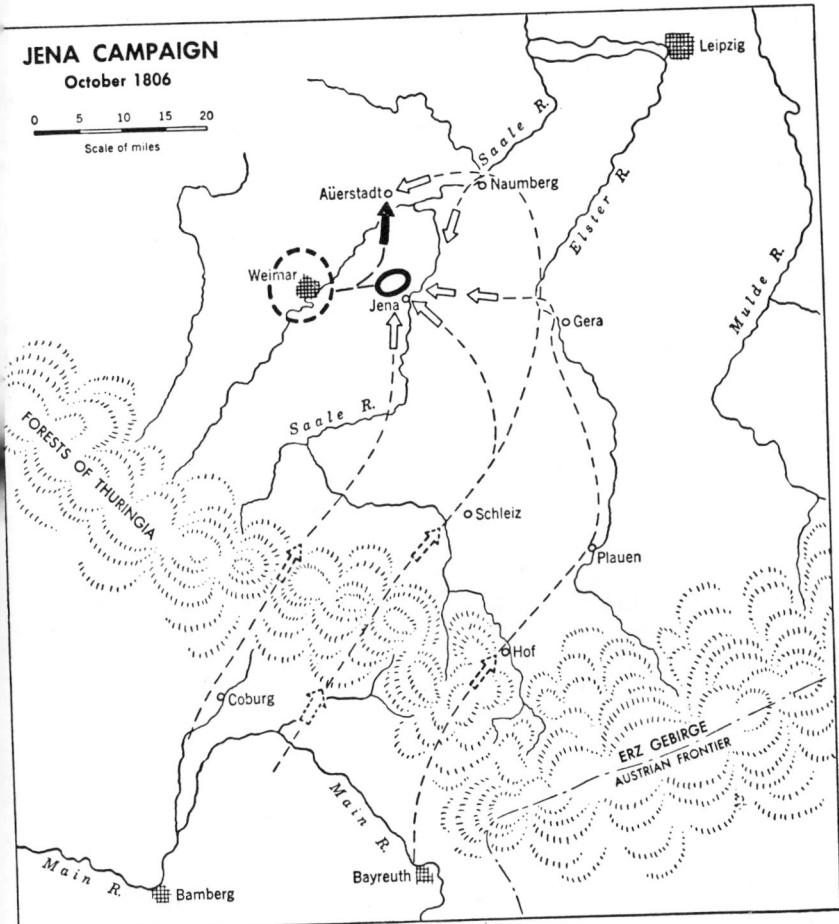

JENA CAMPAIGN
October 1806

0   5   10   15   20
Scale of miles

Leipzig

Saale R.

Elster R.

Mulde R.

Naumberg

Aüerstadt

Weimar

Jena

Gera

Saale R.

FORESTS OF THURINGIA

Schleiz

Plauen

Hof

Coburg

ERZ GEBIRGE
AUSTRIAN FRONTIER

Main R.

Main R.

Bamberg

Bayreuth

the Prussian Army streamed off that battlefield, to join others fleeing from Jena farther south, Scharnhorst reluctantly retreated just ahead of the French skirmish line. He joined one of the few units retaining some cohesion, the division of General Gebhard Leberecht von Blücher. Pugnacious, hard-fighting Blücher retreated northeastward, then northwestward, to Lübeck, closely followed by the pursuing French. Finally, on November 7, when Blücher's troops ran out of ammunition, he and Scharnhorst were forced to surrender. Meanwhile, pitiful remnants of the Prussian Army had retreated with King Frederick William to East Prussia, where they were joined by a Russian army that had belatedly moved to support its Prussian allies.

In an exchange of prisoners a few weeks later, Scharnhorst was released. He joined the one remaining army corps of the Prussian Army, commanded by General C. Anton Lestocq. Serving as Chief of Staff with Lestocq's corps, part of the army of Russian General Levin A. von Benningsen, Scharnhorst was largely responsible for the timely arrival of the Prussians on the blizzardy field of Eylau, transforming a Russian defeat into a drawn battle. In the defense of Königsberg, during the disastrous Friedland Campaign, he gained further favor with King Frederick William III, who observed him frequently.

STEIN AND THE MILITARY REORGANIZATION COMMISSION / Thus it is not surprising that after the humiliating Peace of Tilsit, on July 25, 1807, Scharnhorst—now a Major General—was named head of the Military Reorganization Commission appointed by the King.

Most of the members of the Army Reform Commission were typical officers of the old Prussian Army—poorly educated aristocrats, usually dominated by one or more Junkers* from East Prussia, still convinced that the solution of all military ills was stronger discipline and more rigid doctrine. Their early mistrust of Scharnhorst had not been diminished either by the fact that his dire predictions had become fact or that he had performed well in disaster. But two members of the Commission—like him, non-Prussians—shared Scharnhorst's iconoclasm, and his determination that the reforms should be fundamental, not cosmetic. One of these, the only civilian on the Commission, was the Prime Minister, Baron vom und zum Stein, whose monumental efforts to reform the entire Prussian governmental system gave him little time to join in the military discussions, but who insisted on being a member in order to demonstrate his dedication to new approaches in military affairs. The other was Colonel August Wilhelm Anton Count Neidhardt von Gneisenau.

---

*The term *Junker* stems from a corruption of *Jungherr,* "young master," which was used of the sons of landed gentry who resided on the family estates. It came to denote, often in a derisive sense, members of the East Elbian landed gentry. This group, particularly favored by law, provided the bulk of the leaders of the Prussian Army and the civilian bureaucracy. The term actually carried over into some military titles; for example, *Fahnenjunker* was an officer candidate, and is still the title for an officer candidate in the West German Army after six months of enlisted service.

Stein, a native of the principality of Hesse-Nassau, had been trained for the imperial administrative service. As a young man, he had joined the Prussian government, and he had risen through various levels of local and regional government to become King Frederick William's principal Economic Minister and adviser in 1804. He fled from Berlin to Königsberg in 1806, after Jena, and soon became the most influential member of the rump government there in the winter of 1806-1807. When, early in 1807, he bluntly told Frederick William that the ministers should be freed from interference by the courtiers in the King's personal cabinet, he was dismissed by the outraged monarch. After Tilsit, Napoleon insisted that Frederick William dismiss his Prime Minister and recommended Stein as the replacement. (Napoleon, obviously, had been informed only of Stein's efficiency and his non-Prussian origins, and was unaware of his patriotic dedication and the implications of his ideas for reform of the Prussian government.) Swallowing his pride, Frederick William did as Napoleon suggested, and thereby took the most important possible step toward perpetuation of Hohenzollern rule of Prussia for more than another century.

GNEISENAU / Gneisenau came from a noble but improverished South German military family, tied closely to Austria. He was born at Schilda, near Torgau, on October 27, 1760. His father was an artillery officer in the Imperial (or Austrian) Army. After brief attendance at the University of Erfurt, young Gneisenau served two years in an Austrian cavalry regiment (1778-1780). In 1780, when he was barely twenty years old, he joined the service of Ansbach. This tiny principality based its economy mainly upon the military trade, and in 1782 young Gneisenau was shipped off to Canada with a mercenary contingent hired by the British government in the closing months of the American Revolutionary War. When the contingent reached Halifax, the war was over. After a little more than a year in North America, he returned to Ansbach.

In 1785 Gneisenau applied directly to King Frederick II for a commission in the Prussian Army, and received his appointment the following year after a meeting with the King. For twenty years he remained an obscure company officer, on garrison duty in Silesia. He earned a reputation as an excellent commander, but there were no promotion opportunities, and he was still a captain commanding a company at Jena. Cool, calm, and courageous in defeat, despite being wounded, he led his battalion off the field in good order. He was with those elements of the Army that escaped to East Prussia after the disaster. The reputation he gained in the retreat led to Gneisenau's promotion to major. In April 1807, he was selected to be sent by sea to take command of the beleaguered Pomeranian coastal town of Kolberg. He held the town against repeated French attacks until after the Tilsit armistice. Thus he gained great popularity and the King's favor, as the only successful Prussian commander of the war.

Rosinski describes this man, destined to play such a major role in the recreation of the Prussian Army:

Gneisenau . . . differed as profoundly from [Scharnhorst] in personality as he resembled him in character and fundamental convictions, his hatred of Napoleon and his faith in the resurrection of Prussia; he formed the ideal complement of his chief. A great, impressive, martial figure, the very prototype of a warrior hero . . . he was essentially a man of action rather than of the pen. In the open field, where his enthusiasm and energy, his quickness in seizing the fleeting opportunity, the daring of his plans and actions were able to assert themselves, he was in his element; yet . . . Gneisenau was anything but a mere dashing soldier [and] he combined an unusually well-trained and brilliant intellect with an emotional poetic temperament."[1]

THE TREATY OF PARIS AND THE REFORMERS / Not long after the Military Reorganization Commission began its work, Napoleon's spies brought the Emperor information about its activities and the objectives of its three principal members. He also learned from spies and from intercepted letters how seriously he had misjudged Stein. As a result he demanded that Frederick William dismiss Stein and install a weaker Prime Minister. Then, in the brutal Treaty of Paris, in 1808, Napoleon imposed terms that he believed would prevent any revival of Prussian military strength. The Prussian Army was to be limited to 42,000 officers and men. The soldiers were to be long-service volunteers, and no national militia or any other form of reserve force was permitted.

Thus Napoleon prevented Scharnhorst from putting into effect two important reforms he had in mind. He was not only unable to establish a national conscription system, under which the manpower of the nation would be trained, he was also precluded from creating mobilization procedures that would permit this trained reserve to be called instantly to the colors in time of war.

Despite the failure of Scharnhorst's first plan for fundamental change in Prussia's military system, and despite the loss of Stein's support, Scharnhorst was making headway. He had been able to replace three of the old-line conservative officers on the Commission with younger men of his own choice and by 1808 had a scant majority of like-minded reformists. One of these was Lieutenant Colonel Count Friedrich Wilhelm von Goetzen. The others were two young Majors: Karl von Grolman and Hermann von Boyen. Both of these men had been students of Scharnhorst's at the Academy, and both had distinguished themselves in the recent war against the French. After Count Goetzen was sent to command in Silesia, another former student, Captain Karl von Clausewitz, serving on Scharnhorst's personal staff and as Secretary of the Commission, became virtually a member.

These, then, were the five soldiers, who are known rightly to German history as "the Reformers": Scharnhorst, Gneisenau, Grolman, Boyen, and Clausewitz. Jointly they created a new Prussian Army, and collectively they were responsible for laying the foundations of the military excellence that characterized Prussian and German armies for more than a century.

Although all five shared in this responsibility, it was not distributed equally among them. Greatest was Scharnhorst, an especially gifted and intellectual soldier, the leader, the thinker, the indispensable driving spirit of reform. His spark of genius was extinguished by early death in 1813; he received a minor, but eventually fatal, wound at the Battle of Lützen.

Animated by that spirit, as well as by their own exceptional qualities of intellect and constructive energy, the other four contributed significantly to the early successes of reform, and carried on after Scharnhorst's death. Of these, by virtue of seniority, as well as his inherent qualities of leadership, battlefield coup d'oeil, and moral force, Gneisenau became the most important.

The contributions made by tall, angular Grolman were many; most of them were organizational and conceptual, as will be seen. But perhaps his most important contribution was made during the dark night of June 16, 1815, at Ligny, where Napoleon had once more beaten the Prussian Army. Commanding General Blücher was missing, and presumably dead, and Gneisenau's soaring spirit was for once completely crushed. Yet Grolman persuaded Gneisenau not to issue orders for retreat, but rather to march to join Wellington at Waterloo.

Steady Boyen was the man who had the opportunity to ensure, by personal participation and direction, that the most significant and vital elements of the reform program were in fact carried out, or at least brought to the threshold of fruition. Serving first as virtual Chief of the new General Staff, and later as War Minister, Boyen became an implementer as well as a far-sighted planner, and in time of crisis was recalled as War Minister in his old age, to preserve the institutions he had helped to conceive and to establish.

Young Clausewitz proved to be less a doer than a thinker. This was not because of lack of energy or of operational capacity, but rather a result of the fortunes of war and peace. Unquestionably he is, and always will be, the best known of the five Reformers, his fame secure as the most profound of all military philosophers and writers on war. His record as a soldier and as a man of action was impressive, but brief, in the years immediately following the work of the Commission. His influence on the institutions which emerged from reforms cannot easily be assessed, for a number of reasons which will be noted later. It is unquestionable, however, that his influence was great.

When King Frederick William III appointed the Commission, he sincerely expected that it would produce reforms. Certainly the shattered Army needed new administrative organization. The serious losses of territory under the terms of the Treaty of Tilsit demanded a realignment of the unique canton system, which had been created by Frederick William I and which related the active units of the Army to geographical regions. The events of 1806 had demonstrated a need for an improved staff and command system. Obviously the excellent performance of Scharnhorst himself demonstrated the need for some concessions to bourgeois demands for representation in the officer corps. The King seems to have thought that uniforms should be redesigned, and he was reconciled to an increased budget for more generous rates of pay. Reforms of this kind were substantial and demanded serious consideration. But the end result would have been merely the installation of a modern veneer over a fundamentally unmodi fied army of the early Hohenzollerns.

The five Reformers were determined that the results of the Commission' work should be more drastic and far-reaching than the kinds of change antici pated by Frederick William. Their objective, formulated as their work pro gressed, was a fundamental realignment of the relationships of the Army to the State, to the people, and to the King. There was a simple and essentially military rationale for these drastic politico-military and socio-military objectives. Al though it was only hinted at in the writings of Scharnhorst, and probably not discussed among the Reformers with complete candor, nevertheless, from what they said, what they did, and what they wrote this rationale can be expressed as follows:

Single-minded, determined, and intelligent organizational talent probably can create an effective army from any group of men. The Greeks and Mace donians did it; the Romans did it; two of the English Edwards did it; several French monarchs had done it; Gustavus Adolphus had done it; Frederick the Great's predecessors had done it; and Napoleon had done it recently for the French. But a magnificent army in one generation could not be frozen in a mold and remain equally formidable in a subsequent generation, even if it was faithful to the model in every detail. Human affairs are dynamic, technology changes weapons and equipment, armies must change with the times. When one organi zational talent follows another—as was true of the early Hohenzollern kings of Prussia—then the army will remain dynamic and will change, even if the general pattern remains the same. But when mediocrity follows talent, and the pattern remains the same, decay is inevitable.

So, too, in the operational direction of an army. As Hannibal, Frederick, and Napoleon proved, ordinary generals and ordinary armies cannot easily defeat a genius, even when his army is not as good as theirs. But an operational genius, leading an army created by an organizational genius, is virtually invincible—as was proved by Alexander, Julius Caesar, Gustavus Adolphus, and more recently, by Frederick the Great and Napoleon.

Thus, Scharnhorst and his companions decided that Prussia needed a system under which—insofar as was humanly possible—the Prussian Army would be created by organizational genius and led in battle by operational genius. But how could such an idealistically simple aim be achieved in a world of fallible human beings, among whom genius is rare and utterly unpredictable? While they might not have said it, they must have been thinking of the military ineptitude of the successors of Frederick the Great. Yet certainly as loyal Prus sian officers they had no thought of trying to modify the law and tradition of royal succession.

THE GOAL: INSTITUTIONALIZED MILITARY EXCELLENCE / The Re formers' answer was unique and proved to be earth-shaking: They would try to *institutionalize* genius—or at least try to perfect a system that could perpetuate military excellence through the vagaries of change. Scharnhorst, in fact, once expressed his thoughts on this quite explicitly:

> Normally it is not possible for an army simply to dismiss incompetent generals. The very authority which their office bestows upon generals is the first reason for this. Moreover, the generals form a clique, tenaciously supporting each other, all convinced that they are the best possible representatives of the army. But we can at least give them capable assistants. Thus the General Staff officers are those who support incompetent generals, providing the talents that might otherwise be wanting among leaders and commanders.[2]

Scharnhorst did not, of course, mention that the General Staff might also provide a source of talent wanting among royalty. Such a sentiment could not have been written at that time in Europe, particularly in Prussia. But his readers must have understood what he meant. Certainly the other Reformers did. In any event, the staff procedures which he had organized with the assistance of the other Reformers were certainly a move in this direction. After Napoleon's final defeat at Waterloo two years later, Gneisenau and Boyen, following Scharnhorst's half-completed pattern, established the first true Army General Staff in history. This was to be the key institution, and Gneisenau and his successors turned all their efforts toward finding ways to ensure that it would have the built-in means to maintain the quality of excellence.

The Reformers were not creating an entirely new concept, or even a new terminology. Rather, they were carrying existing concepts and terms to a logical, but never-before-visualized, conclusion. And in the process they were resolving some of the ambiguities which had beclouded all previous military concepts and terminologies. Staffs had existed at least since the days when the Egyptian pharaohs first marched organized armies onto the pages of history. The staff had always been a two-way communications link between the army's commander and the subordinate fighting units. For most of history the staff had consisted merely of a few aides-de-camp, to carry messages back and forth and to keep the commander informed of events that were happening beyond the range of his personal vision. To these aides had been added, over the ages, some clerks to keep records, to write and copy orders, and to make and carry maps. Sometimes the commander's staff would include an especially trusted friend, or subordinate officer, to help him make the difficult decisions; sometimes this adviser, when there was one, would be a respected older man, no longer fit for the rigors of field service, but still capable of giving advice of experience and time-ripened wisdom to a more vigorous but less experienced younger commander.

As armies grew in size, and as weapons increased in complexity, there developed several levels or echelons of staffs. Regimental, brigade, division, and corps commanders required the same kinds of support and assistance, both in dealing with lower levels of command and in responding to the orders of superiors in the chain of command. And so, to make clear the distinction between these subordinate staffs and that of the general commanding the army, there had grown up in the eighteenth century the practice of referring to the latter as "the General's staff."

Also, during that same century, as standing armies became common in peace as well as in war, it had become evident that an overall system was needed, to administer and maintain the peacetime army, as well as to assure its readiness for war. To distinguish this continuing peace-and-war staff from the operational staffs of field armies and lower commanders, and to describe its general, nonoperational functions, these centralized staffs were called general staffs. Since most nations had only one field army, and since the operational staff of the general commanding that army in war was usually made up of the same individuals who performed the more general, nonoperational functions in peacetime, more often than not "the General's staff" was also "the general staff."

In Prussia the peacetime general staff was called the Quartermaster General's Staff, since it assisted that principal administrative staff officer of the King in the performance of his advisory and administrative functions in peace and war. The Reformers, all of whom had served on this Quartermaster General's Staff, saw in it the mechanism for putting their revolutionary ideas into practice, so as to have the best possible army created in peacetime (through the mechanism of "organizational excellence"), and to have available a group of well-trained, well-prepared, carefully selected officers (to assure the "operational excellence") to advise the King in wartime.

This was the rationale and the concept for creating a new Prussian Army. What was needed to make it work?

A PEOPLE'S ARMY / Even if the winds of change unleashed by the French Revolution had not been sweeping new ideas of freedom and popular political responsibility across Europe, the Reformers would have wanted to find ways of making the Army a people's army, for which the Prussian people would have affection, a feeling of association, and a feeling of community of interest. Pervasive popular indifference had greeted the French invasion in 1806. It had been almost as though the common people of Prussia looked upon this as the King's war, fought by the King's army, a conflict that meant little to them except higher taxes and the unpleasant necessity of supporting the armies as they passed across the countryside. The popular disinclination to help the Army resist the invaders, and the rash of desertions that had further reduced the effectiveness of the defeated army after Jena-Auerstadt, was viewed with particular concern by the Reformers.

The absence of a popular feeling of identification with the army might have been a satisfactory state of affairs in the mid-eighteenth century, when a paternalistic state was controlled by a benevolent despot like Frederick the Great—a military and governmental genius capable of brilliantly exercising control. In the early nineteenth century, however, the old paternalism would not do either in political or in military affairs. Napoleon had succeeded in harnessing the new forces of freedom under dictatorial control—but even though he, too, was a genius, it was evident to the Prussian Reformers that his success might well be transitory. At least between 1808 and 1812 they were doing their best to see that it was.

All five of the Reformers were well-educated (although to some extent self-educated), liberal intellectuals—quite different from the vast majority of marginally educated aristocrats who wore the uniforms of Prussian officers.* For all of the strong loyalty these thoughtful men felt to the King and the institution of the Prussian monarchy, they welcomed Stein's plans to respond to, and carry still further in Prussian political life, the concepts of responsible liberty that had been spread by the French Revolution and by Napoleon's armies. Thus they were intellectually and emotionally sympathetic to the concept of the constitutional monarchy that Stein had hoped to create through military reforms, and saw this new political system as an essential concomitant of their idea of creating a new Prussian Army that would be the army of the people as well as the army of the King. They believed—and quite rightly—that a responsible Prussian electorate would be a patriotic citizenry, who would enthusiastically support and contribute to any army which they could look upon as *their* army.

The creation of a people's Prussian Army was both a political reform and a military necessity. But, the Reformers realized, it was a major social issue as well. They were aware of the importance of discipline in any fighting formation. But they saw that discipline would have to be changed to an instrument of control, not a tool of terroristic repression. The need to use disciplinary fear to inspire soldiers to fight would disappear if the Prussian Army were made up of citizens who viewed the King's and the Army's cause as their own. Discipline, a firm, just discipline, would be necessary to assure order, responsiveness to command, and organizational efficiency. But the other side of this disciplinary coin was justice and fairness—treatment and conditions of service that a citizen could and would demand, not the serf's life that had characterized the Frederickian Prussian Army.

Essential to such a transformation of the old Army to a new people's army was assurance that the opportunity to rise to positions of command was not

---

*As to the educational standards and competence of the Prussian officer corps, and particularly of the dominant Junkers, the evidence is contradictory. Frederick the Great, being strongly interested in philosophy and under the influence of the Enlightenment, had taken steps to raise the educational standard of the officers, especially among the cadet corps and the young attendants at court, setting standards which were apparently much higher than was normal in those days. We know the education of 157 of those officers whom Frederick promoted to general's rank. Of these, seventy-four had had secondary education (many of them university), fifty-two had been members of the cadet corps, and forty-three had been pages as attendants at court. Certainly the collective intellectual competence of the five Reformers was high above the standard of the ordinary officer—followers and opponents of the Reformers alike. But how different would this be today? There is no clear evidence whether the normal officer was better or worse educated than the officer of other nations. On the other hand, there was a very strong anti-intellectual sentiment in the Army, a deep suspicion of those officers who had gained exceptional education, and a tendency to consider education in general as evidence of "softness" unbefitting a Prussian officer. (I am indebted to Dr. Uhle-Wettler for facing up to this controversial issue.)

limited to the accident of birth, but was the reward of merit. While Scharnhorst must have felt the importance of this even more than his four associates, all recognized the essential need for this basic reform. One of the principal weaknesses of the old Prussian Army had been Frederick the Great's policy of keeping the officer corps closed to everyone save the nobility, and demanding from these aristocratic officers little more than bravery and obedience. This was adequate so long as the Commander in Chief was a genius who could do all of the thinking necessary to exercise command over a relatively small army. Scharnhorst recognized that bravery and obedience were important qualities for officers, but in a mass army, in which leadership was to be exercised by example and esprit, rather than by regimentation and brutality, the aristocracy must be one of the intellect rather than of birth.

EMERGENCE OF THE GENERAL STAFF CONCEPT / Such a reform, incidentally, would be an incentive to performance by officers and men alike, at all levels of the Army. It would be a reward for ability and for education. It would open the ranks of leadership to a far larger proportion of the population. It would place pressures upon aristocrats to seek the education they had hitherto disdained, in order to be able to compete with the commoners. And in so doing, it would greatly increase the availability of qualified men for the new General Staff, the organ which was to play so important a part in the Reformers' scheme for the new Army.

That General Staff, as the Reformers visualized it, would be a collection of the best and most experienced minds of the entire Army, so organized and dedicated that they could collectively function as a single, coordinated brain, but always be fully responsive to the commands and desires of the Commander in Chief, within the constitutional limits of Stein's political reforms. This was to be done in both systematic and dynamic ways. New General Staff officers would be selected from the brightest of the young officers of the Army. They would be educated carefully and intensively to replace older officers as they lost their sharpness and faded into retirement. The chief of this elite group would be the individual who combined the best in experience, education, imagination, vigor, and intellect. He would not be the Commander in Chief, since that post would still be reserved for the monarch, even under a constitution. But the advice and information that the Chief of the General Staff could give to the King, and the assistance that he and the Staff could also provide in the exercise of command, were expected to assure that wise decisions could and would be made by the least able of monarchs, and that even if a headstrong ruler were to make a blunder, the Staff would be able to retrieve it.

Finally, as an essential element in the transformation of the Army from an instrument of autocracy to an institution of the people, there was the delicate and touchy question of the relationship of the Army to the King, and to the new constitutional government which the Reformers took for granted as an essential political concomitant to their military reforms. A true people's army must not only owe allegiance to the King; it must also be responsible to the constitutional authority which represented the people. This they knew was a concept that would be unacceptable to a majority of the hidebound noblemen of the Army's officer corps. And there was evidence that, despite his sincere desire for reforms in the Army, Frederick William III, as a Hohenzollern monarch, would brook no interference in his command of the King's Army by any other branch of government.

THE KING'S ARMY / The Reformers were only partially successful. Frederick William III was willing to go far in accepting their innovations, even though many of these—particularly those permitting the rise of bourgeois elements in the officer corps—were personally distasteful to him. He remembered Jena and the apathetic acceptance of foreign conquest by the Prussian people too well not to realize that he had to accept some of these innovations if he was to retain his throne—to say nothing of hoping some day to regain his lost provinces. But he would not give up to the people control over the Prussian Army—*his* Army. It was all well and good to grant greater freedom and rights to the people, he obviously told himself, if this would strengthen the nation politically and economically, and would encourage popular support of the Army. But suppose all of this freedom and all of these rights went to the people's heads? The Army must remain his; and even though the officer corps was no longer the exclusive preserve of the nobility, the King was determined that he should be able to select as his principal military subordinates members of the nobility who were as dedicated to the monarchical institution as he was.

The work of the Military Reorganization Commission did not go on in a vacuum. As their recommendations were submitted—and sometimes approved, sometimes modified, by the King—action was then taken by the military high command, which Scharnhorst also directed, to put the reforms into practice. To permit the opening of the officer corps to commoners as well as aristocrats, Scharnhorst established a system of examination, while at the same time leaving it up to regimental officers to approve in their unit all commissions granted to applicants who passed the examinations. Recognizing the importance of the sense of aristocracy, and also of the sense of honor that had always been deemed an essential characteristic of the Prussian officer corps, the Reformers systematized existing courts of honor under the jurisdiction of the unit officers, which tried officers accused of any military or criminal offense.

Three military schools for the preparation of officer candidates to become ensigns were founded at Berlin, Königsberg, and Breslau. In practice there would be a few promotions to officer candidate from the ranks, but these schools were open to all youths who could pass the entrance examination, regardless of social status or origin. Not unnaturally, in the light of traditions and the availability of educational opportunity, most of the applicants still came from aristocratic families, but they could not be admitted without proving their intellectual and educational ability.

The Academy for Young Officers, which Scharnhorst had started to reorganize in the years preceding the 1806 war, was further reconstituted in 1810 under his direct supervision, and was at first called the Military School for Officers. Shortly after this it was renamed the German Military School. In 1859 it became known as the *Kriegsakademie,* or War Academy, and it was long the most illustrious school of higher military education in the world.

ESTABLISHMENT OF THE WAR MINISTRY / In March 1809 Frederick William III had reluctantly moved slightly closer to the constitutional politico-military relationship that was the objective of the Reformers. He established a Council of Ministers and within this a Ministry of War. By this time, the King was becoming resentful of the persistent efforts of the Reformers to weaken, as he saw it, his control over the Army. Therefore he refused to appoint a Minister of War. Scharnhorst was the only logical candidate, other than Army Commander in Chief Marshal Blücher, who was unsuited by training, inclination, and disposition for any command other than field operations. The King instead made Scharnhorst the senior man in the Ministry by appointing him head of the General Department (the genesis of the new General Staff), but offset his influence by placing Count Friedrich Karl Heinrich von Wylich und Lottum, a traditional Prussian aristocratic officer and an old enemy of Scharnhorst, as head of the Ministry's Administrative Department. Nevertheless, Scharnhorst represented the War Ministry on the Council of Ministers, and thus combined in his person the virtual posts of War Minister and Chief of the General Staff.

Within weeks of this major new development in Prussian constitutional government, events elsewhere in Europe intruded upon the work of the Reformers. Since the disaster of Austerlitz in 1805, the Austrian Empire had also been reorganizing its Army, while quietly awaiting an opportunity for revenge against Napoleon. In early 1809, following French setbacks in Spain and Napoleon's departure from Paris to take personal command there, the Austrian government in Vienna thought the opportunity had arrived. In April Austrian troops, under the command of Archduke Charles, invaded French-dominated Bavaria. The Austrian government appealed to Prussia and Russia to join the effort to throw off the French yoke from central Europe.

To the Reformers in Berlin the opportunity seemed as bright as it did to their counterparts in Vienna. Scharnhorst and the others, collectively and individually, did everything they could to persuade Frederick William to declare war, to mobilize the small reserve and the many veterans of the earlier war, and to march against the French. Cautious Frederick William, however, rejected the idea.

Napoleon defeated Archduke Charles in the Ratisbon and Wagram Campaigns, and imposed another humiliating peace on Austria (by the Treaty of Schönbrunn). To Frederick William, Napoleon's success in Austria seemed to justify his earlier caution, since he ignored the possibility that events could have been different if Prussia had promptly joined the war. Napoleon, having learned through his excellent intelligence system that the Reformers had urged Prussian participation, now turned his eyes again on Berlin. He demanded that Frederick William break up the Reformers and reduce their influence. In fact, Grolman had already started this breakup, by resigning from the Army when the King had refused to declare war and journeying to Vienna to volunteer for the Austrian Army. After the defeat at Wagram, he went to Portugal to join General Sir Arthur Wellesley (recently created Viscount Wellington) in the continuing campaign against Napoleon's marshals in the Peninsula.

Now, upon Napoleon's demand, Gneisenau was relieved of his post in the Ministry of War. Frederick William, while increasingly unhappy about the Reformers as a group, had not lost his appreciation for the services rendered by the individual officers, both during the war and since. So he sent Gneisenau on a semisecret diplomatic mission to London. This was, in one sense, an unfortunate move for both Frederick William and for Gneisenau, because it gave Gneisenau a chance to observe, with growing admiration and respect, the functioning of a constitutional monarchy at war.

In 1810 Napoleon, irritated that Frederick William had not dismissed Scharnhorst, increased his pressure on the Prussian King. Despite his occasional annoyance at Scharnhorst's liberalism, Frederick William recognized that this loyal soldier was the strongest pillar of his government, and the King could already see some of the beneficial effects of the reforms Scharnhorst had instituted. Thus the King at first resisted the French Emperor's pressure. But eventually, Scharnhorst, seeing that he had become an embarrassment to his King and a source of friction with the French government, resigned from his post as head of the General Department, and was replaced by Major General Karl George Albrecht Ernst von Hake. Scharnhorst remained the Inspector General of Fortifications and held the title of Quartermaster General, and was still virtual Chief of the General Staff. Hake and his principal assistant, Boyen, received secret orders from the King that they were to consult Scharnhorst on all important matters in the War Ministry. In fact, Boyen probably would have thus sought the advice of his old chief even without such an order.

Meanwhile, relations between France and Russia were growing increasingly strained. In 1811 Napoleon began to prepare for war. Aware of widespread sentiment among Prussian officers for joining Russia, he menacingly demanded that Frederick William provide a contingent for the vast French Army that was being assembled for the coming campaign. Again the Reformers, along with many other Prussian officers, urged the King to join Napoleon's active enemy. Memories of Jena, Friedland, and Tilsit were still fresh, however, and the example of Wagram and Schönbrunn were too recent for the cautious King to follow this advice. He reaffirmed his adherence to the French alliance and the Continental System, and prepared to furnish the demanded military contingent.

At this point many Prussian officers resigned their commissions in disgust. Thirty of them, including Clausewitz, went to Russia, where they were eagerly accepted in the Army of Czar Alexander I. Scharnhorst did not resign his commission, but he did resign from the General Staff. Quietly, he made clear to the King that he would still be available if needed in time of crisis.

TAUROGGEN—THE BREAK WITH NAPOLEON / Napoleon's Russian melodrama became stark tragedy in the late fall of 1812. As the *Grande Armée* dissolved in the Russian snows, one of the few elements remaining intact was the Prussian contingent, a corps of 18,000 men that had been engaged in little of the fighting while guarding Napoleon's northern flank. The commander was General Hans David Ludwig von Yorck,* a typical old-school Prussian officer. Although he and Scharnhorst were poles apart in social and political outlook, Scharnhorst had so respected Yorck's military competence that in 1809 he had appointed Yorck Inspector of Infantry. Now in late December 1912, with secret encouragement from Scharnhorst, Yorck met with Clausewitz (whom he had never previously trusted), who was conducting truce negotiations as a Russian staff officer, at Tauroggen (now Taurage), a few miles northeast of the Niemen River. On December 30 Yorck finally deserted the French, and entered into a truce with the Russians. In vain he had sought guidance from Frederick William, who contented himself with observing events from far-off Berlin.

Yorck's action finally forced the King's hand. Either he would have to denounce the truce immediately and court-martial Yorck (which that General half-expected and which the enraged King almost did), or else he would have to dissolve the Franco-Prussian alliance, which automatically meant war. Even though the King was inclined to the first course, he soon realized that he would be deserted by the Prussian Army and Prussian people if he did not endorse Yorck and join the anti-French coalition. Accepting the inevitable, he moved his capital to Breslau, prepared for war, and sent for Scharnhorst to direct the nation's preparation for that war. Scharnhorst, again appointed Quartermaster General (although Hake remained head of the General Department of the Ministry of War), ordered a mobilization that—thanks to the plans he and his staff had prepared—was hardly less miraculous than that which Napoleon was at the same time carrying out in France. Yet to Scharnhorst's intense disappointment, Frederick William would not give him a senior command. Kings, dictators, and presidents will use the best available men in times of necessity, but they can never forgive such men when their rejected advice has proved to be right.

THE DEATH OF SCHARNHORST / When the Prussian Army took the field in the spring of 1813, Scharnhorst, now a Lieutenant General, had to be satisfied with the post of Chief of Staff to the corps of old Marshal Blücher, who commanded the Prussian contingent of the main Russian Army. At the Battle of Lützen, on May 2, 1813, the green, hastily mobilized levies of Prussia were engaged against equally green, hastily mobilized levies of France. Encouraging

---

*He was made a count in 1814, and given the name and title of Graf von Wartenburg; thus he and his son are usually known as Yorck von Wartenburg.

the unsteady Prussian recruits was Scharnhorst, who was wounded by a rifle ball in his leg. On the other side, the French recruits were being comparably encouraged in the front lines by their Emperor (who is reputed to have used the Imperial boot in encouraging some reluctant young soldiers). Partly because of the outcome of this hard-fought battle, which the French finally won, Blücher would later remark that the mere presence of Napoleon on the battlefield was worth 40,000 men.

Despite his painful but apparently not serious wound, Scharnhorst continued to perform well as Blücher's Chief of Staff, and at Bautzen again helped his chief to limit French victory.

Soon after this an armistice was agreed upon. Russia and Prussia, now joined by Sweden, hoped to persuade Austria to join them in a climactic campaign against the French conqueror. The Austrians, however, remembering how they had been left by Russia and Prussia to fight alone in 1809, were both reluctant and disdainful; they knew that they could not lose by remaining neutral, no matter which side won the war. At this point Czar Alexander and King Frederick William agreed that the logical man to persuade the Austrians to join them was the one who had sacrificed his career by vainly urging Prussia to join Austria in 1809. Scharnhorst was selected to head an Allied mission to Prague, to meet with Prince Karl Philipp von Schwarzenberg, the Austrian Commander in Chief. After a successful meeting Scharnhorst continued on to Vienna, to urge senior government officials to join the war. Unfortunately, his neglected foot wound became inflamed, and blood poisoning set in. Scharnhorst returned to Prague on a stretcher, and died there on June 28, 1813.

Shortly before his death Scharnhorst wrote a letter to his daughter which tells much about the man. Here it is, as quoted by Rosinski:

I want nothing from the world; what I desire she does not give me anyhow; provided that I can soon get about again unwounded, I shall somehow be able to settle things.

A certain post is destined for me, as soon as I am well again, a curious one. That does not trouble me, however. If I were given supreme command I would care much for it, for I believe myself in all respects fully capable of it. As that is impossible, everything else is indifferent to me; in the fight I shall anyhow soon find a position where I can command alone, because my rank and my position will allow me to assume it and because in such moments acts of the kind are not opposed. Distinctions seem nothing to me; as I do not receive what I deserve, everything else is an insult to me and I would despise myself if I thought otherwise. All my seven orders and my life I would give for the command of a single day. It may seem strange to you that what I write here is so contrary to my [usual] nature, that I have not desired anything, never shown myself dissatisfied and now write so differently to you. This is, however, no ordinary letter, but a message to you showing how your father thought (in his heart) when I shall one day no longer be alive, and you will realize that you have not judged me rightly. As you will see I have paid no heed to opinion and acted solely according to what I held to be right and suitable to me.[3]

THE LEIPZIG CAMPAIGN / Scharnhorst's last mission for his King had been successful. Austria did join the alliance, and the result, at the end of the armistice in August, was the Leipzig Campaign, which drove Napoleon forever from Central Europe.

During that campaign an interesting pattern of staff and command relationships emerged, involving all four remaining Reformers. This pattern was to become the model for one of the most unusual features of the subsequent Prussian and German command system. There were four principal allied armies: the Austrians under Schwarzenberg; the Prussians under Blücher; the Russians under Count Bennigsen; and the Swedes under Crown Prince Bernadotte (formerly one of Napoleon's marshals). There was a Prussian corps with Schwarzenberg's main army, in the South, and another with Bernadotte's northern army. Gneisenau had replaced Scharnhorst as Blücher's Chief of Staff; Grolman, back from Spain, was Chief of Staff to General Friedrich Heinrich von Kleist, commanding the Prussian corps with the Austrians; Boyen was Chief of Staff to General Count Friedrich Wilhelm von Bülow, commanding the Prussian corps with the Swedes; and Clausewitz, still in the Russian Army (King Frederick William had refused to accept him back in the Prussian Army), became Chief of Staff of a corps in Bennigsen's Army, after serving as liaison officer for the Russian command at Blücher's headquarters.

Much of the remarkable and unprecedented coordination among the allied armies in the campaign, and in the subsequent successful invasion of France in early 1814, resulted from the mutual understanding that existed, and the constant exchanges of communications that took place, among these four Prussian chiefs of staff.

It was apparently at this time that Gneisenau formulated (presumably with Blücher's approval) one of the unique practices of the Prussian-German Army. The chief of staff of a major command (army, corps, or division) was to share responsibility with the commander. The first test of this system in combat operations in the 1813 and 1814 campaigns worked well.

The abdication of Napoleon in 1814, following his brilliant but doomed campaign against the overwhelmingly superior allied armies, seemed to bring the era to a close. In Prussia Boyen was appointed Minister of War, with Grolman Chief of the General Department. The abrogation of the 1808 Treaty of Paris, as a result of Napoleon's defeat, enabled Boyen to put into effect Scharnhorst's ideas for a new, comprehensive system of national mobilization. The King approved a law requiring compulsory military service by all male citizens. There was to be a standing army, in which the conscripts were to serve for three years, between the ages of twenty and twenty-three. To back up this army there would be an intermediate reserve, and a militia or *Landwehr*. The intermediate reserve would include the two most recently demobilized conscription classes, who would be recalled directly into the standing army in emergency. The *Landwehr*, a separate militia entity, would comprise seven classes of trained reserves, twenty-six to thirty-two years in age, capable of rapid mobilization to fight beside the standing army on short notice. Prussia now had the people's army always visualized by the Reformers.

THE WATERLOO CAMPAIGN / The reorganization was still in process when Napoleon's return from Elba again plunged Europe into war. The Prussian field army of four corps, commanded again by Blücher, with Gneisenau once more his Chief of Staff, marched westward to join the British in another invasion of France. Austrian and Russian armies were soon expected to join these first two contingents on the French frontiers.

Again the Reformers were prominent in the field army. While Boyen remained in Berlin, Grolman left the War Ministry to become Quartermaster General on Blücher's staff, and thus was Gneisenau's right-hand man. Clausewitz (finally forgiven by Frederick William) was back in Prussian uniform and was Chief of Staff to General Adolf von Thielmann, commanding the III Corps. After the defeat at Ligny, when one corps had to fight independently of the rest of the Army to hold off the French right wing at Wavre, Gneisenau selected Thielmann's corps largely because he knew he could rely on Clausewitz. Grolman had already persuaded Gneisenau to make the basic decision to join Wellington at Waterloo with the other three corps.

The victory at Waterloo was due primarily to the timely arrival of the Prussians, in accordance with Gneisenau's promise to Wellington, and thanks to the repulse of Grouchy at Wavre—in large part because of Clausewitz's skill in helping Thielmann direct the battle.

A basic allied decision was necessary after Waterloo. Should the English and Prussian armies await the arrival of the Austrians and Russians, or should they pursue the defeated enemy? There was little hesitation. Gneisenau urged immediate pursuit. Blücher and Wellington both agreed. How this pursuit was conducted, and its results, constitute a very significant chapter in the early history of the new Prussian Army.

In the revitalized General War School in the years between 1809 and 1813, and again in 1814, Scharnhorst first, and later Gneisenau, Boyen, and Grolman, had demanded that the lessons of the 1806 and 1807 campaigns be studied intensively. Particularly emphasized in these classes, and in occasional seminars of high-level commanders, was the fact that French victories of 1806 and 1807 were won by the complete and aggressive responsiveness of French commanders to the will of Napoleon, even without specific directives from the Emperor, and even when they were miles away from his direct supervision. This had not only been significant in the French victories at Jena-Auerstadt and Friedland, but had been even more important in the relentlessness and effectiveness of the French pursuit after these battles. If there was any single historical example which Scharnhorst and Gneisenau cited more than any other in trying to indoctrinate the new leadership of the Prussian Army, it was that of the French pursuit from Jena to the Baltic Sea in 1806.

THE PURSUIT AFTER WATERLOO / Yet now Blücher and Gneisenau discovered, after the victory at Waterloo, that no matter how much the Prussian officers might have been exposed in school and in conference to the importance of aggressive pursuit, it was quite a different matter when it came to carrying out a similar pursuit. A modern German official military history text describes the situation as follows:

> For the most part the Prussian troops pursued the retreating enemy aggressively only when the commander-in-chief or his chief-of-staff drove them to it or took the lead himself at the head of the column. . . . Most Prussian corps and division commanders showed little initiative. . . . Yet Blücher and Gneisenau, thanks to their personal efforts and the consequent rapid advance of their troops, prevented the enemy from taking up a defensive position in front of Paris.[4]

Thus, though the Prussian Army of 1815 was far different from that of 1806, it was evident to the three Reformers who accompanied the army to Paris that Scharnhorst's ideal had not yet been achieved. Still, they felt confident that this would come in time, if their reforms already in process were not undone and if the one additional basic reform of responsible civil-military relationships could also come to pass.

A number of times in history individual military visionaries have been able to plan and carry out remarkable military transformations. This was the first time that comparable changes had been achieved institutionally, by a small group of men below the level of top command. An organizational and operational pattern had been established that would endure for more than a century.

NOTES TO CHAPTER THREE

[1] Rosinski, *op cit.*, p. 61.

[2] Reinhard Hohn, *Scharnhorsts Vermächtnis* (Bonn: 1952), pp. 312-13.

[3] Rosinski, *op. cit.*, p. 79.

[4] *Rückzug und Verfolgung: Zwei Kampfarten, 1757-1944* (Stuttgart: 1960), pp. 235-36; one of a series of publications by the Military History Research Institute of Freiburg im Breisgau, German Federal Republic.

Chapter Four

REFORM & REACTION
Marriage of Convenience

 BOYEN AND GROLMAN–PROGRESS IN REFORM / In 1815, as Prussia finally returned to the peace that had been promised in 1814, the surviving Reformers could be proud of what they had accomplished. They had created a new and popular Prussian Army, based upon the most advanced and most effective system of national conscription that had yet been devised. Not only had they broadened the base of the Army, and substantially improved its quality, they had at the same time made it the focus of a new and unprecedented spirit of patriotism. Admittedly, the large majority of the officers were still members of the aristocracy, but the proportion of bourgeois officers was growing, and the aristocrats had been forced to study their profession in order to remain in the Army. Controlling, directing, and coordinating this greatly improved military instrument was an efficient War Ministry, at the heart of which was an effective General Staff comprising a handful of carefully selected specialists who had proved their competence by superior performance in the new Military Academy and on the battlefield.

The Reformers were conscious, however, that they had failed to accomplish one important objective. There was still no national constitution. There was no body of elected representatives of the people to whom the new people's army could be responsive, as had been originally intended by Stein, Scharnhorst, and their associates. And there were ominous signs that the forces of reaction among the nobility had persuaded the King not to take that final step toward military democratization. There even appeared to be some sentiment among the King's closest advisers to do away with those reforms that might threaten the nobility's domination of the officer corps. Gneisenau, who now commanded Prussian forces in western Germany, was rightly suspected of having liberal tendencies, and found himself increasingly unpopular at the Potsdam court.

War Minister Boyen, perhaps the most liberal public official in the history of Prussia, was aware of the growing difficulties in achieving the ultimate political reform necessary to complement and complete the military reforms. He doubted if this could be done by Chancellor Prince Karl August von Hardenberg. Although Hardenberg shared Stein's hopes for constitutional reform, he lacked

Stein's dynamic force of character. Boyen, however, was determined to provide the backbone that Hardenberg lacked. At the same time he quietly and calmly proceeded to consolidate the military reforms already achieved in a reorganized War Ministry, and in the increasingly effective military-school system which Scharnhorst had established. As Chief of the Second Department, or General Staff, Boyen appointed fellow-Reformer Grolman, who shared Boyen's objectives but was politically more moderate.

Elsewhere in the Army, the forces of reaction were in the ascendancy, gaining the ear and full support of the King. In 1816 Gneisenau resigned from active military service and went into premature retirement because of his strong opposition to the ideas of the King's closest advisers, and to show his dissatisfaction with Frederick William's failure to promulgate a constitution. The King (although appointing Gneisenau nominal Governor of Berlin) never forgave him for this display of opposition, which, with some reason, he interpreted as contempt.

In 1816 Grolman reorganized the General Staff in three principal divisions, one for each of the potential theaters of war: Eastern, which would involve war against Russia; Southern, with Austria the most likely enemy; and Western, to be prepared to fight France again, or possibly a coalition of West German states with or without France. Each of these staff divisions was responsible for studying military conditions and developments within the potential enemy nations in its area of responsibility. Some officers examined the terrain where combat operations were likely, and prepared appropriate strategic plans; others drew up plans for mobilization and deployment in any eventuality.

The following year Grolman—undoubtedly with Boyen's approval—made two further significant modifications in the General Staff organization. A fourth division was established, with the responsibility for studying military history. Henceforward a military-history section would remain a major element of the General Staff, despite many organizational changes.

Grolman's other change was to clarify the relation of the Second Department—now formally called the Staff—to the General Staff officers assisting the commanders of corps and divisions in the field. Henceforward these officers were considered to belong to a fifth division, called the *Truppengeneralstab,* "Troop General Staff," with officers from the central organization in Berlin being rotated to duty with corps and division staffs. There were three such officers—a chief of staff and two assistants—with each corps. There was one General Staff officer with each division. To distinguish the various elements of the Troop General Staff from the central staff planning agency in Berlin, that organization was often called the Great General Staff.

The four years that Grolman was Chief of the General Staff in Boyen's War Ministry were probably more important in assuring the subsequent quality of the General Staff than any other period in the history of that institution. Scharnhorst must be given the credit for the fundamental conception of institutionalized military excellence (even though he had strong intellectual support from Gneisenau, Boyen, Grolman, and Clausewitz). Scharnhorst and Gneisenau had shared in refining the concept and demonstrating its validity in war. But Boyen and Grolman were the ones who established procedures to translate concept into continuing operational reality and who assured the permanence of the institution.

Grolman devoted particular attention to the continuing improvement of officer education, first by establishing high intellectual standards as a prerequisite to obtaining a commission, and second by constantly improving the military schooling system. The emphasis was on scientific education, both in substance and in method. The Prussian officer—and particularly the General Staff officer—was expected to think of the educational process and individual study as objective searches for truth.

Recognizing the inevitably stultifying effect of routine work in compartmented staff bureaus in peacetime, Grolman insisted upon frequent rotation of officers between the line regiments and the General Staff. Within the General Staff there were also frequent rotations between the Second Department offices in Berlin and the troop General Staff assignments in corps and divisions. This had the effect of keeping the General Staff officers closely associated with the thinking and attitudes of the Army as a whole, and also brought regular influxes of fresh blood and fresh thinking to the Staff. Furthermore, it gave the senior Staff officers an opportunity to observe many juniors, and quietly to earmark those who should return permanently to the less intellectually demanding requirements of garrison troop duty.

Another of Grolman's preoccupations was with the improvement of military communications facilities within Prussia. First and most important was assuring a road net adequate for rapid implementation of the various mobilization and deployment plans drawn up by the three theater divisions of the Staff. Related to this was the logistical support of these plans, requiring the strategic positioning of magazines stocked with military supplies and provisions. Grolman gave considerable attention to the Army's network of telegraph towers whereby messages could be rapidly transmitted between Berlin and the principal Army headquarters in the provinces by a visual semaphore code.

REACTION AND THE CARLSBAD DECREES / Grolman was only incidentally involved in the struggle between his chief, Boyen, and the reactionary advisers of the King. However, he generally shared Boyen's views, and like him was shocked by the Carlsbad Decrees. These were the result of a conference at Carlsbad, in August 1819, of the principal ministers of the more important German states, meeting under Austrian auspices as the Diet of the German Confederation. Under the influence of Austrian Chancellor and Foreign Minister Prince Clemens von Metternich, the conferees agreed to take coordinated drastic action to halt the spread of liberal, republican, and nationalist concepts, particularly among the youth of German states. Universities throughout Germany were to be closely supervised and controlled by government officials; periodical publications were to be subjected to censorship; a centralized all-German commission was established at Mainz to investigate and expose the underground network of subversion presumed to exist throughout Germany. Boyen did his best to persuade King Frederick William III to reject these decrees as inconsistent with the principles for which the recent Wars of Liberation against external tyranny had been fought. However, the King heeded his other advisers and endorsed the Decrees.

The King's displeasure with Boyen's opposition to the Carlsbad Decrees seemed to the Army conservatives to provide an opportunity to get rid of the liberal War Minister. There was a handy issue available to fit this opportunity—the question of the status of the *Landwehr*.

THE LANDWEHR ISSUE / Boyen had shared Scharnhorst's original concept that the *Landwehr*—the national militia—should constitute a bond linking the Prussian Army with the Prussian people. To him this was an article of faith matching his unswerving loyalty to the crown. It was intended that the *Landwehr*, maintained at a high level of military efficiency through drills and annual maneuvers, would be ready to fight shoulder to shoulder with the Army in time of war. In peacetime, however, Boyen believed that the *Landwehr* could provide the desired link between Army and people only if completely separate from the Army, with its own system of inspectorates reporting directly to the Minister of War, not through the Army inspectorates. Boyen had succeeded in obtaining endorsement of this concept of separateness by the *Landwehr* Law which the King signed on November 21, 1815.

To Boyen the logical next step to achieve proper status for the *Landwehr* was the national constitution for which he, Scharnhorst, Stein, and other Reformers had striven in the years since 1807. To him it was logical that the duty of military service, performed by citizen soldiers of the *Landwehr*, automatically implied a comparable right to share in the government of the State. However, the fall maneuvers of 1819 provided an occasion for Army conservatives to attack Boyen's *Landwehr* concept and to thwart his hopes for a national constitution.

The performance of the *Landwehr* during the maneuvers was severely criticized by many Army officers, who saw to it that the King was made aware of this allegedly poor performance. Neither Boyen nor Grolman had been satisfied with the maneuvers, nor the role of the *Landwehr*, but they knew that shortages of funds for the past two or three years had made it difficult to maintain the readiness of the *Landwehr* at the desired standards. They hotly protested when Army critics urged the King to end the separate inspection system for the *Landwehr* units and put them under the Army for control and supervision. Boyen and Grolman were convinced that such a change would not in itself improve the quality of the *Landwehr*, and that it would destroy its value as an independent link between Army and people. However, in December the King overruled Boyen, and declared that thenceforth the *Landwehr* would be under direct Army supervision. Boyen resigned in disgust; Grolman immediately followed suit.

The militarization of the *Landwehr* and the resignations of Boyen and Grolman were more significant politically than they were militarily. The three-cornered interrelationship of people, State, and Army—the goal of Stein, Scharnhorst, and their supporters—had been decaying slowly since 1815; now it was in ruins. Without a constitution, without representative institutions, without the emotional pressures of a war for the fatherland, the growing bourgeoisie became increasingly hostile toward autocratic rule, and thus to the Army, the most obvious manifestation of that rule. However, the general population seems to have remained faithful to both crown and Army.

Within the Army the forces of reaction had mixed effects. The proportion of commoners in the officer corps—which had risen to about 40 percent by 1815—declined sharply in the years after 1819. The influential bourgeoisie's growing antipathy for the Army was heartily reciprocated by most of the aristocratic officers. But there was in the Army an institution which had not existed before 1806, and which by 1819 had fully demonstrated its military value to all officers in the Army, whatever their political views or social origins. This was the General Staff. A parallel development was the new system of military education which had also ceased to be thought of as military reform, but rather had become accepted as a basic contributor to Prussian military standards of performance. All Prussian officers were proud that these standards were increasingly admired and copied throughout the world.

Thus, while the reactionary elements in the Army shared in, and to a considerable degree were responsible for, the triumph of political reaction in Prussia, they left untouched most of the major military improvements instituted by Scharnhorst and his devoted band of Reformers. The one significant effect upon the Army of the reactionary triumph must not be underestimated. By destroying the concept of a people's army, which had been one of Scharnhorst's major goals, the reactionaries assured the perpetuation of a pattern of Prussian civil-military relations that was to have the most tragic consequences for Germany and the German people.

CLAUSEWITZ AND THE REACTIONARIES / There was another effect of the triumph of reaction in the Prussian State and Army, one which could not possibly have been foreseen. In 1818, Grolman, as part of his efforts to strengthen the educational system, decided that co-Reformer Clausewitz should be appointed Director of the General War School. Boyen approved, despite some cooling in personal relations between him and Clausewitz due to their differing political outlooks. But not long after newly promoted Major General von Clausewitz took over as Director of the General War School, there came the Carlsbad Decrees, and the fateful debate over the future of the *Landwehr*.

The reactionary leadership of the Army quite properly identified Clausewitz militarily with his fellow Reformers Boyen and Grolman, but failed to realize that Clausewitz's political views were relatively conservative and that he did not share the passionate liberalism of Boyen, or even the somewhat more moderate liberalism of Grolman. Furthermore, the new Minister of War, General von Hake was an old-line, traditionalist Junker officer who was suspicious of the increased emphasis on education, and who was aware that he was held in contempt by the intellectual Clausewitz. While Clausewitz retained administrative control of the school, he found himself frustrated by reactionary employment of the liberal educational machinery he had helped to devise. The council of professors generally ignored him and bypassed him, dealing directly with the Minister of War, or with the equally reactionary educational director in the Second Division.

Thus Clausewitz could do little to influence the curriculum of his own establishment. In frustration he withdrew from most outside contacts and devoted himself to writing. The result was *On War,* which, though never completed, is rightly considered the most important philosophical study of war and warfare. It was a work that would have both good and bad influences on his own beloved Prussian Army. It also brought him, after his death, a far greater international reputation than was achieved by any of the other Reformers.

RÜHLE AND MÜFFLING / Meanwhile the General Staff during this period of political crisis went quietly about its business for slightly more than a year under the temporary leadership of Colonel Johann Jakob Otto August Rühle von Lilienstern, who in December 1819 succeeded Grolman as Quartermaster General and Chief of the Second Department, Although Rühle was promptly promoted to Major General he was not formally appointed Chief of the General Staff. This was probably because in his younger days he had been a close associate of both Stein and Scharnhorst. He seems to have been devoted to his two specialties of military topography and military education, and to have had little direct effect, good or bad, on the functioning of the General Staff.

In January 1821 a much more forceful (and apparently more professionally rounded) man than Rühle was appointed Chief of the General Staff. This was General Philipp Friedrich Karl Ferdinand Baron von Müffling. The relationship between Müffling and Rühle was at first a peculiar one. Rühle remained Chief of the Second Department, with responsibility for military education, while Müffling, senior to him in rank, was nominally his subordinate as Chief of the General Staff. Soon after Müffling took over on January 11, 1821, the name of the General Staff was officially changed to Great General Staff, to assure a clearer distinction between the War Ministry Staff and the general staffs of corps and divisions. At the same time the Chief of this Great General Staff was given considerable autonomy (although still nominally a part of the Second Department) and the prestige of being an adviser to the Minister of War.

While this change seems to have made it easier for Müffling to serve nominally under Rühle, the relationship remained tense. In 1825 the problem was resolved by disbanding the Second Department and giving still greater autonomy to the Chief of the General Staff, whose position as an adviser to the War Minister was confirmed.

EMERGENCE OF THE MILITARY CABINET / During this same period one of the other two departments of the War Ministry—the Third Department—was also struggling for comparable autonomy. It is not clear whether this state of affairs was due to the weakness of Hake or to the exceptionally strong characters of Müffling and the Chief of the Third Department, Colonel Karl Ernst Job Wilhelm von Witzleben, who had the additional advantage of being Adjutant General and a close personal friend of the King. In 1824 the Third Department was redesignated the Department of Personnel Affairs, under the suddenly promoted Major General von Witzleben. Despite its title, this office was initially responsible only for the personnel records of officers. The personal relationship between the King and Witzleben meant that this department, even though still nominally part of the War Ministry, served the King directly. Thus began the recreation of a Military Cabinet, a personal headquarters of the King, which had been one of the first of the old institutions that Scharnhorst had abolished in 1807.

It has been suggested that this near-simultaneous autonomy of the Adjutant General and the Chief of the General Staff was the beginning of a triangular relationship in which War Minister, Adjutant General, and General Staff Chief were all vying for preeminence.[1] While these relationships presaged such a later development, it does not seem actually to have happened at this time. Hake's authority, while somewhat reduced, was still clearly preeminent over both Müffling and Witzleben.

Nor does Müffling seem to have aspired to rival the War Minister. Although politically reactionary, he was a member of the generation of officers that had served under Scharnhorst and Gneisenau and who had been strongly affected by the dynamism of these two men. He had particularly distinguished himself as an operations officer under Grolman in the Waterloo Campaign. He was a very intelligent, very industrious officer, dedicated to the constant improvement of the General Staff, and through it, of the Prussian Army.

NOTES TO CHAPTER FOUR

[1] Walter Goerlitz, *History of the German General Staff* (New York: 1953), p. 58. For another assessment, see Gordon Craig, *The Politics of the Prussian Army* (New York: 1956), p. 78.

Chapter Five

INSTITUTIONALIZING MILITARY EXCELLENCE

 THE GENERAL STAFF AND PRUSSIAN PROFESSION-ALISM / Some modern military and political historians have assumed that the triumph of reaction, the apparent alienation of Army from people (or at least from the most vocal elements of the population), and the lack of military operational experience, combined to create a climate of military decay and decline similar to that which existed in Prussia between the death of Frederick the Great and the Battle of Jena. They apparently attribute the sudden reversal of this supposed military decline, as evidenced by the triumphs of 1864, 1866, and 1870-1871, to the fortuitous historical accident of the almost simultaneous appearance, shortly before these triumphs, of Bismarck, Moltke, and Roon in key positions in the Prussian State, and the revitalization of the General Staff by Moltke.[1] Such a view of Prussian history is factually wrong, and leads to distorted interpretations of the military events of this remarkable era.

Bismarck's rise to power was indeed circuitous and a political accident, and admittedly he enhanced and exploited the military triumphs of the Prussian Army as possibly no one else could have done. The emergence of Moltke and Roon, however, was no accident. The steady, quiet, professional improvement of the Prussian Army during the four decades after 1819 was such that the names of Moltke and Roon were of little importance. Any man who became Minister of War or Chief of the General Staff would have been an officer of great professional competence. The Prussian military triumphs of the mid-nineteenth century were the inevitable result of long-standing Prussian military excellence, not of the fortuitous appearance of one or more military geniuses. Despite the inevitable vagaries of human affairs, and the chance impact of unpredictable events and unique personalities, Scharnhorst's objective had been achieved. The collective brain of the General Staff had brought institutionalized military excellence to Prussia.

Moltke, a competent, even brilliant man, was certainly not a genius of the caliber of Alexander the Great, Frederick, or Napoleon. His ability, however, had brought him to the top in a smoothly functioning system which automatically selected and promoted competence, and which enabled him to coordinate the systematic actions of other competent officers in a collective effort which compared favorably with the performances of geniuses.

How did this happen in four decades?

After Boyen and Grolman resigned, late in 1819, it was only natural in the climate of the times that William would appoint a new Minister of War who would be the most reactionary of the reactionaries. General von Hake was such a man. At the same time, he was a soldier who had been through the experiences of Jena and Waterloo and who, merely by surviving and rising to high command, had inevitably learned something. He would no more have changed the successful military system established by Scharnhorst than he or any other Prussian officer would, in 1786, have changed the successful military system of Frederick the Great. But whether or not Hake appreciated it—and he probably did—there was a fundamental difference in the two systems. Frederick the Great's system was static; change could be made only by Frederick, and Frederick was dead. Scharnhorst's system was dynamic, and was developed to be responsive to the direction of a self-perpetuating institution of highly educated professional men, the General Staff.

There was another difference between the systems of Frederick and of Scharnhorst, flowing from the first. Frederick's system presumed that strategic plans, operational decisions, and tactical control of the main Prussian forces would all be exercised by the Prussian King. To perform these functions the King needed a staff to assist him—officers who could lay out camps, who could supervise collection of supplies, who could write orders, who could carry messages, who could reconnoiter the enemy's positions or possible sites for further battles. These staff officers should be intelligent, quick, and alert. Those with battle experience could expect to be called upon for advice or comment. But their functions required no strategic skill or knowledge. They were extra hands, eyes, and legs, all operating in response to the plans and decisions made by the King alone, even when he heeded the advice of his more experienced staff assistants.

Scharnhorst's system assumed that the King would be the Commander in Chief and that he would make the basic decisions of war and of peace, of national strategy, and even of battlefield tactics—if he wished. But the thinking and planning upon which such decisions were made, the whole process of setting the stage for the King's decisions, would be the responsibility of a carefully selected, specially trained group of professional officers. If the King was a gifted general, like Frederick the Great, his talent would be enhanced by the availability of such a staff. If he was essentially a civilian ruler, with little military ability, he could rely upon this staff to perform the functions of generalship, and to provide him with the military advice needed for political and politico-military decisions.

This had been the system which Scharnhorst had initiated in 1808, when the Prussian Army was being reorganized after its defeats by Napoleon. This was the system which Scharnhorst had in mind in the expanded curriculum of the

School for Young Officers. And the system had worked in the crucible of combat from 1813 to 1915.

The four surviving Reformers and their successors built upon Scharnhorst's prototype of the Prussian General Staff and made it the example for all future General Staffs, both German and foreign, up to the present day.

THE NATURE OF A GENERAL STAFF / The essential purpose of a national General Staff, as visualized by Scharnhorst and his successors, was to serve as Prussia's top military planning, coordinating, supervising agency, thereby assuring the King that the Army was maintained in a state of optimum military readiness.

The first function of the General Staff was planning. This meant the preparation in peacetime of plans to be carried out in the event of war. To perform this function, the Staff not only required as much information as possible about the armed forces and national readiness for war of all potential enemies, but also the same kind of information about allies. Equally complete information was required about the geography of potential theaters of war. Using this information as a basis, each of the three regional divisions of Grolman's General Staff prepared plans for all possible circumstances under which a war might occur and be fought in the area for which it had regional responsibility. The plans of the regional divisions had to be coordinated so as to take care of possible contingencies of a multifront war, as well as of the possibility of coalition warfare, in case Prussia had allies, or if its enemies should include an alliance. These plans were revised and updated periodically, usually every year, and also whenever some important event could affect the planning process. There were many such events between 1815 and 1848 although none of these actually resulted in war.

An important element of the Prussian war plans was the process of transforming the Army from peacetime status to full war readiness. This process of mobilization of the Army had to be rapid and efficient, and had to be fitted precisely to the operational plans for the beginning of combat action. Reserves had to be called to the colors, uniformed, equipped, and supplied for battle. Both regular and reserve formations had to be moved to the positions planned for them at the outset of active operations. Arrangements had to be made to get supplies of food, fodder, and ammunition to these assembled forces, and to keep these supplies coming to the troops as the campaign continued.

Closely related to these mobilization and logistical plans were those for assuring the availability of continuing supplies of manpower to replace the soldiers that were bound to be killed, wounded, or captured in the operations. This meant that a system of wartime recruitment must be planned in advance, and that qualified officers and men were to be kept back from the combat front to train these recruits, so that they could become useful, effective replacements.

After planning, the next most important function of the General Staff was coordination. This provided not only for the coordination of the plans and the operations of the large formations of the Army—corps and divisions—but also for the coordination of activities within these formations, so that each performed its assigned missions in the most efficient manner possible. Coordination, in essence, meant the translation of prewar plans into action, with those same Staff divisions and officers who had been responsible for the various aspects of planning now assuming the responsibility for seeing that the plans were carried out as they should be, or modified, as unforeseen or changed circumstances required, or extemporized when the plans were inadequate.

Closely related to coordination, in fact really part of the same function, was supervision. Scharnhorst believed that the General Staff should not interfere with the performance of lower echelons of staff of command, when these subordinate echelons were functioning efficiently and effectively. But Staff officers were prepared to move in to coordinate when circumstances or poor performance required this. Therefore, there had to be constant supervision of performance at lower levels, with specifically assigned supervision responsibilities for each General Staff agency and for each officer within the agency. It was a result of such supervision that Blücher and Gneisenau, assisted by Grolman and other Staff officers, prodded the Army to effective pursuit after Waterloo.

The third major function of the General Staff was general responsibility for operational readiness. This responsibility was closely related to both planning and coordination, and derived from each of those other functions. It involved such things as officer education, organization and conduct of maneuvers, and the development of new operational doctrine. The First, or Administration, Department of the War Ministry, under the direction of the War Minister, was responsible for the Army's training program through the Army chain of command, and also for the procurement of weapons. But over the years the General Staff exercised an increasing influence on such matters, because both training and weapons had to be related to the doctrine and plans developed by the Staff. Thus, directly or indirectly, the General Staff was concerned with all of the multitudinous things necessary to assure the efficient performance of prewar plans when and if war came. Just as much, the Staff accepted the concomitant responsibility to assure that plans conformed to known and proved capabilities of the Army, and the likely circumstances of possible future wars.

In peacetime the General Staff was obviously more concerned with the planning and operational readiness functions, although that of supervision-coordination was also important. Although Prussia was at peace for more than thirty years after Waterloo, the General Staff was always prepared to move to a war status, in which the planning and operational readiness functions would continue, but increased emphasis would be placed upon the supervision and coordination of combat operations.

A modern military historian[2] has summarized the essence of the nineteenth-century Prussian General Staff system as follows:

The significant features of the Prussian Staff system—all of which went back to the days of Scharnhorst—were (1) the General Staff's quasi-autonomy within the much larger War Ministry, (2) its particular attention to military theory, doctrine, and what can be called postgraduate education for older officers, and (3) the rotation of General Staff officers between the Great General Staff (*Grosser Generalstab*) and positions with the field forces (*Truppengeneralstab*). Entrance to the War College was by competitive examination. Its graduates (at the end of the nineteenth century around a third of the 150 who had been [annually] admitted) were then assigned to the Great General Staff for two years' further experience in topographical work, map exercises, and war games. After they had participated in the annual Staff ride under the personal supervision of the Chief of the General Staff, three or four candidates were made permanent members of the General Staff. (Even when serving in command positions, they were allowed to wear the red trouser stripes of the General Staff.) The others broadcast the General Staff's doctrines, since officers who had completed the War College and General Staff training were usually given better assignments and more rapid promotion. By 1870 most of the higher Prussian officers had been trained in this fashion.

From the example of the nineteenth-century Prussian General Staff we can derive a definition to fit that and all subsequent General Staffs:

A General Staff is a highly trained, carefully selected group of military generalists whose function in peace or war is to assist the nation's military leadership—or a general commanding a field force of combined arms elements—in planning, controlling, directing, coordinating, and supervising the activities of all military subordinate elements in the most effective possible, mutually supporting efforts to achieve an assigned goal or objective, or in maximum readiness to undertake such efforts. The leader or leadership makes decisions and gives commands; the General Staff's responsibility is to provide all possible support to assure that the decisions and commands are timely, sound, and effective.

MÜFFLING AS CHIEF OF STAFF / Müffling made a number of changes in the Staff, its organization, and its procedures in the early and mid-1820s. Soon after becoming Chief of the General Staff, he reinstituted the practice of annual General Staff rides, which Scharnhorst had started before the 1813 campaign, and which had naturally been abandoned during the war. The purpose of those rides was to have the entire Staff gain an intimate acquaintance with one of the potential operational areas for which deployment and combat plans had been so painstakingly prepared. For a period of a week or more, the officers would ride over the countryside, becoming familiar with the terrain, and attempting to visualize on the ground the maneuvers they had developed on maps. Every evening there would be a discussion of what they had seen and done during the day; notes would be taken, Müffling would make suggestions or decisions, and when they got back to Berlin, the plans would be revised accordingly.

In reorganizing the General Staff, Müffling discarded the geographical breakdown instituted by Grolman and assigned responsibilities on a topical basis.

There were still four divisions. The first division was for personnel matters and personnel planning for the Army; its responsibility was largely to coordinate planning with the personnel administration responsibilities of the Third Department of the War Ministry. The second division had responsibility for organization and maneuvers, and for deployment and mobilization plans; it also coordinated war and maneuver plans with the training programs of the Ministry's First Department. The third division was responsible for technological and artillery matters. The small fourth division was still concerned with military history.

Rarely in these years were there more than twenty officers assigned to these four divisions. Another thirty-eight officers, not members of the General Staff Corps, were in the Topographical and Trigonometic Bureaus, attached to the General Staff. About fifty more General Staff officers were with troops.

It was clear that the Reformers' efforts to assure promotion by merit had had considerable success, despite the conservative, reactionary trend in the Army. Shortly before 1830 some twenty out of a total of seventy-one General Staff officers were untitled. At the same time seventeen out of thirty-five officers assigned to the Topographical Bureau, and two of the three officers of the small Trigonometric Bureau, responsible for survey work for the General Staff, were commoners.

Müffling, like all Prussian strategists before and after him, was concerned about the paucity of natural obstacles along Prussia's frontiers to help a defending army delay a foreign invader. East Prussia was completely vulnerable to Russian invasion, Silesia to Austrian invasion, the Rhenish provinces to a French attack. Müffling apparently assumed that there would be an alliance with Austria in the event of war with Russia, or with Russia should the enemy be Austria. But he realized that, in either event, France might also be an enemy. Whatever the opposing lineup, he was forced to assume that the hostile strategy would be to concentrate overwhelming forces against Prussia at the outset. Thus his prime concern was to perfect defensive strategy which would permit Prussia to deal with far more numerous forces invading from two directions. In essence his concept was an updating of Frederick the Great's successful 1757 strategy: the use of interior lines of communcations to permit the concentration of the bulk of the Prussian Army against each threat in turn, while small delaying forces held up the other converging enemy armies. Essential to such a strategy was the ability to mobilize, move, and concentrate forces rapidly and efficiently.

Müffling was as concerned about the quality of military education as were his predecessors, and devoted much time and effort to further refinements of the Army's educational system. To assure thoroughness and consistency, he and his staff compiled the first staff manual. In his spare time he wrote a detailed history of Prussian operations in the final campaigns against Napoleon, 1813-1815. Not surprisingly, he devoted considerable attention to the 1814 strategy, in which Napoleon brilliantly defended France against converging invasion armies.

KRAUSENECK AS CHIEF OF STAFF / After eight years, Müffling retired and was replaced by Major General Wilhelm Johann von Krauseneck. The new Chief of the General Staff had been born a commoner, had risen through the ranks during the Napoleonic Wars, and was later given a patent of nobility as a reward for exceptional service. As a young officer Krauseneck had helped Scharnhorst prepare the training regulations for the post-Jena Prussian Army.

Less aggressive and dynamic than Müffling, Krauseneck was quietly competent. There were no major innovations or changes during his long tenure as Chief, from 1829 to 1848; he was satisfied to follow the examples of his predecessors. Actually, with no new strategic problems to cope with, the inbuilt dynamism of the system was adequate to ensure constant review and updating of plans to reflect new military and technological developments, as well as changing trends in possible enemy armies. In 1833 a thorough modification of the visual telegraph system assured rapid transmission of orders to all subordinate commands, and the prompt receipt of information from frontier outposts. Before Krauseneck retired, the Prussian Army was experimenting with the new electric telegraph, which had first been demonstrated by Samuel F. B. Morse in 1844.

Indicative of the responsiveness and sensitivity of the General Staff to new developments under the Krauseneck regime is the staff reaction to the appearance of the railroad. The first railroad in Germany was a short line between Nürnberg and Fürth in 1835. Within two years the General Staff was preparing studies on the potentialities of the railroad for accelerating Prussian mobilization.

Even earlier the Staff was studying the military potentialities of the Dreyse breech-loading rifle, invented by Johann Nikolaus von Dreyse about 1829. These early studies, initiated by Krauseneck's General Staff, would result, at the time of his retirement (1848), in Prussia's being the first Army in the world to equip its infantry with modern breech-loading rifles.*

During this time the levels of education and professionalism rose steadily in the Army. But at the same time the officer corps was becoming more and more isolated from the population at large. The proportion of titled officers rose during these years, since the regimental officers would almost always select an educated and promising young son of a Junker family in preference to a youth with comparable qualifications whose father was a merchant or a farmer. Nevertheless the balance between titled and untitled officers on the General Staff was not seriously affected by this reactionary development.

At the same time, and contributing to some extent to the widening gulf between middle-class civilians and the military, was the growth of liberal sentiment among the population as a whole. There was also a steady increase in the population of Prussia during this period, and in a few years increasing liberalism and increasing population were to interact to cause a series of major crises in Prussian civil-military relations.

---

*Actually the transition from smoothbore, muzzle-loading musket to breech-loading rifle was not complete until about 1860.

By the early 1830s the effect of population growth forced the General Staff to reexamine its personnel and mobilization planning. More youths were reaching military age each year than could be accommodated within the existing manning levels of the Army. Since the budget and political policy could not afford an increase in the size of the Army, too many young men were being exempted from military service and this, of course, meant that—despite increasing population—the nation's mobilization potential was not being increased; the exempted youths were lost forever to the reserves, and as a practical matter to the *Landwehr* as well. Despite grumbling from the most conservative officers that shorter service would lower the quality of the Army, Krauseneck's General Staff recommended that, in order to permit the conscription of all young men, without increase in size or cost of the Army, the period of active military service be reduced from three years to two, and that the period of *Landwehr* obligation be correspondingly increased by one year. The King approved, and in 1833 this change was made. In fact, as Krauseneck's studies had predicted, there was no reduction in the quality of the Army, and the nation's mobilization potential soon was expanded by nearly 50 percent.

THE FORMALIZATION OF KRIEGSSPIEL / Because of the swelling size of the reserve components of the Army in relation to the active forces, Krauseneck put increased emphasis on the annual fall maneuvers. This assured the readiness not only of the reservists to take their places in the ranks of the Standing Army, but also of the *Landwehr* units to operate effectively beside the regular formations. To prepare officers to perform with maximum efficiency in these maneuvers, Krauseneck introduced throughout the Army a new form of *Kriegsspiel*, or war gaming, which in the 1820s had become highly developed in the General Staff as a logical result of planning analyses and staff reconnaissance rides.

It seems to have been Müffling who recognized the true military potential of *Kriegsspiel* as a tool for war planning. In the previous century complex adaptations of chess had appeared in both Prussia and France. Played on elaborate boards, sometimes with as many as 3,600 squares, they provided the same kind of mental stimulation that comes from chess itself, but had little practical utility for military men, except to help them while away the boring off-duty hours of garrison life.

In the early 1820s, however, a young officer of the Guards Artillery (a Lieutenant M. von Reisswitz) and his father found a way of increasing realism by shifting their playing surface from a checkerboard arrangement to a map. (Possibly they got the idea from reading how Napoleon used colored pins on maps to plan his campaigns.) In any event, young Prince William (second son of Frederick William III, and later Emperor William I), a friend of Reisswitz and also a lieutenant in the Guards Artillery, became interested in the game. In due course Müffling saw Prince William and his friends playing the game, and is said to have exclaimed: "It is not a game at all! It's training for war! It is of value to the whole Army."

Whether or not these were his words, Müffling quickly adopted the map-game concept for the General Staff. Reisswitz soon found himself on duty with the Staff, drawing maps and helping to devise rules. He and his new colleagues produced a manual called *Instructions for the Representation of Tactical Maneuvers Under the Guise of a War Game.*[3] This first manual, dated 1824, was modified in 1825, and again in 1828.*

In the late 1830s, under Krauseneck's direction, use of this simple, but nonetheless sophisticated, military exercise spread throughout the Army. In the lower units—regiment and below—the sandbox was used as much as were maps, to add to the graphic possibilities of the game, to help contribute to its value as a form of entertaining tactical training, and to make it easier to use as a tool for the instruction of noncommissioned officers.

The essence of *Kriegsspiel,* as developed by the General Staff, was the opportunity for officers to operate together as a team of commanders and staffs in dealing with realistic combat situations on maps which might or might not represent actual terrain. One or more umpires assured conformity to practicality and doctrine, while a set of seven dice was available to introduce the "fortunes of war." Each side made its moves in turn. Orders were written out by appropriate officers on one side and submitted to the umpire, who would then rule on the results of these orders, with or without the help of the dice. This permitted movement of markers—paper strips or blocks of wood or lead with appropriate symbols—on the map to conform with the orders and the combat circumstances. The same procedure was then followed by the other side.

Many years later one of the most distinguished products of the General Staff, Prince Kraft Karl August zu Hohenlohe-Ingelfingen, as a military attaché in Vienna, was attempting to explain Prussian *Kriegsspiel* to a group of Austrian officers. One puzzled Austrian asked how points were scored in the game. Hohenlohe patiently explained that the purpose of the game was instruction, that frequently there were no winners, and that points were unnecessary, since the game was not played for money. The Austrian shrugged and sauntered away remarking, "Then what use is it?"

He and his countrymen would learn the answer in 1866.

During the 1830s two promising young officers joined Krauseneck's General Staff. In 1833 Lieutenant Helmuth Karl Bernhard von Moltke, member of a typically impoverished noble family from Mecklenburg, was appointed to the Staff. Three years later Captain Albrecht Theodor Emil von Roon was assigned. It is doubtful if either of these highly disciplined young officers was aware of the contemporary undisciplined activities of an even younger civilian Junker in the Prussian civil service—Otto von Bismarck-Schönhausen—who resigned from the

---

*There were tragic consequences to Reisswitz' sudden rise to prominence. Either because of machinations by his envious former associates, or because of his inability to live modestly with success, the young officer was soon transferred from Berlin to the austere garrison of Torgau. Resentful that neither Prince William nor Müffling had protected him from the fate of dull garrison duty, he became depressed and in 1827 took his own life.

service in 1840, apparently one short step ahead of being dismissed for ineptitude.

NOTES TO CHAPTER FIVE

[1] See for instance Michael Howard, *The Franco-Prussian War* (New York: 1962), p. 12; Hoffman Nickerson, *The Armed Horde, 1793-1939* (New York: 1940), p. 177; and Cyril Falls, *A Hundred Years of War* (London: 1953), p. 62. For a different point of view, see Hajo Holborn, *A History of Modern Germany, 1648-1840* (New York: 1964), p. 459; Gordon A. Craig, *The Politics of the Prussian Army* (Oxford: Oxford University Press, 1955), pp. 77 *ff*; Goerlitz, *op. cit.*, p. 57 *ff.*

[2] Theodore Ropp, *War in the Modern World* (Durham, N.C.: Duke University Press 1959), pp. 137.

[3] For an interesting description of the Reisswitz game and other reference sources on *Kriegsspiel*, see Sidney R. Giffin, *The Crisis Game* (New York: 1965), Chapter I.

Chapter Six

THE PRUSSIAN ARMY &
THE GENERAL STAFF
Mid-Century

BOYEN RETURNS AS WAR MINISTER / The death of King Frederick William III, in 1840, brought to the throne his eldest son, Frederick William IV. The reputation of the new King as a sensitive intellectual brought hope to the growing number of Prussian liberals that his would be an enlightened reign. Young Frederick William, however, was a complex man of many contradictions; despite his essential humanity and his sincere interest in intellectual and cultural pursuits, he was firmly opposed to the two principal objectives of Prussian liberals: a constitution for Prussia and national unity for Germany.

When this royal opposition to liberal reform was recognized by both the constitutionalists and the nationalists, a strong reaction against the new monarch spread among many of the most influential segments of Prussian civilian society. In hopes of appeasing these people, in 1841 the young King reappointed Prussia's archliberal—Hermann von Boyen, one of Scharnhorst's Reformers—as Minister of War. Aging Boyen was still as liberal and still as loyal as he had been when he had clashed with Frederick William's father. He was also as forward-looking in military affairs as he had ever been. Despite considerable difference in political sentiments, he and Krauseneck were able to work well together. Boyen ordered the adoption of the new Dreyse breech-loading needle gun, which Krauseneck's staff had exhaustively tested as the standard infantry weapon. He also supported Krauseneck's efforts to improve the tactical efficiency of the Army and *Landwehr*. He increased the pay and rations of the Army; he instituted a new, more liberal code of military justice; he closely supervised the preparation of a new marksmanship manual for the Army.

However, Boyen found himself powerless to influence the King politically and was more and more shut off from personal contact with the monarch by the increasingly important Military Cabinet, directed by the Adjutant General, Major General Ludwig Friedrich Leopold von Gerlach, a close friend of the King. After more than five years of frustration, Boyen again resigned in 1847.

THE REVOLUTION OF 1848 / The following year, sparked by the February rising in Paris, liberal revolution swept Europe, and for a while seemed to achieve its greatest success in Prussia. In mid-March, there was bitter street fighting in Berlin between the Army and liberal-led mobs, with members of *Landwehr* prominent in the liberal ranks. The King, horrified by the bloodshed, ordered the withdrawal of the Army from the city and apparently capitulated to the demands of the liberals. His promise of a constitution and his prompt convocation of a Constitutional Assembly were hailed by the revolutionaries, while causing deep depression among conservative Army officers. Several generals began conspiring to carry out a royalist coup d'etat, either to restore absolute power to Frederick William or to depose him in favor of his young brother William, the Prince of Prussia. It was during this period that Frederick William began to rely ever more heavily upon the advice of his military aide-de-camp, Major Baron Edwin von Manteuffel, a strongly conservative, aggressive, energetic, and ambitious product of the General Staff.

The people of Prussia in general, and of Berlin in particular, soon found themselves disillusioned by the excesses of the liberal hotheads in Berlin, and by the iconoclasm of ardent leftists in the Constitutional Assembly. Frederick William sensed this popular sentiment and was able to profit from it. In November he ordered the Army to reoccupy Berlin, and suspended the Assembly. Despite loud outcries from the liberals, there was no effective popular opposition to these moves. The King then assured his position on December 5 by magnanimously proclaiming a constitution, in which he included most of the provisions which the Assembly had approved.

THE KING'S CONSTITUTION / For all of his vacillation and indecision during the previous months of turmoil, Frederick William had achieved a significant personal and royal triumph. He had regained the complete loyalty and support of the Army, and he had satisfied the basic demand of the liberals. Although his royal authority was now somewhat limited by the new constitution, its provisions assured to him personally the ultimate power in the State, since the right of supreme command of the Army was reserved to the monarch.

With a clear and unambiguous chain of military command from the King, the most conservative of the Junker officers were satisfied that the best possible solution had been salvaged from the deplorable events of 1848. The Assembly's earlier proposal that the officers take an oath to the constitution—a proposal which Frederick William promised to accept, and which came close to triggering the planned Army coup-d'etat—was omitted from the King's constitution. The only oath required of officers was the traditional one of fealty to the King.

There was one troublesome feature in the new constitution, however. This was the ambiguous relationship of the Minister of War—an Army officer—to the Parliament and to the King. As one of the King's ministers, the War Minister was required to take an oath to support the constitution. At the same time, as the senior officer of the King's Army, he was responsible directly to the King by chain of command and by oath of allegiance. In itself this dual role would not have bothered any War Minister appointed by the King. No general had any doubts as to where his primary loyalty lay. The problem was in the application of this requirement to another provision of the constitution, which gave to the Parliament the right to levy taxes and appropriate funds for the business of government.

There was no doubt that responsible Prussian citizens elected to the Parliament would wish to preserve the security of Prussia with adequate military strength, but civilian and military ideas of adequacy might differ. Thus, whether he wanted to or not, the general who was Minister of War had to take seriously his obligation to the constitution and to the Parliament. Gordon Craig has well summarized this situation in the following words: "Thus in the post-revolutionary period, the Minister of War became the living embodiment of the fateful dualism which characterized the new governmental system, and his required appearances before Parliament tended increasingly to provoke criticism of the Army and the political ideals for which it stood."[1]

The General Staff was too occupied with other duties for its members to be closely concerned with the historic events in and around Berlin during the Revolution of 1848. In fact, for all of the tremendous historical and political significance of the Revolution, and of the Army's major role, and despite the high emotions of the time both within and without the Army, in the end these events had surprisingly little direct effect either upon the Army or on its future role in Prussian history. This fact, paradoxically, was one of the great tragedies of that history.

SCHLESWIG-HOLSTEIN AND THE 1848 DANISH WAR / When the Army withdrew from Berlin in March, the General Staff moved into temporary quarters in Potsdam, and then almost immediately found itself involved in coordinating support for a foreign war with Denmark. Historians have given scant attention to that war and to its relationship with the internal struggle between the King and people of Prussia. To understand the complex background of the conflict and its relation to the upheaval in Berlin, it is necessary to glance back to the Congress of Vienna of 1814-1815.

That diplomatic extravaganza, dominated by Austrian Foreign Minister and Chancellor Prince von Metternich, attempted to restore Europe, as much as was possible, to the frontiers and power balances that had existed before the advent of the French Revolution and Napoleon. Among its myriad decisions was acceptance of the demise of the old Holy Roman Empire in 1806, and its replacement by a German Confederation, a loose association of the thirty-nine sovereign states within the old Imperial, or German, boundaries. A *Bundestag,* or Diet, comprising representatives of these sovereign states, was established at Frankfurt-am-Main. The Diet was not really a legislative body, but rather a mechanism for intra-Confederation consultation, with few powers. It could make recommendations to the respective independent governments of the German states, but such recommendations meant little unless they were endorsed by one or both of the two dominant members of the Confederation, Austria and Prussia.

One of the thirty-nine entities of the Confederation was the North German Duchy of Holstein. Complicating Holstein's membership in the Confederation was its long-standing association with the Danish Duchy of Schleswig, immediately to its north. The population of Holstein was German; that of Schleswig was German in the South, Danish in the North. The Duke of Schleswig had for many years also been the Duke of Holstein—and incidentally the King of Denmark. These relationships in themselves were no more difficult to reconcile with Holstein's membership in the German Confederation than the fact that most of the Austrian Hapsburg dominions were outside the Confederation, just as the eastern lands of the Hohenzollern Kings of Prussia—including the province of Prussia itself—were also outside the boundaries of the Confederation, and just as the King of England had been Elector (1714-1815) and then King (1815-1837) of Hanover.

Complications arose in January 1848 when King Christian VIII of Denmark died and was succeeded by his son Frederick VII, who was childless. This led to a dispute between the new King and the Diet of Holstein as to dynastic succession, since Holstein (being under Salic Law) could not accept a woman ruler, and Frederick's niece was the heiress presumptive of Denmark. The Diet of Schleswig supported Holstein, and on March 24, the two duchies took advantage of the revolutions then sweeping Germany by repudiating the Danish succession, and appealing to the German Confederation for joint membership as the independent State of Schleswig-Holstein.

The Confederation Diet at Frankfurt approved this appeal. Normally both Austria and Prussia would have been asked to enforce the Diet's ruling, but Austria was still in the throes of revolution. Although affairs in Prussia were still tense, the government was operating normally in Potsdam. Frederick William, having unexpectedly espoused the cause of German nationalism, decided to send Prussian troops into the two duchies to preserve their independence from Danish forces which were trying to suppress the rebellions. Early in April a small Prussian Army, commanded by General Count Friedrich Heinrich Ernst von Wrangel, marched into Holstein, and then across Schleswig, sweeping aside the Danish Army with little trouble. The two duchies were quickly occupied, and part of the Prussian Army then invaded southern Jutland, threatening to occupy that indisputably Danish province as well.

Following complicated diplomatic maneuvering and considerable pressure from other European powers, the Prussians withdrew from Jutland and agreed to a truce. Frederick William IV, still engaged in his bitter struggle against liberal rebels at home, was a bit embarrassed to find that he was supporting other rebels against a neighboring monarch. The negotiations got nowhere, and when the Prussians refused to withdraw from Schleswig and Holstein, the Danes renewed the war in April 1849. Once more the Danes were quickly defeated, and once more the Prussians seized portions of Jutland. As before, pressures were brought to bear on Prussia by Russia, Sweden, Great Britain, and France. Frederick William, even more embarrassed, sought a formula that would permit Prussian withdrawal as gracefully as possible. This led to a peace settlement, ratified the next year at Berlin, whereby the ties of Schleswig to Denmark were recognized by Prussia. Since the issue of Holstein's independence was virtually ignored in this settlement, Danish suzerainty had de facto Prussian recognition. As Prussian troops withdrew, the Danes reentered the duchies, but found themselves again opposed by armed rebellion.

King Frederick William, by now wishing that the whole Danish episode had never occurred, was doing his best to ignore the insignificant war in Holstein and continuing rebellion in Schleswig while devoting his attention to new Confederation developments in Frankfurt. There, largely as a result of his earlier unexpected encouragement, a specially convened Assembly was trying to create a new German nation. Austria, still attempting to suppress widespread rebellion, was not represented effectively. In April 1849, the Assembly offered to Frederick William the crown of a new German Empire, which would exclude Austria.

THE "GERMAN QUESTION" AND CONFRONTATION WITH AUSTRIA / In Prussia the issue of a single German state—the German Question, as it was called—had long been debated. A majority of members of the new Prussian Parliament were nationalists. Feelings were mixed in the Army but most of the conservative officers were traditionalists, and their opposition to liberalism almost automatically turned them against nationalism. Furthermore, they had adopted this position in part because Frederick William IV had originally announced his opposition to the establishment of a single German state— influenced, perhaps, because of his belief that such a nation would be dominated by Austria—and they found it difficult to reorient their thinking in consonance with sudden reversals in royal policy.

At the time of the offer by the Frankfurt Assembly, one of Frederick William's closest advisers was General Joseph Maria von Radowitz, who was also a Prussian representative at Frankfurt. Radowitz nearly persuaded the King to accept the offer, but the urgently presented contrary advice of conservatives like Manteuffel gave Frederick William pause. Making it clear that he was receptive in principle, he demanded that the offer come from the German princes as well as from the Assembly.

By this time Austria, under the leadership of Prince Felix von Schwarzenberg, was beginning to recover from the effects of the Revolution of 1848. The growing strength of Prussia was worrisome to Austria, as a threat to traditional Austrian primacy in German affairs. It was also evident to Schwarzenberg that if Frederick William became Emperor of a new German nation, excluding Austria, the power and prestige of the Hapsburg Empire would be seriously diminished. Despite the weakness of the Austrian Empire as a result of the recent revolutions, Schwarzenberg decided to take drastic action to prevent such a development. Apparently he was encouraged by the realization that the most influential elements in the Prussian Army would help him in this effort to prevent creation of a united Germany.

With tension growing between the two major German states, popular unrest in Hesse-Kassel triggered a confrontation. In response to appeals from the Elector of Hesse-Kassel, Austrian and Bavarian troops moved into the electorate to suppress the uprising. This alarmed Prussia, since the principal roads between central Prussia and its Rhenish provinces ran through Hesse-Kassel. Prussian troops moved into the electorate to defend these roads, and war seemed imminent. Both Radowitz—now named Foreign Minister—and Prime Minister Friedrich Wilhelm von Brandenburg urged the King to order mobilization and Brandenburg traveled to Warsaw, seeking an alliance with Russia against Austria.

REYHER AS CHIEF OF STAFF / There had been a recent change in the leadership of the Prussian General Staff. In May 1848 Krauseneck retired and was succeeded by General Karl Friedrich Wilhelm von Reyher, who had been a General Staff officer since 1815. Like Krauseneck, the new Chief was a commoner who had risen from the ranks during the Napoleonic wars and had been admitted to the nobility in recognition of his exceptional military ability. A worthy successor to an increasingly respected position, Reyher was highly intelligent, a student of military history, administratively competent, unswervingly devoted to the King, and single-mindedly dedicated to the professional improvement of the Prussian Army. As in the past, the new Chief of the General Staff was a nominal subordinate of the Minister of War—at this time General Karl Adolf von Strotha—but was in practice quite autonomous as an adviser to the Minister.

Reyher took the threat of war with Austria in stride. He reviewed the mobilization and operations plans, and was prepared to issue orders to implement them upon a moment's notice. He shared the opinion of Prince William, younger brother of Frederick William, that the operational efficiency of the Prussian Army would more than offset the numerical superiority of the Austrians. He awaited word from the King to put the plans in motion.

It was typical of Frederick William that the word never came. As had been the case so many times during the months of the 1848 Revolution, a year earlier, the King suddenly reversed himself. Under great pressure from the conservative traditionalists—who did not fear Austria, but did fear the influence of liberal nationalists in a new German Empire—Frederick William began to back away from the idea of war with Austria, and from the idea of German nationalism. The conservative spokesman was the King's aide-de-camp, Edwin von Manteuffel, who proved to be more persuasive than Radowitz. Suddenly Frederick William repudiated his support of Radowitz, who had no choice but to resign.

Frederick William had always been both fearful and respectful of Austria. Despite assurances—from his younger soldier brother and from Reyher—that Prussia could defeat Austria, the unsoldierly King was unable to assess the risks and was fearful of the gamble. His conservative Army advisers, despite their personal convictions of Prussian superiority, emphasized the imponderables of such a war, in the hope of stopping Prussia's drift to nationalism. Moreover, with Radowitz removed from the scene, the King's old objections to a national German union returned. The sudden death of Brandenburg permitted the King to appoint Otto von Manteuffel, brother of Edwin, as Prime Minister.

THE CONVENTION OF OLMÜTZ / On November 29, 1849, Otto Theodor Baron von Manteuffel and the Austrian Chancellor, Prince von Schwarzenberg, signed a convention at Olmütz in which Prussia agreed to withdraw troops from Hesse-Kassel and to help Denmark reestablish its authority in Schleswig and Holstein; the question of the future of Germany was referred to a conference at Dresden, at which Austria would be represented. Thus the idea of a new German Empire, without Austria, was clearly abandoned by Frederick William. The old weak Confederation was reaffirmed.

Even the Army conservatives were a bit abashed by the results of the "humiliation of Olmütz." But they and the King, who had now forgotten his flirtation with the nationalists, were willing to accept the embarrassment in the light of the setback given to the twin causes of liberalism and German nationalism.

As a result of the Treaty of Olmütz, a joint Austrian-Prussian force again invaded Holstein and Schleswig, but this time for the purpose of restoring Danish royal authority. The policy reversal was complete!

One unexpected result of the insignificant Prussian-Danish War of 1848-1849, and the subsequent joint pacification of Schleswig-Holstein, was its effect upon the Austrian Army. Thoughtful Austrians were shocked by the contrast between Prussian efficiency in dispersing both Danish troops and Danish-German insurgents, and the inefficiency of the Austrian armies in their bumbling efforts to suppress the 1848 revolts in Austria, Bohemia, Hungary, and northern Italy. Imperial authority had been restored in the Hapsburg dominions only with the assistance of a major Russian invasion of Hungary. Senior Austrian governmental officials and Army officers began to recognize that in the event of war with Prussia, Austria's tremendous numerical superiority might not be sufficient to win. Schwarzenberg's bluff at Olmütz had worked, due mainly to a behind-the-scenes understanding with the Prussian conservative advisers of Frederick William. But the Austrians realized that on other issues these same conservatives would have no hesitation in urging Frederick William to fight Austria. An intensive effort to revitalize the Austrian Army was undertaken in the early 1850s.

THE REGENCY OF PRINCE WILLIAM / On October 7, 1857, gifted General von Reyher died suddenly. Before King Frederick William could fill the vacant post, he suffered a severe stroke. The King never recovered; he lived out the remaining three years of his life an invalid, totally incapable of ruling. The Cabinet hastily called upon Frederick William's younger brother, William, Prince of Prussia, to serve first as Deputy to the ailing King, then as Regent.

Prince William, who was born in 1797, had served since the age of seventeen as a soldier. When summoned to Berlin, he was the Military Governor of Rhineland Province, with headquarters in Koblenz. For the next thirty-one years William was the ruler of Prussia: one year as Deputy, twenty-seven months as Regent, and twenty-seven years as King; for the last seventeen years of his life he was also the German Emperor.

As a military man, one of William's first concerns after his arrival in Berlin was to assure continuity and leadership in the General Staff. On October 29 he announced the appointment of Major General Helmuth Karl Bernhard von Moltke, fifty-seven years old, as the acting Chief of the General Staff. At first, William was reluctant to make permanent appointments, since he expected to return the reins of government to Frederick William in a few weeks or months.

THE CAREER OF GENERAL VON MOLTKE / Helmuth von Moltke was born in 1800, the son of a Prussian Army officer, member of an impoverished Mecklenburg noble family. During Helmuth's youth his father resigned from the Prussian Army and joined the Danish service. As a result, young Moltke was educated in the Danish Royal Cadet Corps in Copenhagen; he graduated as lieutenant at the age of nineteen and joined a Danish regiment. Moltke, however, was not close to his father, and he did not feel at home in Denmark. In 1822 the young lieutenant applied for a commission in the Prussian Army. Not only was the application approved, but he did so well in his examination, and in his first year as a regimental officer, that he was admitted to the General War School in 1823.

Clausewitz then was Director of the General War School but, as we have seen, had little direct contact with students. There is no evidence to substantiate myths of a master-student relationship between the two. Clausewitz was probably totally unaware of Lieutenant von Moltke.

It was not until 1832 that Moltke first really felt the impact of Clausewitz, on reading the posthumously published *On War,* which Moltke immediately recognized as the most important exposition of military philosophy to appear in print.

After completing the intensive three-year course, Moltke returned to his regiment for two years. But in 1828, on the basis of his record at the General War School and the evaluations of his superiors and instructors, he was assigned to the General Staff—where he remained on active service for sixty years. Until he commanded a group of armies, in 1866, Helmuth von Moltke had never commanded a unit as large as a company.

In his youth as an impecunious lieutenant, Moltke was able to pay for his uniforms only by cultivating his exceptional writing talent. His short stories and historical articles were published in popular magazines and scholarly journals; he translated English classics into German. (He was practically bilingual; in 1842 he married Mary Burt, an Englishwoman.) In these years he sharpened his writing skills to the point that a German-American historian has written that he "became one of the most eminent masters of German prose."[2]

Moltke's staff service in Berlin was interrupted by two foreign tours of duty. From 1835 through 1839 he served in Turkey as a military adviser to Sultan Mahmud II. The Sultan was attempting to revitalize the Turkish Army after its humiliating defeat at the hands of a nominal vassal, Mohammed Ali of Egypt, and his soldier son Ibrahim Pasha. When Turkey invaded Egyptian-held Syria in 1839, seeking revenge with its improved Army, Moltke accompanied Hafiz Pasha, the commander of the Turkish Army. On June 24 the Turks met Ibrahim's Egyptian Army at Nezib. Hafiz preferred the advice of his astrologer to that of his young Prussian adviser, and Ibrahim won again. In disgust Moltke requested to be transferred back to Berlin, and was again with the General Staff by the end of the year. He was soon promoted to major.

It was about this time that railroads were beginning to spread across Europe. The first railway in Germany was opened late in 1835. Before construction had started on this Nürnberg-Fürth line, Moltke had recognized the military potential of the new invention for mobilization and supply of armies, and had urged General Staff support of railways. He could also see the economic significance of the new means of transportation. Having by now saved some money from his writings and the increased pay of a field officer, he invested all of his savings in the Prussian railroads. Unfortunately, he and his wife never had children to whom their resulting wealth could be passed on.

Early in 1845 Moltke was sent to Rome, to become the military aide to Prince Henry of Prussia, recluse, bachelor uncle of King Frederick William. Less than two years later the Prince died, and in 1847 Moltke—now a lieutenant colonel—was assigned as Chief of Staff of the IV Army Corps at Koblenz in the Rhineland. In that capacity he must have frequently seen Prince William, the soldier prince, military governor of the Rhineland. In 1848, at the time of the war with Denmark, Reyher called him to the Great General Staff, then temporarily at Potsdam.

During the following years Prince William apparently kept track of Moltke's work in the General Staff. In 1855 King Frederick William appointed recently promoted Major General von Moltke to be the aide-de-camp of twenty-four-year-old Prince Frederick William, the only son of the soldier Prince. Presumably this was at William's request, since such an assignment was unusual for a general officer.

During the next two years Prince William had many opportunities to observe and to talk to his son's military mentor. It was the admiration and respect inspired by these contacts that in 1857 led William to select Moltke as acting Chief of the General Staff. Having made the appointment, the Prince then devoted his attention to military organization, satisfied that he could leave the planning to Moltke.

Moltke's appointment was puzzling to many Prussian officers not on the General Staff. To them the unassuming Moltke was either completely unknown or was recognized only as a military historian and the author of some indifferent fiction. Indeed, the fifty-seven-year-old officer had recently been talking of retirement.

GENERAL VON ROON AND THE ARMY REFORMS / During his years of command in the Rhineland, William had come to the conclusion that the Prussian Army was in need of a substantial reorganization. Now, as Prince Regent, he had an opportunity to do something about it. He recognized, however, that a proposal to expand or reorganize the Army would arouse the suspicions of the liberal *Landtag,* lower chamber, of the Prussian Parliament. (He felt certain of support from the autocratic *Herrenhaus,* or upper chamber, whose members were either officers, former officers, or closely related to officers.) To overcome political suspicions and opposition in the lower chamber, any reorganization proposal would require solid military justification. William believed he had found such justification in a document submitted to him in July 1858 by Major General Albrecht von Roon, commanding the 14th Division at Düsseldorf, where he had served under Prince William before the King's stroke.

Roon's paper, which he called a "military constitution for the fatherland," proposed to increase the size of the standing army by returning to a system of three-year conscript service. The annual conscription call-up of 40,000 men was based upon Krauseneck's conscription plan of 1833 when the population of Prussia had been a little over 12 million; it was more than 18 million in 1859. Despite the shortened period of service instituted in 1833, a quarter of a century later approximately one third of the available Prussian manpower was not receiving military training; these men were lost not only to the Army, but to the reserve as well. Roon recommended an annual call-up of 63,000; this and a three-year period of service would permit an increase of about 40 percent in the size of the active Army, to about 200,000 men, and would also mean a substantial increase in the numbers of trained reserves.

The other major purpose of Roon's reforms was to improve Prussia's military readiness by raising the standard of effectiveness of the *Landwehr.* Theoretically, under the law of 1815, the size of the Standing Army would be automatically doubled by mobilization of the so-called first levy of the *Landwehr.* But regular-army men had long been maintaining that this was misleading, since—despite the changes made in 1819—the *Landwehr* was not trained to match Army standards. The Franco-Austrian War of 1859 had demonstrated that an immediately deployable field army of more than 200,000 men was needed, but it had to be capable of better performance than would be the case if half of it was composed of the poorly trained *Landwehr.*

Roon's proposal, then, was to enlarge the active Army to the desired size by doubling the number of infantry battalions, and increasing the cavalry and artillery each by about 25 percent. (For the cavalry this would be accomplished by an increase of service from three to four years.) This reform would eliminate the need for the first levy of the *Landwehr,* which was unsatisfactory anyway. Instead, the partially autonomous *Landwehr* would be amalgamated with the regular Army's reserves, under full Army control, to provide a better-trained, and substantially augmented reserve for a prolonged conflict.

Although some Army officers doubted whether an increase in the length of conscript service was desirable, most were in full agreement with the general objective of Roon's reform measures. Only a few, like the newly appointed Minister of War, General Eduard von Bonin (who had served in the same post from 1852 to 1854), recognized the serious political implications of the proposals. The general popular support of the Army among Prussian citizens in the years following the Wars of Liberation had declined, although the *Landwehr,* only partially under Army control, was still thought of as a people's militia. The events of 1848 had, of course, clearly demonstrated that the Army still belonged to the King. It was largely because of the *Landwehr* that a feeling of popular military participation persisted among large elements of the population, despite the uneasy relationship existing between the aristocratic officer corps and most of the middle class. Thus to eliminate the *Landwehr,* or to reduce its role and importance in the security of the nation, would seriously undercut one of the most important and most effective of the Scharnhorst reforms. Bonin, a great admirer of Boyen, recognized the need for new military reforms but doubted if Roon's proposal was the way to go about it. He knew that the Parliament would be unwilling to appropriate funds for an Army almost doubled in size.

Roon was fully aware of the political implications of his proposals for the *Landwehr.* Remembering with some bitterness the role of the *Landwehr* in the 1848 Revolution, he considered that this subordination of the hitherto unreliable militia provided a political bonus to a plan which was essentially based on military considerations. William, who fully shared Roon's political conservatism, was perhaps even more pleased by these political implications. During late 1858 and early 1859 the Prince Regent appears to have consulted Roon frequently about the best manner of implementing the proposed changes. Also sitting in on these consultations, apparently, were Colonel von Manteuffel, now the Chief of the War Ministry's personnel division, and Major General Gustav von Alvensleben, the Adjutant General. It is not clear to what extent the Prince also consulted War Minister von Bonin, who was strongly opposed to the politico-military confrontation with the Parliament that Manteuffel and Alvensleben appear to have sought.

MOLTKE AS CHIEF OF STAFF / The Acting Chief of the General Staff, General von Moltke, was not concerned with these discussions. The Prince believed that organization and politico-military matters were outside the province of the General Staff, and Moltke seems to have been more than satisfied not to be involved in the difficult military-reform controversy. He found enough to keep him busy in considering Prussia's strategic problems, and in contemplating a major reorganization of the General Staff.

Soon after Moltke was appointed permanent, instead of acting, Chief of Staff, on September 18, 1858, he began to introduce the organizational changes he felt were necessary. He decided to return partly to the geography-oriented or strategy-oriented organization of Grolman and Müffling, without completely abandoning the more function-oriented system that had been initiated by

Krauseneck and retained by Reyher. Moltke's 1858-1859 reorganization gave the Staff four principal planning divisions, or departments as they were newly named.

The Eastern Department was responsible for strategy and planning relating to possible hostilities and alliances involving Russia, the Austro-Hungarian Empire, Sweden, and Turkey. The German Department was concerned with all of the German states (including Austria), plus Denmark, Switzerland, and Italy. The Western or French Department was concerned not only with the France of Napoleon III, but also Great Britain, the Netherlands, Belgium, Spain, and the United States. A new Railways Department was established; it was responsible for general coordination of military use of railroads with the Ministry of Commerce, and also for coordinating such use with the mobilization and operational plans developed by the three geographical departments.*

Although it had no planning responsibilities, the Military History Department was retained as a major element of the General Staff, dividing its efforts between response to requests for information or support from the other departments, and preparation of monographs analyzing the strategy and tactics of historical operations of the immediate and distant past.

THE FRANCO-AUSTRIAN WAR AND PRUSSIAN MOBILIZATION / The first important test of the modified organization, and particularly of the new Railways Department, came in mid-1859. In April of that year, war broke out in northern Italy between Austria and the Kingdom of Sardinia (or Piedmont), with France supporting Sardinia. The invasion of Austrian Lombardy in early June by a French and Piedmontese Army under the personal command of Napoleon III led to an appeal from Austrian Emperor Francis Joseph to the Prince Regent of Prussia for coordinated action against the traditional French foe. On June 4 the French won a victory over the Austrians at Magenta, and four days later King Victor Emmanuel of Sardinia entered Milan in triumph. The Franco-Sardinian Army advanced slowly eastward toward Venice.

On June 14 William ordered a mobilization of the Prussian Army against France. The orders, based on Moltke's plans, were promptly issued, and for the first time railways became the principal means of moving troops and material to mobilization assembly areas. Mobilization, however, had not yet achieved either the economic or psychological significance which was to be the logical development of Moltke's concepts when applied to "nations in arms." It is doubtful that Prince William would have ordered mobilization had this been considered by him or by others as an irrevocable decision for war. In fact, he does not seem to have taken this action because of any strong convictions regarding the issues

---

*Americans fondly believe that the military significance of railroads was not recognized until demonstrated in the American Civil War. Moltke, however, was twenty years ahead of us, and the sophistication of the German General Staff in this respect is demonstrated by the establishment of a Railways Department as a major section of that Staff in early 1859, more than two years before the outbreak of the Civil War.

of the war, or even necessarily to demonstrate Prussian solidarity with Austria as a fellow-member of the German Confederation. It was simply the fact that the conflict between Prussia's two principal rivals appeared to offer an irresistible opportunity for Prussia to gain something at the expense of one or both. He began negotiating with Emperor Francis Joseph of Austria for a concerted invasion of France by the German Confederation.

While the bulk of the Prussian Army was assembling in the Rhineland Province, more slowly and with more confusion than Moltke had anticipated, Francis Joseph left Vienna to take command of the Austrian armies in Italy. A few days later on June 24, rival Emperors Napoleon III and Francis Joseph ineptly maneuvered their armies into contact at Solferino. In a sanguinary battle the Austrian Emperor outblundered Napoleon, and the French Army held the field. The Austrians withdrew behind their formidable Quadrilateral: the fortified cities of Mantova, Peschiera, Verona, and Legnago.

Unexpectedly Napoleon III opened peace negotiations with Francis Joseph. To the disgust of his Italian allies, who thought they had his promise of invasion and conquest of Venezia, and to the annoyance of William of Prussia, who had not yet extracted any concessions from either side, the French and Austrian Emperors reached a settlement at Villafranca on July 11, and the war was over.

Moltke felt neither relief nor frustration at this sudden end of the Franco-Austrian War. He merely busied himself and his staff in moving as rapidly as possible to take advantage of the lessons learned directly in the abortive mobilization, and indirectly from the experiences of the campaign in northern Italy. He worked closely in person with his Railways Department, his German Department, and his Military History Department on these major staff efforts. The results were evident in 1862.

That summer the annual Prussian maneuvers took the form of a railroad mobilization and transportation exercise, directed toward a possible war in North Germany or against Denmark. This time the troops and the railroads functioned in concert, a marked improvement over the confusion of 1859.

Also that year Moltke completed and published a monograph on the 1859 Italian Campaign. From press coverage and the reports of Prussian observers in France, Italy, and Austria, he was able to put together a cohesive and thorough picture of the operations, which had been the first major field campaign in Europe since Waterloo. The factor that seems to have impressed Moltke most was the difficulty experienced by the opposing high commands in maintaining control over field forces of nearly 200,000 men. The efforts of both sides to assure coordination broke down completely at Solferino, and it was evident to Moltke that this was not merely the result of the meddling of the two amateur Imperial commanders. Once the armies of the opposing sides had assembled in northern Italy—and despite use of railroads by both sides for movement of troops and supplies—the tempo of operations was slower than had been the case in the Napoleonic Wars. Although the French and Austrian subordinate commanders and their troops performed well when orders were clear, Moltke noted that they generally stopped and awaited further instructions when orders were lacking or conflicting.

Moltke probably did not think that Prussian commanders, all indoctrinated with a common adherence to the concept of offensive warfare, would have been as indecisive as their French and Austrian counterparts, but he was determined to do what he could to avoid any such possibility. The examples of the Italian Campaign reaffirmed his view that commanders should be assigned general missions, related to fundamental, clearly understood objectives, and then instructed to accomplish those missions by carrying the fight aggressively to the enemy. It was also evident to him that the old Napoleonic precept, "Separate to live, unite to fight" needed to be slightly updated for the larger armies of the mid-nineteenth century: "Separate to *live and to move*; unite *only* to fight."

These lessons were implicit in Moltke's monograph; he made them explicit in his instructions to his staff, in the guidance given to instructors at the War Academy, and in his lectures at that institution. Thus the institutionalized excellence of the Prussian General Staff derived more benefit from the lessons of the 1859 Italian Campaign than did either the French or Austrian officer corps that had fought the campaign.

THE ARMY REFORMS CRISIS / While he and his staff had been concentrating on these lessons of the 1859 war, Moltke had held himself completely aloof from dramatic politico-military events in Prussia. Early in 1859 Prince William had instructed the Minister of War, Bonin, to prepare the legislation and orders necessary to carry out Roon's 1858 proposal for Army reform.

Bonin vainly tried to explain to the Prince Regent the political implication of the proposed reforms. More important, he tried to point out how unpopular these changes would be with the Parliament. He soon realized that William rather liked the idea of demonstrating to the Parliament that the Prussian Army belonged to the monarchy, and neither to it nor to the people it represented. Bonin's efforts to get William to modify the proposed reforms, to keep the two-year term of service, and to retain some significant autonomous role for the *Landwehr* were being effectively undercut by the persuasive arguments of Manteuffel and Alvensleben.

It was evident to Prince William, as well as to Roon, Manteuffel, and Alvensleben, that the mobilization of 1859 provided an excellent opportunity for initiating Roon's proposed reform. The *Landwehr* regiments called to active service could be kept activated, at reduced strength, with regular Army cadres, when the citizen soldiers were demobilized. Then they could be filled out when the next class of young conscripts was called to service. In September 1859, in the light of Bonin's opposition to the idea, the Prince was persuaded by Manteuffel and Alvensleben to bypass the War Ministry and appoint Roon to head a special Military Commission that would draft the reform proposals for submission to Parliament. At the same time William formally revived the old Military Cabinet, appointing Manteuffel as its chief; all officer appointments were withdrawn from the Minister of War, to be handled in the future by the Military Cabinet.

With this evidence of royal disfavor, Bonin resigned as War Minister in late October. For nearly a month William sat on Bonin's resignation. When, however, late in November, Roon and his Commission had their proposal ready, Prince William acted. He accepted Bonin's resignation, and on December 5 appointed Roon as the new Minister of War. That same day Roon presented the reform proposal in the *Landtag*.

The reaction was exactly as Bonin had foreseen. However, when William saw this, he simply withdrew the bill from the Parliament, thus preventing debate. Instead he demanded from the Parliament 9 million thalers as a "provisional" appropriation. As constitutional Commander in Chief, he had already retained the mobilized *Landwehr* regiments on active service, even though the part-time soldiers had been sent back home.

It is doubtful that William had any thought of being cunning in submitting his unitemized demand for a "provisional" appropriation. Nevertheless, the Chamber chose to see his withdrawal of the bill as an indication of a royal willingness to negotiate, and they were certainly not discouraged in this assumption by Roon, Manteuffel, or Alvensleben. So, to show comparable goodwill, early in 1860 the Chamber voted 7.3 million thalers, on the express understanding that this was provisional, and implied no permanent parliamentary commitment to the reform. It was clear from the debate that this "provisional" approval meant that no expenditures were to be made for such permanent facilities as barracks. In the debate in the Chamber, the responsible leaders made clear their patriotic support of "adequate" military protection, but their opposition to "uncontrolled military strength."

Prince William and War Minister von Roon paid scant attention to these parliamentary observations. They had their increased Army, and the *Landwehr* had automatically been relegated to the reserve. Furthermore, since under the Act of 1815 the War Minister had authority over *Landwehr* training and readiness, but outside Army command channels, Roon now simply exercised that responsibility through the Army. As to the Chamber's implicit limitations on funds for barracks, this too was ignored.

The issue lay dormant for more than a year, but in 1861 the Parliament indicated its willingness to appropriate "provisionally" another 7.3 million thalers, but only on condition that a new, compromise Army bill be submitted within a year, or at most two years. (Roon had suggested the two-year compromise.) But William, who had been King since his brother's death in January, saw no reason to compromise. It was now up to the Parliament to ratify and to support the existing Prussian Army, which Prussia's King felt necessary for the security of the realm. In the light of this position by his sovereign, Roon withdrew his compromise agreement. When in March 1862 the Parliament refused to budge further, William dissolved it and called for new elections. But the new Chamber, assembled a few weeks later, was equally adamant.

BISMARCK STEPS ON THE STAGE / At this point—early September 1862—William threatened to abdicate. He was dissuaded by his advisers, but Roon sent a telegram to Otto von Bismarck, a stalwart monarchist and brilliant politician, then Prussian Ambassador to France, to return to Berlin to help resolve the impasse. Bismarck arrived on September 22, and next day was appointed Prime Minister.

Bismarck finessed the dispute with a brilliant political ploy. The constitution provided that the budget had to be agreed between the Lower and Upper chambers. Since the aristocratic Upper Chamber naturally supported the King, Bismarck was able to maintain that there was a "gap" in the constitution. Since taxes were being collected, since the funds were available, and since the government had to operate, Bismarck asserted that the King was responsible for making necessary expenditures until an agreed budget could be prepared. The predominantly liberal Chamber protested in vain. There was nothing in the constitution that prevented the King from making expenditures without a budget, and there was no way they could achieve a constitutionally valid budget.

NOTES TO CHAPTER SIX

[1] Craig, *op. cit.,* p. 125.

[2] Holborn, *op. cit.,* p. 185.

Chapter Seven

MOLTKE
TAKES COMMAND

AUSTRIA, PRUSSIA, AND SCHLESWIG-HOLSTEIN / Bismarck's advent at the helm of Prussian diplomacy had an immediate effect upon Moltke and his General Staff. It soon became evident that Bismarck was seeking a showdown with Austria over preeminence in Germany, and that his political objective was a union of Germany—without Austria—under Prussian leadership. During the winter of 1862-1863 there was a dispute resulting from Austrian efforts to strengthen the Confederation Diet at Frankfurt; since representation in the Diet was by state, Austria—supported by a majority of the German princes—would have gained authority by the proposed change. On the other hand, Bismarck's counterproposal of a popularly elected German Parliament would have assured the predominance of populous Prussia, since most of the Hapsburg dominions lay outside the Confederation boundary.

Hardly had this crisis quieted down when another arose with France, because of Prussian support for Russia in the suppression of the 1863 revolt in Poland. Moltke quickly shifted the focus of the General Staff's concerns from a southern to a western orientation. But Bismarck was not yet ready for a confrontation with France, so he withdrew the support to Russia.

Almost immediately there was new trouble with Austria over the German Confederation. Emperor Francis Joseph suggested a conference of the German princes at Frankfurt, to consider possible reforms in the Confederation. Bismarck immediately recognized this as another Austrian effort to increase influence in Germany; with difficulty he persuaded William not to attend. Relations with Austria became further strained in November when Bismarck was able to isolate Austria economically from the rest of Germany through a trade agreement between France and the *Zollverein,* the German customs union, which Prussia dominated.

The same month childless King Frederick VII of Denmark died. The Schleswig-Holstein issue, which was a question of dynastic succession to the crown of Denmark and to the ducal coronets of Schleswig and Holstein, had been simmering since the Danish-Prussian War of 1848-1849. In the Treaty of London of 1852, the European powers had established a formula for succession

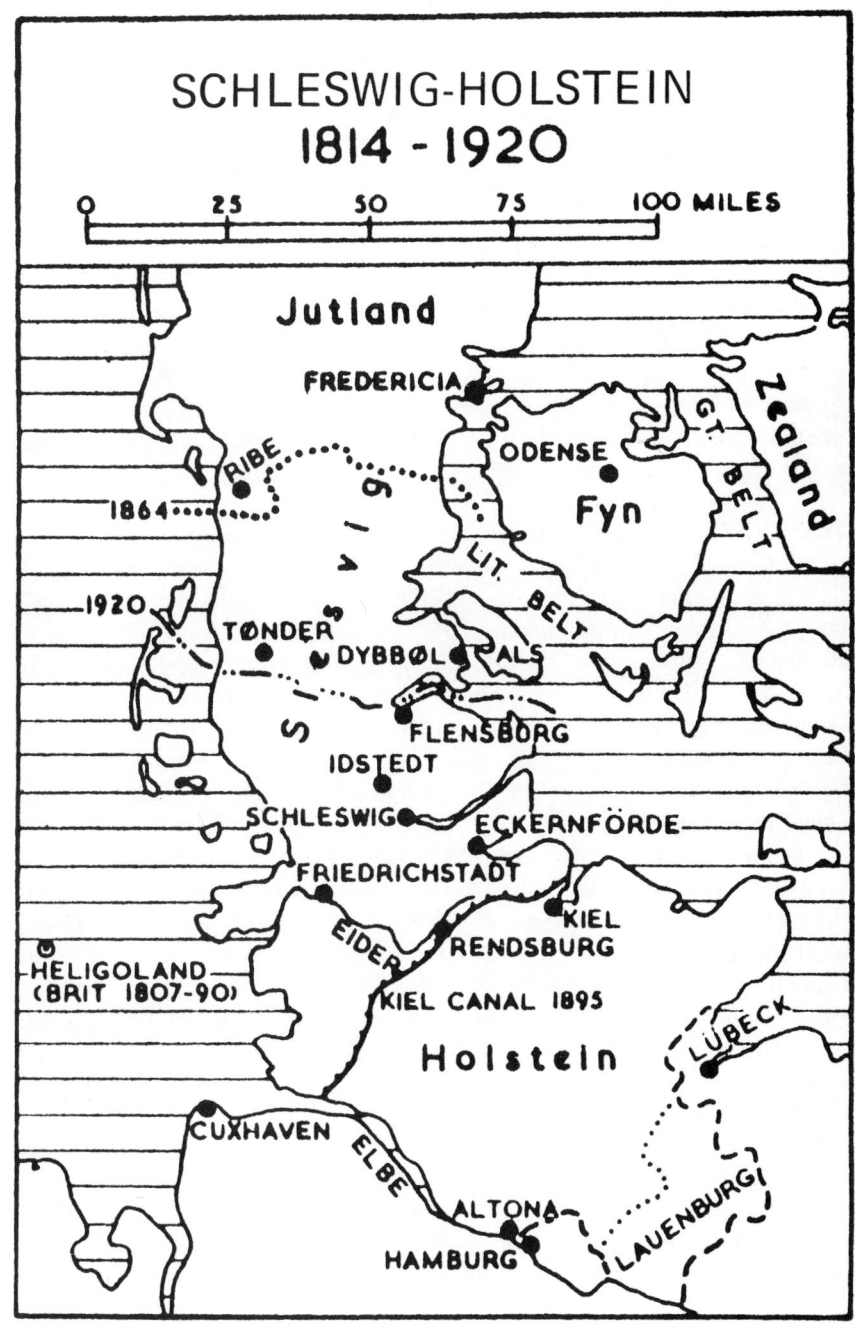

SCHLESWIG-HOLSTEIN
1814 - 1920

0   25   50   75   100 MILES

Jutland

FREDERICIA

Zealand

RIBE

ODENSE

1864

Fyn

Slesvig

LIT. BELT

GT. BELT

1920

TØNDER

DYBBØL ALS

FLENSBORG

IDSTEDT

SCHLESWIG

ECKERNFÖRDE

FRIEDRICHSTADT

KIEL

EIDER

RENDSBURG

HELIGOLAND
(BRIT 1807-90)

KIEL CANAL 1895

LÜBECK

Holstein

CUXHAVEN

ELBE

ALTONA

LAUENBURG

HAMBURG

of the combined realm of Denmark-Schleswig-Holstein under a Danish King. But this was now repudiated by the two duchies, which both proclaimed Prince Frederick of Augustenburg as their Duke, while Denmark proclaimed Christian IX as its new King, in accordance with the Treaty of London. On the basis of some technicalities in that treaty, most of the German princes, including Francis Joseph of Austria and William of Prussia, recognized Frederick's claim to the two duchies. Denmark, naturally, did not, and moved to reestablish central authority in the two recalcitrant duchies.

Moltke at once realized that this was almost certain to lead to hostilities between Denmark and Holstein, and possibly Schleswig as well. Since Holstein was a member of the German Confederation, some sort of military action in northern Germany was almost inevitable. Less clear was the question whether Austria and Prussia would stand together on this issue, as they had in the past, or whether a two-front war might result. Moltke calmly reviewed and updated both sets of plans, then awaited developments and instructions from the King.

THE SECOND DANISH WAR / These were not long in coming. Neither Austria nor Prussia was willing to allow the other to appear more devoted to support of the Confederation's sympathies for the German people of Holstein. In December both nations approved the dispatch of a federal Army of Saxon and Hanoverian contingents that occupied Holstein, while Danish troops were moving into Schleswig. On January 16 Austria and Prussia signed a treaty of alliance against Denmark, and jointly presented an ultimatum to Denmark to withdraw from Schleswig. When this was rejected by the Danes, Austria and Prussia declared war on Denmark on February 1, 1864, and sent a joint invasion army into Schleswig, under the command of Prussian Field Marshal Friedrich von Wrangel.

Moltke's position at this time was an anomalous one. In prewar conferences between King William, War Minister von Roon, and the senior generals of the Army, Wrangel had contemptuously rejected the suggestion that Moltke or one of the senior officers of the General Staff should serve as Chief of Staff of the invasion army. According to one historian, this suggestion gave Wrangel a long-awaited opportunity to express his personal opinions about the General Staff, which he declared to be wholly unnecessary, adding that it was disgraceful for a royal Prussian Field Marshal to have to put up with a lot of "damned clerking."[1] Instead, Wrangel chose for his Chief of Staff General Karl Ernst Eduard Vogel von Falckenstein, a like-minded, bull-headed aristocrat. Equally contemptuous of the General Staff, for which he had never been selected, Vogel von Falckenstein did not bother to keep Moltke informed of the progress of field operations. Fortunately for Moltke, however, he had frequent and thorough reports from Colonel Karl von Blumenthal, a General Staff officer, who was Chief of Staff of the corps commanded by Prince Frederick Charles (the King's nephew).

Actually Blumenthal did not have very much to report. As Moltke had foreseen in a prewar strategic planning memorandum to Roon and the King, the Danes had quickly fallen back from the frontier, avoiding a major battle in which they might be overwhelmed and destroyed. They had withdrawn to the fortifications of Dybböl (Düppel) in eastern Schleswig, guarding the approach to the island of Als (Alsen) across the Alsensund, and to Fredericia on the Little Belt in southeast Jutland, controlling the land approach to the island of Fyn (Fünen). Düppel (to use the German name) was one of the strongest fortifications in Europe at the time.

Moltke's strategic memorandum had pointed out that, without a fleet capable of challenging the Danish Navy, it would be impossible to do serious harm to Denmark other than by occupying the fertile province of Jutland. But the Austrians feared the possibility of intervention by the other signatories of the Treaty of London (Britain, France, Russia, and Sweden) if operations were carried into Denmark proper, and so opposed any move into Jutland. Accordingly, at Bismarck's instigation, that aspect of the General Staff plan was deleted from the order issued in the King's name to Wrangel by Roon.

Wrangel's Austro-Prussian Army quickly occupied all of Schleswig, save for the Düppel fortifications. Recognizing that an assault against those defenses would be costly at best, and that without seapower it would be impossible to starve the Danes into submission, Wrangel notified Berlin that he was going to invade Jutland. At Bismarck's behest, orders were rushed to him to call off this planned invasion and to avoid crossing the Schleswig-Jutland frontier. Nevertheless, one Prussian unit did cross, on February 17, and next day occupied the Danish town of Kolding. Despite repeated orders not to cross the frontier, in early March another Prussian thrust probed a few miles into Jutland.

MOLTKE AS FIELD ARMY CHIEF OF STAFF / General Edwin von Manteuffel, Chief of the Military Cabinet, believed that General Vogel von Falckenstein was more responsible for these violations of instructions than was the old Field Marshal. He persuaded the King to send Moltke to replace Vogel as Wrangel's Chief of Staff. Moltke arrived at Wrangel's headquarters in late April, just as the first phase of the war was coming to a close.

The Austrians, in March, had been persuaded that further operations against Düppel and Als would be endangered by the possibility of interference by the Danish forces in Fredericia. The Austrians therefore agreed to an advance that would blockade Fredericia, but insisted that the principal focus of operations should be against Düppel and Als. (Since the Austrian contingent was on the western side of the peninsula, they would not have to suffer the inevitable heavy casualties from such operations.)

This Austrian insistence reinforced Bismarck's position in an argument he was having with King William and the Prussian generals. The British, supported by the other great powers, were endeavoring to get a cease-fire agreement as a basis for peace negotiations. But Bismarck did not want to go to the conference table without the bargaining power that would come from a major Prussian victory. The only possibility of such a victory, as he saw it, would be an assault against Düppel and the occupation of Als.

Prince Frederick Charles, who had been left in front of Düppel when Wrangel moved north to blockade Fredericia, opposed the projected assault as being militarily meaningless. He and Blumenthal had prepared plans for an amphibious crossing to Als which could bypass Düppel, and might permit the eventual starvation of that fortress. Frederick Charles and Blumenthal asked permission to carry out that plan instead of the assault. Moltke supported their arguments and so did Roon. But Bismarck knew that he could not stall negotiations long enough to force the surrender of Düppel by starvation. A victory was needed—and needed quickly. Reluctantly the King gave the order, and on April 18 Prussian troops stormed the fortress to win an overwhelming victory.

Bismarck had his victory (and the Austrians, too late, recognized how they had helped him gain a strong bargaining position at the conference due to begin soon in London). A month's armistice was agreed, and the negotiations began in late April. To the annoyance of the Prussian Army, the armistice was extended for a month, near the end of May, because of lack of progress in London. On June 28, as the second month of the armistice was about to expire, the London conference collapsed, and hostilities began anew.

In mid-May King William, at the urging of Roon and Manteuffel, had diplomatically relieved Wrangel from command of the allied forces in Schleswig and Jutland, and placed Prince Frederick Charles in overall command. Moltke remained Chief of Staff of the field command. Anticipating that the conference would probably fail (and probably recognizing also that Bismarck wanted it to fail), Moltke obtained Frederick Charles' approval for a revised plan for an amphibious assault against Als. He also prepared plans to complete the occupation of Jutland.

Thus, when the war was renewed on June 28, the Prussian troops were ready. Within two weeks Als and Jutland had been occupied, and Denmark was suing for peace. The smooth efficiency of these operations contrasted sharply with the confusion and controversy that had attended the initial invasion of Schleswig. King William, who was in the field with the Army during the final weeks of the campaign, recognized that the difference was due to Moltke and to the system of coordination that linked the Chief of the General Staff to the chiefs of staff of the subordinate commands.

Shortly after the conclusion of the Danish War, Moltke decided it was time for him to retire and make room for younger men in the General Staff. After all, he was sixty-four years old. However, it was not to be; retirement was still twenty-four years away. Roon and the King had always respected Moltke, but now both began to consider that he was indispensable. Roon sensed that Manteuffel, who now combined the positions of Adjutant General and Chief of the Military Cabinet, had become somewhat jealous of the sudden attention Moltke was receiving from the King and the royal Princes. Ever the military diplomat, early in 1865 Roon was able to ease Manteuffel out of the court by persuading William to promote him and to place him in command of the Prussian troops in Schleswig-Holstein. The new Chief of the Military Cabinet was

Major General Hermann von Tresckow, who had served under Moltke in the General Staff. It did not take much persuading by Roon and Tresckow to have the King begin to include Moltke in meetings of the Crown Council when military matters were discussed.

MOLTKE AND BISMARCK / It was in such a Crown Council, on May 29, 1865, that Moltke had his first serious disagreement with Bismarck. The issues were familiar: relations with Austria and the future of Schleswig-Holstein. Bismarck was determined that Prussia should either annex, or otherwise gain control of, both Schleswig and Holstein. Austria, with the support of most of the members of the German Confederation, was strongly opposed to this. Moltke, speaking for the generals present in the Council, agreed with Bismarck's objective for the duchies, and urged the King to decide on war against Austria. But then Bismarck seemed to shift course. Despite the assurances of Roon and Moltke, he did not wish to risk war against Austria and the entire German Confederation. He insisted that a decision for war should be taken only if Prussia were able to arrange an alliance with France. After a brief argument between Moltke and Bismarck, the king intervened. The idea of an alliance with the hated enemy, particularly under the Imperial rule of a Bonaparte, was too much for William. Siding with Bismarck, he decided to compromise with Austria, and an agreement was reached whereby Austrian troops would occupy Holstein and Prussian troops Schleswig.

Despite William's evident distaste for an alliance with France, Bismarck pursued the possibility of at least an understanding with Napoleon III. After two meetings with the French Emperor convinced him that France was unlikely to intervene against Prussia in a war with Austria, the wily Chancellor sought the desired alliance with another traditional foe of Austria: Italy. On April 8, 1866, Prussia and Italy signed a treaty that committed Italy to join Prussia if war broke out between Prussia and Austria within three months.

To Moltke it was obvious that the die was cast. If the natural course of events did not precipitate war, Bismarck would create a casus belli in May or June. Although the military problems were formidable, Moltke was not dismayed; after all, less than a year before, he had argued with Bismarck in the Crown Council that Prussia could fight and defeat Austria and all of the other German states, even without allies. Although he was not counting on the Italian alliance to divert much Austrian strength from Germany, he recognized that there was a psychological benefit.

PLANNING FOR WAR WITH AUSTRIA / In Germany the odds against Prussia appeared substantial. Out of an Army of more than half a million men, Austria could mobilize more than 240,000 in Bohemia for an immediate offensive against vulnerable Berlin; Austria's German allies, with forces totaling close to 200,000 men, could interfere with the concentration of troops from Prussia's western provinces and could at the same time support the Austrian drive on

Berlin. Moltke knew that he could mobilize field forces totaling nearly 300,000 troops in four weeks—almost twice as fast as Austria could mobilize.* Close neighbors like Saxony could be overwhelmed before Austria could help them; the more distant and more formidable southern German states like Bavaria, Baden, and Württemberg would be held off with about 50,000 troops from Prussia's Rhenish provinces; another 10,000 would secure Silesia. This would permit the employment of field forces nearly 250,000 strong against Austria. Since Prussian mobilization was faster, even with the delays necessary to take care of Saxony and Hesse-Kassel, Moltke believed he could concentrate the scattered Prussian armies in northern Bohemia before the Austrians were ready to start their expected offensive against Berlin. With near equality in disposable forces, Moltke believed that the faster mobilization, and the better quality of the Prussian troops, combined with speed and boldness, would permit him to concentrate superior forces on the battlefield, and thus achieve an overwhelming victory in a one-battle, Napoleonic-type campaign.

Moltke knew that the Austrian Army had improved since 1859, but he was counting on three aspects of Prussian superiority: equipment, training, and leadership. In equipment the principal advantage was in the Prussian infantry rifle—the breech-loading Dreyse needle gun adopted in the late 1840s, and now issued to all regular and reserve troops of the Army. This could be reloaded by soldiers in a prone position, while the equally-new Austrian muzzle-loading rifled musket, although more accurate and with a considerably longer effective range, had a slower rate of fire, and could be reloaded only from a standing position.

Moltke recognized that the Austrian artillery weapons, even though predominantly muzzle loaders, were more accurate, and longer-ranged than those of the more rapid-firing Prussian artillery, now about two-thirds breech loaders. But here he was counting on generally higher Prussian training standards, maintained by a former General Staff officer, Lieutenant General Gustav Eduard von Hindersin, Inspector General of Artillery, to offset the slight Austrian technological superiority in cannon. Moltke was confident that the Prussian infantry units were also superior to their Austrian counterparts. Only in cavalry did he concede Austrian superiority, based on their long experience in combat with the Turks.

Leadership, of the sort provided to the artillery by Hindersin, was considered by Moltke to be the primary Prussian advantage. He had had an opportunity to study the Austrians in the 1864 war in Denmark, and felt they were not much improved over their 1859 standards of leadership; he was confident that the Prussian commanders, and their efficient chiefs of staff, would outperform the Austrians, and he expected comparable superiority at the lower levels of command.

---

*There were about 100,000 additional Prussian troops, mostly mobilized reserves, in garrisons and depots throughout Prussia; Austria, of course, had about 80,000 field troops in Italy, and more than 200,000 others in garrisons throughout the far-flung Hapsburg Empire.

Having started the wheels of war turning with the Italian alliance, Bismarck found that there was little need for him to stir the witches' broth further. Saxony, fearful of a sudden Prussian surprise attack, ordered a partial mobilization on April 14. The Italians went about their preparations so enthusiastically that Austria, on April 1, began mobilizing its southern Army, some 80,000 men under the command of Archduke Albert. On April 27 Austrian mobilization began in Bohemia, under General Ludwig August Ritter von Benedek. In the following days the southern German states also began partial mobilizations.

By the beginning of May, Prussia was the only German state that had not ordered some form of mobilization; Moltke was becoming concerned as William, still not convinced that war was inevitable, hesitated. Bismarck, who fully recognized the inevitability of war, refrained from pressing the King to order mobilization; he was confident of the Prussian Army and Moltke, and he wanted to avoid any charges by the other powers that Prussia was the aggressor. Finally, on May 3, the King ordered partial mobilization, and on the eighth a full mobilization.

Now both Moltke and Bismarck went into action; the general, fully occupied with his military problems, did not realize that he was acting in concert with the Chancellor—who fully recognized and planned it that way. While vigorously defending Prussia against the accusations of the other German states in the Frankfurt Diet, Bismarck assured the governments of France, Britain, and Russia—attempting to establish a European Congress to preserve peace—that Prussia was willing to negotiate. And he encouraged Prussian General Anton von der Gablenz to enter into negotiations with his brother, Austrian General Ludwig von der Gablenz, to seek a peaceful solution to the German and Schleswig-Holstein questions.

On June 1, however, Austria played into Bismarck's hands by raising in the Frankfurt Diet charges against Prussian aims in Schleswig-Holstein. This was a violation of the Treaty of Gastein, in which Austria and Prussia had agreed that they would resolve between themselves all differences regarding the two duchies. Knowing that Moltke had now had his four weeks for mobilization, Bismarck accused Austria of treaty violation, and on June 3 informed the other powers that their proposed European Congress was impossible until Austria conformed to its treaty obligations. On June 7 Prussian troops in overwhelming numbers marched into Holstein.

WAR WITH AUSTRIA / On June 12 Austria broke diplomatic relations with Prussia, and the Austrian representative at the Frankfurt Diet called for joint Confederation action against Prussia. Bismarck, knowing that a vote in the Diet would be overwhelmingly against Prussia, merely announced on June 14 that the Confederation was abolished. Next day Prussian ultimatums were presented to Saxony, Hanover, and Hesse-Kassel, demanding their neutrality. When these were rejected, Prussian troops invaded the three small countries. There was no declaration of war. The closest approximation was a message from Crown Prince

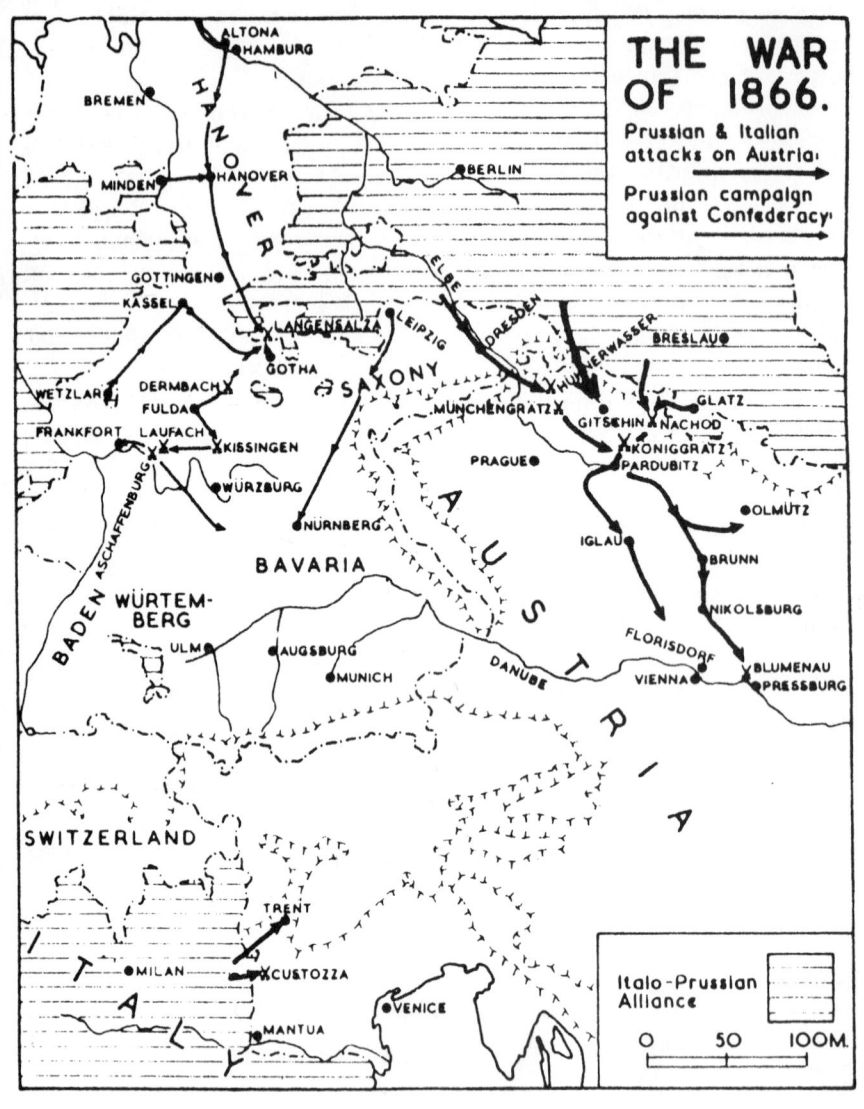

THE WAR
OF 1866.

Prussian & Italian
attacks on Austria:

Prussian campaign
against Confederacy:

Italo-Prussian
Alliance

0   50   100M.

Frederick William, commanding the Prussian Second Army, concentrating in northern Silesia, to the nearest Austrian commander in Bohemia, announcing the existence of a state of war.

Meanwhile, as Moltke kept close contact with all of the subordinate chiefs of staff, the mobilization had gone well. Late in May, however, an incident occurred that was to have important repercussions in both the long- and short-term military history of Prussia. Fearful of possible intervention by Emperor Napoleon III, Bismarck—without Moltke's knowledge—persuaded the King to issue orders countermanding the mobilization instructions of the VIII Corps, which Moltke had directed to move eastward from the Rhineland Province to join the main Prussian concentration in south-central Prussia. Moltke was furious; he and Roon had an interview with the King. William, good soldier that he was, meekly accepted Moltke's diplomatic but firm remonstrance, and revoked his last order.

MOLTKE AS FIELD COMMANDER / Then, on June 2, with the approval of War Minister von Roon, the King issued a brief but momentous order. Until further notice, the Chief of the General Staff was authorized to issue orders directly to subordinate units in the Prussian Army, without the delay of getting the approval of either King or War Minister.

It was a substantial command, stretched in an arc more than 300 miles long, from the Neisse River on the east to the Aller River in the west. In central Silesia was Crown Prince Frederick William's Second Army of about 115,000 men. Based on southern Brandenburg, and now sweeping through eastern Saxony, was the First Army, 93,000 strong, under Prince Frederick Charles. Farther west, marching south from Torgau on Dresden, was the Army of the Elbe, 48,000 men under General Karl Eberhard Herwarth von Bittenfeld. General Vogel von Falckenstein's Western Army, about 50,000 men, was concentrated in Prussian Saxony.

Vogel von Falckenstein's mission was to knock Hanover out of the war, to turn south to repeat the process against Hesse-Kassel, then to advance in a southeasterly direction to attract the attention of Bavaria (and incidentally of Hesse-Darmstadt, Baden, and Württemberg) away from the main theater of operations in Bohemia. The three main Prussian armies were meanwhile to advance into Bohemia, converging east of Prague, then to march eastward toward Olmütz, the expected concentration center for General Benedek's Austrian Army.

During the mobilization and preliminary operations Moltke remained in Berlin, tied to the telegraph, making certain that his dispositions were going according to plan. It was fortunate that he did because the irrepressible Chancellor again interjected himself into the military picture.

On June 19 Bismarck, without notifying either the King, Roon, or Moltke, sent a telegram direct to Vogel von Falckenstein, now in southern Hanover, suggesting that an advance southwestward to Frankfurt would prevent the concentration of the Confederation armies and "would easily lead to a second Rossbach." Vogel von Falckenstein had just discovered that the Hanoverian Army was moving south toward Bavaria, and had begun pursuit. While pondering over this message from Bismarck, he lost contact with the Hanoverians on the twenty-second. Never having been sympathetic to the General Staff, and holding a grudge against Moltke since the Danish War, when Moltke had taken his place as Chief of Staff of the Field Army, Vogel decided to follow Bismarck's advice. He began marching toward the southwest. Not surprisingly he did not bother to inform Moltke.

Moltke soon realized, however, that something was seriously wrong in the area of the Western Army. The Hanoverians, taking advantage of Vogel's disappearance, were marching southward unopposed, across the western tip of Prussian Saxony, toward a possible junction with either the Bavarians or the Austrians. Moltke rushed several contingents of garrison troops to delay the Hanoverians, and peremptorily ordered Vogel to return to carry out his assigned mission. The result was a battle at Langensalza just north of Erfurt, on June 27, where General Alexander von Arentschildt's Hanoverians sharply defeated Vogel von Falckenstein's advance guard. Before the day was over, however, the remainder of Vogel's Army reached the field, blocking further advance by the outnumbered Hanoverians. On June 29 blind King George V of Hanover surrendered his Army to Vogel.

THE KÖNIGGRÄTZ-SADOWA CAMPAIGN / Meanwhile the three main Prussian armies were advancing steadily toward Bohemia. The Army of the Elbe took Dresden on June 19, then pursued the Saxon Army of 35,000 men toward the Bohemian mountains. On June 22 Moltke ordered the three army commanders to cross the mountains and meet near Gitschin, in front of the main Austrian Army, now advancing from Olmütz. They were to move rapidly to avoid the danger of defeat in detail.

As they approached the frontier, the Army of the Elbe and the First Army converged, and pushed ahead into the mountain passes under the overall command of Prince Frederick Charles. Less than 100 miles further east, the Second Army was streaming through the passes south of Breslau. Moltke, receiving daily telegraphic reports in Berlin, recognized that there was still some danger that Benedek might be able to concentrate his Army against either the combined First and Elbe armies to the West, or the Second Army to the East, to defeat one, and then the other. However, the reports he received late on June 27—the same day as the Battle of Langensalza—convinced Moltke that the Austrians were neither bold enough nor concentrated enough even to try to defeat the Prussians in detail, and much less able to accomplish it.

There had been three sharp clashes in Bohemia that day. North of Prague the advanced guard of the First Army encountered the Austrian I Corps of General Count Eduard von Clam-Gallas, and rear-guard elements of the Saxon Army. After half-hearted, brief opposition, Clam-Gallas fell back toward Gitschin.

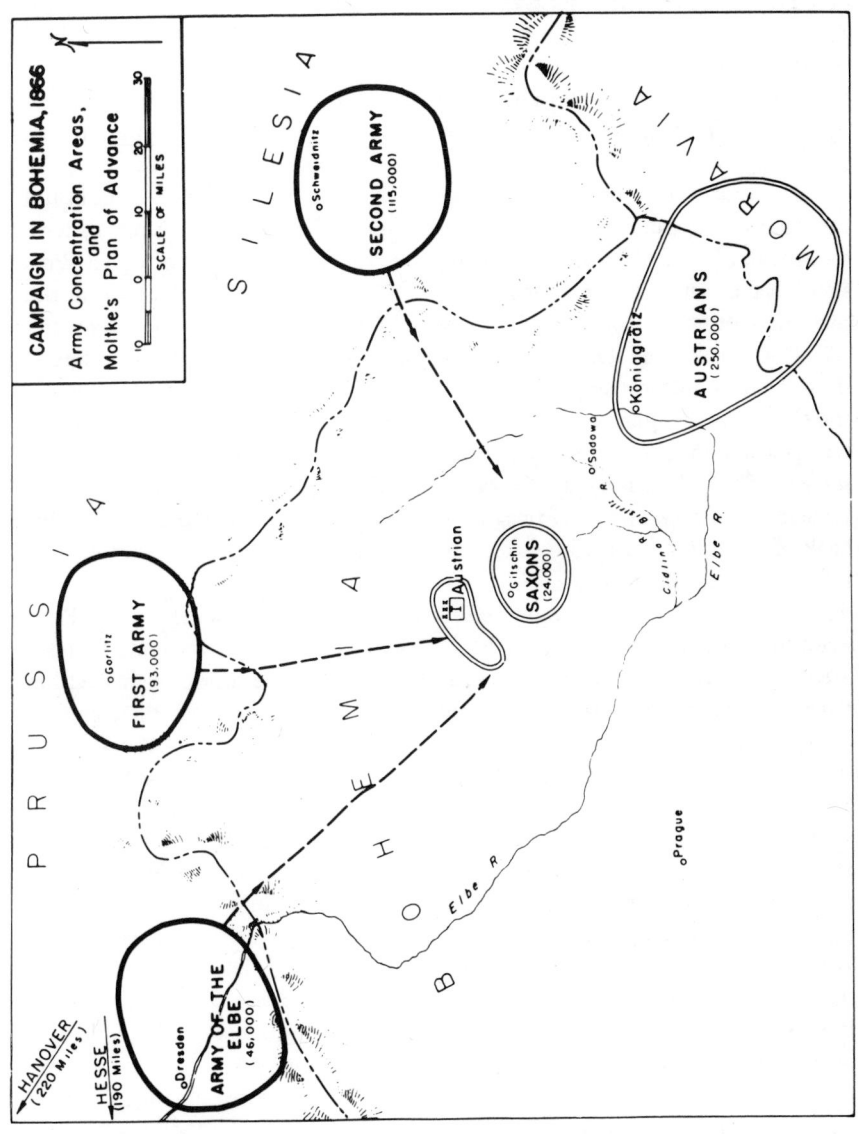

Further east the Second Army, also debouching from the passes, had two engagements that same day. At Trautenau, General Adolf A. von Bonin's I Corps, right-wing element of Frederick William's Army, encountered an Austrian corps under General von der Gablenz. After an initial Prussian success, Gablenz, despite heavy losses from the Prussian needle guns, counterattacked, and drove the Prussians back into the defile in confusion. The exhaustion of his troops, and their heavy casualties (5,700 killed and wounded, as opposed to Prussian losses of only 1,300 men), combined with the threat of other Prussian columns advancing through passes to his right, kept Gablenz from following up his success.

The results were different, however, at Nachod, sixteen miles to the Southeast. There Prussian General Karl Friedrich von Steinmetz' V Corps was opposed by Austrian General Wilhelm Ramming von Riedkirchen's VI Corps. The Prussian advance guard, at the head of the defile, threw back an Austrian attack; Steinmetz rushed forward with his main body, and drove the Austrians back.

The reactions of the opposing commanders to the reports they received of these actions on the twenty-seventh were markedly different. Benedek, despite the success at Trautenau, found his worst fears confirmed. He was also encountering severe logistical difficulties. When, the next day, the Prussians offset the results of Trautenau by a victory over Gablenz in a sharp action at Soor, Benedek sent back a gloomy telegram to Vienna, warning of disaster, and pulled back his scattered corps to concentrate for a defensive battle west of the upper Elbe River, near the fortress of Königgrätz.

For his part, when Moltke received word of the engagements of June 27, he knew that a major battle would be fought in northeastern Bohemia in a few days. He issued orders for a concentration of the three armies near Gitschin, then suggested to the King that the royal headquarters should join the combined armies of Frederick Charles and Bittenfeld. On the thirtieth the Prussian high command—including William I, Bismarck, Roon, Moltke, and a small General Staff contingent—reached the First Army near Gitschin, where another encounter had just taken place. A telegram was soon received from Frederick William, reporting that he had driven the Austrians out of Skalitz some thirty miles to the east. There was no cavalry reconnaissance, but General Staff study of newspaper reports, and interrogation of local civilians indicated that the main Austrian Army was concentrating in the vicinity of Königgrätz. The incomplete information suggested that the concentration was taking place east of the river; at least Moltke assumed that Benedek would not prepare for battle with an unfordable river in his rear.

Moltke, seeing an opportunity to encircle the Austrians, on July 1 ordered the First Army to advance to the south toward Königgrätz; the Second Army was to continue its southwesterly advance against the Austrian right; the Army of the Elbe was to cross the Elbe south of Königgrätz to strike the Austrian left flank and rear. Moltke anticipated a battle on July 3 or 4; possibly the third if Benedek decided to advance from Königgrätz against the First Army and the Army of the Elbe, more likely the fourth if the Austrians awaited the Prussian

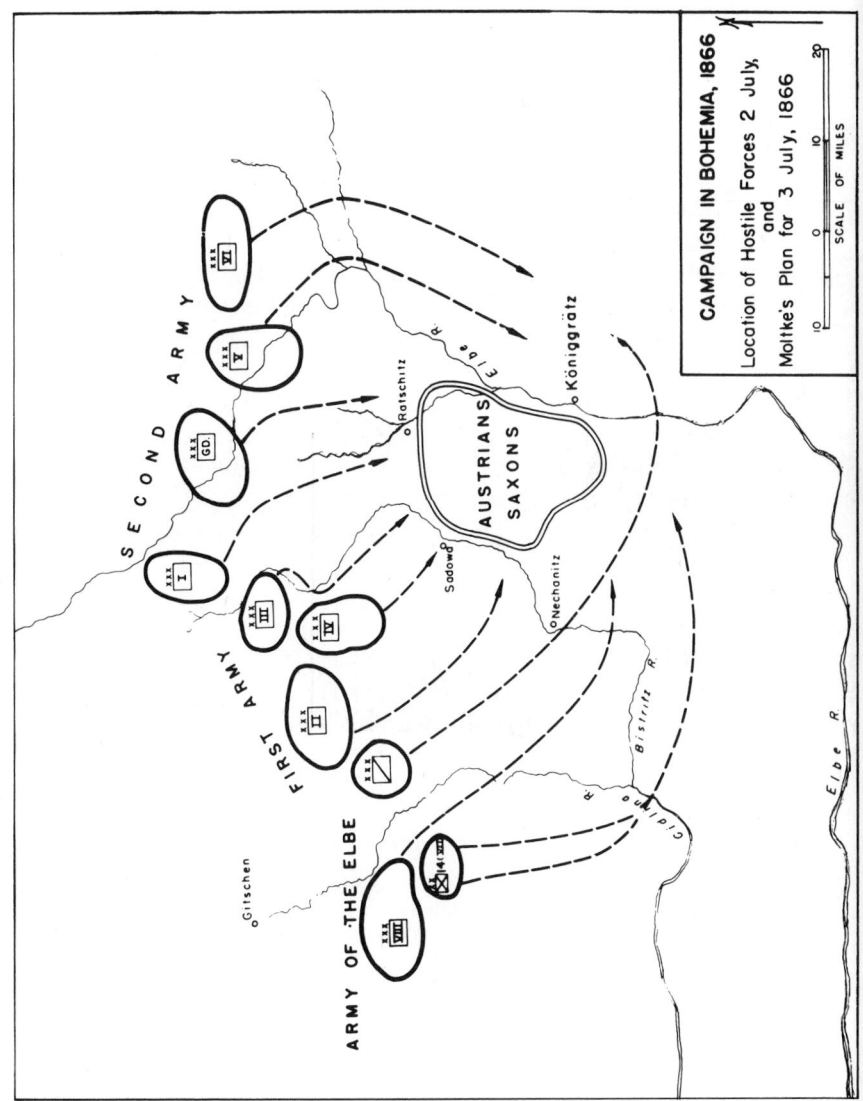

CAMPAIGN IN BOHEMIA, 1866

Location of Hostile Forces 2 July, and Moltke's Plan for 3 July, 1866

advance behind the Elbe.* In either event he felt that an encirclement should be possible, since an Austrian advance on the second and third (which Moltke considered unlikely) would merely reduce the distance that Frederick William's and Bittenfeld's armies would have to travel.

Moltke has been criticized, with some reason, for not having used his cavalry reserve for screening and scouting, and for not having insisted that his subordinate commanders make better use of their cavalry than they did in this campaign. But in their defense, it must be remembered that the Prussian generals were more respectful of the Austrian cavalry than of any other element of Benedek's army. Thus the Prussian cavalry was being held in reserve to exploit expected infantry success. The Prussian leaders did not realize that Benedek, more reprehensible in his failure to use his best troops, was also holding his cavalry in reserve, rather than using it aggressively in front of his army. In any event, the result was that neither army was as well informed of the dispositions of its enemy as it should have been. Moltke, still assuming that the Austrians were east of the river, was thus unaware of the fact that he was offering Benedek a fleeting opportunity to hit the flank of the First Army, advancing across his front. Benedek was equally unaware of the opportunity, which he probably would not have tried to seize, since he had avoided similar but better opportunities four days earlier.

Late on July 2, however, First Army patrols informed Prince Frederick Charles that there were at least three Austrian corps deployed to his left, near Sadowa. Quickly the Prince shifted direction to the east, and issued orders for an attack the following day. While his own army would strike what appeared to be the main Austrian position between Sadowa and Königgrätz, he ordered the Army of the Elbe to shift its advance from southeast to east; Bittenfeld's mission was still to turn the Austrian left flank, but now he was to do so west of Königgrätz instead of east of the Elbe. Frederick Charles also sent a message to

---

*During this flurry of telegraphic orders there may have occurred an event which is probably apocryphal. In his article on Moltke in *Makers of Modern Strategy* normally reliable historian Hajo Holborn makes the point that Moltke, even though he had been Chief of the General Staff for nine years, was still virtually unknown in Prussia, and not even well-known in the Army. A division commander is supposed to have received a message directly from Moltke, and to have commented, "This is all very well, but who is General Moltke?" Gordon Craig, in his *The Politics of the Prussian Army*, repeats the story somewhat doubtfully in a footnote, citing Holborn as the authority. Walter Goerlitz, in his *History of the General Staff* reports the same incident and although the quoted words are slightly different, and there is no source cited, it is hard to avoid the suspicion that Goerlitz was merely embellishing the Holborn story. There are two compelling reasons for doubting the story's authenticity. In the first place, it is difficult to accept the thought that the respected Chief of the General Staff would have been unknown to a division commander, even of a reserve division (which almost certainly would have been commanded by a regular officer), with a chief of staff almost certainly from the General Staff. Furthermore, Moltke's entire concept of directing modern war, reinforced by his study of the 1859 campaign in Italy, was for the provision of very general instructions to the senior subordinate commanders, making clear the objective and the mission, then allowing the subordinate to arrange the details. Thus, for Moltke to send a message directly even to a corps commander, to say nothing of a division commander, is almost inconceivable, and totally out of character.

Prince Frederick William, requesting his Second Army to cover the left flank of the First Army, and to strike the Austrian right. Another message was sent back to Gitschin to inform Moltke of the situation, and of Frederick Charles' plans and orders.

Some authorities have criticized Frederick Charles for "headstrong impetuosity," and for attempting "to take charge of the campaign." They have suggested that possible disaster was averted only by Moltke's prompt corrective action. These criticisms are unfair to both Frederick Charles and Moltke.

Frederick Charles's orders to his own army and to Bittenfeld were fully consistent with the general instructions he had received from Moltke, and with the objective set by the Chief of the General Staff. The Prince was merely responding to a situation which, while unexpectedly different in detail, did not affect his mission. To have waited for the Second Army to arrive, in order to carry out the maneuver as originally envisaged by Moltke, would have given the enemy an opportunity to change the situation still further, either by concentration on one or the other of the two main Prussian forces or, more likely, by withdrawal from the trap. And if the Austrians to his front had been only three corps, as the Prince apparently believed, the delay would have been even less justifiable. Frederick Charles's one mistake was in failing to make clear to his cousin—the Crown Prince—the potential urgency of the new situation.

It is doubtful if Moltke would have wanted Frederick Charles to do anything differently from the way he did, save for the wording of the message to the Second Army. Moltke was awakened from his sleep shortly before midnight when the report from Frederick Charles reached the royal headquarters. He read the messages the Prince had sent and recognized the danger of inadequate response by Frederick William, since Moltke was certain that the First Army was opposed, not just by three corps, but by Benedek's entire Army. The General did not even consider ordering Frederick Charles to delay his attack until the Second Army arrived. He merely sent a message of his own to Frederick William to march at once, with all possible force and all possible speed, against the Austrian right flank. To make certain that the urgency of this message was appreciated, he wakened the King at midnight, and asked him to countersign the order.

Frederick William, and his Chief of Staff Blumenthal, had already replied to the message from Frederick Charles, telling him that only one corps would be available to support the First Army on the third. When Moltke's order reached them at 4:00 A.M., however, they changed their minds and issued urgent march orders to the entire Army. The leading elements of the Second Army reached the battlefield by 11:00 A.M..

Moltke's order to Frederick William was undoubtedly the key to the scope of the victory won that day. Major General Eduard P. K. von Fransecky, commanding the 7th Division on the First Army's left flank, had allowed himself to be carried away by initial early-morning success. His orders were merely to push back the Austrians' outposts to the line of the Bistritz River, a tributary of the

Elbe, but, despite rain and early morning fog, he had impetuously attacked across the river into the center of the Austrian Army. To avert disaster, and to assure a junction with the Second Army, Frederick Charles had to feed more divisions into the fight on his left, which was touch-and-go when Frederick William's advance guard reached the field.

Moltke's hopes for an encirclement of the Austrians were frustrated, however, by the excessive caution of Bittenfeld. Fearful of becoming isolated, that general turned his Army of the Elbe eastward too soon, overlapping the right wing of the First Army. Thus the Austrian left flank, instead of being turned, and cut off from Königgrätz, was merely driven back toward the river and fortress.

By 2:30 Benedek's right wing was in confusion, under the hammer blows of the Second Army, and his left wing was also falling back. The battle was clearly lost; his army was trapped in front of a river. The Austrian general, who had saved his Emperor's army from disaster by masterly conduct of the rear guard at Solferino in 1859, again demonstrated his capabilities as a defensive commander in disaster. He ordered a general withdrawal, then employed his cavalry, ably supported by his artillery, in a series of counterattacks that slowed down the Prussian advance. Despite fearful losses, the Austrian horsemen performed their mission well. Under this gallant cover, the disorganized Austrians were able to get across the Elbe fords and bridges without further serious loss.

The Prussians, exhausted by intensive marching and fighting in midsummer heat, were in no condition to pursue. Benedek, still making good use of his cavalry in withdrawal, fell back to Olmütz. Austrian casualties had been about 40,000, half of these being prisoners; Prussian casualties were about 10,000.

END OF THE SEVEN WEEKS' WAR / After a day to reorganize, the Prussians resumed the advance to the south, closely pursuing Benedek, who fell back toward Linz and Vienna. Bismarck and Moltke both kept close touch with developments elsewhere by telegraph. Even before Königgrätz the Prussians had learned that the Austrians had inflicted a major defeat on the Italians at Custozza, thus making it likely that reinforcements could be sent to Benedek's Army before it reached Vienna. In fact, Archduke Albert, the victor of Custozza, had already been ordered north to replace Benedek.

In Germany Vogel von Falckenstein's command—now called the Army of the Main—was advancing on Frankfurt, after victories over the Bavarians at Dermbach and Kissingen. But Bismarck was becoming increasingly concerned about the possibility of French intervention. It was clear that Austrian Emperor Francis Joseph was willing to make peace, if the terms were right. If, on the other hand, Prussia tried to humiliate Austria, Moltke told Bismarck that in a prolonged war Prussia would be forced, at least temporarily, to the defensive. On top of that, Bismarck was thinking ahead to the likelihood of eventual war with France. It would be important that the Hapsburg Empire be friendly, or at least

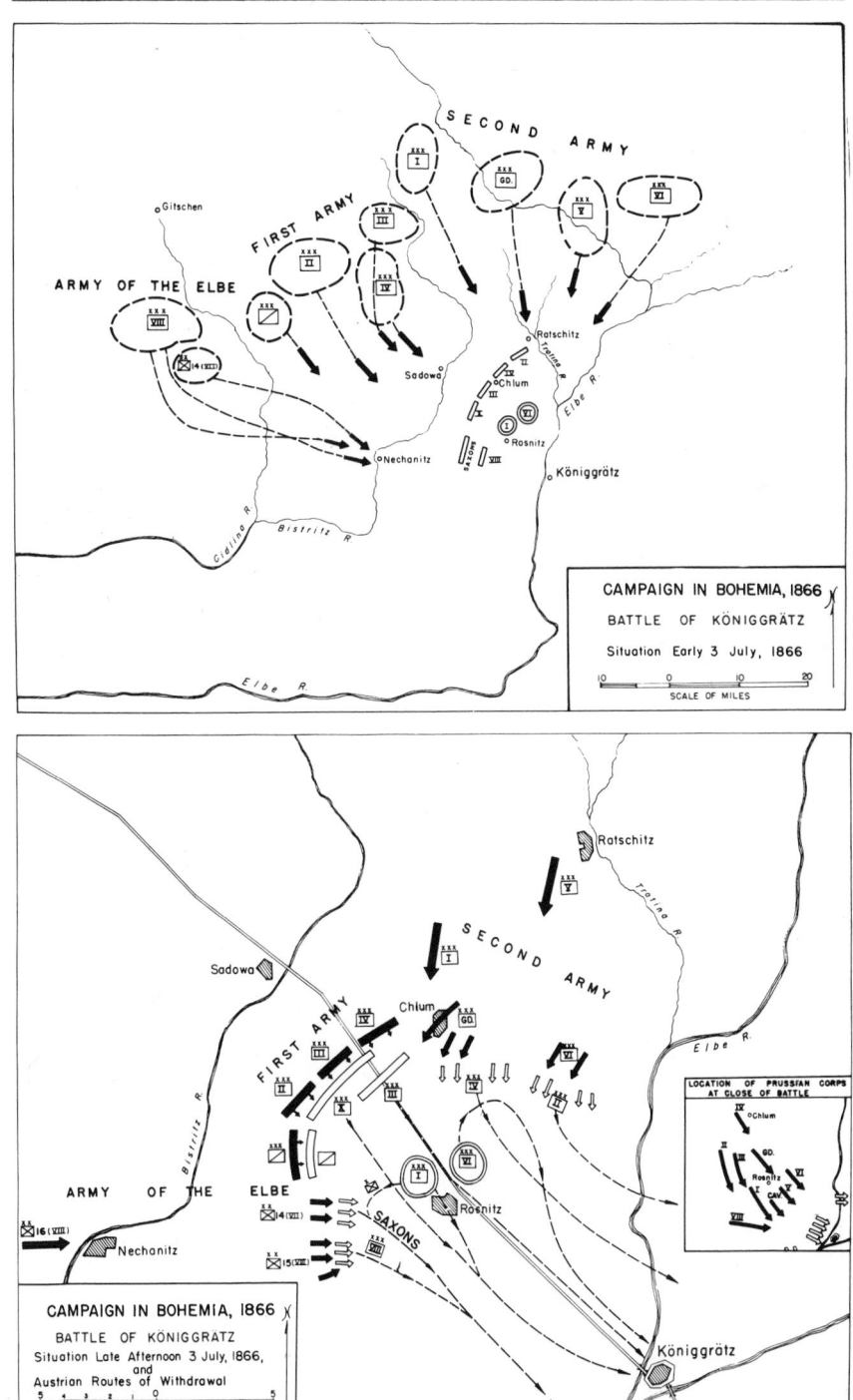

CAMPAIGN IN BOHEMIA, 1866

BATTLE OF KÖNIGGRÄTZ

Situation Early 3 July, 1866

SCALE OF MILES

CAMPAIGN IN BOHEMIA, 1866

BATTLE OF KÖNIGGRÄTZ

Situation Late Afternoon 3 July, 1866,
and
Austrian Routes of Withdrawal

SCALE OF MILES

LOCATION OF PRUSSIAN CORPS
AT CLOSE OF BATTLE

neutral, when that eventuality came. And so peace was quickly made with an Austria that was chastened, but not humbled.

NOTES TO CHAPTER SEVEN

[1] Goerlitz, *op. cit.,* pp. 83-84.

Chapter Eight

THE GENERAL STAFF
The Franco-Prussian War

 APPLYING THE LESSONS OF THE SEVEN WEEKS' WAR /
Despite the sudden fame and acclaim he had received from his
decisive victory over Austria in 1866, Moltke was far from
satisfied with himself or with the General Staff or with the
Prussian Army. This was not because of any excess of modesty
—false or otherwise—on his part. Quiet and self-effacing
though he was, Moltke knew his strengths and was aware of his worth. Furthermore, his confidence in the superiority of the Prussian Army over potential
foes had been fully confirmed by Königgrätz, and he was quite aware of the
importance of his contribution, and that of the General Staff and its plans, in
demonstrating that superiority. Nevertheless, as an objective and historically
oriented professional soldier, he knew how many things had gone wrong, and
recognized some deficiencies in Prussian organization, weaponry, and doctrine;
any of these shortcomings might have been exploited by an alert foe, with
incalculable results.

Moltke was particularly chagrined by his failure to use the Prussian cavalry
properly, and by his realization that all of the commanders at lower levels had
been equally inept in the employment of the horsemen in their commands. Here,
clearly, was a fundamental failure in Prussian doctrine that might have had
disastrous consequences in the week before Königgrätz, as the Prussian armies
were blindly pushing their way through the Bohemian mountain passes, and as
their individual advanced elements literally blundered their way into unforeseen
meeting engagements around the periphery of northern Bohemia. Henceforward
he would see to it that commanders at all levels were reminded of the crucial
importance of cavalry for reconnaissance, to establish contact with the enemy,
and then to maintain constant surveillance over all hostile activities. Equal stress
was laid upon the use of cavalry to screen the movements of the main elements
of the Army, to prevent enemy cavalry from gaining comparable information,
and to provide outpost cover to delay and harass an approaching foe.

Hardly less important were the deficiencies discovered in Prussian artillery
weapons and doctrine. As for the weapons, the answer was clearly to hasten and
complete as soon as possible the partial conversion of the Prussian artillery to

steel, rifled, breech-loading cannon. But more fundamental was the employment of these cannons. It had been the Prussian practice to have the artillery toward the rear of the marching columns, on the understandable premise that the artillery would generally be deployed behind all of the infantry except the reserves and rearguard. But what this meant was that the columns debouching from the mountain passes were unsupported by artillery, when they met the Austrians in the Bohemian foothills. The same problem of delay in providing artillery support to the engagement elements was also evident, although less seriously, on the main battlefield of Königgrätz.

The new Prussian artillery doctrine that soon replaced the previous practice was probably devised by General von Hindersin, Inspector of Artillery, and certainly endorsed by Moltke. Hindersin, originally an infantryman, had spent most of his early career on the General Staff, and had served as the Chief of Staff of the Confederation contingent that reestablished peace in Baden in 1849. His skill in commanding the artillery in the attack on Düppel had led to his appointment as Inspector of Artillery shortly before the Austrian war. He was generally satisfied with the performance of the Prussian artillery once it got into action, but was concerned by the fact that this was often late in the engagements. He had two doctrinal solutions.

In the first place, a substantial detachment of artillery was to be assigned to the advanced guard of a division, corps, or army. The remainder of the artillery was to be placed close to the front of the main body of any march column, so that in a meeting engagement it would be able to offer the earliest possible support to an engaged advance guard, and to cover with fire the deployment of the main body. Secondly Hindersin recommended that the old practice of holding out a reserve of artillery be abandoned. All available artillery should be engaged in battle at the earliest possible opportunity. Hindersin seems to be the man who devised the modern concept that the artillery's reserve is its ammunition.

Moltke had also been embarrassed by the confusion which existed on the battlefield of Königgrätz after the Austrian retreat. The mingling of units and individuals from the First and Second armies, and the time-consuming necessity to reorganize, was largely responsible for the success of the Austrian cavalry in the closing hours of the day, and prevented immediate initiation of the pursuit that Moltke wished for. By the time the Prussians renewed their advance, the Austrians were a full day ahead of them, the retreat well covered by their cavalry.

The solution to this problem was not as obvious as the doctrinal changes initiated for the cavalry and artillery. In order not to deter individual commanders from seeking to press forward as aggressively and energetically as possible, Moltke continued to emphasize the importance of initiative and aggressiveness at all levels of command. (Adherence to that doctrine, after all, had had much to do with the early and decisive entry into battle by the Second Army's advanced elements in the late morning and early afternoon of July 3.) There was increased emphasis on coordination between adjacent units—again at all levels of command. At the same time commanders were impressed with their responsibility to maintain complete control over all their subordinate units at all times—which meant knowing where they were and being able to get messages to them—while at the same time making sure that their own immediate superiors were kept more adequately informed of what was going on.

Perhaps the most important tactical-doctrinal lesson of the war was its confirmation of Moltke's prewar assessment of the growing importance of infantry firepower, primarily as a result of the introduction of the infantry rifle, with its long-range, accurate conoidal bullet. This was enhanced in the Prussian Army by its marriage to the breech-loading action of the Dreyse needle gun. As a result of his observations of the effectiveness of Danish defensive fire in the 1864 war, and also possibly as a result of reports on the American Civil War,[*] Moltke recognized that a true revolution was taking place in weapons effects. In mid-1865 he wrote:

> The attack of a position is becoming notably more difficult than its defense. The defensive during the first phase of battle offers a decisive superiority. The task of a skillful offensive will consist of forcing our foe to attack a position chosen by us, and only when casualties, demoralization, and exhaustion have drained his strength will we ourselves take up the tactical offensive. . . . Our strategy must be offensive, our tactics defensive.[1]

There was not time before the outbreak of war with Austria for this concept —almost as revolutionary as the weapons effects which prompted it—to be translated by the conservative Prussian Army into effective tactical doctrine, although Moltke may have had this in the back of his mind when he formulated his encirclement plan at Königgrätz. But the effects of firepower on that and the other battlefields of the war provided further evidence that the concept was sound, and he was determined that it should become doctrine.

Moltke had no personal authority to introduce these doctrinal changes for cavalry, artillery, and infantry into the Army. With the return of peace, he had reverted to his position subordinate to the Minister of War. But not only was there a cordial personal relationship between Roon and Moltke; the bluff War

---

[*] Moltke's writings reflect little interest in the American Civil War, but there does not seem to be any solid authority for the reputed contempt attributed to him in the apparently apocryphal remark that the Union and Confederate armies were "armed mobs." His own experience in the 1864, 1866, and 1871 wars confirmed much of the Civil War experience, in which infantry rifles inflicted 85 to 90 percent of the casualties, while artillery accounted for only 9 to 10 percent. This was in marked contrast to early nineteenth century experience, evidenced as recently as the U.S.-Mexican and the Crimean Wars, in which artillery accounted for nearly 50 percent and infantry firearms for barely 50 percent of casualties. The increasing effectiveness of infantry small arms also raised the total casualty rates significantly above those of the early nineteenth century, even above the rates of Napoleon's bloodiest battles.

Minister had been tremendously impressed by the success of Moltke's plans, and by the smooth and efficient way in which they had been implemented. As a soldier he fully understood the reason for and the need for the changes, and he saw to it that the necessary orders were issued. Both Roon and Moltke consulted frequently with the Inspectors of Artillery, Infantry, and Cavalry in the years following the war. The validity of the new concepts, and the success with which they were incorporated into the Army's doctrine would be well demonstrated within four years of Königgrätz.

GENERAL STAFF REORGANIZATION / During and just after the war Moltke had also initiated some internal changes in the organization of the General Staff. These were confirmed by royal order on January 31, 1867. The staff was divided into two major elements, a Main Establishment (*Hauptetat*) and a Supporting Establishment (*Nebenetat*). The mission-oriented Main Establishment initially consisted of the three traditional geographical mission-related departments with a slight reordering of areas of responsibility: The First Department was concerned with plans relating to Austria, Russia, Scandinavia, Turkey, Greece, and Asia; the Second Department was responsible for Prussia, Germany, Switzerland, and Italy; the Third Department dealt with matters concerning France, Great Britain, Belgium, Holland, Spain, Portugal, and America. Within the Second Department was a section responsible only for the Prussian and German railroads; it was practically a fourth department, and a few years later it was officially reorganized as such.

The functionally concerned Supporting Establishment had five departments: Military History, Geographical-Statistical, Topographical, War Room, and Land Triangulation Bureau.

POLITICAL HARMONY AND THE NORTH GERMAN FEDERATION / Meanwhile, there had been two important political developments of indirect military significance. In the first place, on September 3, 1866, Bismarck and the liberals of the *Landtag* agreed upon an Indemnity Act, which resolved the parliamentary impasse which had existed since Bismarck became Prime Minister, after the 1862 defeat of the Army Reform Bill in the Parliament. Counting rightly on the liberals' recognition of the new popularity of the Army, and the effects of the battlefield demonstration of its efficiency as reorganized by the King and Roon in 1858, Bismarck thought the time was ripe for a compromise. He was willing to agree that the collection of taxes since 1862 had been unconstitutional, if the *Landtag* would now give its approval to a five-year budget accepting the King's original Army Reform Bill. He hinted at the same time that this would facilitate cooperation of Chancellor and *Landtag* in diplomatic moves toward greater German unity. The *Landtag* eagerly agreed. This was a stroke of political genius, which pleased almost all elements in Prussia: King, Army, liberals, and the general populace.

Political harmony having been restored in Prussia, Bismarck then moved promptly to consolidate politically the military victory of 1866. In return for French neutrality in that war, he had promised Napoleon III that Prussia would not try to annex or dominate the South German states. However, his hand was free in North Germany, which had been virtually conquered by Prussian troops. On April 17, 1867, he established a North German Federation, with a constitution approved by representatives of Saxony, Hesse-Darmstadt, Mecklenburg, Oldenburg, and all of the minor German states north of the Main River. This, of course, was a political organization which the South German states might also be induced to join at a politically propitious moment.

The North German Federation, while nominally an association of sovereign entities, was actually a cohesive state, built around Prussia, with a functioning centralized constitutional government, and a *Bundestag* elected by universal suffrage. To the annoyance of Roon, Bismarck refused to include a War Ministry in the government of the new Federation. He feared political problems like those of 1862 if the North German *Reichstag* were given a reason for assuming any responsibility for the Army other than budgetary. Thus, though the *Reichstag* could call upon the Prussian War Minister for advice and information on military matters relating to the budget, his constitutional responsibility was clearly limited to the political institutions of Prussia—King and *Landtag*—and not those of the Federation: Federation President (who was the King of Prussia), his Chancellor (who was Bismarck), and the *Reichstag*.

THE LUXEMBOURG CRISIS WITH FRANCE / The establishment of this new Federation led immediately to a dispute with France, which was alarmed by this sudden increase in the size and power of Prussia. After vague demands for compensation by German cession of the left bank of the Rhine, or French annexation of neutral Belgium—both of which were rejected by Bismarck—the government of Napoleon III saw the possibility of a diplomatic compromise in French annexation of Luxembourg. Bismarck, at first sympathetic to that solution, rejected it when German public opinion protested against surrendering traditional German territory to France. French fears and wounded pride, combined with the renewed nationalist fervor which the incident created in Germany, raised real possibilities of a war.

Luxembourg, whose Grand Duke was also the King of the Netherlands, had been a part of the German Confederation until Bismarck dissolved that organization in June, 1866. As part of the Confederation, it had been garrisoned by Prussian troops, and they remained in the city of Luxembourg even though the principality was not a part of the new North German Federation.

Through adroit diplomacy, Bismarck now offered a compromise of his own, which was accepted by France at an international conference convened in London to deal with the crisis. Luxembourg was to become a completely independent and neutral state, with no further political connections either with the Netherlands or with the North German Federation, and the Prussian garrison was to be withdrawn. The Prussian withdrawal satisfied French pride, and the war clouds dissipated.

This grave crisis had worried Moltke, since there was no immediate possibility of integrating the military potential of the rest of North Germany with that of Prussia in the event of war with France. He felt confident of Prussian military superiority over France, but the situation could be dangerous if France and Austria were to join in an alliance—and his intelligence system told him that both nations were exploring this possibility.

At Moltke's urging, therefore, Bismarck had moved quickly to establish a legal basis for a centralized North German Army for the new Federation. Like Moltke, he was aware of the informal military and political conversations between the French and Austrian governments, and he agreed with the Chief of the General Staff that, in the event of a military alliance between these two potential enemies, Moltke should be able to plan to employ a military force commensurate with the military conquests of 1866, and the political achievements of 1866 and 1867.

Even though the Luxembourg crisis finally was resolved in September, Bismarck pressed ahead with legislation to consolidate the military establishments of the Federation. The result was a compulsory military service law for all of North Germany, passed by the *Reichstag* on November 9, 1867, to be effective for seven years. This provided for annual conscription sufficient to maintain a standing army that was 1 percent of the population, approximately 401,000 enlisted men and noncommissioned officers. For all practical purposes, this was merely an extension of the Prussian military system to all of North Germany, for three more years than was provided for by the Prussian Indemnity Act of the previous year. This new army was virtually an expanded Prussian Army, although Saxony was permitted to retain a nominally independent contingent.

CONTINUING CONFRONTATION WITH FRANCE / Moltke welcomed the new law, which increased the size of the Prussian Army by more than 30 percent. However, he knew that France, suddenly aware of Prussian military power, was beginning to undertake major military reforms. Austria was also reorganizing, on the basis of lessons learned in 1866. Moltke therefore suggested to Bismarck that a preventive war against France should be started, at Prussian initiative, before either Austria or France was ready. Bismarck, although recognizing that a war with France was probably necessary before his goal of German unity could be achieved, nonetheless refused to consider the possibility of a preventive war. He understood Moltke's desire to have the war started under circumstances propitious to Prussia, but was determined that this would have to be under political circumstances in which Prussia could not be accused of aggression. Meanwhile, also in response to recommendations from Moltke, he concluded an alliance with the South German confederation of Baden, Bavaria, and Württemberg.

Actually, events in Spain were about to set the stage for the political showdown with France that Bismarck was seeking. In September of 1868 Queen Isabella II of Spain was overthrown by a revolution. The Prime Minister of the interim government established early in 1869 was General Juan Prim, who immediately went shopping for a new Spanish King among the royal families of Europe, In May 1869 Bismarck secretly suggested Prince Leopold of Hohenzollern-Sigmaringen, a distant cousin of the King of Prussia. When Prim approached Leopold, the Prince at first refused. Under pressure from Bismarck and (with some reluctance) King William, the young prince finally agreed, in late June 1870.

In early July, before the Spanish Cortes had a chance to vote an invitation for Leopold, the French government learned of the plan for him to become King of Spain. (By coincidence a French emissary was at that very time in Vienna, attempting to complete arrangements for an alliance of France, Austria, and Italy against Prussia.) Fears of a pro-German King on France's southern frontier created alarm in France. Napoleon III decided that the time had come for a showdown and sent a demand to Prussia that Leopold's name be withdrawn. Bismarck, seeing in this affair the possibility of a French insult to Prussia, and thus a cause for war, checked with Moltke on Prussian military readiness. Assured that the Army was ready, Bismarck began stirring up Prussian and German public opinion against "unwarranted" French interference in Spanish and German affairs. To his disgust, however, on July 12 Leopold, encouraged by William, announced that he was withdrawing his candidacy to the Spanish throne.

THE EMS INCIDENT–WAR WITH FRANCE / Foolishly, Emperor Napoleon III was not satisfied with this diplomatic victory. He ordered the French Ambassador to Prussia, Vincent Benedetti, to obtain William's assurance that he would never again allow Leopold to be a candidate for the Spanish throne. Benedetti went to Ems, where William was vacationing, and met with the King on the morning of July 13. In a meeting that was cordial and correct, William said that he approved Leopold's decision to withdraw, but refused to make the promise demanded by the French Emperor. After receiving another telegram from Paris, the Ambassador again asked to see the King. William sent a firm but courteous message to Benedetti, saying he saw no reason for further discussion, but felt that the morning meeting should provide adequate assurances to France. The French Ambassador said he was satisfied.

That evening Bismarck, Moltke, and Roon were having dinner together when a telegram arrived from Ems, sent by a member of the King's diplomatic staff, informing Bismarck of the meeting, and of the subsequent exchange of messages between the King and the Ambassador. Bismarck, as he later admitted, slightly "edited" the telegram from Ems, by deleting some sentences. The edited version gave the impression that the French Ambassador had been undiplomatic in his request for the King's promise never to permit Prince Leopold to accept the crown of Spain, and that in consequence of this the King of Prussia had been rude and abrupt in his refusal to talk further to the French Ambassador. Bismarck then released the doctored telegram to the press. His intention was to arouse passions in both France and Germany. He was fully successful.

Napoleon, after an all-night meeting with his Council of Ministers, decided upon war before dawn on July 15 and ordered immediate mobilization. Publication later that day of a parliamentary note to provide funds for war was considered, by both sides, as a declaration of war. A few hours later Moltke, with the King's approval, sent out the telegrams for a Prussian mobilization. The formal French declaration of war was not delivered in Berlin until July 19.

Meanwhile the governments of the three South German states—Bavaria, Baden, and Württemberg—had on July 16 and 17 ordered mobilization in support of Prussia and the North German Federation, in accordance with their obligations under the recent treaty. This meant that the total German force immediately mobilizable was about 475,000 troops, with more than half a million more in reserve, available for mobilization within a few weeks.*

Moltke estimated that the maximum French Field Army that could be committed to battle by early August, when the German mobilization would be complete, was about 340,000 men; a more likely figure was about 250,000. His only worry was that the French might advance into the Rhineland with about 150,000 regular troops between July 20 and 30, while the German armies were still concentrating. The French would have two reasons for such a bold and dangerous move. In the first place, an early French success might induce Austria, and even Italy, to join in an alliance against Prussia; Moltke was aware of the continuing conversations among these three governments. Secondly, the French might count on such a blow to disrupt the German mobilization, giving them an opportunity to occupy the entire west bank of the Rhine.

Moltke was not seriously worried about this latter possibility and was prepared to counter it with forces at least as strong as those the French could employ in late July. After the beginning of August, the German superiority in numbers would mount daily. He was more concerned about the possibility of Austrian intervention, and so kept back about 95,000 troops from the Rhine mobilization. Even so, by July 30 he had assembled some 380,000 men west of the Rhine in three armies: The First Army, about 60,000 men, under General Karl F. von Steinmetz, was concentrated south of Wittlich, with advance elements near Trier and Saarbrücken. The Second Army, 175,000 men under Prince Frederick Charles, was in the Kaiserslautern-Homburg area. The Third Army, 145,000 men under Crown Prince Frederick William, was concentrated near Landau and Germersheim.

On July 30, the day Moltke left Berlin with King William's royal headquarters, he sent orders to the Third Army to commence an advance toward the frontier. The other two armies were to wait for a few more days. Moltke expected a French advance from Saarbrücken and Metz, and planned a battlefield

---

*By the first week of August the total German moblization was 1.183 million men. The maximum French mobilized strength at about the same time, was 567,000, including overseas garrisons and the ill-trained *Guarde Mobile.*

concentration, probably northeast of Saarbrücken, to envelop the French in an improved Königgrätz.

Two days earlier, July 28, Napoleon III had arrived at Metz to assume command of his armies in northeastern France. Actually they were not organized as armies; they were eight separate army corps, spread across the northern frontier area from Thionville to the Rhine. There was no centralized army command, merely the Emperor and the War Minister, General Edmond Leboeuf, with small personal staffs. Like Moltke, Napoleon issued his first orders for an advance on July 30, thus voluntarily moving the French corps toward the encirclement trap that the German Chief of Staff was setting for them.

It is probable that the slow, disjointed, and uncoordinated advance of the eight separate French corps toward the frontier would have brought them within the encirclement Moltke planned north of Saarbrücken, had it not been for the impetuosity of General von Steinmetz, commanding the German First Army. Without orders, he pressed forward to Saarbrücken, where the first engagement of the campaign took place. It was a minor action, but brought the French advance to a full halt. The Emperor had not realized that major Prussian forces were so near at hand.

Belatedly Napoleon III ordered a consolidation of command in two armies: the Army of Lorraine, five corps in the Metz-Saarbrücken area, under one of the corps commanders, Marshal François Achille Bazaine; and the Army of Alsace, the three corps in the northeastern corner of France, under another corps commander, Marshal M. E. Maurice de MacMahon. There were no army staffs; the new army commanders had to use their own corps staffs to direct their armies, as well as to perform their regular functions of corps operational control. The delay and confusion resulting from this series of events saved the French from destruction in the first week of August; it was to be a prolonged agony, even though the result would be the same.

OPERATIONS OF THE FIELD GENERAL STAFF / The outcome of the Franco-Prussian or Franco-German war was never in doubt. There were occasional Prussian blunders, there were a number of miscalculations by Moltke and by other Prussian commanders and staff officers. But even if Prussia had not had overwhelming numerical superiority from the outset of the war, French defeat would have been assured by the consistently superior quality of Prussian staff work, and the general superiority of Prussian leadership, particularly at the higher levels of command. All three of these Prussian superiorities—a much larger and more rapidly mobilized force, more efficient staff work, and the higher leadership qualities—were all due, directly and without question, to the exceptional effectiveness of the Prussian General Staff.

Moltke brought with him from Berlin only a fraction of the entire General Staff: fourteen officers, ten cartographers, seven clerks, and fifty-nine other enlisted men as messengers, assistant clerks, and general handymen. This Field General Staff was the operational nerve center of the large and cumbersome

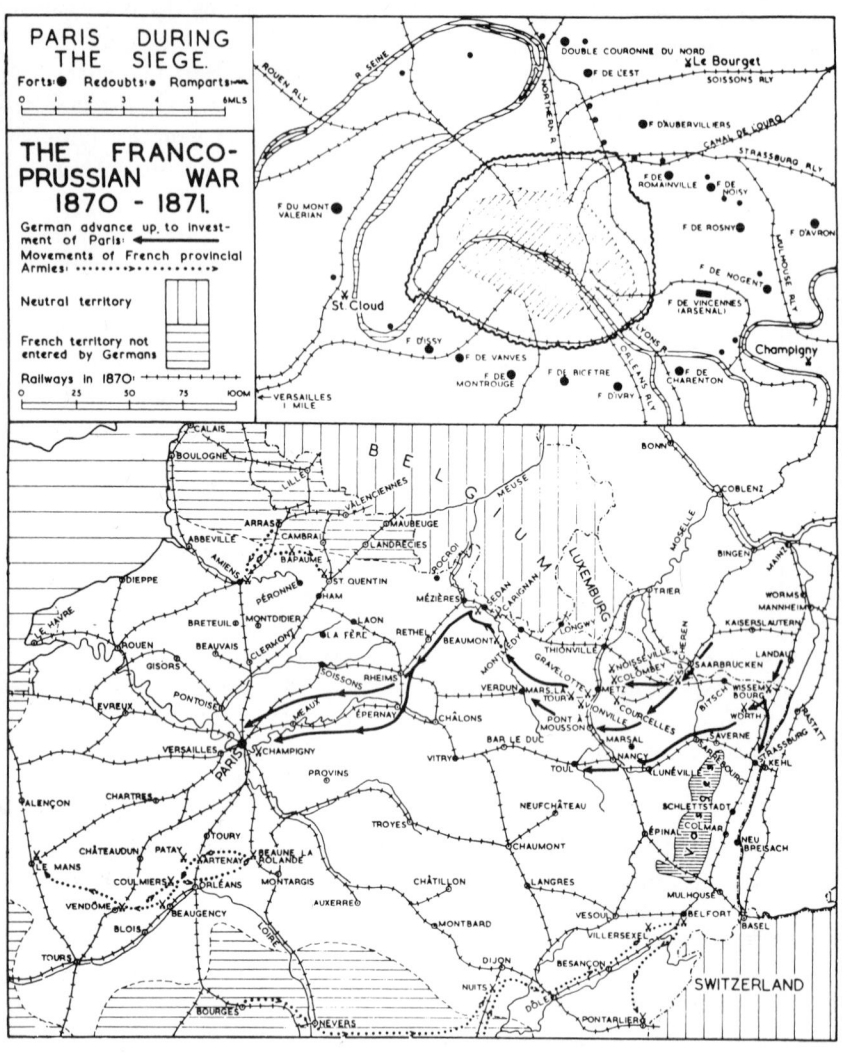

royal headquarters that accompanied King William into the field. This latter included a large contingent from the War Ministry, under Roon. Two senior War Ministry officers worked so closely with Moltke and his immediate subordinates that they were virtually a part of the Field General Staff: Lieutenant General Theophil von Podbielski, the Quartermaster General (or chief operations officer), and Lieutenant General Albert von Stosch, the Intendant General (or chief administrative officer).

The Field General Staff was organized in three functional sections operating directly under Moltke's close personal direction: an operations and movement section, under Colonel Paul Bronsart von Schellendorf; a railways and supply section, directed by Colonel Karl von Brandenstein; and an intelligence section under Colonel Julius von Verdy du Vernois. Verdy du Vernois also functioned as the chief administrative officer, or adjutant, of this small but effective staff. These three section chiefs were known throughout the Prussian Army—with grudging respect and jealousy—as Moltke's Demigods.

COMPARISON OF THE FRENCH AND GERMAN ARMIES / Despite the steamrollerlike efficiency of the Prussian armies under the direction of Moltke and his headquarters staff, the French made a surprisingly good showing in a number of isolated engagements. The training and combat experience of the long-term French soldier, generally a veteran of combat in North Africa and Italy, made him at least a match, man for man, with his Prussian counterpart. And the gallantry, devotion, and typical French élan of the low-level leaders compared favorably with the effectiveness of the junior Prussian officers. And even among the top leaders, the best of the French—Chanzy, Trochu, and Faidherbe—were probably every bit as good as the best of the Prussians. But by the time these generals had a chance to demonstrate their ability, the French regulars were either dead, imprisoned, or besieged, and the leaders had only ill-trained levies "stamped from the ground" by Leon Gambetta, and they still had no chance of success.

And so, even if France had made as efficient use of its military manpower as the Prussians (unlikely, without a counterpart of the Prussian General Staff), even if its best leaders had been in the key positions of responsibility at the outset (also unlikely without a military system in which the General Staff procedures assured the selection of excellence in peacetime), the French combat operational processes could never have matched the swift, sure efficiency of General Staff officers like Moltke's Demigods.

One of the best commentaries on the general nature of the Prussian superiority may be found in some assessments by a French military historian, Lieutenant Colonel Leonce Rousset, in a work based on lectures which he gave at the Ecole Supérieure de Guerre in the years after the war:

> The Chassepot rifle constituted, without question, our sole material
> superiority. It was a relatively light piece, with remarkable accuracy and

precision, with a long range (1800 meters), substantially surpassing the famous needle-gun (Dreyse) of the Germans. The sword bayonet which could be fixed to its extremity was so constructed as not to diminish its ballistic qualities in the slightest, and assured to our infantry the ability to employ its favorite method of attack. Thus in this respect we were better served than our enemies, and the bloody losses which they suffered in the early part of the war, as well as their numerous partial setbacks, were due as much to the excellence of our weapon as to the steadiness of our infantrymen. . . .

But on the credit side the German soldier had a very solid background of training which assured strict fire discipline, and at least part of the success must be attributed to this training, as well as to the sense of duty and military honor which inspired this training at all levels of the hierarchy. As a result the officers shared a determination to retain the initiative by all possible means, and to deliver the maximum effort of which they were capable; while the soldiers were stimulated to zeal and individuality, each man being obliged to think, to analyze, and to formulate his own ideas. The Prussian commanders kept the [peacetime] garrison tasks of barracks maintenance, guard, and fatigue duty to the absolute minimum to permit the allocation of most of the men's time to purely military duties; thus the soldier was diverted as little as possible from the final objective: to learn his profession. By intelligent decentralization, responsibility for the soldier's training was confided to his direct superiors, noncommissioned officers, lieutenants, and captains, thus a reasoned and progressive development encouraged a level of perfection not to be found elsewhere. In this respect, the Prussian Army was incontestably the best in Europe, and its system of training, facilitated by German respect for the principle of authority, contributed as much as its remarkable organization to its surprising triumphs.[2]

In comparing the Prussian cavalry to the French, Rousset had the following observations:

As for the cavalry—whose role is essentially to act with rapidity and to precede the army, in order to cover and protect it—French unreadiness was disastrous. Instead of throwing itself to the front, to clear the advance of the columns, even to endeavor to interfere with the mobilization and concentration of the enemy, the cavalry was united with the operational forces too late, and was forced to subordinate its movements to those forces, without sufficient space ahead of them to operate with the necessary independence. . . . It was merely an instrument of combat, from which the enemy firearms promptly removed most of its power and nearly all of its effectiveness. . . .

The Prussian cavalry was . . . better trained, more proficient in reconnaissance, and from its leaders, generally young and vigorous, it derived a bold aggressiveness. The uhlans, in particular, were past masters in the art of patrolling long distances in front of the marching columns. . . . The cavalry . . . was both the eyes and the legs of the Prussian army.

Rousset's comments on the inferiority of the vaunted French artillery, in comparison with their initially poorly considered Prussian counterparts, are even stronger.

While our adversaries had for some time been equipped with steel, rapid-fire artillery pieces, we retained bronze, muzzle-loading cannon which had been outmoded even in 1859. While the Germans had long recognized, from experience, the advantages of great masses of artillery, which were coordinated in operation, and employed converging fire, our batteries were still committing the error of going into action one at a time; this sterile and feeble procedure meant that the number of French pieces in position was never sufficient to achieve fire superiority. Finally, while we kept a number of reserve artillery batteries in the rear of our columns, so they could not open fire until too late, the corps artillery batteries of our adversaries were, if necessary, engaged exactly like divisional batteries as soon as an action began, thus assuring their troops an immediate and insurmountable superiority.

Rousset clearly understood the role of the Prussian General Staff in assuring both prewar German superiority and the extraordinary efficiency of the German field operations:

The principal support of the high command was the General Staff corps, recruited from the best officers of all arms who had successfully completed the War Academy. Its Chief devoted to this Staff a jealous care and constant attention which prepared it without cease or remiss, for the business of war. Moltke directed this service in person, choosing his key officers from an elite from whom the mediocrities were carefully eliminated, assuring him of that fertile impetus which produced such great results in 1870.

Moreover, the entire officer corps, with almost all of its members from the nobility or upper middle class, was exceptional. Prussia had maintained the cult of the profession of arms, which assured to the officer corps a preponderant social position and special honors, to the point of making it a kind of caste, possessing a spirit of discipline, a feeling of dignity, and almost excessive professional self-esteem. The training, the relative independence which this corps enjoyed within its area of responsibility, the regulations which guided it, and finally the high concept which it made of its mission, all served to develop a spirit of initiative and of solidarity which was repeatedly demonstrated during the war. Its devotion to the sovereign was unlimited.

As to the noncommissioned officers, they provided the true power of the Prussian troops. They were recruited for the most part from special military schools, having received a solid military education which they then passed on in their regiments, where they were precious auxiliaries of the officers. This special position, surrounded by a respect and a well-being unknown in other armies, assured them of an honorable and enviable profession. By the role assigned to them in the command structure, these noncommissioned officers could practice and develop their military qualities. The Prussian Army was proud of them, and justly considered them as one of the principal elements of its future successes.

Rousset's comments, from a respectful enemy, provide much food for thought.

Clearly there had been a transformation in the employment of the Prussian cavalry since 1866. Not since the time of Napoleon I had cavalry been so effectively employed on European battlefields. No army has ever been better informed of hostile dispositions and movements than was the Prussian Army of 1870.

The improvement in the Prussian artillery in the four years since Königgrätz was equally marked. The fascinating *Letters on Artillery* by Prince Hohenlohe-Ingelfingen, Commanding General of the Guard Artillery Brigade, provides emphatic corroboration of Rousset's assessment. The Battle of St. Privat, for instance, could have been won by the French due largely to some mistakes by General Steinmetz of the First Army. More than any single factor contributing to Prussia's ability to hold the field was the superb handling of the Prussian artillery, particularly Hohenlohe's guns of the Guard Artillery Brigade. He describes one part of the battle, when his brigade of thirty guns, with only a handful of infantry, found itself in the way of a French division's counterattack:

> We had not long to wait for the first movement which the enemy's infantry was to make in our direction. It advanced in quarter column from Amanvillers, and attacked us energetically. When the head of the column became visible over the hill, our ranging shots reached it at a range of 1900 meters, and my 30 guns opened a rapid fire. The enemy's infantry was enveloped in the thick smoke which the shells made as they burst. But after a very short time we saw the red trousers of the masses which were approaching us through the cloud. I stopped the fire. A ranging shot was fired at 1700 meters range; this was to show us the point up to which we should let them advance before reopening the rapid fire; we did the same for the ranges of 1500, 1300, 1100, and 900 meters. In spite of the horrible devastation which the shells caused in their ranks, these brave troops continued to advance. But at 900 meters the effect of our fire was too deadly; they turned short round and fled; we hurled shells after them as long as we could see them. Here was an infantry attack which was repulsed purely and simply by the fire of artillery.[3]

There could be no better examples of the coordinated operation of great masses of artillery which, as Rousset pointed out, gave the Prussian infantry "an immediate and insurmountable superiority."

It was also an example of the "spirit of initiative and of solidarity" of which Rousset wrote with grudging admiration. He obviously appreciated, as have few other non-German analysts of German combat operations, how precision in drill and unquestioning obedience in discipline could be utilized in paradoxical fashion to instill initiative, to require intelligent and thoughtful independence on the part of all leaders, from corporals to army commanders. Rousset recognized that the Prussian excellence in all aspects of "the business of war" was the result of a system which appeared rigid in its training requirements, but was flexible to the extreme in the battlefield employment of the fruits of that training. Most significant of all Rousset's comments is that which recognized that it was the General Staff which was responsible for all of "that fertile impetus which produced such great results in 1870."

This lesson, learned by Rousset and a number of other far-sighted French officers, resulted in the development of a comparable French staff system in the years between the Franco-Prussian and First World wars. That staff was to provide the military organization and leadership which in 1914 could survive crushing defeat on its way to victory at the Marne. The French General Staff of 1914 was almost—but not quite—as good as the German General Staff of that same year. How and why that difference persisted (despite intensive French efforts), and the significance of that difference, can be found in the military records of the forty-three years between the wars, as well as in the combat records of World War I.

MOLTKE, THE GENERAL STAFF, AND THE PRUSSIAN ARMY / Rousset's assessments of the Prussian Army and its proven fighting qualities in the Franco-Prussian War, reveal to us an army organized, trained, motivated, led, and directed in a fashion which could be matched in earlier history only by the armies of the greatest military geniuses, such as Alexander, Hannibal, Caesar, Genghis Khan, Gustavus Adolphus, Frederick the Great, and Napoleon. But the record of that war, as reported by Rousset and other competent military critics, also demonstrates that, for all of his exceptional ability, Moltke was not a genius of that caliber. J. F. C. Fuller, possibly the most competent military commentator of the twentieth century, is overly critical of Moltke. It is, nevertheless, instructive to read what Fuller has to say:

> Moltke . . . was a supremely great war organizer, who relied on logic
> rather than opportunity. For success his art depended on adherence to a
> somewhat static doctrine set in motion by *directives* rather than by orders.
> To him a war of masses was a war of accidents in which genius was sub-
> ordinate to the offensive spirit. Whereas Napoleon I led and controlled
> throughout, Moltke brought his armies to their starting points and then
> abdicated his command and unleashed them. [At Sedan] he never issued
> an order except for a few suggestions to General Blumenthal, Chief of
> Staff of the Third Army. He never foresaw the encirclement of the French,
> which was due to their stupidity, the initiative of the Prussian Army
> commanders and the superb handling of the Prussian artillery. Moltke is
> not a general to copy but to study. His reckonings were wonderful, yet

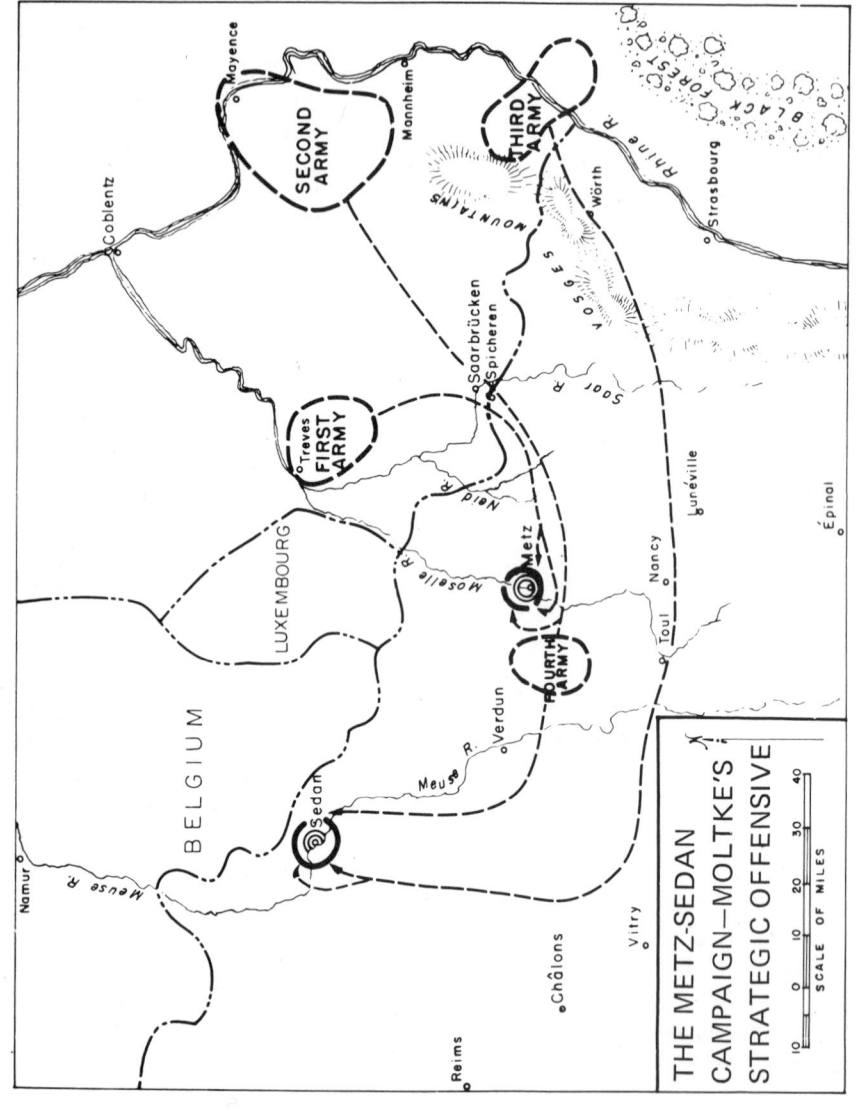

THE METZ-SEDAN
CAMPAIGN—MOLTKE'S
STRATEGIC OFFENSIVE

his risks against an able opponent might easily have proved damnable; for he was apt to be run away with by his subordinates.[4]

Fuller is perhaps unfair in some of these comments—as in his suggestion that Moltke, despite his directive system, could not seize opportunities, and that he had not foreseen the French encirclement at Sedan. That encirclement—though not so clearly and dramatically as at Gravelotte-St. Privat—was the deliberate and effective translation into tactical doctrine of the Moltke concept of "strategic offensive—tactical defensive." In both the Metz and Sedan Campaigns Moltke's directives to his subordinates were designed to place the Prussian armies on the French lines of communications. The course of battle in each case then followed the prophetic words of his 1865 memorandum: "The task of a skillful offensive will consist of forcing our foe to attack a position chosen by us, and only when casualties, demoralization, and exhaustion have drained his strength will we ourselves take up the tactical offensive."

Despite his underestimations of Moltke, Fuller provides a more balanced assessment than blind admirers. Moltke was an excellent general, but not so gifted a leader as either Grant or Lee, his great American contemporaries. He was a product of the system of selection from the exceptional elite described by Rousset—a system which he did not create but merely inherited. As such, he was outstanding. Yet he probably was no better than a number of other products of that same system, like Roon, Hindersin, Hohenlohe, Alvensleben, Manteuffel, Manstein, and the two princes.

This all leads to the inescapable conclusion that the structure that Scharnhorst had created and that had been refined, updated, and adapted by Gneisenau, Grolman, Müffling, Krauseneck, and Reyher, had proven itself under Moltke to be the institutionalized excellence—indeed institutionalized genius, since its performance can be compared favorably to the leadership of the Great Captains—intended. To an extent unparalleled in history, the Prussian General Staff was a self-regenerating institution, not dependent upon the random appearance of great leaders, because—among many other things—it automatically produced outstanding leaders.

FLAW IN THE SYSTEM—CIVIL-MILITARY RELATIONS / There was, however, even in this period of its greatest triumph, some hint of a flaw within the Prussian military establishment: its lack of responsibility to the nation as a whole. This was a flaw that would have been fully appreciated by Scharnhorst and his four fellow-Reformers, all of whom had foreseen the possibility and had hoped to prevent it by the establishment of the constitutional monarchy that Frederick William III had vetoed. And, just as Moltke is the perfect exemplar of the military strength of a system which used competent men to create institutional excellence, so too he is a perfect exemplar of the one significant weakness of the system.

In the latter part of the war, after having destroyed the French Army,

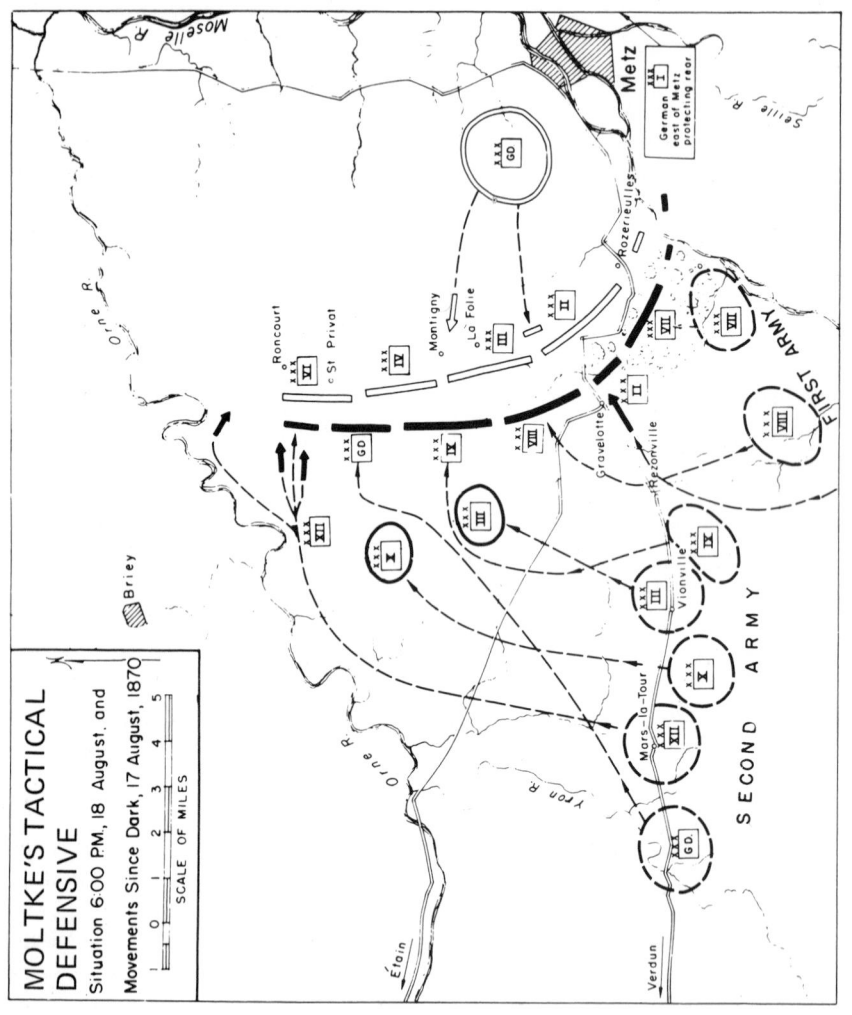

Moltke and his splendid military machine were for several months frustrated in completing the subjection of a defeated enemy that would not acknowledge defeat. For the second time in less than a century, France became a revolutionary nation in arms in a great patriotic response to a Prussian-led invasion from Germany. This time—because of the General Staff—the outcome was different. Nevertheless, as a result of the unexpected rising of the French people under Gambetta's inspiring political leadership, the concluding months of the war were in some respects more difficult for Moltke and his armies than were the first four weeks, in which the French Army was destroyed on the battlefields from Worth, past Metz, to Sedan. But even during those later trying months, the most formidable opposition encountered by Moltke was from Bismarck, who was with the royal headquarters in the field. The rising hostility between these two prewar friends came to a head during the siege of Paris.

Moltke, a devoted student of Clausewitz, understood the primacy of civilian leadership in peacetime, and in the diplomacy which preceded and followed war. But he frequently expressed his firm conviction that once a war began, the politician must step into the background and leave all aspects of warmaking to military leaders. He seems to have focused on only one passage in Clausewitz's eloquent discussion of the relationship of war and policy: "The conduct of war ... takes up the sword in place of the pen." He virtually ignored the several statements of Clausewitz, which put that transition in proper perspective, as for instance:

> That the political point of view should end completely when war
> begins would ... be [inconceivable]. The subordination of the political
> point of view to the military would be unreasonable, for policy has created
> the war; policy is the intelligent faculty, war only the instrument, and
> not the reverse. The subordination of the military point of view to the
> political is, therefore, the only thing which is possible.[5]

Bismarck, who may never have read Clausewitz from cover to cover, understood far better than Moltke what Clausewitz meant in his discussion of the relationship of war and policy. And so, in the early days of the war, he became increasingly upset and finally furious, when he found that he was not being kept fully informed of the progress of the combat operations. He finally protested to the King, who ordered Moltke to provide the Prime Minister with full information.

Then, during the siege of Paris in the fall of 1870, Bismarck feared that he would be forced by the mediation efforts of the other powers to enter into peace negotiations with the war still unwon, with Gambetta's armies still in the field and harassing the Prussian outposts, and with the French capital still boldly defying Moltke's besieging armies. He demanded that Moltke bombard the city to force its early surrender. Moltke refused. This reluctance to use his artillery against Paris was not a matter of morality in Moltke's mind, although he saw no reason for what he considered unnecessary bloodshed since Paris would inevitably be forced to surrender from starvation. His principal reason was that he also saw no need for tying up the railroad lines by unnecessarily transporting siege artillery and ammunition for the big guns, when the supply situation of his far-flung units across northern France was critical.

In late November Bismarck, infuriated by the attitude of the Chief of the General Staff, again complained to the King, who sternly asked Moltke to explain the delay in bombarding the city. Moltke's response was typical: "The question of when the artillery attack on Paris should or can begin, can only be decided on the basis of military views. Political motives can only find consideration insofar as they do not demand anything militarily inadmissible or impossible." Apparently he felt that it was inadmissible to begin the bombardment before it was proved to be necessary, and it was impossible to get the guns or ammunition to the scene any quicker (unless—he omitted to say—he changed priorities on the railroads). He went on to make it clear that he considered bombardment an expensive and inefficient procedure, to be undertaken only if starvation failed.[6]

Roon, always politically more perceptive than Moltke, now became as annoyed as Bismarck. On December 17, at a council of war, the King put increasing pressure on Moltke, and in the following two weeks the artillery and ammunition began to accumulate.

The bombardment began on January 5. Politically the gesture of the bombardment was extremely important, internationally, in France, and above all in Germany, where the apparent stalemate was creating an understandable but unnecessary alarm—which Bismarck apparently kept well stirred up during his confrontations with Moltke.

The bombardment of Paris, under the able leadership of Prince Hohenlohe-Ingelfingen, was a symbol restoring—as Bismarck had known it would—German confidence in an early, successful conclusion of the unexpectedly protracted war. It was in this political climate that on January 18, less than two weeks after the bombardment began, and only eight days before the French garrison asked for an armistice, Bismarck achieved his greatest ambition: the unification of Germany as a new empire, with William its first Emperor. The ceremony took place in the famed Hall of Mirrors of the Palace of Versailles.

Yet Moltke was right in his prediction that the military effect of the bombardment would be negligible. When the garrison and the city government sought an armistice, a week after the coronation of William as Emperor, it was because of starvation, as Moltke had predicted, not the pinpricks of bombardment.

As Fuller wrote, Moltke's "reckonings were wonderful," and his military assessment of the siege of Paris was typical. Indeed, he is even more worthy of study than Fuller's somewhat faint praise would suggest; truly he was one of the most successful generals of history. But what would Moltke have been without a Bismarck both to guide and restrain him? Interestingly enough, history gives us an opportunity to get a tantalizing glimpse of such a situation in Germany less than half a century later. It is difficult to avoid the conclusion that a Moltke without a Bismarck would very possibly have been a prototype Ludendorff.

NOTES TO CHAPTER EIGHT

[1] As quoted in Eugene Carrias, *La Pense militaire allemande* (Paris: 1948), p. 250. See also Howard, *op. cit.,* p. 7.

[2] Lieutenant Colonel Leonce Rousset, *Histoire Generale de la Guerre Franco-Allemande* (Paris: 1886, 2d edition 1911), pp. 22, 34.

[3] Prince Kraft zu Hohenlohe-Ingelfingen. *Letters on Artillery,* translated by N. L. Walford (London, 1898), 3d edition, p. 86 (some terminology modified).

[4] J. F. C. Fuller, *A Military History of the Western World* (New York: 1956), Vol. III, p. 134.

[5] Karl von Clausewitz, *On War,* translated by O. S. Mathis Jolles (Washington, D.C.: 1950), p. 589.

[6] These comments on Moltke's memorandum are based, with only slight modification, on the sound assessment of Howard, *op. cit.,* p. 325. There is another viewpoint, however, which cannot be ignored. Without starvation, as soon became evident, the bombardment would certainly have been a failure politically, since it first would have raised high hopes and then demonstrated to the public the futility of Prussian efforts. Thus, it has been suggested, Bismarck demanded something which was militarily nonsense and could have been politically detrimental. Why, ask these critics, should Moltke not resist? This was only one example of the constant interference of Bismarck with truly military matters, often without even bothering to inform Moltke. Bronsart von Schellendorf's diary contains many more examples of unnecessary political meddling.

Chapter Nine

AVOIDING THE
NEMESIS IN WARFARE

 **AN EXCEPTION TO TOYNBEE'S LAW** / In discussing what he called "the Nemesis in Warfare," Arnold Toynbee, in a widely quoted passage, has linked the progress of armed conflict among nations to an ever-lengthening chain:

Each link has been a cycle of invention, triumph, lethargy and disaster; and, on the precedents thus set by three thousand years of military history, from Goliath's encounter with David to the piercing of a Maginot Line and a West Wall by the thrust of mechanical cataphracts and the pin-point marksmanship of archers on winged steeds, we may expect fresh illustrations of our theme to be provided with monotonous consistency so long as mankind is so perverse as to go on cultivating the art of war.[1]

There has been at least one exception to Toynbee's Law. The amazing series of Prussian-German successes in the seven-year period from 1864 to 1871 did create in Germany and its Army the arrogance that almost invariably follows triumph. But there was neither the lethargy nor complacency which also often beset victors. The institution which Scharnhorst and his fellow-Reformers had created was designed to be proof against the lethargy that had characterized Prussia and its Army after Frederick the Great, and the institution now performed just as they had hoped and expected it would. The nemesis would eventually appear to exact retributive justice, but in a fashion that Toynbee overlooked—although its manifestation, ironically, would not have been surprising to Scharnhorst, Gneisenau, Boyen, Grolman, or even Clausewitz.

Thanks to the successes in the three midcentury wars, the Army had become the most popular, most admired, most respected, and most influential entity in the new German Empire. Furthermore, political developments in the third quarter of the nineteenth century also contributed to feelings of national pride in, and identification with, the German Army as an obvious manifestation of Prussian leadership in highly popular German unity. The bourgeoisie, fearful of socialist ideas, were becoming loyal monarchists; many of the most fervent

110

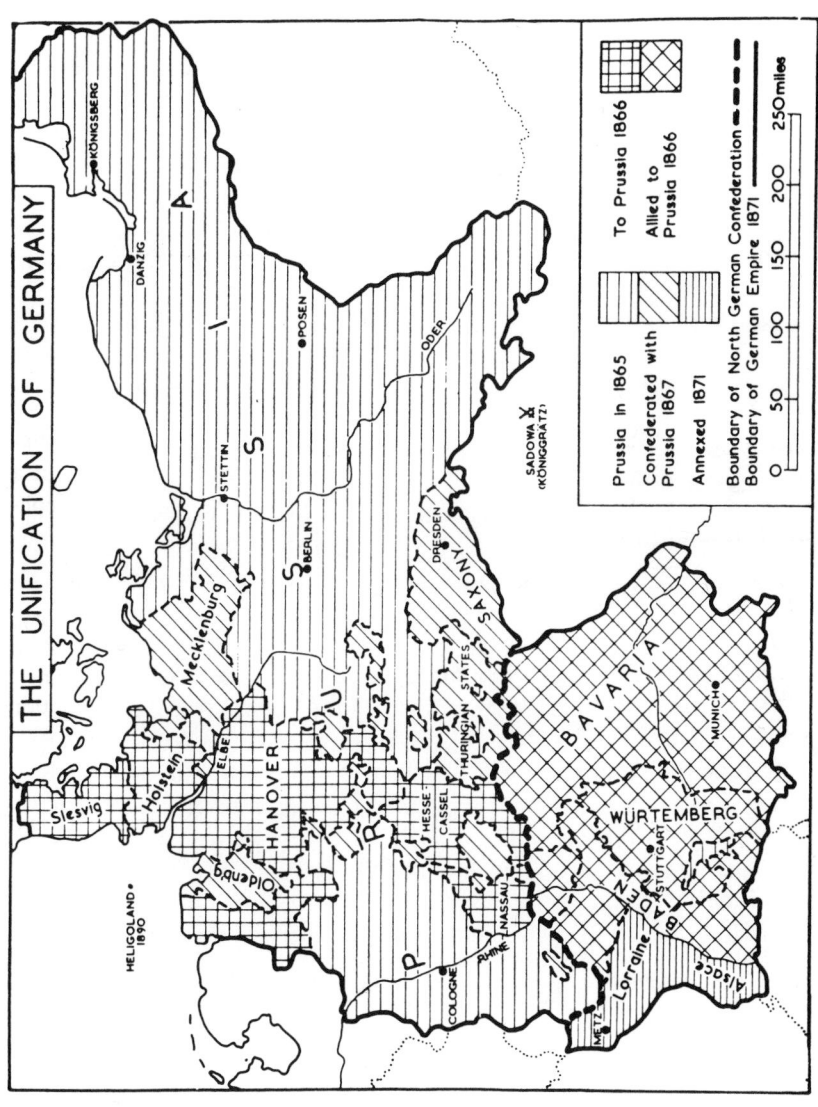

supporters of Bismarck and German unity had been revolutionaries in 1848. To most Germans their Army—the Emperor's Army—represented stability as well as honor and glory. Superficially it seemed as though the Reformers had achieved complete success, despite the failure of one element of their plan. Yet the fatal flaw remained. Germany's and Prussia's constitutions excluded the Army from the control of the people and their elected representatives. Unfortunately, the flaw would not make itself evident for nearly half a century.

During the years immediately after the Franco-Prussian War the activities of Moltke and his General Staff were focused on three major tasks, which they probably considered of almost equal importance, even though they required varying amounts of attention: refinement and improvement of strategic planning; technical developments and improvement of the German Army in general, and the General Staff in particular; and enlargement and reorganization of the German Army. The third of these tasks—Army enlargement and reorganization—was, of course, closely related to the first: strategic planning. General Staff efforts to deal with both tasks went hand in hand.

For forty-four years of peace the General Staff—now the German General Staff—prospered and grew, but did not allow either prosperity or growth to affect performance of its one major mission: perpetual quest for military preparedness and excellence. The prestige, which the General Staff and its distinguished Chief had won in the victories over Denmark, Austria-Hungary, and France, was reflected in increased peacetime influence and responsibility for the training, organization, and equipping of the Army, in addition to the planning functions to which its direct responsibility had previously been limited.

The Emperor, as Commander in Chief of the German Army, exercised that command through the machinery of the Prussian War Ministry.* (Bismarck had thoughtfully organized the new Imperial government so that there would be no *German* Minister of War responsible to the *Reichstag,* although the *Prussian* War Minister did have this responsibility so far as Prussia was concerned.) The personnel administration of the German Army's officer corps was even more closely held by the monarch, through the Chief of his Military Cabinet, now almost completely autonomous, and only nominally connected with the War Ministry. The Chief of the General Staff, who as recently as five years earlier had rarely been consulted by the King, was now the Emperor's principal military adviser, and while Moltke scrupulously held himself aloof from interfering in the affairs either of Roon, the War Minister, or Major General Emil L. von Albedyll, the new Chief of the Military Cabinet, his opinion on matters of command, organization, training, and weapons development was sought by War Minister Roon and his subordinates, while Albedyll invariably requested his advice on appointment of officers to senior command and staff positions.

Moltke did believe, however, that the General Staff should become directly

---

*The War Ministries of Bavaria, Württemberg, and Saxony were responsible for administration of the semi-autonomous armies of those principalities.

responsible for two important peacetime activities which it already strongly influenced: control of the Directorate of Communications and Railroads and of officer education. The performance of the communications and railroads directorate was essential to the vital mobilization plans prepared by the General Staff, and thus it was logical that Moltke would wish to be in a position to assure that this performance was completely responsive to his planning. Responsibility for officer education would give to the General Staff control over the preparation of young officers for staff and command positions, and thus facilitate the selection of the most promising of these for the General Staff. It would also assure the Staff that training and doctrine were fully consistent with war planning.

In accordance with Moltke's desires, he was given authority over the Directorate of Communications and Railroads on June 2, 1872. On November 21 the War Academy was also placed under his direction, giving him effective control over the entire process of officer education, since all of the other officer schools—from cadet academies through branch schools—had to gear their curricula to the requirements set for the War Academy.

FOREIGN IMITATORS OF THE GENERAL STAFF / Meanwhile, the wartime successes of the General Staff were influencing military affairs in other nations throughout the world. Early in 1872 France established its own General Staff, as the first step down the long road France was determined to travel to avenge the defeats of 1870, and to recover the lost provinces of Alsace and Lorraine. Initially the French copied the Prussian mission-oriented staff organization. Later they would reorganize the staff into functional groupings: personnel administration, intelligence, training and operations, and logistical affairs. This change was made partly because of typical French concern for consistency between theory and practice, and in part because the French had only one front and one enemy to think about, whereas the Germans had to be ready for a major war on any of three major fronts, or simultaneous wars on all three. In any event, the French General Staff remained faithful, after its own fashion, to the institutional concept borrowed from the Germans. This was to have much to do with the amazingly rapid recovery of France from the defeats of 1870-1871, and with the excellent performance of French armies when next they went to war.

Austria-Hungary, too, was in the process of adopting a General Staff on the Prussian model. Like a number of other armies, that of Austria-Hungary had nominally had a General Staff before the Austro-Prussian War, but it had been largely composed of favored nobles who had obtained easy headquarters positions and rapid promotions through nepotism, preference, and favoritism. In Vienna spirited debates about this state of affairs had naturally followed the Königgrätz disaster; these abruptly ended in 1871, after the Austrians observed the outcome of the Franco-Prussian War. The old Austrian General Staff corps was abolished. After a brief period of confusion, in 1875 the Austrians followed the French example of creating a new General Staff, on the Prussian model. For the next forty-five years the Austro-Hungarian General Staff remained a faithful imitation of the Prussian or German model, but—unlike the French—never achieved a comparable level of excellence.

Like Prussia, Russia had nominally had a General Staff for nearly a century before Scharnhorst created a true General Staff in 1808. Sixty years later, however, the Russians, having been impressed by Prussian performance in the Danish and Austrian wars, adopted a new organization, very much like that of Prussia. In the following years the Russians made a number of minor changes and adaptations, bringing their staff organization still closer to the Prussian or German model, but lacking the latter's spark of genius.

In the following years, all of the important armies of the world—with varying degrees of eagerness or reluctance—followed the example of the Prussian General Staff. Among the last to follow the example were Britain and the United States. The obvious efficiency resulting from a centralized, coordinated General Staff overcame only with difficulty the fears of many in the Anglo-Saxon democracies that it would be militaristic to follow a Prussian example, and that military efficiency was somehow, in itself, a manifestation of militarism.

GENERAL STAFF REASSESSMENT AND SELF-IMPROVEMENT / While the military establishments of other nations were trying to improve themselves by copying the German General Staff, that institution kept a sharp eye on them, not only to be able to assess their military capability, but also to be alert to any foreign innovations that could be usefully introduced into the German General Staff. Intensive historical studies were also in process, particularly to review the operations of the recent wars. These included exhaustive analyses of the effects of weapons; German, Austrian, and French mobilization procedures and tactical performance of all participants in both wars.

Simultaneously a major study program was initiated to reassess the role of the General Staff in its relationship to its mission and to the preparedness of the rest of the Army, in the light of recent wartime and peacetime experience. The result was general confirmation of the principles that had guided General Staff policies and procedures in the period before 1870. There was a complete reorganization of the General Staff, although this did not result in any major changes in internal relationships or organization charts. At the same time, it was proposed that there be closer links between the General Staff and the remainder of the War Ministry, and between the General Staff and the Army as a whole. These recommendations were approved by Roon and by his successor, General Georg Arnold Karl von Kameke, who became Prussian War Minister when Roon retired on November 9, 1873.

One result of all of this activity was that the work of each major division within the War Ministry was kept under general surveillance (supervision would probably be too strong a word) by some individual or agency within the General Staff. Similarly, the German regional division of the Staff was responsible for keeping abreast of the training activities of the Army corps and their subordinate units, and for keeping in close touch with all of the branch inspectors, who were responsible for the state of training of the field army.

At the same time, the military historical studies were being reviewed in other agencies of the Staff, to ascertain what lessons they could provide for training guidance to the Army as a whole, and for the instructional program at the War Academy and the other service schools for officers and noncommissioned officers. This led to the preparation of a series of training directives for the field forces, for the branch inspectors, and for the schools.

These historical analyses were also scrutinized by the Staff agencies responsible for keeping track of War Ministry procurement of weapons and equipment. From this emerged guidance to be followed by the War Ministry in establishing requirements and procedure for design, development, and purchase of material for the Army.

Moltke assigned to Colonel Paul Bronsart von Schellendorf (one of his Demigods in the Franco-Prussian War field GHQ) the responsibility of preparing a manual of General Staff procedures and policies. This was originally entitled *General Staff Service in Peace and War* and was first published in two volumes in 1875 and 1876. (It immediately became a major text in the War Academy.) It was and is an important source of information on the general nature of the activities of the Great General Staff and of General Staff officers assigned to field units. Translations of this manual soon appeared in other countries, and were carefully studied in the officers' schools and General Staffs of the major powers. Although such study undoubtedly provided some valuable intelligence insights into the control and operational procedures of the German Army, they were particularly valuable in helping other armies improve their own staff procedures.

Imitation by other armies was naturally a source of pride for Moltke and his assistants, and they undoubtedly recognized that they were, to some degree, contributing to the military improvement of potential foes. This, however, was an inevitable consequence of their own improvement, and they were rightly confident of their own ability to retain the intellectual initiative, and keep constantly in front of rivals. They also realized a fact which had been well demonstrated by the history of Prussian military improvement between the Wars of Liberation and the Wars of Unification: knowledge and understanding of military theory and principles is not enough to assure truly effective battlefield performance; the ability to perform in accordance with theory must be so thoroughly ingrained in all leaders—and the soldiers too—that they will automatically perform their wartime tasks intelligently and flexibly.

For this reason there was a continuing emphasis on field maneuvers as the culmination of each year's training program. The plans for these maneuvers were drawn up by the General Staff. They were designed to take place in regions which might become theaters of war, and to emphasize responses to technical or tactical problems which seemed most currently significant to Moltke and to the branch inspectors. In addition, Moltke continued the practice of annual Staff rides in critical frontier areas each year, to give the Staff officers extra experience, and practice in dealing with unexpected problems (which Moltke would throw at them without warning).

AUFTRAGSTAKTIK—MISSION TACTICS / It was during this period of postwar introspection and evaluation that one of the fundamental military concepts of Scharnhorst and Gneisenau coalesced into a clearly defined doctrine understandable to and understood by all officers in the Army. This was the concept of *Auftragstaktik,* or mission tactics. Moltke himself inserted in the draft of a new tactical manual for senior commanders the following lines:

> A favorable situation will never be exploited if commanders wait for orders. The highest commander and the youngest soldier must always be conscious of the fact that omission and inactivity are worse than resorting to the wrong expedient.

Those words have appeared in every subsequent edition of that manual.

This, of course, was what Gneisenau and Blücher were trying to drum into their subordinate commanders during the pursuit from Waterloo to Paris; it was what—after indoctrination by Grolman, Müffling, Krauseneck, and Reyher—Moltke could expect from his subordinates once he gave them missions in the Seven Weeks' and Franco-Prussian wars.

Nothing epitomized the outlook and performance of the German General Staff, and of the German Army which it coordinated, more than this concept of mission tactics: the responsibility of each German officer and noncommissioned officer—and even Moltke's "youngest soldier"—to do without question or doubt whatever the situation required, as he saw it. This meant that he should act without awaiting orders, if action seemed necessary. It also meant that he should act contrary to orders, if these did not seem to be consistent with the situation.

To make perfectly clear that action contrary to orders was not considered either as disobedience or lack of discipline, German commanders began to repeat one of Moltke's favorite stories, of an incident observed while visiting the headquarters of Prince Frederick Charles. A major, receiving a tongue-lashing from the Prince for a tactical blunder, offered the excuse that he had been obeying orders, and reminded the Prince that a Prussian officer was taught that an order from a superior was tantamount to an order from the King. Frederick Charles promptly responded: "His Majesty made you a major because he believed you would know when *not* to obey his orders." This simple story became guidance for all following generations of German officers.

DEVELOPMENT OF NEW STRATEGIC PLANS / The principal mission of the General Staff remained, however, the preparation of mobilization and operational plans for any and all conceivable conflicts. No matter what else they might be doing, the thoughts and attention of the General Staff officers never wandered far from this critical function.

Less than three months after the surrender of Paris, Moltke and his staff produced a new strategic plan for a possible two-front war against France allied with Russia. He did not really expect such an alliance, between the new French Republic and the conservative Romanov Empire, but he could see the possibility that a common fear of the powerful new German Empire might bring these two nations together in an unlikely partnership. (That was the year that Charles Dudley Warner, in his "Fifteenth Week" essay in *My Summer in a Garden,* wrote that "politics makes strange bedfellows.")

Bismarck, of course, also recognized this danger. One can speculate that, despite the recent strains on their official relationship, this was a subject often discussed between two old friends who continued to see each other frequently and informally. It would be easy to suggest that politically more perceptive Bismarck alerted the soldier to the danger; on the other hand, historian Moltke would not have needed this advice. Both probably recognized the situation instantly, and each took appropriate action in his own sphere of activity. Bismarck guided German diplomacy so as to prevent such an alliance, if possible, and to circumvent it should it ever materialize. Moltke, meanwhile, planned to deal with it, should Bismarck's diplomacy fail.

Moltke saw the strategic implications of the immediate threat of a reorganized and rejuvenated French Army, and the longer-term threat of the ponderous mobilization of Russia's vast manpower. His initial reaction to this strategic problem was to seek to avoid the situation that had almost destroyed the Prussia of Frederick the Great: fighting a two-front war against vastly superior forces invading simultaneously from east and west. Interestingly, in the light of the events and controversies of the next three quarters of a century, the thought that immediately came to his mind was to concentrate overwhelming force, created by the more rapid German mobilization, to defeat France, and drive that nation out of the war, and then to turn all of this force against the Russians, before they had time to invade Prussia. After some study, however, he came to the conclusion that such a strategy would not work. "Germany cannot hope to rid herself of one enemy by a quick offensive victory in the West in order then to turn against the other. We have just seen how difficult it is to bring even the victorious war against France to an end."[2]

Moltke's decision, then, was to plan a mobilization that would divide the German Army approximately equally between the two fronts, to be employed strategically in offensive-defensive operations that would make maximum use of the defensive-offensive tactics he had so well mastered in the recent wars with Austria and France. He planned to move into the enemy countries, to seize an easily defendable glacis to protect the frontiers of Germany, undertake local offensives against approaching enemy armies whenever the opportunity presented itself, but in general to let the French and the Russians dash themselves to pieces against German defensive firepower.

FOREIGN THREATS AND BISMARCK'S DIPLOMACY / All three of the neighboring major potential foes of Germany—Austria, France, and Russia—soon adopted mobilization plans modeled on that with which Prussia had amazed the world in 1866 and 1870. Thus if Germany were to go to war with any one of them, the strategic problem would be greater than it had been in the two recent wars. And if, as Moltke and Bismarck both feared, it were to be against any combination of these neighbors, the danger of German defeat by overwhelming numbers was a very serious one. Thus, the General Staff believed, there was an urgent need for major increases in the strength of the standing army and of the mobilization potential of the nation.

Such increases, however, were not easy to obtain. When the North German Federation was established, Bismarck had adopted a policy of seven-year military programs, in order to avoid in the Federation *Reichstag* the constant political bickering over annual military budgets which had so embittered Prussian politics in the 1850s and 1860s. He adhered to this policy within the framework of the Empire, although he did later reduce the periods to five years in length. He firmly believed that he could assure maximum military budgets in this fashion. Thus, despite the arguments presented to him by Roon and Moltke, he refused to go back for any major increases in military appropriations in the early 1870s. He made it clear that he would of course seek more funds in an emergency, but he did not see an emergency at that time. In fact, his successful diplomacy was avoiding an emergency.

In 1873 Bismarck established the League of the Three Emperors, or *Dreikaiserbund,* linking the three major Continental monarchies—Germany, Austria, and Russia—in a loose conservative partnership which was, more than anything else, an expression of monarchical solidarity in the face of the republicanism represented by France. This informal alliance almost fell apart in the disputes between Austria and Russia over their Turkish and Balkan policies in the period 1875-1878. Bismarck, however, was able to prevent a war between the other two empires by skillful diplomacy which culminated in the Congress of Berlin, which at least temporarily resolved "the Eastern Question." He followed this with another series of adroit diplomatic moves. To demonstrate to Russia his displeasure with the threat to the peace of Europe resulting from the Russo-Turkish War of 1877-1878, as well as his determination to preserve Austria as a great power, he concluded a defensive alliance with Austria-Hungary on October 7, 1879. Then he was able to convince Russia that by this action he had kept Austria-Hungary from joining Great Britain in an anti-Russian alliance.

Although Russia and Austria-Hungary remained somewhat distrustful of each other, they joined with Germany in a reaffirmation of the League of the Three Emperors on June 18, 1881. Then, to assure further the isolation of France from any other Continental power, Bismarck engineered the Triple Alliance with Italy and Austria-Hungary, in which Germany guaranteed to support Italy should that monarchy become involved in war against France, in return for Italian commitment to neutrality in the event of war between Austria-Hungary and Russia.

FRANCE, RUSSIA, AND THE DANGER OF TWO-FRONT WAR / Imperturbably Moltke, while recognizing that the diplomatic legerdemain of Bismarck would probably obviate a two-front war, nonetheless continued to keep updated Germany's plans for the worst possible situation, which he still considered to be a two-front war against Russia and France. By 1877 it had become obvious that the French threat was more acute than that of Russia. France had been able to increase her military manpower dramatically by a national conscription policy adopted in 1872, and had developed an efficient, rapid mobilization system comparable to that of Germany. Moltke decided to increase the size of the force to be mobilized against France, at the expense of that in the East, and to expand somewhat the scope of the previously limited offensive planned against France since 1871.

Moltke made this change in the planned initial deployment most reluctantly, because the Russian Army, also, had shown signs of improvement. Russia was making progress in correcting defects in military policy, organization, and doctrine made evident in the Russo-Turkish War of 1877-1878, and was becoming a more formidable potential foe. But this fact merely made more serious the considerably greater and more immediate threat of France. It was doubtful if the previous German strategy of approximately equal allocation of forces and simultaneous limited offensive-defensives on the two fronts was still viable for either front.

Moltke's new strategy, therefore, provided for massing the bulk of the German armies first against France and then Russia. He still intended that the initial offensive against France should remain limited. When the French armies had been overwhelmed in major battles in eastern France, he hoped Bismarck would be able to negotiate a reasonable peace with France—but on terms still favorable to Germany. If France refused relatively generous peace terms, she would have been so weakened that substantially reduced German armies could remain indefinitely on the defensive in eastern France (falling back slowly to the Rhine if necessary) while the bulk of the German forces could be transferred to the East to deal with Russia.

The most worrisome feature of this new plan from Germany's standpoint was the risk that Russia, despite slow and cumbersome mobilization, might be able to start an invasion of East Prussia and Silesia before the transfer of the bulk of German forces from France could be accomplished. Otherwise the General Staff considered this plan to be an improvement over that of 1871.

The only solution to this threat to Silesia and East Prussia was to obtain a substantial increase in the size of the German Army. There had been a modest augmentation of both the standing army and the reserve mobilization base in May 1874, when the Reich Military Law, providing for a standing army of 401,659, was passed by the *Reichstag* after serious debate. In 1880 the Standing army was increased by the *Reichstag* to 427,724. While this was less than Moltke had hoped for, he was able to plan to place the additional troops, including those that would be provided from the increased mobilization base, in the East. This would secure vulnerable East Prussia and Silesia while the main German Army was concentrated in the West.

New developments in France, however, soon forced Moltke and his General Staff to make still another significant change in their strategy and mobilization plan. By 1879 a new French fortification system had progressed far enough to render doubtful the possibility of a quick decision in the West. At the same time, this French fortification system provided a base from which the improved French Army could undertake an early offensive into Germany—particularly into the former French provinces of Alsace and Lorraine. Early in 1879, therefore, Moltke began to urge more vigorously upon Bismarck to conclude an alliance with Austria.

Informal discussions had already taken place between the German and Austrian General Staffs, in Vienna as well as in Berlin, and as soon as the treaty was signed later that year, Moltke had his new plan ready. As before, the concept was for the initial concentration of overwhelming force on one front, in order to gain an early decision there, with a rapid shift of this massed military power to the other front. Now, however, the initial focus of the concentration was shifted from West to East, with half a million German and Austrian troops pouring across the frontiers into Russian Poland, while a small German army delayed the French in the West.

Moltke recognized that it would take longer to reach a major decision in the East than in the West, but the Austro-Hungarian Army could be most rapidly deployed there, and with that reinforcement he could afford to leave a respectable army to defend Alsace-Lorraine and the Rhenish provinces, and if necessary that army could even fall back to the Rhine without any serious danger or damage to Germany.

Nevertheless, Moltke had the staff prepare an alternative deployment plan, providing for a major mobilization against France, should unforeseen events either result in a different alliance lineup in wartime, or permit a one-front war against France. This general strategic concept of preparedness for both two-front and one-front wars was retained in effect for the next nine years, with two updated alternative mobilization plans being produced by the General Staff each year. In 1882 the conclusion of the Triple Alliance permitted Moltke the luxury of planning for the possibility of shifting six Italian corps to the upper Rhine, permitting the concentration of still greater forces against Russia or—in the one-front alternative plan—enabling him to concentrate a vast army in Lorraine, based on the new fortress of Metz, to smash through the northern French defenses in order to reach the favorable maneuvering ground of Champagne and an unobstructed road to Paris.

WALDERSEE AS MOLTKE'S DEPUTY / By this time Moltke was beginning to feel the weight of his eighty-two years, and he again asked his monarch for permission to retire. But William was growing old too, and the thought of having to entrust the planning for the security of his Empire to anyone other than Moltke frightened him. He insisted that Moltke retain his post, but acceded to the Chief of Staff's request that in such circumstances he be provided with a deputy to whom he could shift much of the day-to-day responsibility for supervision and administration of the General Staff.

The man that Moltke selected as his deputy and likely successor was fifty-year-old General Count Alfred von Waldersee. He had first joined the General Staff in 1866 at the age of thirty-five, somewhat older than most new entrants into the General Staff. After a year on the Staff in Berlin, he had gone to Paris as military attaché, and soon gained the favorable attention of Moltke by his thorough reports. When war was declared, Waldersee returned to Berlin, and soon went back to France with the royal headquarters as King William's aide-de-camp. As a member of the royal household in the field, he naturally was seen frequently by Moltke, just at the time the accuracy of Waldersee's reports from Paris were being confirmed by the course of operations. The military future of the young officer was assured. Now, with the title of Quartermaster General, he became Moltke's deputy, and was granted considerable authority by the old Chief of Staff.

During the Austro-Prussian and Franco-Prussian wars, Moltke had enjoyed the personal right of reporting directly to the King—now the Emperor—and after the wars the old monarch occasionally summoned him for conversations on General Staff matters. Theoretically, however, as the nominal subordinate of the War Minister, Moltke was supposed to report to the monarch only through him. He was always meticulous in keeping his old friend Roon informed of such private conversations with William, until Roon resigned as War Minister in early November 1873. The same cordial, easy relationship continued between Moltke and Roon's successor, General von Kameke.

Some of Moltke's subordinates, however, resented the fact that their Chief—acknowledged as the greatest soldier of the era—was forced to play a subordinate role to a younger and less distinguished man. They felt, furthermore, that the preeminence of the General Staff in German military affairs had been so demonstrated in the great victories over Austria and France that it was not proper for the Chief of the General Staff to be the subordinate of a governmental functionary—even if that person was always a military man and almost always a former General Staff officer.

INTRIGUE: WAR MINISTRY, GENERAL STAFF, MILITARY CABINET / Waldersee was one of those who felt most strongly that the General Staff should not be subordinate to the War Ministry, but should be directly under the Emperor. Now that he was in a position of considerable power, he decided to do something about the situation. When it became apparent that Kameke had no intention of abdicating his responsibilities as War Minister, Waldersee began to intrigue against him. He found an immediate confederate in intrigue: General von Albedyll, Chief of the Military Cabinet.

Albedyll had been a protege of Manteuffel, and succeeded to the position of Chief of the Military Cabinet five years after Manteuffel became Governor of Schleswig, in 1865. Like Manteuffel, Albedyll was dedicated to the objective of obtaining complete independence of the Military Cabinet from the War Ministry, and at the same time of gaining control over the principal matters of military administration. Albedyll had no apparent desire to become responsible for the planning functions of the General Staff, thus he and Waldersee were natural allies. Equally natural as their enemy was War Minister von Kameke, who, while a loyal lieutenant of the Emperor, was also an adherent of the Scharnhorst-Gneisenau-Boyen philosophy of centralized Army control, responsive to the elected representatives of the people.

An unexpected third ally against Kameke was Bismarck. The Chancellor apparently had no personal difference with Kameke, but disagreed totally with the concept of legislative authority over the Army. Growing liberalism—and even hints of socialism—among the legislators had made Bismarck distrustful of the entire *Reichstag* and of democratic processes. Since he saw in the Army the nation's last resort against possible revolution, he felt that it was desirable to do everything possible to weaken legislative authority over the Army. He therefore sought to reduce the power of the War Minister—the only military official who had even indirect responsibility to the *Reichstag*. This could best be done by transferring some of this power to the Military Cabinet and the General Staff, both of which owed primary responsibility to the Emperor.

Bismarck's philosophical differences with Kameke became an important issue early in 1883, when a group of legislators accused the Army of fiscal inefficiency. They combined this with criticism of the Prussian Guards regiments as parade-ground troops with little actual military effectiveness. As these attacks against the Army mounted in intensity in *Reichstag* debates, the aging Emperor became infuriated. Albedyll hinted to William that Kameke was not defending the Army with sufficient vigor; Bismarck may have added fuel to the monarch's burning fury. William wrote a long, imperious directive to the War Minister, telling him to do better in making clear to the *Reichstag* that the Army was controlled by the Emperor, not the legislature. Kameke, rightly interpreting this as evidence that the Emperor no longer reposed confidence in him, resigned on March 3, 1883. Bismarck immediately advised William to accept the resignation.

Albedyll and Waldersee seem to have agreed—presumably with Bismarck's approval—that the logical replacement for Kameke was General Paul Bronsart von Schellendorf, who had been one of the principal Staff officers in Moltke's field headquarters in the Franco-Prussian War, and was the author of *Duties of the General Staff*. Bronsart well understood the issues involved. He seems to have shared Bismarck's desire to weaken *Reichstag* control over the Army, and thus was willing to take the position of War Minister with reduced powers. As an experienced General Staff officer, also, he sympathized with the desire of direct approach of the Chief of the General Staff to the Emperor. In fact, he had been one of those who urged this move. He was probably less enthusiastic about increasing the power of the Chief of the Military Cabinet, but transferring control over military personnel affairs from the War Minister to the Military Cabinet seemed to be the simplest way of reducing the responsibility of the War Ministry without completely destroying that institution.

IMMEDIATVORTRAG–DIRECT ACCESS TO THE EMPEROR / On March 8, 1883, therefore, an Imperial order was issued abolishing the Division of Personnel in the War Ministry, and transferring responsibility for all military personnel matters to the Military Cabinet. On May 24, another Imperial order granted to the Chief of Staff and his deputy the right of immediate access (*Immediatvortrag*) to the Emperor.

It has been suggested by Gordon Craig that Bronsart, by his willingness to increase the power of the General Staff and the Military Cabinet at the expense of the War Ministry, had enabled Albedyll "to destroy the administrative unity which the Army had enjoyed since the days of Scharnhorst and Boyen, and, in doing so, he had introduced a degree of interdepartmental rivalry that had been unknown before 1883. The War Ministry, the Military Cabinet, and the General Staff had become mutually independent agencies, but it was virtually impossible to define the limits of their spheres of competence and, between 1883 and 1914, disputes were frequent, acrimonious, and damaging to the efficiency of the Army."[3]

Without necessarily disagreeing with all of this assessment, it must be recognized that there can be another evaluation. Interdepartmental rivalry, when carried to excess, can be bad; on the other hand, as has been argued frequently in the United States, it can prevent the growth of "monolithic militarism," and can encourage healthy competition. The difficulty, of course, is to define the operative words "carried to excess" and "healthy competition." Inefficiency is not inevitably the handmaiden of argument and acrimony. In fact, from a purely military standpoint, these changes probably had absolutely no effect on the efficiency of the German Army. Certainly Bronsart did not think so, and it is doubtful if there was a greater authority on the subject. The pervasive influence of the General Staff on all matters that really affected military efficiency certainly was not lessened; on the other hand it was also probably not significantly increased by the right of *Immediatvortrag*.

The damage that was done was indeed significant, but all in the political and politico-military fields of which Bronsart and other General Staff officers had little understanding. The battle which Scharnhorst and Boyen, and more recently Kameke, had waged to assure some measure of popular control over military affairs was now irretrievably lost. The authority and power of the crown over the Army had been reestablished more firmly than it had been since the days of Frederick the Great. The will of the people—democracy—had been significantly, perhaps fatally, weakened in Germany. As long as affairs of state were managed by a brilliant pragmatist like Bismarck, there was little danger that the vast, unfettered military power of Germany would be employed irresponsibly. But given a weak and vacillating Emperor and a weak Chancellor, unwise decisions were a distinct likelihood, and so was the possibility of irresponsible employment of military power by soldiers—like Moltke, say, or Ludendorff—inexperienced in affairs of state. Furthermore, a pattern was established which would facilitate the misuse of German military power by an evil madman as head of state.

Waldersee's rise to power in the General Staff was a demonstration of the strengths and weaknesses of institutionalized military excellence. The institution was, after all, human, and composed of human beings. Waldersee was unquestionably a man of great military competence, and his influence on the Staff's activities during his years as deputy and, later, Chief of Staff certainly had no adverse effect on its performance of its mission as the "brain" of the German Army. (It was during this period that Spenser Wilkinson wrote his brilliant analysis of the German General Staff, which he entitled *The Brain of an Army*.)[4]

For all of his competence, however, Waldersee lacked the intellectual brilliance either of his predecessor or his successor. He was an intriguer, and while his intrigues did not damage the military efficiency of the General Staff, they could have. He was vain, arrogant, and inordinately ambitious. The German Army was not faced with any major crisis—other than those he created—during his period at or near the head of the General Staff, so it is not possible to assess how he would have performed under the pressure of great responsibility in a time of national crisis.

WILLIAM II BECOMES GERMAN EMPEROR / Early in 1888 Emperor William I died, and was succeeded by the Crown Prince, who became Frederick III* for a brief reign of slightly more than three months. Dying of cancer at the time of his accession, Frederick had lost his voice as a result of a tracheotomy performed in January 1888. When he died, on June 15, he in turn was succeeded by his son, young William II.

Moltke had hoped to retire shortly after the death of William I, but had withheld submission of his resignation as Chief of the General Staff until the outcome of the new Emperor's illness became clear. Now that a young, vigorous Emperor had succeeded to the throne, Moltke delayed no longer. His resignation was graciously accepted by William II, and on August 10, 1888, the eighty-eight-year-old Field Marshal finally left the post he had held for thirty-one years. He was succeeded by Waldersee, who had for years been a friend of the new Emperor.

---

*Interestingly, William had been the first of his name both as King of Prussia and Emperor of Germany; the decision of his son—known formerly as Prince Frederick William—to call himself Frederick III instead of Frederick I shows that the Hohenzollerns considered that the royal succession as Kings of Prussia took precedence over the Imperial title.

CONTINUING INTRIGUES OF WALDERSEE / Waldersee was now in a strong position to proceed with other intrigues which he was planning or in which he was already involved, plots against the three men who had been his allies a few years earlier: Albedyll, Bronsart von Schellendorf, and Bismarck.

Waldersee's differences with Albedyll were the first to come to the surface. He knew that the new Emperor was a close friend of Major General von Hahnke, commander of the 1st Guards Infantry Brigade, who was also a friend of Waldersee's. So, Waldersee began quietly to undercut his former confederate in conversations with William, at the same time encouraging the Emperor to consider the possibility of appointing Hahnke as Chief of the Military Cabinet. Late in 1888 the change was made; Albedyll left Berlin to spend his last few years of active service in relative obscurity as commander of the VII Army Corps. The new Chief of the Military Cabinet promptly joined forces with his benefactor in a more convoluted intrigue against the War Minister, General Paul Bronsart von Schellendorf.

His experience as a Cabinet Minister and legislator had caused Bronsart to realize that the weakening of the power of the War Minister was really totally unrelated to the performance of the General Staff. At the same time, he was concerned by the fact that, despite his general administrative and fiscal responsibility for the Army as a whole, he had no control over the individuals who made up that Army. He found this to be not only administratively frustrating, but also politically embarrassing. It was sometimes convenient to be able to avoid answering difficult questions in the *Reichstag,* when these related to personnel or planning matters. More often, however, this efficient man was embarrassed to be forced to admit to the legislators that he had no knowledge of important military matters of which the Prussian *Landtag* or German *Reichstag* felt that they had every right to be kept informed.

This situation was particularly galling to Bronsart during the septennial debate over the Army budget in the spring of 1887. It was only with great difficulty and much embarrassment that the Chancellor and War Minister persuaded the *Reichstag* to agree to an increase in Army strength to 468,409 enlisted men. The difficulty was repeated in December of that year, as Bronsart doggedly pushed through a bill for reorganizing and enlarging the reserve forces.

Thus the War Minister was annoyed when he began to detect that the young Emperor was paying increasingly more attention to the advice he received from the new Chief of the Military Cabinet and from the new Chief of the General Staff, than he did to that he was receiving—with decreasing frequency—from his experienced War Minister. A coolness had already affected the previous cordial relationship of Bronsart and Waldersee; now the War Minister realized that he was engaged in a power struggle with the Chief of the General Staff. Early in 1889 Bronsart wrote two memoranda to William, pointing out that he could not perform his functions properly in the *Reichstag* unless he could answer questions intelligently about the Army, rather than avoid such questions, and unless it was clear that he had the confidence of the Emperor.

Not receiving satisfactory imperial responses to his memoranda, Bronsart resigned, and on April 8, 1889, was replaced by his old General Staff colleague, Julius von Verdy du Vernois. This was seen by Waldersee and Hahnke (who was a true spiritual successor of Manteuffel and Albedyll) as an opportunity to transfer further power from the War Ministry to their agencies. Verdy agreed, somewhat ruefully remarking to Waldersee, "The new War Minister must make his debut in his office as a kind of suicide."[5]

Waldersee had secretly been intriguing against Bismarck since 1886. He became convinced that the aged Chancellor's shifting diplomacy with respect to Russia and Austria was a meaningless seesaw, and that Bismarck had lost his sharp, ruthless energy. Waldersee believed that the growing strength of Russia, with its obvious ambitions for expansion as far as Constantinople, was the greatest threat to Germany. The time had come, he believed, for Germany and Austria-Hungary to destroy Russian power. And if France came into the war, so much the better. There is little doubt that Waldersee was already beginning to have ambitions to become Chancellor,[6] so that he could carry out this policy.

It is not clear whether Bismarck realized that Waldersee was intriguing against him. When Moltke was retiring, the Chancellor seems to have had some doubts about Waldersee's qualifications as the new Chief of the General Staff, but apparently he was reassured by Moltke's strong endorsement of Waldersee, and Bismarck in turn recommended approval to the new Emperor. He was repaid, less than two years later, by Waldersee's contributions to the Emperor's decision to get rid of Bismarck. But, to Waldersee's apparent surprise, he was not selected to replace the old Chancellor. Instead William selected General of Infantry Count Leo von Caprivi, a former General Staff officer.

Meanwhile, Verdy du Vernois, apparently sharing the disillusionment that had contributed to Bronsart's resignation as War Minister, also resigned. On October 4, 1890, he was replaced as War Minister by General Hans Karl Georg von Kaltenborn-Stachau.

It was about this time that Waldersee began to realize that he had lost the confidence and friendship of William. This was partly the result of Waldersee's sound assessment of the strategic implication of the Emperor's determination to build up the German Navy. William became cool when Waldersee tried to persuade him that Germany, as a continental power, already dangerously surrounded by more numerous potential enemies, could not afford to divide its strained resources between a great Army and a great Navy. Waldersee tried to retire, but William persuaded him, instead, to accept the command of an Army corps. On February 9, 1891, General Count Alfred von Schlieffen was appointed Chief of the General Staff.

NOTES TO CHAPTER NINE

[1] Arnold J. Toynbee, *A Study of History,* Somervell abridgment of vols. 1-6 (New York: 1947), p. 336.

[2] As quoted in Gerhard Ritter, *The Schlieffen Plan* (New York: 1958), p. 18.

[3] Craig, *op. cit.,* p. 230.

[4] Spenser Wilkinson, *The Brain of an Army* (London: 1890).

[5] Alfred von Waldersee, *Diaries* (Berlin: 1928), p. 325.

[6] See Goerlitz, *op. cit.,* pp. 111-126, for an interesting discussion of Waldersee's ambition in relation to his post in the General Staff.

Chapter Ten

THE SCHLIEFFEN PLAN
Failure in Perfection

 ALFRED VON SCHLIEFFEN / The new Chief of the General Staff, a member of an old Prussian noble family and the son of a Prussian officer, had been born in Berlin in 1833. In 1837, his father, Major Magnus von Schlieffen, retired because of poor health, and moved to his estate in Silesia. There Alfred von Schlieffen lived until he went off to school, in 1842. Unlike some of his military contemporaries, who were boastful of their aristocratic origins, young Schlieffen was proud not only of his aristocratic forebears, but also of the fact that many of them had been wise enough to marry commoners. He was fond of attributing to this injection of less-than-blue blood his own qualities of energy, industry, and painstaking thoroughness.

In his youth, Schlieffen did not show any interest in military life, and in fact had trouble deciding on a career. Thus he did not attend one of the traditional Prussian cadet academies, and had enrolled as a law student at the University of Berlin when he entered the Army in 1853 to perform his compulsory military service as a one-year volunteer. This was in accordance with a provision of the law that permitted educated men to become officers after one year of active enlisted service, in anticipation of subsequent appointment to a reserve commission. To his surprise, however, the slight, almost frail young man decided —without much enthusiasm—that military life was not unpleasant. Instead of joining the reserves, in 1854 he was appointed an officer candidate in the 2nd Guard Uhlans. In 1858, he was admitted to the General War School at an age somewhat younger than usual, on the basis of strong recommendations from his commanders. When in 1861 he graduated from the War Academy (renamed in 1859), with high honors, his future as a General Staff officer was assured.

After a year as adjutant of his regiment Schlieffen was assigned to the Topographic Bureau of the General Staff in 1862. In 1865 he was transferred to the Staff itself. He served in the Austro-Prussian War as a staff officer in the cavalry corps of Prince Albert of Prussia and was at the Battle of Königgrätz. He was married to his cousin, Countess Anna Schlieffen, in 1868. Schlieffen had already acquired a reputation as a hard worker, but after the premature death of his beautiful wife in 1872 after the birth of their second child, the griefstricken young officer immersed himself completely in his work, and for the rest of his life seemed to have no interest in pleasure or recreation of any sort.

Schlieffen was serving on the Great General Staff in Berlin at the time of the outbreak of the Franco-Prussian War, and to his intense disgust feared that he would miss active field service. He did not feel much better when he was assigned to the staff of Grand Duke Frederick II of Mecklenburg-Schwerin's newly organized XIII Corps, protecting the North Sea coast from a possible French amphibious invasion. When, however, the Grand Duke Frederick was summoned to France, in November, to take command of a small army operating in the Loire Valley between Orleans and Le Mans, Schlieffen accompanied him. Thus he achieved his hoped-for active-combat service experience as a trusted and influential staff officer in one of the most difficult campaigns fought by the Prussian Army in that war. He was promoted to major.

Between 1871 and 1884 Schlieffen's service alternated between his regiment and the General Staff. In the latter year Colonel von Schlieffen was again assigned to the General Staff in Berlin, in charge of the Military History Division. Obviously being groomed by Moltke and Waldersee as an eventual Chief of Staff, Schlieffen served as the director of several Staff divisions between 1885 and 1888. On December 4, 1886, he was promoted to Major General. Soon after the retirement of Moltke and the appointment of Waldersee as Chief of Staff, Schlieffen became Deputy Chief of Staff (there were two other deputies) and Quartermaster General and was promoted to Lieutenant General on December 4, 1888.

Unlike his Chief, Schlieffen avoided political affairs and intrigue, devoting himself with equal diligence to supervision and active involvement in the two main tasks of the General Staff: the preparation of war plans, and furtherance of the preparedness of the German Army for war. Like Moltke, he had become gravely concerned by the growing rapport between France and Russia, and the fact that these potential enemies could mass far superior forces against the vulnerable eastern and western frontiers of Germany. He was convinced that Germany's only hope of victory, should Germany become involved in a war against a Franco-Russian coalition, was not only a more effective mobilization system, and superior strategic plans, but also the maintenance of a substantial superiority in the combat effectiveness of the fighting forces, from generals to privates. Yet he could see that by imitation of the German General Staff system the French and Russians were increasing the efficiency of their armies.

Schlieffen is known to history primarily as a stategist and planner. It is generally forgotten that implicit in his strategic concepts was a military force whose combat effectiveness would be substantially superior to that of its enemies. Thus the new Quartermaster General devoted at least as much attention to training, military education, and the adaptation of modern technology to military purposes as he did to strategic planning. However, he was not to be Quartermaster General for long. Two and a half years after his appointment, he found himself Chief of the General Staff, replacing the embittered

Waldersee. On January 27, 1893, he was promoted to the rank of General of Cavalry.

THE FIRST SCHLIEFFEN PLAN / Up to this time Schlieffen had not made any attempt to change the basic war plans that had been adopted by Moltke and had then been retained with little change by Waldersee. But in the light of the increasing danger of a Russian-French entente, he was beginning to have doubts about the wisdom of the current strategic concept of a two-front defensive-offensive, with first priority to the East. When the entente became a fact in 1893, Schlieffen concluded that the time had come for a fundamental change in strategy. He agreed with Moltke that Russia was a less formidable foe than France, but he doubted whether an early and decisive victory could ever be obtained against Russia in time to avert the danger of a powerful French invasion of Germany. Schlieffen remembered what had happened to the far more efficient, and numerically superior, army of Napoleon when it invaded Russia in 1812. The Russians could again trade space for time, drawing German armies ever deeper into the vast reaches of Russia until France was ready to overwhelm the smaller army that Moltke had believed adequate to hold the line of the Vosges Mountains or the Rhine River.

Adding to this concern was the growing rapprochement between France and Britain, in large part a British reaction against the flamboyant and expansionist colonial and naval policies of Emperor William II. Since Schlieffen—who had seen what had happened to Waldersee—saw no possibility of any change in those policies, the danger of British manpower being added to the already substantial numerical superiority of a Russo-French entente was a threat which he could not ignore. Although Germany's alliance with Austria-Hungary and Italy to a large extent offset the manpower superiority of France and Russia, there was a clause in the Triple Alliance which specifically excused Italy from joining the other two allies if they were engaged in war with Great Britain.

The basic concept of the new war plan which had been taking shape in Schlieffen's mind was simple. Relatively small German forces in the East could hold off a Russian threat to Prussia and Silesia, not only because of the slow and ponderous Russian mobilization plan, but also because of the clear-cut German combat superiority over the Russians. While Schlieffen was confident that the German Army was also better than that of France, he knew that the French had greatly improved, and probably had the second best army in the world. (This, of course, was a still further reason why Schlieffen considered that a delaying strategy against France in the West was less realistic than against Russia in the East.) Counting on at least a measure of German superiority over the French, however, Schlieffen decided that he would hurl the bulk of the German Army—nine tenths of its mobilized strength—against France, to seek a decisive result before the French were completely ready for battle. Employing maximum speed, and making the optimum use of maneuver, he would seek to destroy the French armies and capture Paris so quickly that Britain would not intervene in the war or—if the British were already committed—before that intervention could be effective on the Continent.

Moltke had been thinking in somewhat similar terms in the late 1870s, but had changed his mind because of the formidable nature of the new French fortifications in Lorraine. Schlieffen recognized that his proposed plan for an offensive through those forts would be costly, and that there was a considerable risk attached to it. But he considered that the cost of a prolonged war would be far greater, and so would the risk, with Britain, France, and Russia combined against Germany and (only possibly) Austria-Hungary.

The new plan was adopted in 1894. At the same time Schlieffen and his staff intensified their efforts to seek ways of increasing German combat effectiveness, and adding greater mobility and speed to the field armies. Schlieffen turned to modern technology for assistance in this effort.

SCHLIEFFEN AS CHIEF OF STAFF / The greatest threat to the success of his new plan, Schlieffen realized, was the possibility that the French armies, based upon their strong fortifications in eastern Lorraine, could stop the German advance, and create a stalemate along the frontiers. The answer to this, Schlieffen reasoned, was to provide the fighting troops with much greater firepower than had ever before been employed on open battlefields. He would make heavy artillery, traditionally known as siege artillery, mobile enough to accompany the field armies, where the guns could be employed not only to augment the firepower of conventional field artillery on the battlefield but also to smash the French fortifications quickly, and without the delay normally associated with "bringing up siege batteries."

Conventional German soldiers—including artillerymen—were appalled. They had visions of the rate of advance of the entire army being slowed down to that of giant cannon, towed at snail's pace by vast teams of straining horses; thus they saw the introduction of heavy artillery to the battlefield as having an effect just the opposite of what Schlieffen wanted. The Chief of the General Staff was not deterred by this opposition, however. He was planning not only to make more effective use of the railroads to transport the artillery—and most of the rest of the army—closer to the battlefield than had ever been attempted before; he was also considering the use of steam engines to pull the cannon on roads, either with or instead of horses. But before this idea had reached the development stage, the newly perfected internal combustion engine provided Schlieffen with the towing mobility he sought.

Meanwhile, his thoughts on integrating the railroads even more closely to battle plans than Moltke had envisioned caused Schlieffen to create a new branch of the service: railroad engineers. Their principal mission was to keep railroads operating as close behind the front lines as possible, so that the fighting troops would not be dependent for supply upon long, slow wagon trains, traveling many, and ever-lengthening, miles between the advancing armies and the German frontiers. The captured railroad lines could be utilized, even if partially destroyed by the retreating French, if they could be quickly and effec-tively repaired and operated by engineer troops properly trained, prepared, and equipped. Again there were screams from the preponderantly conservative German officer corps that Schlieffen was making a dirty, grubby business out of the noble art of war. Schlieffen probably retorted, in his often-sarcastic manner, that war had always been dirty and grubby, and that blind adherence to custom and practice was no reason to keep from waging it efficiently.

Schlieffen was very much concerned about the danger that custom and practice could lead to procedures which, perhaps once essential, later became unnecessary routine, preserved in the mistaken belief that they were matters of tradition to be revered. As demonstrated by his artillery and railroad engineer innovations, he was perhaps less a conformist than even the most enlightened of his predecessors had been. Schlieffen was determined that routine matters should be handled routinely, quickly, and efficiently, to leave time for thinking about the really important problems.

Accordingly, shortly after he became Chief of Staff, Schlieffen introduced minor changes in the organization and procedures of the General Staff. These were for the most part small matters that had seemed to him desirable during his many years with the General Staff, and now he was in a position to do some-thing about them. These changes were mostly incorporated in a third edition of Bronsart von Schellendorf's *Duties of the General Staff,* which was revised and updated under Schlieffen's direction in 1893.

For the most part, however, the procedures were little changed from those that had been in practice even before Moltke had become Chief of Staff. Schlieffen retained the annual staff rides that had been a custom for three quarters of a century, because the reasons for such staff rides had been sound when introduced by Müffling, and they were still sound. He continued the emphasis on military history, since he was as much a believer in the value of the study of historical examples as even Moltke had been. In fact, in his spare-time— and although he devoted practically every waking hour to his work, he was always able to find a few minutes every day—he began to write a historical treatise on the subject of maneuver in history, a matter which had long intrigued him, and which he found particularly important as he pondered the problems of a possible two-front war against France and Russia.

SCHLIEFFEN AND CANNAE / This treatise, which he later published under the title *Cannae*, had two purposes. First to clarify in writing his own concepts of maneuver, and particularly the maneuver of envelopment, in relationship to the other fundamentals of warfare. Second—and perhaps more important, since his own thoughts were completely crystallized long before he finished the work —it was to be an instrument of instruction for the Staff, for the War Academy, and for the Army as a whole.

A significant military evaluation of the book is found in two para-graphs from an introduction to a 1925 edition, by an officer who had served on the General Staff under Schlieffen, General Baron Hugo von Freytag-Loringhoven.

The work of General Field Marshal Count von Schlieffen, as Chief of the General Staff of the German Army, took place remote from publicity. Since the World War, however, his name is mentioned by all. It came to be known that it was his spiritual heritage which, at the beginning of the war, brought to the German arms their great success. Even where his doctrines were misapplied, his schooling of the General Staff remained, nevertheless, a priceless possession.

Strictly, the Cannae studies of Count Schlieffen are not presentations from Military History. They comprise, rather, a conversational document of instruction. Just as the Field Marshal, in his activity as Chief of the General Staff of the Army, always endeavored, during the long period of peace, to keep alive in the General Staff, and thus in the Army at large, the idea of a war of annihilation, so likewise, is this expressed in his writings. Germany's situation demanded a quick decision. Though the Count set great store on the efficiency of the German Army, he was, nevertheless, always preoccupied with thoughts of how our leaders would acquit themselves when the time came. Hence, in his writings he often attributes his own ideas to the leaders of the Past—among them Moltke—when he wishes to prove that to achieve a decisive victory of annihilation *outflanking*—preferably from two or three sides—must be resorted to, as Hannibal did at Cannae. In everything which Count Schlieffen wrote the two-front war which threatened Germany hovered before him. In such a war we would be victorious only if soon after its outbreak we succeeded in obtaining an annihilating defeat of France. Modern battles Count Schlieffen characterizes even more than earlier battles as a "struggle for the flanks." Therefore he stresses the necessity, in case parts of an army have made frontal contact with the enemy, that the neighboring columns be allowed to march further so that they may be able to turn against flank and rear. In this method of presentation the Count is not always just to the actors of war history, especially the subordinate leaders of our own Army of 1866 and 1870-71. However, he explains their conduct as born of the Napoleonic traditions in the absence of war experience by their own generation. Notwithstanding the severity of his judgment, the writings of the Field Marshal show a real appreciation of true military art, for within him there abided an incomparable military fire. The reckless urge to the offensive of our Infantry he emphasizes as the prerequisite to victory.[1]

From the beginning of his tenure as Chief of the General Staff, Schlieffen considered that one of his primary tasks was to prepare the younger officers of the staff to accept responsibility, and to think imaginatively. Much to the annoyance of more senior officers, Schlieffen frequently assigned to younger members of the staff responsibility not only for planning maneuvers, but also for directing the movements of the maneuvering troops.

SCHLIEFFEN THE STRATEGIST / Some modern writers have created for Schlieffen a reputation of inflexible adherence to strategic and tactical patterns. Such writings reflect a lack of understanding both of the man and of his concepts of war. Schlieffen, as a student of Clausewitz, was probably even less committed to patterns and rules than was Moltke, archadvocate of flexibility. On the other hand, Schlieffen, like Clausewitz, and probably to a greater extent than Moltke, recognized the existence of certain fundamental principles of war. The modern shorthand codification of the principles in terms of key words was not yet in vogue in his lifetime, but his writings and actions show that he thought of war primarily in terms of four principles which today would be called The Offensive, Maneuver, Mass, and Economy of Forces. The actual application of these principles, he taught, would depend upon the situation, upon the forces available, and upon the actions and dispositions of the enemy. But by aggressively taking the offensive, and thus seizing the initiative, Schlieffen believed that one could require the enemy to conform substantially to one's own battle plan. Like Napoleon, he believed in attempting to maneuver the mass of one's own forces against the flanks of the enemy, not only to avoid the costly losses of frontal attacks against the weapons of modern firepower, but also to throw the opponent off balance, and force him to respond to the initiative. This mass of maneuver could be collected, and applied at a decisive point, he taught, by exercising economy of forces at places where the enemy could do the least harm, or where geography permitted a few men to fight successful defensive actions against more numerous attackers.

Schlieffen taught that these principles were equally valid for tactical and strategic operations. His model of perfect tactical battle of maneuver and envelopment, in which an army with inferior forces was able to bring to bear superior strength against both flanks of the more numerous opponent, was Hannibal's classic double-envelopment victory at Cannae, in 216 B.C. Thus the title of his book, in which he went on to show how Frederick the Great, Napoleon, and more recently Moltke, had successfully applied these principles in strategic campaign operations, and in tactical battlefield maneuvers.

Schlieffen did not allow a certain amount of chauvinistic pride in the accomplishments of both Frederick the Great and Moltke to blind him to the still greater genius of Napoleon. But he felt that the principal military value of military history was in the analysis of modern battles—in which weapons, equipment, and conditions were closest to those of the time of the student—within the context of a general understanding of how the great military masters of the past had applied similar principles with different kinds of weapons and forces. Thus, in his book and in his talks to his staff, Schlieffen devoted more attention to Sedan than to any other battle. That was not only the most recent major battle, it was also a splendid demonstration of the employment of the maneuver of envelopment strategically as well as tactically.

Schlieffen was fond of posing tactical problems to his staff officers. Not only would he do this in staff discussions and during the annual staff rides, he would do so whenever he perceived an opportunity—often at times when the opportunity was not perceived by the others. For instance, his annual Christmas greetings to selected members of the Staff was to present them with a tactical problem early on Christmas Eve, expecting to get a solution by the evening of Christmas Day. Being completely bound up in his work, he apparently never realized that this created no minor problem to his subordinates, almost all of whom were married, most having children at home.

By 1897 Schlieffen had modified his original 1894 plan (for a power thrust into Lorraine) to a more sophisticated, massive version of Moltke's strategic envelopment in the opening phases of the Sedan operation. In order to avoid the costly frontal assaults against the French fortresses, he had developed a plan for going around them to the north with the bulk of the German Army. In a gigantic wheel he would then sweep the French Army back against the Vosges Mountains and the Swiss frontier, where they would be forced to fight a climactic battle under circumstances closely resembling those under which Napoleon III and MacMahon faced Moltke's encircling armies just short of the Belgian border. The only problem with this plan was that, in order to bypass the French fortresses, it would be necessary to march through Belgium, Luxembourg, and Holland, countries whose neutrality Germany was pledged to support.

In each of the following years the plan was refined. In 1905 further improvements were planned, which he intended to introduce piecemeal, over the next few years. (This gradual approach would permit testing each innovation in annual war games and maneuvers.) That year, however, Schlieffen—who two years earlier had been promoted to Colonel General—was severely injured in a fall from his horse, and had to retire. Accordingly, in December 1905, just before retiring, he prepared a detailed memorandum for his successor, showing how he had intended to have the plan evolve in the next few years. (This memorandum was not actually completed and delivered to the new Chief of Staff until February 1906.) It became the basis for the operational plan with which the Germans entered World War I that is usually referred to as "the Schlieffen Plan."

THE ESSENCE OF THE SCHLIEFFEN PLAN / What was this plan, that has been praised by some admirers as the quintessence of strategic brilliance, and castigated by some sharp critics as a bold but rash gamble in violation of sound military principles?

Actually there were four different but similar Schlieffen Plans, including the second one, which was in effect at the time of Schlieffen's retirement. This was the plan of 1904-1905, the last operational war plan prepared in complete detail by the General Staff under Schlieffen's guidance. It provided for approximately twenty divisions to be deployed in the Aachen-Trier region, to advance through southern Belgium and Luxembourg toward Mezieres and Stenay, with the mission of enveloping the French left; twenty-two divisions

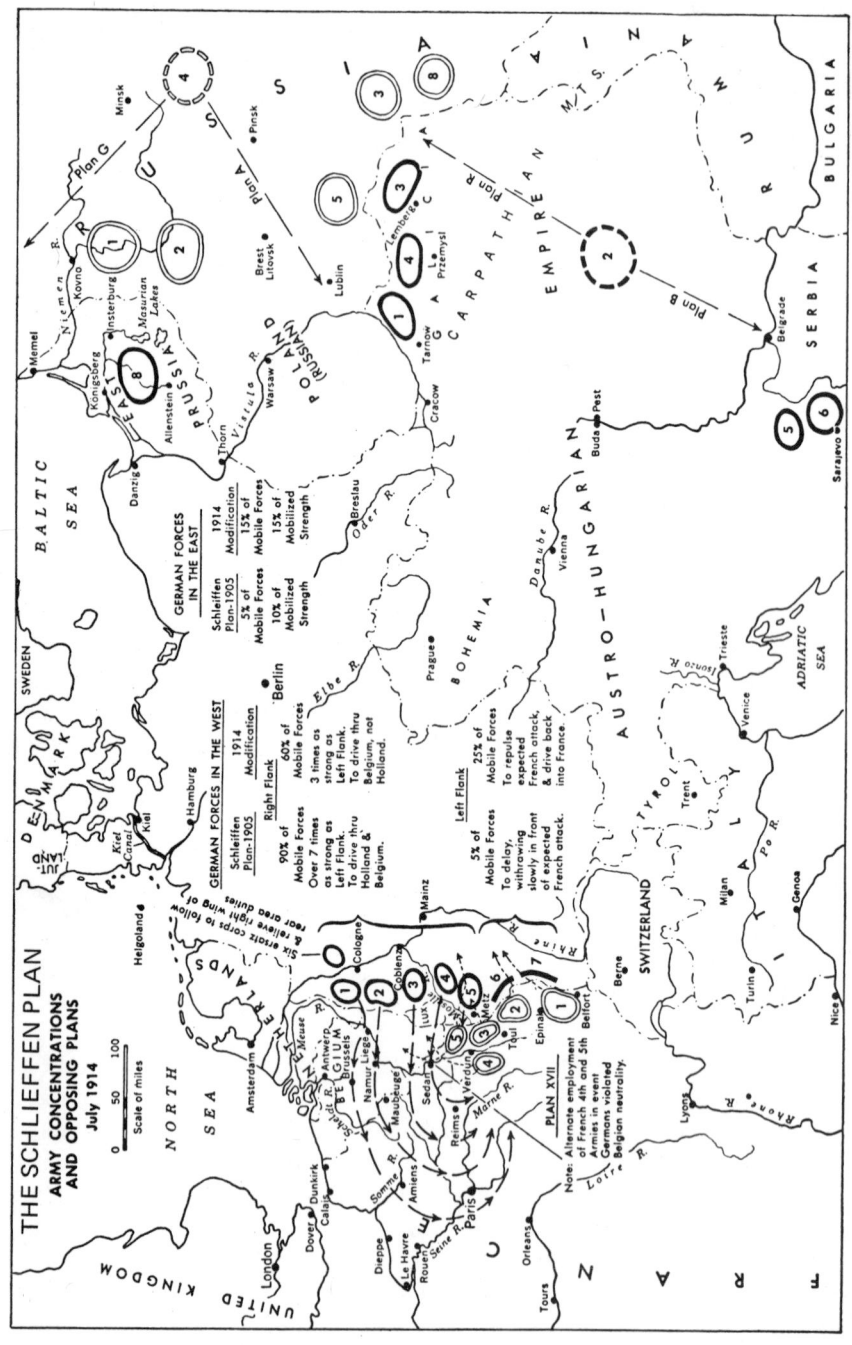

from the Thionville-Metz area were to conduct defensive-offensive operations to pin down the main French armies, which were expected to undertake an offensive from the Côtes de Lorraine; approximately nineteen divisions were to hold Alsace against the right wing of the expected French offensive. This meant, therefore, that approximately 52 percent of the German Western Army would be deployed north of Metz, and 30 percent of the Army would comprise a mass of maneuver to carry out a major strategic and tactical envelopment of the French left. Or, since about ten divisions were to be employed initially on the Eastern Front, to hold off the Russians until a decision was gained in the West, some 45 percent of the entire mobilized strength of the German Army was to be deployed north of Metz, 41 percent south of Metz, and 14 percent in the East.

War games in 1904 and 1905 convinced Schlieffen, however, that the force north of Metz was not strong enough to be certain of decisively smashing the French left wing, nor did it comprise a sufficient threat to the French rear and lines of communication to perform the truly strategic function of envelopment. Furthermore, in these games the German forces in Lorraine and Alsace were even more successful in their attack than Schlieffen had anticipated, but were not strong enough (and could not be made strong enough) to expect to make a breakthrough of the French fortifications. On top of this, the weaknesses of the Russian Army were being exposed in a disastrous war against Japan, and the internal weaknesses of the Russian Empire were demonstrated by an outbreak of revolution in Russia itself in early 1905. These were the considerations that were leading Schlieffen to project a major change in his plan at the time his accident forced his retirement.

The resulting memorandum, therefore, was not a plan; it was only a thoughtful presentation of a modified strategic concept for a revised plan. It remained, nevertheless, despite some adaptations that will be noted below, the conceptual basis for the German war plan at the outbreak of World War I, the concept usually called the Schlieffen Plan.

Schlieffen recognized, as he wrote in his memorandum, that an offensive invasion "calls for much strength and also consumes much, that this strength dwindles constantly while the defender's increases, and all this particularly so in a country which bristles with fortresses." Thus in order to reinforce the right wing it would be necessary not only to reduce substantially the forces south of Metz, and those scheduled for deployment in the East, but also to create a larger army. He pointed out that this should not be difficult, however, since France, with a population of 39 million, was able to mobilize an army as large as the planned mobilization strength of Germany with a population of 56 million. To permit the maximum possible reduction of forces in Lorraine and Alsace, Schlieffen recommended a major fortification construction program at Metz. He also recommended a change in the existing conscription laws and practices in order to make more effective use of German manpower and raise more troops.

Assuming that these recommendations would be carried out in the next few years (they were), Schlieffen postulated his revised plan on the availability of a mobilized army of approximately eighty-four divisions, regular and reserve, to be augmented at mobilization by twelve ersatz—newly created reserve divisions— to bring the mobilization total to ninety-six divisions. (His 1904-1905 plan provided for seventy-one divisions.) Of these ninety-six divisions, seventy-one would be deployed in the enveloping force of five armies, north of the Metz fortifications. There would be only ten divisions south of Metz in two armies in Lorraine and Alsace. The two right-wing armies, which would sweep through southern Holland and across Belgium toward Lille and Amiens in northern France, between them would have a total of thirty-two divisions. The other three armies in the right wing, pivoting more slowly above Metz, would have thirty-nine more divisions. Behind this gigantic wheeling movement would come the twelve new divisions. Also with this follow-up force would be four divisions shifted north from Alsace and Lorraine, after the anticipated French offensive was halted in those provinces, as Schlieffen confidently expected.

In his memorandum Schlieffen did not even mention the East, but it is known from other things he wrote and said that he was thinking in terms of skeleton forces, garrison, *Landwehr* and ersatz units, totaling not more than about three divisions in equivalent strength. These units were to conduct an active defense, falling back if necessary behind the Vistula. Schlieffen expected that the task of this small force would be greatly facilitated by an Austro-Hungarian offensive into southern Poland from Galicia, which should keep the Russians from massing overwhelming forces against the tiny German holding forces in East Prussia and Silesia. Schlieffen was confident that by this time—after five to seven weeks—a decisive victory would have been gained over France, and that the bulk of the ninety-three divisions in the West could be rapidly shifted, via the efficient German railroads, to meet the Russians at or east of the Vistula.

It will be seen then that Schlieffen envisaged, initially, a 7-to-1 ratio of German forces north of Metz in comparison to those to the south. But as forces were shifted from south to north, and as newly mobilized troops were shifted from the interior of Germany to the northern part of the front, the five enveloping armies could comprise as much as 96 percent of the entire mobile field forces mobilized by Germany in the West. Or, in other terms, taking into consideration the small forces in the East, this enveloping force could comprise between 86 and 91 percent of the entire mobilized field strength of the German Army.

During the next six years, even though in retirement, Schlieffen continued to devote his waking hours to the strategic problems of a two-front war. He also was thinking about the practical problems of controlling armies of unprece- dented size. At that time each German army corps consisted of two divisions. He came to the conclusion that this rigid army corps organization was unnecessary, and involved too many people in corps and army headquarters. By this time, as a result of the augmentations he had recommended in his 1905 memorandum, the mobilized field army had grown to a strength of more than 100 divisions, with fifty-two corps headquarters.

In December of 1912, therefore, seven years after his 1905 memorandum,

Schlieffen wrote another (his fourth plan) dealing generally with the same subject. Part of this memorandum was devoted to Army reorganization; he suggested that savings in manpower, and particularly efficiency, could be achieved by reorganizing the fifty-one corps as divisions. These would then be organized in four armies: the First Army, of twelve divisions, after crossing the Waal and the Meuse in Holland and Belgium, would advance toward Abbeville and St. Quentin; the Second Army of eight divisions would advance south of the Meuse-Sambre toward La Fere and Laon; the Third Army of ten divisions would move toward Mezieres and Verdun; the Fourth Army, of twelve divisions, would keep the main French armies pinned down between Verdun and Belfort. Behind the First and Second Armies a follow-up force of about nine divisions would occupy the overrun regions of Holland and Belgium, and invest bypassed fortresses.

This time Schlieffen mentioned the East, but he was hardly more specific than he had been in 1905. After somewhat unrealistically suggesting that Russia would hesitate to invade East Prussia and Silesia if there were no evidence of German offensive forces in those provinces,* Schlieffen justified leaving insignificant forces in the East by writing: "Frederick the Great was ultimately of the opinion that it was better to sacrifice a province 'than split up the Army with which one seeks, and must achieve, victory.' The *whole* of Germany must throw itself on *one* enemy—the strongest, most powerful, most dangerous enemy: and that can only be the Anglo-French!"[2] Presumably, however, he was still contemplating the deployment of skeleton defensive forces in the East, probably about the equivalent of two of the proposed new divisions.

It will be seen that Schlieffen had come to the conclusion that a slightly larger force was needed south of Metz, in order to prevent the French from shifting forces from the South to meet the northern envelopment. Nevertheless, the three northern armies, the enveloping force, was to comprise more than 76 percent of the Western Army, and at least 74 percent of the entire mobile strength of the German Army.

THE YOUNGER MOLTKE AND THE SCHLIEFFEN PLAN / Schlieffen's successor, General H. J. L. von Moltke, not only had adopted Schlieffen's existing plans when he became Chief of the General Staff on January 1, 1906, he also accepted without serious challenge or change the entire concept of the 1905 memorandum. He did, however, make some modifications in detail, and as time went on, continued to make more minor changes. For instance, in order to avoid adding the Netherlands to the list of German enemies, he decided to find some way of adhering to the Schlieffen concept without invading that country. He concluded that this could be done if Liege could be captured quickly, thus

---

*In a marginal note on the memorandum, General H. J. L. von Moltke, Schlieffen's successor as Chief of Staff, comments, "There can be no question under present-day political circumstances and treaties of Russia's hesitating to invade Prussia if no defense forces are left there."

permitting both the First and Second Armies to advance simultaneously through the narrow gap between the Ardennes and the Dutch frontier. This very idea, and its successful performance in war, are enough to demonstrate that the younger Moltke, if not of the caliber of most of his predecessors as chiefs of the General Staff, was nonetheless a competent and resourceful soldier.

In 1910 Moltke eliminated the idea of shifting two corps from the left-wing armies. He shifted the follow-up force of reserve divisions to Metz, where he felt they could be employed either to the North or to the South, as the situation might seem to warrant. And, as still larger forces were authorized by the *Reichstag,* the additional divisions thus created were allocated to the Sixth Army in Lorraine and the Seventh in Alsace. Moltke also rejected Schlieffen's idea of only skeleton forces in the East. He established an Eighth Army which, with nine instead of three divisions, would hold East Prussia; although he recognized that superior Russian strength might require even this augmented force to withdraw behind the Vistula. The six additional divisions were all taken from the right-wing armies.

Moltke never took any serious action on Schlieffen's 1912 memorandum.

The result of Moltke's changes in the 1905 concept meant that when war came in 1914, the right wing began its great wheeling movement with only fifty-five divisions, instead of the seventy-one Schlieffen planned, and without the sixteen divisions of follow-up force. This meant that the right wing was only 65 percent of the western army strength. Instead of being between 74 and 90 percent of the entire mobilized strength of the German Army, as Schlieffen had recommended, it was only about 54 percent. Critics of Moltke, and blind admirers of Schlieffen, have asserted that by thus watering down the original Schlieffen Plan, Moltke had vitiated it, and assured its eventual failure. This is somewhat unfair to Moltke because the events of 1914 demonstrated that, if the Schlieffen Plan was in fact really viable, fifty-five divisions could have accomplished the job that Schlieffen had envisaged, and that Moltke had planned, for them. What the so-called watering-down indicated, however, was the inherently cautious nature of a general who, in Napoleon's words, "saw too much," and who therefore would not be able to carry through the concept with the single-minded vigor and boldness that were the essential ingredients of the Schlieffen Plan.

CRITICISMS OF THE SCHLIEFFEN PLAN / However, a number of modern historians, led by Gerhard Ritter and Sir Basil Liddell Hart,[3] see things quite differently. They criticize Moltke for not seeing—despite his change of the concept for the invasion of the Netherlands—that the plan was politically self-defeating, and militarily impossible to implement. Thus the principal criticism of these historians is directed against the formulator of the concept—Schlieffen himself—and only incidentally against his successor, Moltke, who after all became responsible in 1906.

The political criticisms can be summarized as follows: By the formulation of his plan, Schlieffen committed Germany to an unpardonable breach of the neutrality of Belgium and Luxembourg (and, as he planned, the Netherlands as well), despite Germany's solemn pledge in 1839—reaffirmed in 1870—to honor, and if necessary protect, the neutrality of those small states. According to these critics, he failed to recognize that the defeat of France (even in the doubtful event this could be accomplished with the speed and decisiveness Schlieffen envisaged), would not necessarily force Britain to make peace. On the contrary, the threat of German hegemony over Europe would probably induce in Britain a reaction comparable to that of the Napoleonic wars, in which the collaboration of British seapower and Russian manpower eventually overwhelmed Napoleon. Finally, Schlieffen is criticized for not having recognized that the diversion of German resources in manpower, money, and materials to the Navy meant that German ground-force strength would be seriously weakened. Therefore, we are told, Schlieffen should have found ways to keep William from making this dangerous diversion, and also from espousing expansionist policies that would inevitably lead to war.

In the light of the reputation which Schlieffen enjoyed in Germany and among military men around the world for so many years, the military criticisms are even more serious. Foremost among these are his recklessness in gambling the future of his nation upon a desperate strategy which demanded a quick victory over a competent, numerous, and exceedingly well-prepared enemy. Schlieffen had no assurance that this bold gamble would succeed; in fact, the critics say, his study of history should have suggested to him that it was less than likely to be successful. One important reason why it could not have been successful was the fact that the logistical requirements for support of the two right-flank armies—particularly the First—were beyond the technical capabilities of the German Army, or any army, in the early twentieth century. Finally—according to the critics—Schlieffen demonstrated a rigidity of mind and of strategic thinking that was unworthy of the German General Staff and of a successor of the great Moltke. Unlike the first Moltke, who (Schlieffen's critics assert with admiration) never planned a campaign beyond the opening engagement, and who recognized that war is not capable of being cast in rigid patterns, Schlieffen prepared a strategy which prescribed an inflexible course of action in a critical campaign, against a resourceful, resilient enemy, from the opening move to the final victory. Among other incidental criticisms of Schlieffen are his misreading of military history by falsely assuming that military success could be achieved only by flank movements or envelopments, and the fact that he was, as Ritter writes, "almost an octogenarian" when he was proposing the final modifications to his plan in 1912.

THE POLITICAL CRITICISM / Although the criticisms of Schlieffen's political insensitivity are to some degree justified, there are some arguments in his favor which should be examined. Schlieffen considered himself a servant of the state, whose duty was to guide the employment of its land armed forces in support of the interests and national policy of the state. It was his duty, in particular, to prepare realistically for the kind of war that Germany might get involved in, and do so in such a way that German interests and territorial integrity were best preserved. It was his opinion—shared with Bismarck and the elder Moltke—that a multifront war against more numerous opponents would gravely threaten the security, possibly even the existence, of the German state he knew.

As to the political, legal, and moral implications of the proposed invasion of Belgium and Holland, Schlieffen the scholar undoubtedly remembered Cicero's saying: *Silent enim leges inter arma* (In war the laws are silent).*

Schlieffen served a monarch who to him represented the state. Schlieffen was in no way responsible to the people, either directly or through their elected representatives. It is unfair to judge his formulation of strategy by the standards which a soldier of a democracy takes for granted. His proposed strategy, designed sincerely and patriotically to win a potentially dangerous and disastrous war as quickly as possible for Germany—with the least dislocation of its institutions, and its social and economic structure—was obviously satisfactory to the monarch, who approved the war plans. Perhaps Schlieffen should have sought to explore the political implications and to expose those to the Emperor. Perhaps he did; we don't know. On the other hand, Schlieffen had been brought up to believe, and the operation of the German monarchy was such as to support that belief, that all political implications were matters for the monarch, his Foreign Minister, and his Prime Minister to consider. If Schlieffen had raised such matters, it might have been considered an impertinence by William.

It has been noted that Schlieffen had seen what had happened to his predecessor when Waldersee tried to suggest to the monarch that a matter of strategic policy, outside the realm of ground-force strategy, was wrong. Schlieffen may or may not have had opinions about the dangers of German naval policy, or about the dangers of German foreign policy, or the possible political implications of military strategy. But if he did not mention these opinions, it was because he believed it inappropriate for him to do so.

Thus the justified criticisms of the political insensitivity of Schlieffen's strategy should not really be leveled at the man, but at the system, and at the flaw in that system resulting from the failure of Scharnhorst and his colleagues to achieve their objective of assuring that their new Army would be responsible to the people.**

Historical evidence is inconclusive as to the likely political results of a quick victory over France—if it was indeed attainable militarily. Would France of the

---

*Invoked for World War II by no less an authority than Winston Churchill to justify the joint British-Soviet occupation of Iran. See *The Grand Alliance,* Volume Three of *The Second World War,* p. 482.

**Obviously the specifics of a secret war plan would not have been published to obtain popular approval, or even approval of the duly elected representatives of the people. But in an Army subject to democratic controls, the plan would have been subject to review and approval by a responsible head of government; in Germany it was not.

early 1900s have reacted to catastrophic military defeat as France did in 1940, or would it have been like the France of 1793 and 1870? The tenacity of French resistance in the critical days of 1914 suggests that a people's war might have continued, as in 1870. Probably the French mutinies of 1917 and the incipient French collapse in June 1918 were the result of war weariness. But there was no war weariness in 1940. Furthermore, from Schlieffen's point of view, continued French resistance after the defeat of the French armies would not have interfered in the slightest with the continuation of the second phase of the plan, against Russia. A military victory once achieved, the ultimate outcome in France would have been as inevitable as it was in 1871.

As to Britain, a negotiated, face-saving peace between the kingdom of Edward VII (or George V) and the empire of William II could have been quite possible. Whatever one may think of William, he was not a Hitler, in either fact or image; a negotiated peace was probably more likely than unlikely, if the military events went the way Schlieffen wanted them to.

And so, granting that Schlieffen was not, did not aspire to be, and could not have been, a Napoleon politically, nonetheless he cannot justly be accused of political irresponsibility, either.

THE MILITARY CRITICISMS / What of the military criticisms? What, for instance, of the charge of taking unjustifiable risks in a desperate gamble with one throw of the dice?

What were the alternatives, other than recommending an Olmütz-type surrender without going to war? Really there was only one. That was to return to some form of the Moltke strategy of a two-front defensive-offensive, hoping that some unexpected eventuality would permit a favorable solution before the stalemate bankrupted the world (as Schlieffen was confident would be the case) economically and socially. In the 1870s and 1880s, when there was political maneuver room in Europe, this might have been a viable alternative. To Schlieffen it was completely unacceptable as long as it was avoidable. The effects of World War I, lasting as they did through World War II, were certainly not inconsistent with his fears of what the effects of a stalemate might be; his sophisticated prescience suggests, also, that he was not the shallow interpreter of history that some have suggested.

Looking at it the other way, what was the consequence if the one-shot gamble failed? We know the answer to that, from the record of World War I. It was the stalemate that might possibly have been avoided. But a stalemate under circumstances better for Germany (at least initially) than for her foes, and a stalemate from which a negotiated peace statisfactory to Germany was conceivable, even as late as 1917.

The charge of military recklessness simply will not stand up. It was, in fact, the kind of strategic gamble of which Napoleon was so fond, in which even the worst outcome was not likely to be disastrous, and in which the possibility of a good outcome was extremely attractive. In concept it was, in fact, truly

Napoleonic, comparing favorably in its brilliant, concentrated simplicity with the campaigns of 1800, 1805, and 1806.

The suggestion that Schlieffen misread the importance of flanking maneuvers in history is best refuted by reference to the remarks of one of his principal critics, Liddell Hart, who was fond of writing about "the strategy of the indirect approach." Historically both strategic and tactical maneuvers against flanks have almost invariably provided the key to significant victory. Schlieffen was neither distorting, concealing, nor exaggerating—nor was he deceiving himself or his General Staff—as he surveyed the examples of ancient and early modern history, and discovered, as had Napoleon, that operations against hostile flanks were the touchstone of victory. Furthermore, the lessons of the American Civil War, and the Franco-Prussian War, reaffirmed by the Russo-Japanese War, demonstrated that tactical success in modern war against modern firepower was possible only by operating against hostile flanks. Under some circumstances, as Schlieffen recognized, those flanks might have to be created by a breakthrough. But a frontal attack for any purpose other than creating a flank for maneuver was both suicide and murder.

Ritter's lack of objectivity in his criticisms of Schlieffen is revealed by his contemptuous dismissal of Schlieffen's 1912 plan as coming from a "nearly octogenarian author." Actually Schlieffen was seventy-two when he prepared *the* Schlieffen Plan, against which Ritter's criticisms are focused. Furthermore, his comment must be compared with Ritter's lavish approval of Moltke's plans from 1881 through 1887, for Moltke became an octogenarian in 1880.

In his critique of the Schlieffen Plan, Liddell Hart agrees that "it was a conception of Napoleonic boldness," but he adds:

> Schlieffen failed to take due account of a great difference between the conditions of Napoleonic times and his own—the advent of the railroad. . . . The great scythe-sweep which Schlieffen planned was a maneuver that had been possible in Napoleonic times. It would again become possible in the next generation—when airpower could paralyze the defending side's attempt to switch its forces, while the development of mechanized forces greatly accelerated the speed of encircling moves, and extended their range. But Schlieffen's plan had a very poor chance of decisive success at the time it was conceived. . . . The German advance dwindled in strength and lost cohesion as it pressed deeper into France. It suffered badly from shortage of supplies, caused by the French and Belgian demolition of the railways, and was on the verge of breakdown by the time the French launched a counter-stroke, starting from the Paris area—which sufficed to dislocate the German right wing and cause a general retreat.
>
> In the light of Schlieffen's papers, and of the lessons of World War I, it is hard to find reason for the way he has so long been regarded as a master mind, and one who would have been victorious if he had lived to conduct his own plan.[4]

This argument—like the more serious one of logistical infeasibility—is best answered by the historical record of 1914, which is there for all to see.

THE MARNE CAMPAIGN; MOLTKE'S SCHLIEFFEN PLAN IN ACTION / Moltke the younger had watered down Schlieffen's plan so that the right wing was only 53 percent of the Army, instead of 74-90 percent as Schlieffen had urged. Then he took away four divisions (two corps) to send on a useless trip to the East; these troops were in mid-Germany when the crucial battles of the Marne and Tannenberg were in process. Then he lost control of the operations of his two right-hand armies, and sent them confused and confusing instructions. And yet the right-wing army, after one of the fastest, most exhausting infantry marches in history—575 kilometers (360 miles) in twenty-five days, while fighting two battles and a number of skirmishes—was far from being on the verge of a breakdown.

As Maunoury's fresh French Sixth Army moved out from Paris, expecting to strike the exhausted, unsuspecting Germans on the flank, it found itself instead struck by a savage counterattack, with the initiative immediately seized by the Germans. Kluck was actually winning the Battle of the Ourcq from the more numerous, rested French troops when he was ordered to retreat to the Aisne River by Moltke's staff officer, Lieutenant Colonel Richard Hentsch. The record of the Battle of the Ourcq shows clearly that this army was not on the verge of a breakdown; it was not about to collapse because of lack of sufficient food and ammunition. It was a tired army, but not so tired that its toughness and effectiveness as one of the finest fighting armies in the history of warfare was not conclusively demonstrated.[5]

This is not to suggest that the Battle of the Marne was a German victory, misrepresented in history. Far from it. Despite Kluck's success on the Ourcq, overall the Marne was a clear-cut German defeat, brought about partly by the failure of the German commander (Moltke) to seize one of the greatest opportunities ever within the grasp of a military leader, and partly because he was outgeneraled by his indomitable French opponent, Joffre. But the performance of Kluck's army, before and during the Battle of the Ourcq, demonstrated beyond question that the Schlieffen Plan was viable, and that it was well within the performance capability of the German combat forces and logistical support services. And it demonstrated that Schlieffen's pride and confidence in the army he had improved and prepared for this tremendous task was in every way justified. It also answers conclusively the surprising assertion that "Schlieffen's Plan had a very poor chance of decisive success at the time it was conceived." The proof of the pudding is in the eating.

However, there is still one point in the Liddell Hart quotation which must be dealt with: his suggestion that Schlieffen was not abreast of modern technology, since he did not even understand the military capabilities and limitations of the railroad. In the light of what Schlieffen did to adapt the railroad to military use, even beyond the accomplishments of his great predecessor, this is a remarkable argument. Liddell Hart perhaps did not realize, either, that one element of the technological superiority of the Germans over the French and British in 1914 was in their more effective use of aerial reconnaissance. Schlieffen—again overruling more conservative contemporaries—had established the first regular military air arm in history.*

Finally, what about the rigidity of the Schlieffen Plan, and the argument that it was an unrealistic pattern for operations that could not possibly be planned in as much detail as was done by Schlieffen? The mere fact that the First Army performed well does not answer the criticism that, nonetheless, the operation did not go exactly as Schlieffen had planned it.

Schlieffen would no more have thought of planning the details of combat operations through a campaign than would the elder Moltke. As every competent planner must, he had a clear conception of how he hoped the operation would go—in general terms, not specifics. He had a timetable; he had arrows and phase-lines on maps. But his concept for the employment of more than a million men was simple, and presented in fewer than twenty typewritten pages. He was confident (and rightly as it turned out) that the combat superiority of the German troops would permit them to retain the initiative, and thus enable them to impose their general operational concept on the enemy—provided the Commander in Chief had will, determination, and skill to match those qualities in his troops. Schlieffen had given his successors, and the combat commanders, a concept, and with it a painstakingly prepared mobilization and preliminary movement plan. The only rigidity in his plan was in his insistence on adherence to fundamental principles of war: maintain the objective; apply mass in an enveloping maneuver designed to encircle the opposing army; use economy of forces to assist in achieving the mass necessary for the maneuver. This was no more rigid than Napoleon's strategic plans for the Ulm or Jena Campaigns, or Moltke's plans in 1866 and 1870.

Like the other criticisms of Schlieffen on military grounds, this one simply will not stand up. The objective military analyst can reach only the conclusions so ably presented in Herbert Rosinski's brilliant and completely favorable analysis of the plan and the planner.[6]

As with Scharnhorst, the harsh facts of history prevented Schlieffen from ever demonstrating whether or not he was truly a military genius in his own right. But, in any event, Schlieffen, his General Staff, and his Army, are clear demonstrations of the validity of Scharnhorst's initial concept of the institutionalization of military genius.

In passing, it is worth mentioning that the most surprising development of August 1914 to the French General Staff was the fact that German reserve corps were deployed in the initial campaigns beside the regular army corps—and performed with comparable effectiveness. This was a result of Schlieffen's untiring

---

*An argument can be made that this was an American innovation, with balloonists, in the Civil War. It is not a very good argument, however, since the Union corps of civilian balloonists disappeared from the Union Army and from history before the war was over.

efforts to improve German readiness and German mobilization, efforts effectively continued by Moltke. Such a development, so totally unexpected by the French, was merely one more example of the skill of the German General Staff.

NOTES TO CHAPTER TEN

[1] Count Alfred von Schlieffen, *Cannae,* authorized translation (Fort Leavenworth, Kan.: 1931), pp. vii-lx.

[2] As quoted in Ritter, *op. cit.,* p. 172. The emphasis is Schlieffen's.

[3] In particular, see Ritter, *op. cit.,* and Basil Liddell Hart's Foreword to that book.

[4] Liddell Hart, *op. cit.*

[5] See also Edmund L. Spears, *Liaison, 1914: A Narrative of the Great Retreat* (Garden City, N.Y., 1931), pp. 558-572, passim; and Hermann J. von Kuhl, *The Marne Campaign, 1914* (Fort Leavenworth, Kan.), p. 219.

Kuhl and Spears saw the battle from opposite sides of the line. Both reached the identical conclusion: General von Kluck's First Army was defeating General Maunoury's more numerous, less exhausted French Army when the First Army had to withdraw to avoid envelopment by the British Expeditionary Force. The discussion of this subject by Ritter and Liddell Hart in Ritter, *op. cit.,* and in Larry H. Addington, *The Blitzkrieg Era and the German General Staff* (New Brunswick, N.J., 1971), pp. 19-20, however, ignores fundamental points in sources to which they refer.

[6] Rosinski, *op. cit.,* pp. 134-139, 144-147.

Chapter Eleven

TRENCHES, BARBED WIRE & DEFEAT

THE YOUNGER MOLTKE AS CHIEF OF STAFF / The new Chief of the General Staff, General Helmuth Johann Ludwig von Moltke, inherited what may have been the finest military force ever created. History has been doubly unkind to Moltke. In the first place, he has inevitably been compared both with his illustrious uncle and with his equally illustrious prede-cessor, and not many soldiers in history could fare well in such comparisons. Secondly, because he was not up to the task of carrying out Schlieffen's strat-egy, he has been unfairly dismissed by most historians as an inept person who reached high rank only because of his name and family influence.

In fact, however, when World War I broke out the German General Staff and the German Army were still every bit as good as when Moltke had assumed responsibility, almost nine years earlier. He had done a good job as a peacetime Chief of Staff. Had Moltke gone into the war as one of the eight army com-manders, his reputation today might be much different.

The younger Helmuth von Moltke was born on May 25, 1848, at Gersdorff in Mecklenburg. He was named after his uncle, then Colonel H. K. B. von Moltke. When the Franco-Prussian War broke out young Helmuth was a lieu-tenant of grenadiers, and he served with distinction in several battles. After the war he attended the War Academy and qualified for General Staff duty. His first service on the General Staff was as aide-de-camp to his uncle. In the early 1890s he was a personal aide to young Emperor William II, with whom he established a close and cordial friendship. In fact, more of his early service was spent as an aide-de-camp than with troops. On March 25, 1899, he was promoted to Major General, and on January 27, 1902, he was advanced to Lieutenant General, while commanding a Prussian Guards division. In late 1903, William assigned him to the General Staff. At the Emperor's request Schlieffen somewhat reluctantly appointed Moltke First Quartermaster-General, and thus his deputy. Schlieffen's doubts were apparently not caused by any lack of confidence in Moltke's ability, but rather because he had had little practical experience in lower and inter-mediate Staff positions. Schlieffen still had some doubts two years later, at the time of his retirement, when Moltke was named to replace him as Chief of the

General Staff. On October 16 Moltke was promoted to General of Infantry.

William II, a vainglorious person, disliked his father, but idolized his grandfather, William I. Thus a major motive in his decision to appoint Moltke to replace Schlieffen may have been a conscious or unconscious desire to emulate his grandfather by having a Moltke as his Chief of Staff.

In the next nine years, the new Chief of Staff acquitted himself well. He earned the respect of his associates on the Staff as an intelligent, thoughtful, and competent soldier. He quickly recognized the potential of aircraft for reconnaissance and communication, and followed Schlieffen's initiative by encouraging the development of military aviation in the German Army. He gave comparable attention to improvement of weapons, particularly the new machine gun and heavy artillery. Staff procedures in the General Staff and training throughout the Army were also matters of great importance to him. On January 1, 1914, he was promoted to Colonel General.

In the field of strategic planning, on the other hand, Moltke showed little imagination. He adopted without question the strategic concept Schlieffen presented to him in February 1906. As we have seen, he did make changes in details, of a sort to demonstrate a lack of complete understanding of what Schlieffen was trying to accomplish. His cautious and unimaginative nature was more naturally attracted to measures which seemed to reduce or lessen the risks which Schlieffen had been perfectly willing to accept, than to seeking ways to enhance, or even to maintain, the power and momentum of Schlieffen's combination of manuever and mass.

COMPARISON WITH JOFFRE / An able administrator, a competent organizer and trainer, a good field soldier, Moltke lacked the spark of genius required for outstanding performance as a war commander in chief. But even in this respect the institutionalization of military genius might have saved him from catastrophe, and even brought him victory and fame, had history not dealt him a third unkind blow. It was his bad luck to be opposed by a man who did have that spark of high-level command genius: French General Joseph J. C. Joffre.

Joffre was served by a staff only slightly less competent than that of Moltke. He commanded an army that was not so good as that of Germany, but that was, nonetheless, very good indeed. He entered the war with a plan that was at best mediocre, but when that plan failed, Joffre immediately understood why it failed, and grasped the essence of the Schlieffen concept that was unfolding itself in a terrifying threat to northern France and the French armies.

Joffre did not panic, and adapted to his own hastily devised plan those same principles of mass and maneuver that were threatening to destroy France. With excellent staff work, making maximum use of French railroads, initiating several inspired changes in the echelon of command below him, he exploited to the utmost the resilience and élan of the French soldier. Above all, while the reins of control of the German armies were slipping from Moltke's hands, Joffre retained a complete and clear picture of the situation, as well as absolute control of all of

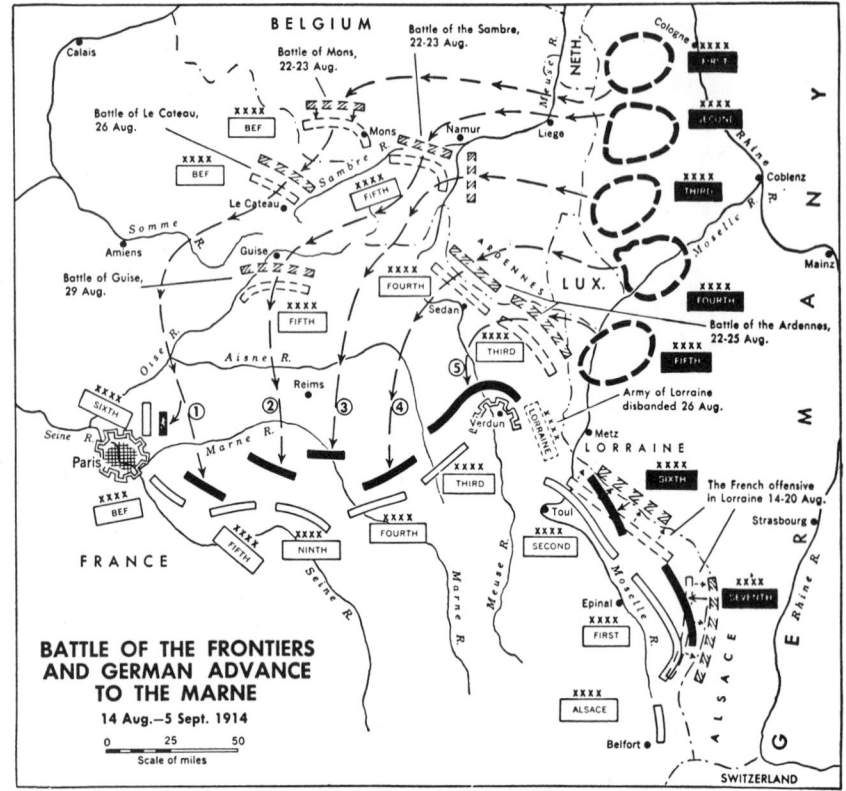

BATTLE OF THE FRONTIERS
AND GERMAN ADVANCE
TO THE MARNE
14 Aug.—5 Sept. 1914

his armies—save the British. By eloquent, emotional appeal to the British commander, however, he was able to assure full Allied coordination, then issued his orders for a counterstroke at exactly the right moment. As it was, it was a close thing, and had a Falkenhayn or Ludendorff been in Moltke's place, Schlieffen probably would have been vindicated, and Joffre gone down to gallant defeat.

As it was, even after losing the Battle of the Marne, the beaten German armies were occupying most of northern France, and were generally in a more favorable strategic position than the victorious Allies. This unique outcome to a battle considered generally one of the decisive encounters of history says much regarding both the institutionalization of military excellence, and the question of whether or not Schlieffen's plan was a reckless gamble.

The performance of the German Army and of German commanders in World War I was everything that Schlieffen had expected.

GRONAU AND THE BATTLE OF THE OURCQ / There was, for instance, Hans H. K. von Gronau, sixty-four years old in 1914, an artilleryman who had risen to the rank of General of Artillery in 1908, and who had been called out of semiretirement to command the IV Reserve Corps as part of General Alexander von Kluck's First Army. Gronau had graduated from cadet school just in time to see service as a lieutenant in an artillery battery in the Franco-Prussian War, in which he was decorated for gallantry. He graduated from the War Academy in 1878, and spent most of the rest of his career rotating between General Staff assignments and artillery commands. In 1903 he became a division commander, and from 1908 to 1911 was military Governor of Thorn. He then retired, until unexpectedly recalled to active field service on the outbreak of the war.

On September 5, 1914, the IV Reserve Corps was marching southward, about thirty-five kilometers east of Paris, and just north of Meaux, on the Marne River. Gronau was covering the right rear of the main body of Kluck's army, whose four other corps were already south of the Marne River. By midmorning, after about five hours of marching, the corps had reached its assigned objectives, and was preparing to go into bivouac. Gronau began to receive from his efficient cavalry patrols disturbing reports of much French activity to his west, in the general direction of Paris and St. Denis. Since German cavalry had swept through this same area during the two previous days, and had not noticed any such activity, Gronau was concerned about these reports. He sent out more cavalry patrols, but these were blocked by large numbers of French cavalry or halted by heavy volumes of long-range infantry fire. All of the Army's reconnaissance planes were busy south of the Marne. Shortly before noon Gronau turned to his chief of staff and said: "Colonel, there's no use delaying any further. We must attack."

Attack he did, sending both of his divisions westward toward Paris. German light-artillery fire, followed by determined German infantry, threw into confusion three divisions of the assembling French Sixth Army, moving toward their jump-off positions in anticipation of a surprise attack early the following

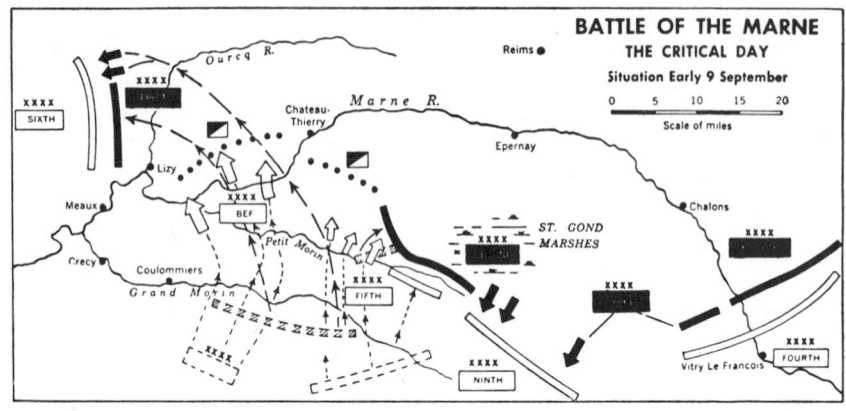

morning, September 6. This French attack, planned by Joffre against the right flank and rear of the German First Army, was to initiate the French counter-offensive, known to history as the Battle of the Marne. But, thanks to the sound, trained military instincts of Gronau, it was the surprisers who were surprised.

Although the French quickly recovered from their initial panic, the German momentum resulting from the surprise was not stopped. Against odds of nearly 3 to 1, Gronau's two divisions pushed slowly ahead, not halting till dark. Gronau, recognizing that he had stirred up a nest of hornets and suspecting the mission of the large forces he had uncovered, demonstrated how German doctrine tempered boldness with caution. Sending a brief radio message to his Army commander, reporting the engagement and requesting reinforcements, he pulled back during the night to defensive positions west of the Ourcq River to await an inevitable attack.

More than any single person in either the French or German armies, Gronau influenced the outcome of the Battle of the Marne. Had he not attacked when he did, the German First Army could have been badly defeated, perhaps destroyed, by the French counteroffensive. As it was, by a successful defensive-offensive battle on the Ourcq, the First Army saved itself, and was able to withdraw in good order when a British penetration threatened to cut it off from the beaten and withdrawing right wing of the Second Army.

HINDENBURG AND LUDENDORFF TO THE EASTERN FRONT / While nearly 3 million fighting and marching men were engaged in this tremendous drama in eastern France, between Paris and the Alps, about one sixth that number were participating in activities at least equally dramatic in East Prussia. At the urgent appeal of threatened France, Russia had hurried its mobilization and sent two hastily concentrated armies on converging paths into East Prussia: General Pavel K. von Rennenkampf's First Army crossed the Niemen River at the eastern extremity of that German province, while General Alexander Samsonov's Second Army drove north across the flat, southern, unfortified East Prussian frontier. Facing them, with less than half their combined strength, was the German Eighth Army of Colonel General Max von Prittwitz und Gaffron.

The Germans moved first to meet Rennenkampf's army, but because Prittwitz was also concerned about the approach of Samsonov, to the southwest, he was overcautious, and could do no better than a drawn battle with Rennenkampf at Gumbinnen on August 20. Fearful of encirclement, Prittwitz lost his nerve and decided upon a precipitate retreat to the Vistula River. He put in a long-distance telephone call to Moltke, at his headquarters in Koblenz, asking for reinforcements to hold the Vistula River line. Moltke, amazed at this turn of events, made two characteristic decisions, one good and one bad. The good decision was to order Prittwitz relieved of command, and to call another old General Staff alumnus out of retirement: Colonel General Paul von Hindenburg und von Beneckendorff. As Hindenburg's Chief of Staff, Moltke appointed Major General Erich Ludendorff, one of Germany's most respected General Staff officers. Ludendorff had recently been assigned to Second Army Headquarters, and was planning to capture Namur, having just helped capture Liege by personally leading a bold and daring assault on the citadel. Upon receipt of urgent orders, Ludendorff rushed back to Koblenz, was briefed on the situation in the East—as it was known at GHQ—then got on a special two-car train to pick up Hindenburg at Hanover. At 4:00 A.M. on August 23, Hindenburg got on the train, and met his new chief of staff.

Moltke's bad decision was to withdraw two corps from the Western Front (one each from the Second and Third armies), to send eastward to reinforce the Eighth Army. It should have been evident to Moltke that those two corps could not arrive before the Eighth Army was forced to deal with Samsonov's threat. Moltke should have recognized that he was seriously reducing the preponderance of right-wing strength to which Schlieffen had attached so much importance, and which he, Moltke, had already dangerously weakened. The four divisions of those two corps were still crossing central Germany by railroad while the great battles of Tannenberg and the Marne were being fought. As the ghost of Schlieffen could have told him, they were not really needed in the East. And had they been present in the West, the Second and Third Armies probably would have been victorious in their hard-fought battles on the Petit Morin and the St. Gond marshes; the Battle of the Marne would have been a German victory, and the name of the younger Moltke would have lived forever in German history as the second Moltke to conquer France. In fact, after his arrival in the East, General Ludendorff—understanding the Schlieffen Plan better than Moltke—

informed GHQ by telephone that these corps were not needed in the East, although they would of course be welcome.

HOFFMANN, LUDENDORFF, AND THE BATTLE OF TANNENBERG / Meanwhile, however, at the Eighth Army headquarters of Mühlhausen, East Prussia, late in the afternoon of the twentieth, the senior staff planner, forty-four-year-old Lieutenant Colonel Max Hoffmann, had persuaded General Prittwitz and his Chief of Staff, Major General Count Georg von Waldersee, that the proposed retreat to the Vistula would be a tragic mistake. Samsonov's army was closer to that river than were the Germans. The only result of such a move would be a desperate battle for the river crossings, under unfavorable circumstances, with the Eighth Army probably destroyed against the river by the combined forces of the Russian First and Second Armies.

Rather, Hoffmann proposed, there was still time to adapt Schlieffen's original Eastern Front plan to the changed situation. A small force of cavalry, and as much infantry as necessary, could delay the advance of Rennenkampf's army, while the rest of the Eighth Army was concentrated against Samsonov. Prittwitz immediately saw the logic of Hoffmann's argument, and directed him to issue the necessary orders. Unfortunately for Prittwitz and *his* place in history, he did not think to call back to Moltke to tell him of his new decision to fight east of the Vistula.

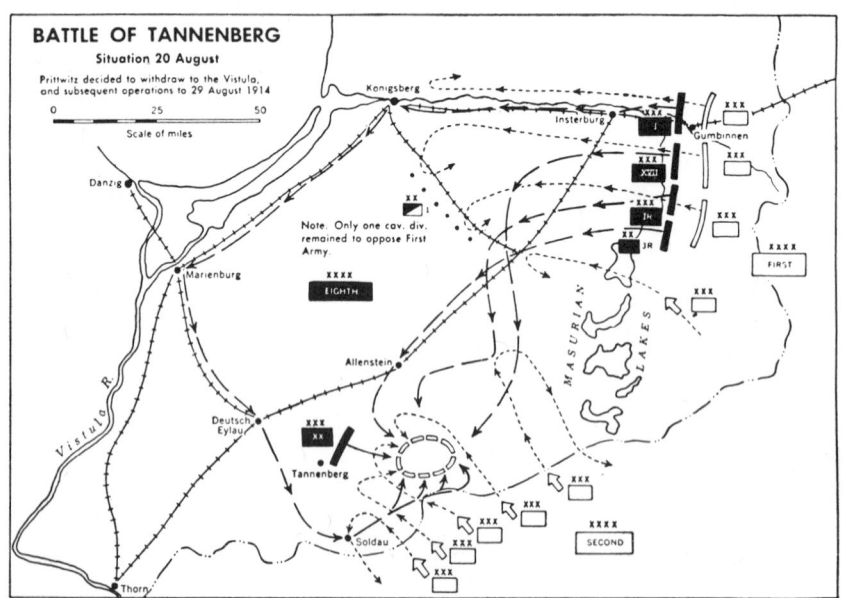

It was no coincidence that, on the special train that was carrying him and Hindenburg eastward to their appointment with destiny, Ludendorff had been studying a map similar to the one that Hoffmann had used in the conference at Mühlhausen. Before leaving Koblenz, on the twenty-second, Ludendorff had marked on his map the situation in East Prussia as it was then known to GHQ. He came to the conclusion that an aggressive delaying action by a part of the Eighth Army could hold back Rennenkampf, while the bulk of the army stopped, and possibly defeated, Samsonov. He discussed this with Hindenburg, who approved. At the next station Ludendorff sent off telegrams to Eighth Army headquarters and to the individual corps commanders, to make the necessary moves. He was unaware, of course, that more than a day earlier Hoffmann—with Prittwitz' approval—had issued almost identical orders. In fact, when Hindenburg and Ludendorff reached Marienburg the next day, where they had ordered the new Army headquarters to be established, they discovered that—since Rennenkampf had not moved—Hoffmann had actually ordered all of the Army except for one cavalry division to concentrate against Samsonov.

It is idle to speculate whether Hoffmann or Ludendorff was the more responsible for the resultant triumph at Tannenberg, in which Samsonov's army was encircled and destroyed in a modern version of Cannae. In fact, if one person has to receive credit, it should be Schlieffen, because he was the one who had trained all of his General Staff officers to seek and boldly exploit such opportunities. Most judiciously, however, the credit should go not to an individual, but to the German General Staff system, institutionalized excellence, which had caused two individuals with extremely different personalities— Ludendorff and Hoffmann—to analyze a military situation thoroughly and objectively, so that the same set of facts led both of them to identical solutions for making the most effective, aggressive employment of the forces available.

On other matters, however, although they had been old friends, Hoffmann and Ludendorff rarely saw eye to eye. As a result, while Hoffmann was probably one of the most gifted German officers in the war, he was not promoted to Major General until late 1917, after he had become Chief of Staff of the combined German armies on the Eastern Front, under the nominal command of Prince Leopold of Bavaria. He was never again promoted, although from that time until the end of the war he was virtually the Commander in Chief of that front, and more than any one man was responsible for the victories which finally caused the collapse of the Russian Empire. He disagreed particularly with Ludendorff about the annexation of Poland (of which more later) but carried out his orders in conducting negotiations with the new Communist government of Russia at Brest Litovsk. When Trotsky procrastinated, Hoffmann, by judiciously combining force and diplomacy, forced the Bolshevik leader to sign the Treaty of Brest Litovsk, which sealed the German victories in the East—until they became unsealed by the 1918 Armistice on the Western Front.

SCHEFFER-BOYADEL AND THE BATTLE OF LODZ / Another elderly alumnus of the General Staff who was brought back to active service to command a reserve corps was General of Infantry Baron Reinhard von Scheffer-Boyadel, who had retired in 1913 at the age of sixty-two. In the fall of 1914 he was placed in command of the newly organized XXV Reserve Corps, which was incorporated in the new German Ninth Army, under the command of General August von Mackensen.

In early November the Russians, now under the overall command of the Grand Duke Nicholas, finally completed their mobilization, and had at least partially recovered from the psychological effects of the Tannenberg disaster. The Grand Duke, with about a million men north of the Carpathians, concentrated overwhelmingly superior forces in western Poland for an invasion of German Silesia. Hindenburg and Ludendorff decided to disrupt the Russian's plan by sending the Ninth Army—about 260,000 men—on a limited counter-offensive toward Kutno and Lodz, to penetrate between the widely deployed Russian armies, and to destroy as many Russian units as possible between Lodz and the Vistula River. About 100,000 additional German troops were spread out to the north and south, in mobile defense.

On November 11, 1914, the Ninth Army began its advance from the German frontier south of Thorn. On the extreme left, marching at first along the left bank of the Vistula, was Scheffer-Boyadel's XXV Reserve Corps. Between November 12 and 16, the XXV Reserve Corps, in cooperation with two other Ninth Army corps, completely smashed the left wing of the Russian First Army south of the Vistula. At the same time, the corps marched seventy-five miles in five days, which would have been very good marching without any fighting. A clean breakthrough had been achieved. Meanwhile the rest of the Ninth Army continued its advance toward Lodz, where the Russian Second Army was hastily assembling and preparing for defense.

Scheffer-Boyadel pressed southeastward until, by November 21, his corps, reinforced by one division, was east of Lodz, completely behind the Russian Second Army. Advancing through Brzeziny, he turned west, and attacked the defenders of Lodz from the rear.

Russian reactions were much slower than those of the Germans, but the Russian commander—Grand Duke Nicholas—was a competent soldier. Elements of his Fifth Army from the South, his First Army from the North, and his reserves from Warsaw to the East, closed in on Scheffer's command, some 50,000 German troops, complete with divisional and corps artillery. At the same time, about half of the Russian Second Army, with the remainder securely entrenched in front of Lodz, turned to complete the encirclement of the German corps.

At first Scheffer continued his drive toward Lodz from the East, sending strong detachments to cover his flanks and rear. He soon found that the Russian forces in front of him were too strong, and he had no reserves to commit. Late on November 22, General Mackensen informed Scheffer by radio that the defenses of Lodz were too strong to crack from the front, and so Scheffer was to

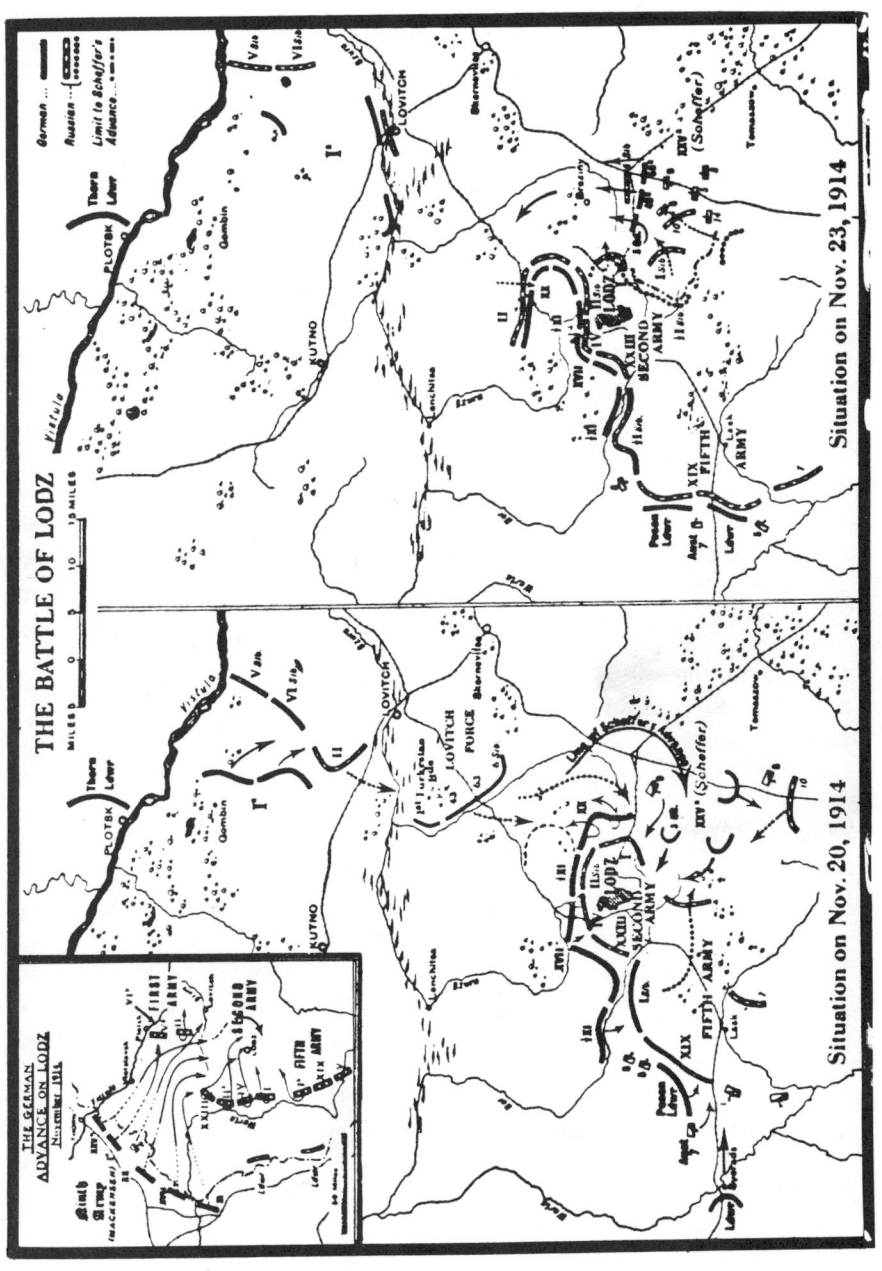

THE BATTLE OF LODZ

Situation on Nov. 23, 1914

Situation on Nov. 20, 1914

THE GERMAN ADVANCE ON LODZ
November 1914

extract his corps from its situation as best he might. Mackensen probably never expected to see Scheffer again. The Russians, who now had about 200,000 men encircling the German XXV Reserve Corps, ordered trains from Warsaw to carry away the expected prisoners.

After making a hasty estimate of the situation, Scheffer did the one thing the Russians expected least: He attacked eastward, toward Warsaw and Moscow. He broke through the ring of surprised Russians, then marched north, as the Russians hastily tried to reestablish the encirclement. But the German XXV Reserve Corps, now about fifteen miles behind the Russian front lines, marched north in a combat formation like Napoleon's "battalion square." After over-running and destroying a Russian division in its way, Scheffer's corps turned west, rejoined the Ninth Army, and on November 26 took its place in the German line north of Lodz.

In two weeks of almost continuous fighting and marching, Scheffer-Boyadel and his corps had suffered slightly more than 4,300 casualties, and had inflicted at least three times that many on the Russians. He not only brought out of encirclement most of his wounded, all of his heavy equipment, and all his artillery, he also escorted 16,000 Russian prisoners and sixty-four captured guns. It was an almost unbelievable feat, one of the greatest of the war, and of all military history.

FALKENHAYN AS CHIEF OF STAFF / Back in northern France, following the Battle of the Marne, each side tried to go around the other's northern, open flank. This resulted in the so-called "race to the sea," culminating in the bloody Battle of Ypres late in November.

On September 14 Moltke had been relieved of his position as Chief of the General Staff and virtual Commander in Chief of the armies in the West. (The Emperor, of course, was the nominal Commander in Chief.) Moltke's place was taken by General Erich von Falkenhayn, who had been Minister of War of Prussia since June 6, 1913, and thus for all practical purposes, Minister of War of Imperial Germany. To avoid public admission of the extent of the Marne defeat, no announcement of this change was made for several weeks. For more than four months, Falkenhayn was both Chief of Staff and War Minister (until January 21, 1915).

Faced now with the stalemate that Schlieffen had feared, it was Falken-hayn's thankless task to devise a new strategy. His first reaction was to try to seize as much of the English Channel coast as possible, to make it difficult for Britain to send reinforcements to France, and then to attempt to concentrate as much of the German Army as possible against the French. He hoped to defeat the French armies before Britain—which had only a small, volunteer army before the war—could build up a conscript Army large enough to exert a major in-fluence on the Continent. His first step then had been to rush several newly raised corps from Germany toward Dunkirk and Calais, together with divisions pulled out of the now-stabilized front along the Aisne Rive and farther south.

But Falkenhayn was forestalled by the withdrawal of the Belgian Army and some attached British units from Antwerp to establish a new anchor for the Allied line between Nieuport and Ypres, in western Belgium. These units were then reinforced by the arrival by train, from the south, of Sir John French's British Expeditionary Force, leading to the bloody struggle for Ypres in October and November.

Following the inconclusive battles of Ypres and Lodz, the stalemate became hardened, both in the East and the West. Falkenhayn, after studying the situation on both fronts, still believed that the best possibility of victory lay in the West. He believed that the size of Russia, combined with the numerical superiority of the Russians in manpower, would make it very difficult to achieve an early solution in the East. Yet at the same time it had been demonstrated that relatively small German forces could contain much larger Russian forces.

In the West, on the other hand, France was already scraping the bottom of its manpower barrel, whereas Germany had a much larger reserve of untrained but mobilizable manpower. Falkenhayn thought that the war could be ended only by the defeat of Britain. But if France were defeated first, British manpower could not be brought to bear on the Continent. France had suffered more than a million casualties in 1914. Although Germany had lost nearly 900,000, she could better afford such losses, staggering though they were. Finally, the British Expeditionary Force had been almost wiped out in the Battle of Ypres, and Britain would not be able to put significantly large new forces into battle until mid-1915. Falkenhayn began to build up reserves for a spring offensive in the West in 1915. He believed that Joffre was making his task easier by mounting an offensive in Champagne in December; the French were suffering enormous casualties. The Germans, taking advantage of better entrenchments, more machine guns, and much more heavy and medium artillery, were suffering relatively few losses.

Falkenhayn's strategic decision soon encountered formidable opposition. The Eastern Front commander and his chief of staff—Generals von Hindenburg and Ludendorff—believed that their successes against far more numerous Russian forces were clear evidence that ultimate victory in the East would be both quicker and less costly than in the West. They were strongly supported by the Austro-Hungarian Chief of Staff, General Franz Conrad von Hötzendorf.

On January 8, 1915, the Emperor made his decision—against the Chief of his General Staff and for the popular victors of Tannenberg. Falkenhayn reluctantly but obediently began to shift reserves to the East, and moved his own headquarters to Pless, in Poland, to supervise the plans and preparations. At the same time, however, he began to build up a new reserve, of divisions of freshly mobilized men, which he planned to use in the West as soon as the Eastern offensive either succeeded or failed. But the entry of Italy into the war on the side of the Allies in early 1915 ruined that plan, also. The new reserves had to be shifted east also, so that Austria-Hungary could rush troops to the new Italian Front.

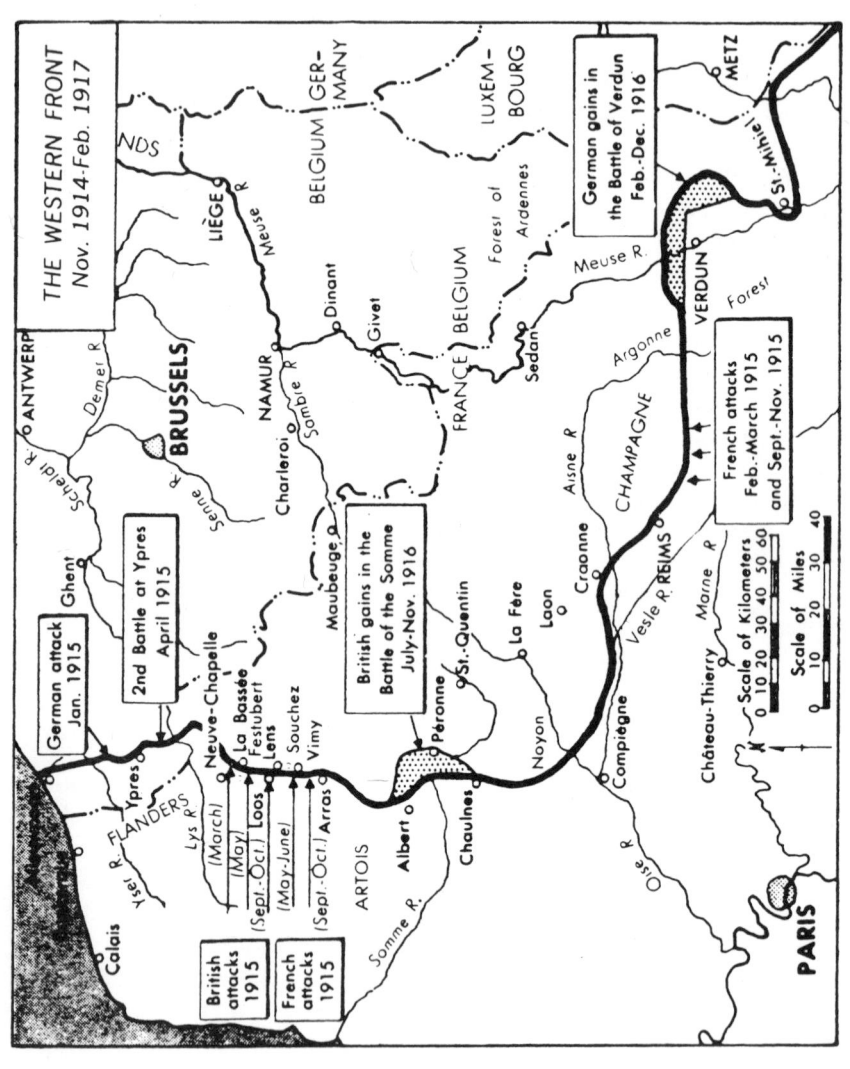

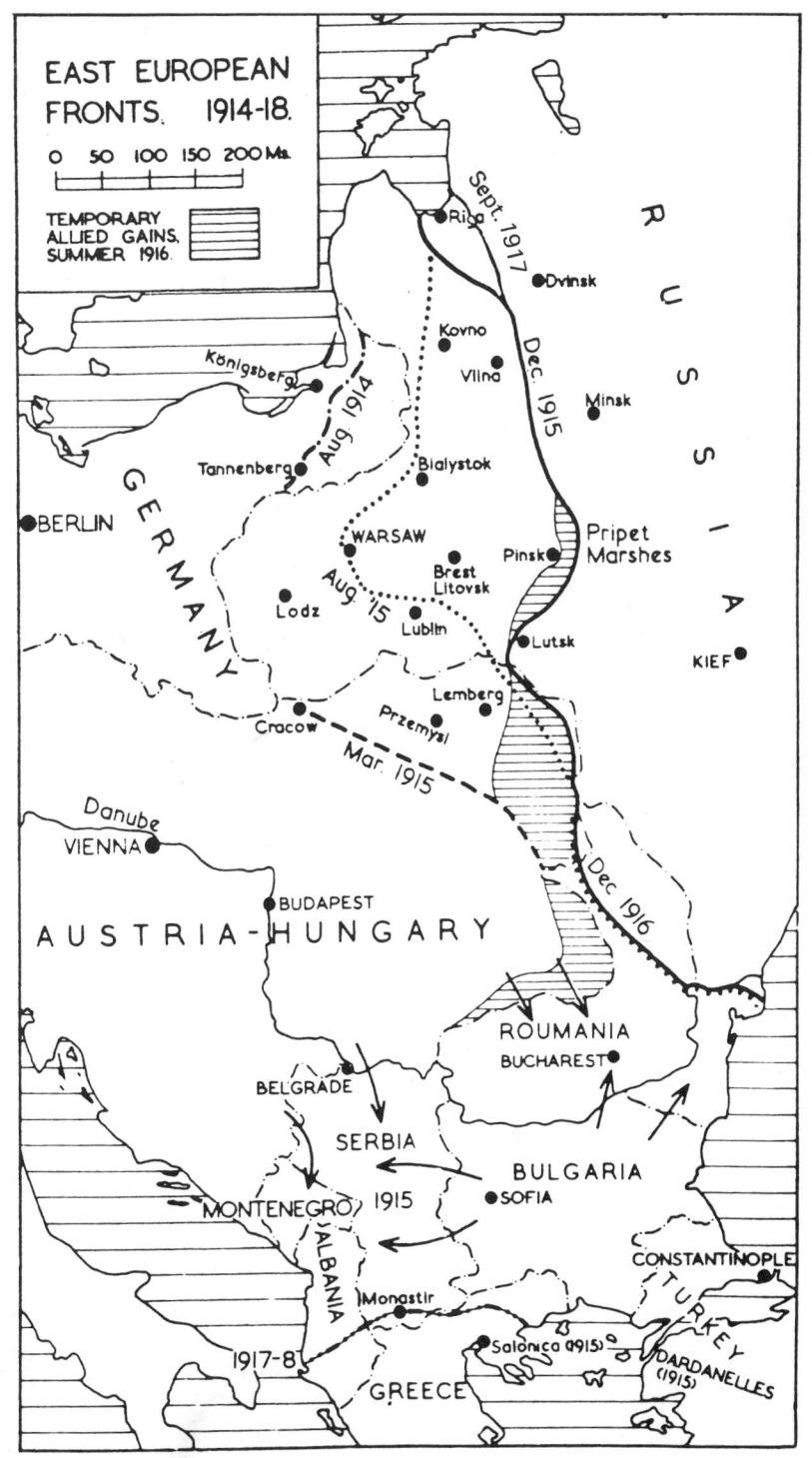

EAST EUROPEAN
FRONTS. 1914-18.

0   50 100 150 200 Ms.

TEMPORARY
ALLIED GAINS,
SUMMER 1916.

RUSSIA

Rīga

Dvinsk

Kovno

Vlina

Minsk

Königsberg

Tannenberg

Bialystok

BERLIN

GERMANY

WARSAW

Pripet
Marshes

Pinsk

Brest
Litovsk

Lodz

Aug 15

Lublin

Lutsk

KIEF

Lemberg

Cracow

Przemysl

Mar. 1915

Danube

VIENNA

Dec 1916

BUDAPEST

AUSTRIA-HUNGARY

ROUMANIA

BUCHAREST

BELGRADE

SERBIA

BULGARIA

MONTENEGRO

1915

SOFIA

CONSTANTINOPLE

ALBANIA

Monastir

TURKEY

1917-8

Salonica (1915)

DARDANELLES
(1915)

GREECE

Sept. 1917

Dec 1915

Aug 1914

THE GORLICE-TARNOW BREAKTHROUGH IN THE EAST / Aside from forcing Falkenhayn to shift the new reserves to the East, the Italian declaration had little effect upon the planned German offensive. This followed an overall plan developed by Falkenhayn, with details worked out by Lieutenant Colonel Hans von Seeckt, the forty-eight-year-old Chief of Staff of General von Mackensen's Eleventh Army. The Germans, with some Austrian support, assaulted the Russian Third Army on May 1, in a massive offensive through the Galician cities of Tarnow and Gorlice, and made a clean breakthrough by the fourth. Hindenburg and Ludendorff, to their annoyance, were allowed to make only a limited offensive from East Prussia, in coordination with the main Austro-German effort in southern Poland.

The Gorlice-Tarnow breakthrough initiated a steady German advance through Poland, which continued through June, July, and August. By that time, however, after the sacrifice of thousands of square miles, the Grand Duke Nicholas was able to establish a new line, running from the Gulf of Riga, west of the Dvina River, through Lake Narotch and the Pripet Marshes to the Carpathians in eastern Galicia. The Germans had conquered practically all of Poland and White Russia, but they had hardly made a dent in the Russian Empire, and the Russian armies, in barely diminished numbers, were beginning to receive newly manufactured ammunition for guns which had been almost useless during much of the summer.

Falkenhayn, who had never expected a decision in the East until France was defeated, was doubly satisfied with the results. Russia had been badly hurt, but, as he had predicted, not knocked out of the war. Furthermore, the Eastern Front had been stabilized; now he could concentrate most of the German Army in the West, if William approved. Hindenburg and Ludendorff, on the other hand, could claim that the results would have been decisive if they had been allowed to conduct the offensive in their own way. Again they pleaded for a free hand in the East.

VERDUN AND THE SOMME / This time, however, the Emperor approved Falkenhayn's concept. The Chief of the General Staff began to prepare for a massive breakthrough offensive in the West. He expected to destroy the French armies, and to force the British to withdraw back across the Channel. His plan was "to bleed France white" by an offensive that would threaten the historically symbolic fortress of Verdun, which had also been an anchor of the French defensive line since the Battle of the Marne.

In the great Battle of Verdun that began on February 21, 1916, and did not end until December 18, France was indeed almost "bled white," suffering more than half a million casualties. But Germany lost 434,000, and in return for this sacrifice had gained only a few square miles of raw, shell-torn land. France, though close to collapse, still held Verdun, and had won a moral victory.

In the middle of that great battle, the British—who now had nearly a million men in France—launched a major counteroffensive on the Somme River. On the first day the attacking British suffered 60,000 casualties, the greatest one-day loss in the history of the British Army. But the British persevered, and this bitterly contested struggle lasted until a mid-November blizzard finally brought the operations to a halt. The negligible British territorial gains on the Somme barely offset the French losses at Verdun; the greatest advance in those four and a half months of battle was eight miles. The human losses were even greater than at Verdun: 475,000 British, 195,000 French, and 500,000 Germans. Although German total casualties in the two great 1916 battles were substantially less than the combined Allied losses, nevertheless they were also substantially greater than those suffered either by the French or by the British. Falkenhayn's strategy had backfired; in 1916 Germany bled more than France. The result was William's decision to remove Falkenhayn as Chief of the General Staff; he was to be replaced by Hindenburg—who had been promoted to Field Marshal on November 27, 1914—with Ludendorff as the First Quartermaster General.

HINDENBURG AND LUDENDORFF TO COMMAND / By this time the war was completely stalemated. Hindenburg and Ludendorff—virtually supreme military commanders—planned no major efforts in the West for 1917, but were looking ahead to 1918. There were only two ways out of the impasse—a general negotiated peace in which neither side would be the victor, or a new ingredient in the war that would decisively shift the balance. The new German military leaders, with the support of the Emperor, completely rejected the first alternative. But to take the second course required either a new strategy, a new tactical system, a new weapon, a new ally, a defection from the Allies, or some combination of these.

A separate peace with Russia seemed possible in late 1916, and this would have allowed Germany to concentrate all her armies against the Western Allies, and force a victorious settlement. Here, however, in the complicated and unfamiliar world of politics and diplomacy, Hindenburg and Ludendorff stumbled badly.

HINDENBURG-LUDENDORFF AND GERMAN POLITICAL POLICY / The German Governor-General of Warsaw had proposed that a nominally independent Polish state be formed out of German-occupied Russian Poland, and that a Polish Army be raised to fight for the Germans. The Governor-General dangled before Hindenburg's eyes the prospect of five trained divisions by spring and a million men once conscription started.

The German Chancellor, Theobald von Bethmann-Hollweg, protested, since peace contacts had been made with Russian representatives in Sweden. He knew the Russians would never make peace unless their Polish territories were returned. Hindenburg also drew back, for a different reason. Old Prussian that he was, he feared the establishment of a Polish state that would undoubtedly want to repossess part of Prussian Poland. And knowing that most Poles hated Germany, he doubted that a Polish Army would rally to the German cause. Beyond these feelings, he had few opinions and less knowledge about the complex political factors involved and believed soldiers should not meddle with such matters.

However, Ludendorff persuaded Hindenburg to push for the establishment of the Polish state on purely military grounds. Bethmann reluctantly went along because of the influence Hindenburg and Ludendorff had with William. The Polish state was established, and the Russian peace feelers abruptly vanished. Not surprisingly, the military gains to Germany were nonexistent. Since Hindenburg and Ludendorff did not want a powerful Poland, no boundaries were set for the new state and no guarantees of its permanent existence were made. Rightly suspicious, the Poles were in no hurry to volunteer to fight Germany's battles.

American President Woodrow Wilson made an appeal to the warring nations on December 18, 1916, urging peace on terms of no annexations and the return of Alsace-Lorraine to France. Britain agreed to these terms, but also demanded payment of reparations. Germany would not think of paying reparations at that stage of the war, for this would have been an admission of war guilt. Nor was Germany—its armies deep in hostile territory—ready to accept either peace without annexations, or the cession of Alsace-Lorraine.

The war had been presented in the press to the German people as Russian aggression, with France and treacherous England joining in the attack. The invasion of Belgium was portrayed as a necessary defensive measure. The German press assured the people that Germany was winning the war. The casualty lists from the Somme and Verdun had shaken their confidence somewhat, but to make peace in 1917 without territorial gains to repay their sacrifices and protect the nation against future aggression was unthinkable. With Hindenburg and Ludendorff, the victors of the East, in overall control, most people felt the war would now go well.

Of the political parties in the *Reichstag,* only the Social Democrats were receptive to the idea of a negotiated peace in early 1917. The others were willing to back the military leadership in whatever it considered necessary to win the war.

Bethmann-Hollweg was exploring another peace possibility when Hindenburg and Ludendorff were appointed to the supreme command. He believed that the most effective offer Germany could make would be the return of Belgium to national independence. The violation of Belgium was the act that had brought England into the war and had done more than anything else to turn world opinion against Germany. The restoration of Belgium offered a real hope of peace.

Hindenburg and Ludendorff, however, protested to the Emperor about this proposal. Hindenburg felt Germany must occupy Belgium until that country could be relied upon to be a loyal political, military, and economic ally. He and Ludendorff were reinforced in their view by such groups as the supernationalistic Pan-German League and various associations of industrialists.

The annexationists, who wielded great political power, wanted permanent control of Belgium and also the annexation of northern French coastal districts down to the mouth of the Somme, of rich coal-mining areas of France, and several French fortresses, including Verdun. They also wanted annexation of Polish agricultural areas in the East to balance the industrial areas that would be seized in the West. Bethmann-Hollweg opposed annexation but lacked the political backing to do so openly and firmly. William agreed with the annexationists, both by personal inclination and because his weak and impulsive character made him susceptible to pressure from the military and industrialists. In accordance with German tradition, the Emperor was little influenced by parliamentary leaders, and certainly not by Socialists.

Hindenburg and Ludendorff were both proud of their educations, which had been strictly military, technical, and nationalistic. Ludendorff once said that he had never read a serious book that did not deal with military matters. (This, of course, suggests a weakness in the General Staff system.) Now the weakness of the German political system and German political leadership was forcing these gifted soldiers into policy-making decisions where their political ignorance led to tragic errors.

BLOCKADE AND THE SUBMARINE WARFARE ISSUE / Germany's greatest strategic problem was its isolation from sources of food and raw materials overseas. Britain's powerful Royal Navy had instituted a blockade of Germany at the outset of the war, and despite the German government's extraordinary and effective efforts to channel supplies efficiently and to develop and use substitute products, the blockade began to feel more and more like a noose.

Germany had a weapon against the blockade—its fleet of submarines, or U-boats. The rules of international law, however, made it hard to use the submarines effectively. Their chief advantage was surprise; if they gave warning before they struck, they were highly vulnerable, and their intended victim could take evasive action. Although they could strike enemy warships without warning, under international law merchant ships had to be notified before a naval attack could be made, and passengers and crews had to be given a chance to escape in lifeboats. But if such warning was given, most merchant ships could outrun the slower U-boats and escape. Furthermore, the British were arming their merchant vessels, thus making it impossible for the German submarines to carry out the stop-and-search procedures required by international law.

The Germans believed that armed merchant ships were just as legitimate war targets as warships. They believed they had as much right to cut off Britain's food and military supplies as the British did to blockade Germany. On May 7, 1915, the great British passenger liner *Lusitania* was just two hours from her destination of Liverpool on a transatlantic voyage from New York when she was struck by torpedoes (one of which may have ignited explosives stored in her hold). She sank in twenty minutes, before lifeboats could be lowered, taking with her 1,198 people, including 128 Americans. Germany justified the sinking on grounds that the *Lusitania* was also carrying 173 tons of rifle and artillery ammunition, but most people in the United States and other neutral countries were outraged by the Germans' flouting of international law, and ignored the British violation.

After an American protest following another sinking that took American lives, the German government announced, on August 30, 1915, that U-boats would no longer sink merchant ships without warning. Fear of United States' entry into the war had persuaded Bethmann-Hollweg and Emperor William that this step must be taken.

By the end of 1916, however, with the war stuck at a bloody stalemate, Hindenburg and Ludendorff were easily persuaded by the naval high command that unrestricted submarine warfare could win the war for Germany by starving Britain of weapons and food. Even if the United States should enter the war in response to such a policy, the naval leaders argued that America was militarily weak and could never make her potential strength felt in time to affect the outcome. Hindenburg and Ludendorff agreed, and began to persuade the Emperor. Bethmann-Hollweg held out to the last, stressing the solemn promise made to the United States in 1915, and his fear of the disastrous results that could come from United States entry. He stood alone.

Although the decision had the gravest political implications, it was really made by Hindenburg and Ludendorff. Their crowning and unanswerable response to Bethmann's arguments was that they "could not be responsible" for the military consequences if their advice were not followed. They said, on the other hand, that they would accept full responsibility for these consequences if the Emperor decided to order unrestricted submarine warfare. On January 31 the German government notified the United States that on the following day all shipping in waters around Britain and off the shores of the other Western Allies would be sunk without warning, regardless of nationality. The Germans were as good as their word, and in February, sinkings jumped dramatically.

THE UNITED STATES ENTERS THE WAR / After five sinkings that brought loss of American lives, and after a blundering German effort to gain Mexican support for a war against the United States, on April 2 President Wilson asked the United States Congress for a declaration of war. Four days later he got it by an overwhelming vote. The power of the United States was in the war and—despite the German Navy's promises to Hindenburg and Ludendorff, and their consequent promises to William—Britain was not knocked out of the war by the submarines. For a while the British feared they might be starved into surrender, but by summer a newly devised convoy system was working effectively, with large groups of merchant vessels being escorted across the Atlantic by warships.

Millions of young Americans were meanwhile in training for battle. Hindenburg and Ludendorff had made another tragic blunder, by forcing the German government to make political decisions entirely on the basis of military considerations.

THE "DICTATORSHIP" OF HINDENBURG-LUDENDORFF / The two German military leaders had meanwhile been responsible for a number of other political decisions, all of them justified by "military necessity." In November 1916 Hindenburg forced the resignation of the Foreign Minister, Gottlieb von Jagow, on the grounds that he was not strong enough—an "intelligent man, but not one who can bang his fist on the table."

Soon, however, the Chief of the General Staff came to believe, as Ludendorff repeatedly told him, that Bethmann-Hollweg was the cause of all Germany's internal troubles. After various maneuvers to undercut the Chancellor, Hindenburg and Ludendorff finally used their ultimate weapon; they both threatened to resign unless Bethmann-Hollweg left office. The reluctant Emperor asked for the Chancellor's resignation on July 13, 1917.

One of Hindenburg's and Ludendorff's major criticisms of Bethmann-Hollweg had been his failure to keep the *Reichstag* from debating a peace resolution. One was passed on July 19, shortly after Bethmann-Hollweg resigned. It called for a "peace of understanding and the permanent reconciliation of all peoples," and rejected annexations as a war aim. The resolution was strongly resented by the General Staff leaders.

Bethmann-Hollweg's successor, approved in advance by the General Staff command team, was Georg Michaelis, who had performed well as Food Minister. He had been recommended by General Hans Georg Hermann von Plessen, commandant of the Military Headquarters, but neither Hindenburg nor Ludendorff had met him. Nevertheless, they recommended him to William, who also had never met him. This was the sad state of political leadership in Germany in 1917. Not surprisingly, Michaelis turned out to be a weak and ineffective Chancellor. By this time the real leaders of Germany, with power unchallenged, were Hindenburg and Ludendorff. The Field Marshal and the General had not seized power; Germany's political leaders, pale imitations of Bismarck, had abdicated power to them.

The idea of seizing power as military dictator almost certainly never occurred to Hindenburg. Ludendorff, also, consistently refused to consider the possibility that he or Hindenburg should become a dictator in name, or to take formal responsibility for political control of the country. He kept searching and hoping for a "strong man" who could provide the forceful civilian leadership he felt Germany needed. Much of his and Hindenburg's political meddling was devoted to this end. However, Ludendorff could not restrain himself from making political and economic decisions, always in the name of "military necessity." In effect, he did become a dictator, without real responsibility and with no training or experience that would qualify him to make national political policy.

Hindenburg recognized his own inadequacies. "It would be perfectly accurate to say that mine is a nonpolitical temperament," he wrote after the war. "It was against my inclination to take any interest in current politics." Yet he also admitted, "I grant that I have covered many expressions of opinion on political questions with my name and responsibility even when they were only loosely connected with our military situation at the time." What this often meant was that Ludendorff ruled the country in Hindenburg's name while the Emperor, Chancellor, Cabinet, and *Reichstag* stood by ineffectually.

LUDENDORFF'S MILITARY BRILLIANCE / Even while Ludendorff blundered and stumbled in matters of high government policy, he was showing his brilliance as a military thinker and leader. Wisely ordering no German offensives on the Western Front in 1917, and voluntarily yielding most of the Noyon salient, his defense-in-depth doctrine ensured the collapse in April of a massive French effort under General Robert Nivelle. All Allied offensive efforts in the West had come to nothing.

In the East, toward the end of 1916, Romania had entered the war on the Allied side and had almost immediately been soundly defeated and overrun by German and Bulgarian forces under Generals von Falkenhayn and Mackensen. Then in mid-1917 came the Russian collapse. Later in the year Italy was dealt a decisive defeat at the Battle of Caporetto. Submarine warfare had brought dramatic successes at first, but by the summer of 1917 it was clear the Allied countermeasures would make it increasingly ineffective.

Ludendorff realized that, despite temporary advantages, in the long run Germany could not hope to win a war of attrition. The total manpower and material resources of Germany and its allies were far less than those of the

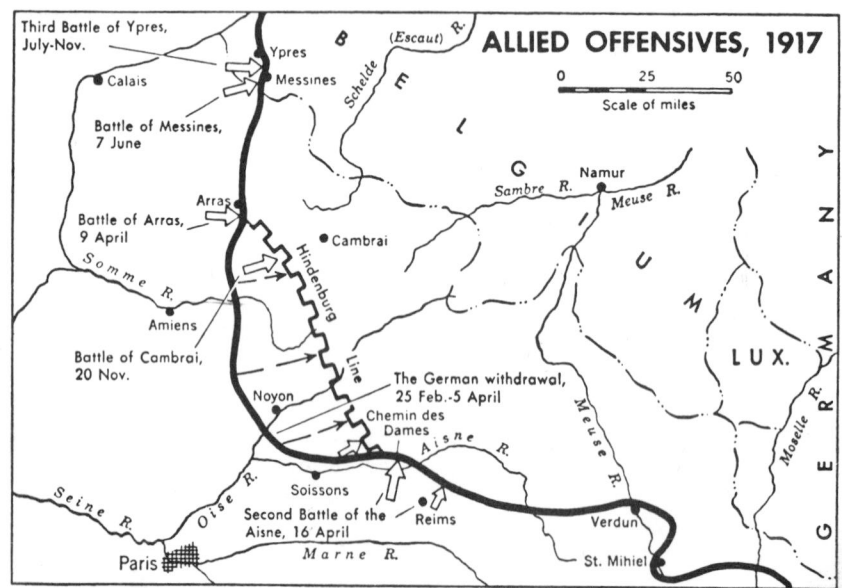

Entente, since the United States' entry in the war offset the exit of Russia. A decision had to be reached early in 1918, Ludendorff knew, before United States strength could be brought to bear. Taking advantage of manpower made available by victory in the East, a decisive success must be won in the West. Since there were no flanks to turn on the Western Front, it must be a penetration of the Allies' lines, a penetration at a decisive spot so deep, and so quickly and fully exploited, that the enemy would decide that the war was lost and make peace.

Deep and massive penetrations had been tried before, over and over again, on the Western Front, most recently and disastrously by Nivelle. The pattern was always the same. First there was a devastating preparatory artillery bombardment, sometimes lasting a week. Then the infantry would go "over the top," leaving their trenches and rushing across "no-man's-land" to the enemy trenches. The artillery preparation would have killed and dazed the occupants of the first line of enemy trenches, and good progress was usually made during the first few hours of these infantry attacks.

But the long artillery preparation had also given the enemy ample warning of the impending attack, and plenty of time to rush reserves to the threatened sector. As the attackers encountered the reinforced secondary lines of defense, their artillery support and supplies were lagging behind; it was hard to bring up heavy guns and equipment over the shell-cratered terrain. There were also always strongpoints of resistance that the preliminary bombardment had missed, and these could hold up the advance for hours. Yet the commanders kept pushing forward, hopeful that one more try would achieve the longed-for breakthrough. Then the cavalry, always held in readiness, could rush through to exploit the success. The result was a very few miles gained, and thousands of lives lost. The cavalry never had its opportunity for glory.

The two opposing sides chose different ways to try to solve this "riddle of the trenches." The Allies, under British leadership, inspired particularly by Winston Churchill, the First Lord of the Admiralty, sought a mechanical solution. They developed the tank, whose caterpillar tracks enabled it to cross trenches, crush barbed wire, and negotiate shell-pocked terrain, and whose armored sides protected its crew and firepower from all ordinary infantry weapons.

The German General Staff, first under Falkenhayn, and then under Hindenburg and Ludendorff, sought a tactical rather than a technical answer. First the Germans changed their divisional organization from a "square" division of four regiments in two brigades to a more maneuverable and flexible "triangular" organization of three infantry regiments. Then, within the division a new battle drill was developed, built around the flexible maneuver of smaller subordinate echelons, down to basic battle groups within each company.

Ludendorff's elastic defense-in-depth tactics had already proved themselves in stopping the Allied 1917 offensives with relatively light German casualties. At the same time he had directed the General Staff to carry out studies of offensive tactics. The war had already given them a number of hints on the solution of the riddle.

In the initial German assault on Verdun, surprise had been achieved by an intensive preliminary bombardment which lasted only a few hours, rather than days. Small groups of infantrymen had gone forward as infiltration teams, probing for weak spots, instead of hundreds of thousands moving toward the enemy in long, unbroken lines. These tactical innovations had been effective, but at Verdun they were used only on a very narrow front, with no attempt at large-scale exploitation.

On the terrible first day of the Battle of the Somme, only the British XIII Corps had achieved any real success. General Walter Congreve, the corps commander, apparently owed this success to his use of a creeping, or rolling, barrage in which the preliminary artillery bombardment continued after the infantry went over the top, gradually moving forward just ahead of the foot soldiers. The Germans thus had had no opportunity to recover from the preparation fires before the attacking infantry arrived.

THE NEW GERMAN TACTICS / The German General Staff had been continuously studying these limited successes by both sides, and devising a tactical system that would apply to the conditions of contemporary warfare such basic principles of war as surprise, mass, economy of forces, maneuver, and security. The critical feature of modern warfare was the deadliness of high-speed automatic weapons, the high-explosive shells of quick-firing cannon, and the tremendous advantage these weapons—combined with trenches and barbed wire—gave to the defenders. New offensive tactics had to overcome this defensive advantage.

Surprise was the key to the new German tactics. Surprise was to be achieved by making the preliminary bombardment fierce but short—a few hours at most. Great care would also be devoted to keeping troop concentrations secret; they would be moved up only at night and as shortly before the time of assault as possible. Special attention would be given to deceiving the enemy with convincing feints and deceptions. New techniques for accurate, surprise placement of artillery fire were developed.

The tactical unit was to be a squad of fourteen to eighteen men. Each squad would have its own base of fire—a light machine gun or automatic rifle and a light mortar. Specially trained assault infantry, called storm troops, were to advance on a broad front, behind a rolling barrage, probing for weak spots. All strong centers of resistance were to be bypassed. The guiding principle was to maintain the momentum of the offensive, to keep pushing forward.

As the assault units pushed the penetration at full speed, reserves would be committed where the progress was greatest, to strengthen the breakthrough. "Soft spot" exploitation, this was called. Other reserves would mop up the bypassed pockets of resistance. Larger units, of regimental and division size, would enlarge the penetration by attacking into and behind the newly created

HUTIER OFFENSIVE TACTICS

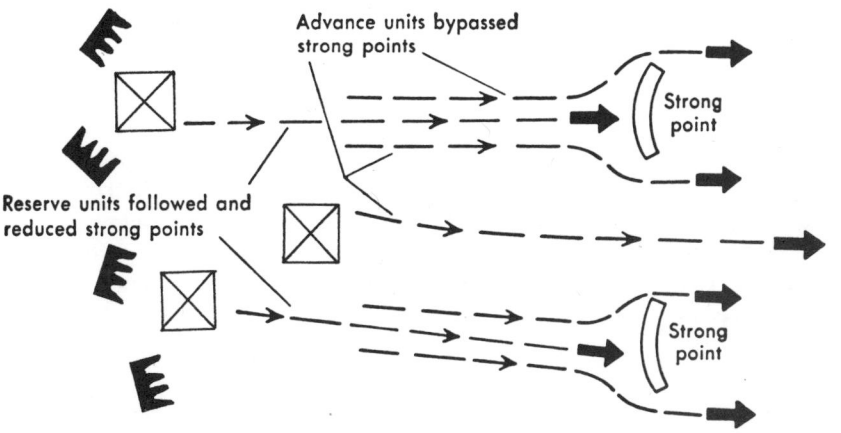

enemy flanks, on either side of the breakthrough. Artillery was to be emplaced at irregular distances from the front lines, and to move forward in bounds behind the infantry, maintaining a constant rolling barrage. Aircraft, now becoming a significant influence on war, were to provide constant close support, strafing and bombing enemy pockets of resistance and enemy reserves moving up.

There was no dramatic innovation in the new tactics. All the commanders since 1914 had been trying to apply the principles of war under modern conditions to achieve surprise, to make a breakthrough, and then to exploit it. What the Germans did was to devise systematic and practical ways in which these things could be done under the new circumstances of combat, and to provide detailed procedures for training and supporting the men who were to do the job.

HUTIER, RIGA AND CAPORETTO / After the failure of the last Russian offensive in July 1917, the whole Russian southwest front had collapsed, but still the new Russian government did not ask for an armistice. The Germans decided, therefore, to capture the important port of Riga, far to the north. Riga was a fortified outpost of the capital city, Petrograd, three hundred miles to the northeast. The current commander of the German Eighth Army, General Oskar von Hutier, was directed by the high command to apply the new General Staff tactics to attack Riga, which had held out against the Germans for two years.

Hutier kept his assault troops back from the front until the last possible moment. He used a short, intense preparation bombardment, carefully planned by his artillery officer, Colonel Georg Bruchmüller. Both the bombardment and the infantry attack were launched on September 1. The infantry went forward in small infiltration units, each well supported by its own base of fire. On September 3, Riga fell. From that day "Hutier Tactics" was the name given this German answer to the riddle of the trenches.[1]

Far to the south, in the Italian Alps, Hutier Tactics were used again in October by General Otto von Below, who had been a corps commander at Tannenberg. Attacking an ill-prepared Italian Army, Below won an overwhelming victory at Caporetto, crippling Italian military morale. All that saved Italy from complete collapse was the movement of large British and French reinforcements across the Alps to bolster the threatened Italian Front.

These victories gave Ludendorff and the General Staff confidence that they could now succeed on the Western Front, where all efforts at breakthrough had failed since 1914. They were convinced that they now knew how to break through the trenches to decisive victory.

THE GERMAN 1918 OFFENSIVES / Having devised successful new tactics, the General Staff now had to prepare a strategic plan to put them to the best use. At a major staff conference in November 1917, at German GHQ at Spa, Belgium, Ludendorff presented the problem to the principal division chiefs. Hindenburg was not present at this conference, and played little part in the strategic decision that emerged from it.

After long hours of discussion of many possible plans, Ludendorff decided that the attack should be made against the British. He now believed, as Falkenhayn had, that Britain was the crucial enemy. Britain, he felt, could go on fighting without France, but France would be helpless without Britain. He expected that victory would be won before the United States could play any significant role.

The General Staff drew up at least six different detailed plans for operations in various parts of Flanders and the Somme area, and a number of others for such possible alternatives as the French-held front at Verdun. The plan finally selected, code-named "Michael," was for a hammer blow against the right wing of the British armies in an area that stretched between the town of St. Quentin on the River Somme, to Arras, forty-seven miles to the north. The sector was lightly held by the British Fifth Army. Once the breakthrough was accomplished, the remaining British forces would be destroyed on the shores of the English Channel.

The German blow was struck on March 21. Specially selected and trained German storm troops were as successful with their new tactics as Ludendorff had expected. Following artillery barrages that were brief, but more intensive and destructive than anything previously seen on the battlefield, small German battle groups infiltrated the British positions. They smashed their way through weak resistance, while bypassing and isolating strongpoints of defense, which

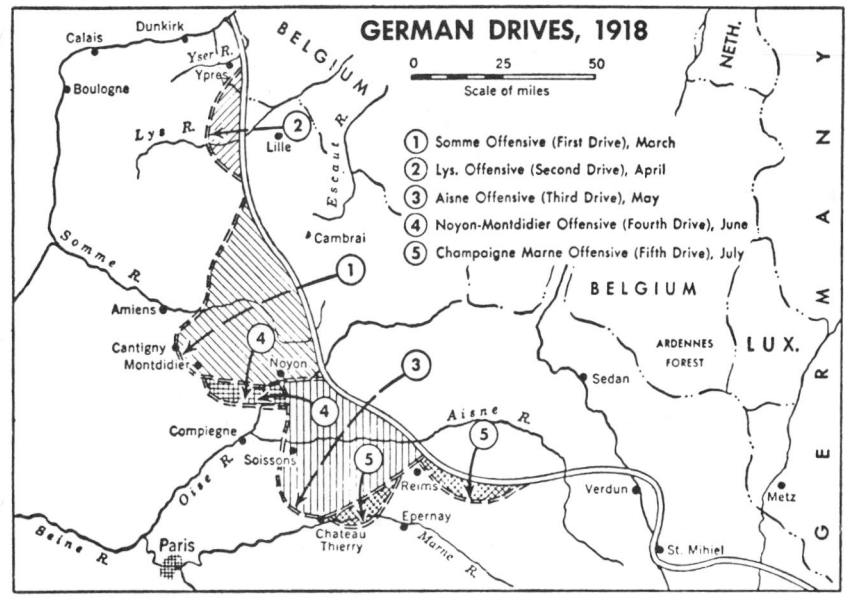

were then mopped up by following waves of storm troopers. The front of the British Fifth Army was ripped apart, and the German tide poured through in a spectacular success. Field Marshal Sir Douglas Haig appealed to General Philippe Pétain for help, but the French Commander in Chief was rushing reserves to block the Germans from advancing against Paris. He said he had no more troops to send to Haig's assistance. This was what Ludendorff had expected.

Despite severe losses, Haig and his generals conducted a skillful retreat. The frontline German troops were tiring, and they had pushed ahead so fast that their artillery, reinforcements, and supplies could not keep up with them, due to the difficulties of moving trucks and wagons across the shell-torn countryside. Because of this, the German momentum began to slow down, and the tenacious British soldiers, with good support from the Royal Air Force, started to form an effective defensive line again.

Meanwhile, at Haig's urgent request, the Supreme Allied War Council had met. It followed his recommendation that brilliant, energetic General Ferdinand Foch, Chief of Staff of the French Army, be appointed as the overall Allied Commander in Chief of the Western Front. Foch now began to provide French reinforcements to help the British. By April 4 the great German drive was brought to a halt. Although the British had suffered terrible losses, their armies were still intact.

Ludendorff believed, however, that one more severe hammer blow would destroy Haig's forces. On April 9, the Germans struck again, this time against the northern portion of the British line in Flanders. The Germans once more came very close to breaking through. But again they were foiled by the tenacity of the British soldier, by the leadership of Haig, and, above all, by their own inability to keep supporting artillery, supplies, or reinforcements close behind the front-line storm troops.

At the height of the crisis, American General John J. Pershing told Foch that he could have American troops, recently arrived in France, to use as reserves or replacements at any point along the front. In response to Foch's request, units of the American 1st Division were rushed to the front near Amiens.

Ludendorff still believed that one more great blow could destroy the British armies, but first he wanted to force the Allies to shift away the reserves which Foch had now gathered behind the British Front. To do this, he decided to attack across the Aisne River, in the center of the French lines, and to advance directly toward Paris. Then, as soon as the Allied reserves were shifted to protect the French capital, Ludendorff planned to strike the final decisive blow against the British in Flanders.

The German attack across the Aisne River on May 27 was even more successful than Ludendorff had expected. The French armies were so badly hurt, and his storm troopers were advancing so rapidly, that he decided to let them keep going toward the Marne River, then on to Paris. But at the Marne the German advance was brought to a halt by a combination of American and French units rushed to the front by Foch.

Once again the Germans had achieved spectacular tactical successes, but had failed to gain their strategic objective. The most serious development, from their point of view, was the fighting ability shown by the Americans.

In an effort to connect the new salients he had created in the Somme and Aisne-Marne sectors, Ludendorff launched another offensive against the French in the Noyon-Montdidier area in early June. But this time there was no break-through; the German advance was stopped after making only small gains.

A month later, Ludendorff tried again, after having made the most careful preparations. This time the Germans broke across the Marne River, and on July 15 and 16 it seemed, for a few hours, that they would win this Second Battle of the Marne and that they would go on to take Paris. But the next day French and American troops halted the drive.

Ludendorff realized that time was now running out for the Germans. The Americans were beginning to make their presence felt. Although the five German offensives had inflicted terrible losses on the British and French, the Germans had suffered just as badly; indeed, they had lost most of their specially selected and trained storm troopers. But Ludendorff believed that he had both time and strength enough to make one more massive effort against the British in Flanders. And since his last three offensives had been made far to the south, he believed that his new Operation "Hagen" would catch the British by surprise, and win the victory he had been seeking. He ordered limited attacks to continue against Rheims, while he personally rushed to the Flanders front to supervise the final preparations for Operation Hagen.

LUDENDORFF AND THE FAILURE OF THE 1918 OFFENSIVES / It was a blow that would never be struck. Ludendorff's offensives had indeed made possible a decision in 1918. But it was not to be a German decision. On July 18 Foch launched French and American troops in an offensive toward Soissons. The Allies had seized the initiative, and the Germans never again regained it.

This does not mean that Ludendorff's strategy had been hopeless from the outset. The Germans had come very close to decisive victories in their first three offensives in March, April and May. These successes could well have been so crippling to the British and French armies that a compromise peace might have been secured on terms that would have left Germany the leading European power. Who can say what the reaction of the British, French, and Italian governments—or of their discouraged, war-weary peoples—would have been if Paris had fallen, if the British had been driven across the Channel, and if Italy had been threatened with the full might of the victorious German armies? What would or could the American government and people have been able to do?

But the first two offensives, for all their startling tactical gains, had failed completely in their strategic objectives, for reasons we have seen. By the end of Ludendorff's third offensive—even though it made comparable tactical gains—he had lost all chance to win the war in 1918, or even to get a compromise peace in 1918 or 1919. All that he was accomplishing by that offensive, and by the two that followed it, was to deplete the German Army of its best troops, while lowering the morale of the survivors, thus making it progressively easier for the Allies to win. Ludendorff should have recognized this, but the strain of decision making was taking its toll; he had lost his formerly brilliant analytical objectivity.

THE ALLIED COUNTEROFFENSIVE / The situation, however, was understood clearly by General Foch, who was already in the process of seizing the golden opportunity which he saw emerging. The very fact that Foch was in a position to do something about this situation was directly attributable to Ludendorff's offensives. By bringing the Allies to the verge of catastrophe, he had made them take the final step toward unity of effort and purpose which—for selfish national reasons—they had been so long reluctant to take. More than any single factor, the Allied opportunity to achieve a victory in 1918 or 1919 was due to the fact that Ludendorff's offensives had made them resort to a unified command and appoint a Commander in Chief who proved to be strong, brilliant, and effective.

The next Allied blow came on August 8, when Field Marshal Haig launched British and American troops toward Amiens. By the end of the day, the Allies had penetrated seven miles into the German defenses along a fifteen-mile front. Six German divisions had collapsed; many prisoners had been taken, and German morale had sunk to an all-time low. Reinforcements marching to the front were greeted with curses by retreating troops, who cried: "You're prolonging the war."

Ludendorff recorded afterward that August 8 was "the Black Day of the

German Army. . . . It put the decline of the fighting power beyond all doubt. The Army had ceased to be a perfect fighting instrument. . . . The war must be ended." August 8 smashed all of his dreams for the offensive in Flanders, or elsewhere. He informed the Emperor that peace negotiations must be opened before the situation became worse, as it surely would.

However, the tough resilience of most of the German troops, and the defensive skill of their commanders, postponed the inevitable end for three months. Ludendorff in fact regained some of his old confidence, but not his objectivity. He began to plan the establishment of a new defensive line along the German frontier. Here, he thought, his armies could hold indefinitely and thus persuade the war-weary Allies to negotiate a peace favorable to Germany.

COLLAPSE–EXIT LUDENDORFF, ENTER GROENER / Other events, however, had already made this impossible. While Ludendorff's armies were desperately striving to stem the Allied advance during September and October, their comrades on other fronts were being crushed in defeat. On September 30, the Bulgarians signed an armistice which was a virtual surrender. Turkey capitulated on October 30. That same day Austria-Hungary requested an armistice, which was signed on November 3.

And in Germany itself the civilian population was close to collapse. The German failure to provide for a prolonged war, combined with the terrible stranglehold of the blockade, had caused unbelievable hardships; people were actually starving. The nation was no longer willing to support continuation of the war and to suffer another winter of famine.

On October 3, Emperor William II called on liberal Prince Max of Baden to become Chancellor and to negotiate peace terms. Two days later Prince Max received Hindenburg's urgent appeal to negotiate an armistice before the German armies collapsed.

The next day, on October 6, the new Chancellor dispatched a note to President Wilson, stating that "to avoid further bloodshed, the German Government requests the President to arrange the immediate conclusion of an armistice on land, by sea and in the air." But Wilson refused to enter negotiations save with responsible representatives of the German people, making it clear that the Allies did not believe the Imperial Government was truly representative.

The new German government hastily instituted measures designed to bring all the powers of the state under the control of the *Reichstag* and on October 20 assured Wilson that the armistice was asked in the name of the German people as well as by their leaders. In his reply on October 23, Wilson agreed to take up the question of armistice negotiations, but stated that there could be no negotiations "with the military . . . and monarchical masters of Germany."

Wilson's stern warning caused the Emperor, upon the insistence of Prince Max, to force Ludendorff to resign on October 26. The tall, corpulent figure who for so many months had dominated the war on the Western Front—dwarfing both Germany's political leaders and Hindenburg, his nominal commander—went into exile in Sweden. He was replaced as Hindenburg's deputy by General Wilhelm Groener.

GERMAN COMBAT PERFORMANCE IN WORLD WAR I / Did the German defeat, and the disappearance of the disgraced Ludendorff, mean that institutionalized military excellence was really a myth? Let's examine the record.

First some general statistics. In World War I the Germans mobilized military forces totaling about 11 million men, and suffered almost exactly 6 million casualties. Against Germany alone, the Allies mobilized approximately 28 million, more than two and one-half times as many. Allied casualties in combat against Germany totaled about 12 million (ignoring losses against Austria-Hungary, Turkey, and Bulgaria). Thus on the average each mobilized German soldier killed or wounded slightly more than one Allied soldier; it took five Allied soldiers to incapacitate one German. However, the Germans were more often than not on the defensive, the posture which Clausewitz called "the stronger form of combat." Experience has shown that troops on the defensive have advantages such as position, observation, and fortifications which enable them, man for man, to inflict more casualties than the more exposed and more vulnerable attackers. Recent research has demonstrated that this advantage in World War II was a factor of about 1.3; it may have been slightly less than that in World War I, but certainly not much less. If it is assumed that 1.3 was the multiplying factor for defensive advantage over the attacker, then on an equal, or normalized, basis, there was an overall German superiority of 4 to 1 in inflicting casualties.

A modern method of historical analysis of combat[2] calls the quantitative, per-man capability of a force to inflict casualties upon its opponents "score effectiveness." Throughout the war the Germans consistently had a substantially greater score effectiveness—which of course is a measure of combat effectiveness—than the Allies. This German combat superiority was demonstrated time and again, from the opening battles in 1914 to the final desperate defensive struggle in late 1918.

Consider, for instance, the sweep of the German armies across France in August and early September 1914, as General von Moltke threw away the formula for victory bequeathed him in the Schlieffen Plan. His subordinate commanders and his soldiers performed magnificently. On their way to the Marne the seven German armies in the West, some 1.2 million men, suffered more than 200,000 casualties in the battles of the frontier. But the French, more than 1.3 million mobilized by that time, lost 300,000 men, and were driven back in bloody defeat. Considering the ten days of most intensive combat of this period, the Germans had a score effectiveness of 3.1; the French only 1.8. Meanwhile, the German right-flank armies were marching about twenty miles a day and fighting at the same time.

At the Marne, Moltke's ineptitude and Joffre's amazing powers of recuperation combined to halt the Germans in decisive defeat. Through strategic mistakes they had maneuvered themselves to the brink of disaster. Nevertheless, in that grim, bloody, and bitterly contested battle, they still were inflicting more casualties on a man-to-man basis than the French: 5.8 to 5.2.

The French were never again to be as effective in the more than four years of war that remained. Thereafter German score effectiveness would invariably be much greater than that of the French, whether they were on the offensive or the defensive, whether they outnumbered the French, or were outnumbered.

The same thing was true of the German battles against the British. In the great British offensives of the Somme, Arras, and the Third Battle of Ypres, the Germans invariably inflicted twice as many casualties per man as they received. The same thing was true when the Germans attacked, as at the first two battles of Ypres, and in the opening phases of the Somme and Lys offensives of early 1918. In the latter two offensives, however, when Ludendorff required his over-extended and exhausted shock troops to continue fruitless attacks against fresh British and French reserves, and under constant strafing from the Royal Air Force, German casualties rose sharply, while the loss rate of the Allies dropped, so that the final score shows that German casualty inflicting effectiveness in those offensives was only about 90 percent that of the British.

Appendix C lists the basic statistics—including the score effectiveness of each side—for fifteen of the most important battles of World War I, ten on the Western Front, five on the Eastern Front. In summary, against the British, the German score effectiveness superiority averaged 1.49 to 1; against the French it was 1.53 to 1 (almost identical); against the Americans, in the Meuse-Argonne, the German divisions that our own intelligence reports described as "tired and depleted," had a score effectiveness advantage of 1.04 to 1. These figures have been adjusted to allow for the increased effectiveness of defensive firepower, so that they indicate that on the offense as well as defense two German soldiers could on the average fight three Allies to a standstill.

On the Eastern Front the statistics are less reliable, and score effectiveness calculations may be distorted by the tremendous and exceptional hauls of prisoners which the Germans captured in such battles as Tannenberg, Masurian Lakes, the Winter Battle, and Gorlice. Omitting the Russian prisoners in those battles, the result is a German score effectiveness superiority of 2.8 to 1; including the prisoners, German score effectiveness superiority was 7.9 to 1; the average is 5.4 to 1. This suggests that—on a broad front, with plenty of room to maneuver and to employ their strategic and tactical leadership superiority—German armies could hold off Russian armies three to five times as large as their own.

The Battle of Lodz tends to confirm that this was what actually occurred. It will be recalled that in late 1914 a Russian offensive toward Silesia and Breslau was met in western Poland, almost head on, by a German offensive through Lodz toward Warsaw. Hindenburg and Ludendorff had collected a force of about 260,000 men in their Ninth Army just west of Lodz. The Grand Duke Nicholas had available north of the Carpathians something over a million men.

Georg von Kameke
(*Military History Institute,
East German People's Army*)

Paul Bronsart von Schellendorf
(*Military History Institute,
East German People's Army*)

William II, with Hindenburg (l.) and Ludendorff (r.) (*U.S. National Archives*)

Count Alfred von Waldersee (*Keystone Service*)

Julius von Verdy du Vernois
(*Prussian Cultural Picture Archives*)

Walther Bronsart von Schellendorf
(*Prussian Cultural Picture Archives*)

Count Alfred von Schlieffen
(*German National Archives*)

Heinrich von Gossler
(*Military History Institute,
East German People's Army*)

Helmuth von Moltke—the younger
(*U.S. National Archives*)

Theobald von Bethmann-Hollweg
(*U.S. National Archives*)

Erich von Falkenhayn
(*U.S. National Archives*)

Paul von Hindenburg, center
(*U.S. National Archives*)

Erich Ludendorff
(*U.S. National Archives*)

Baron Reinhard von Scheffer-Boyadel
(*German National Archives*)

Alexander von Kluck, with cape (*U.S. National Archives*)

Friedrich Ebert (*Keystone Service*)

Max Hoffmann (*U.S. National Archives*)

Gustav Noske (*Keystone Service*)

Wilhelm Groener
(*Military History Institute,
East German People's Army*)

Walter Reinhardt, seated (*Keystone Service*)

Wilhelm Heye (*U.S. National Archives*)

Hans von Seeckt (*U.S. National Archives*)

Wolfgang Kapp (*Keystone Service*)

Baron Walter von Lüttwitz
(*Keystone Service*)

Otto Gessler (*U.S. National Archives*)

Of these about 400,000 were actually engaged by the Germans in the Battle of Lodz. The remaining 600,000 were either in unused reserves, or scattered along the front opposite fewer than 100,000 Germans. Thus the Russians, with a strategic superiority of about 3 to 1 over the Germans, were able to bring to bear in the battle a superiority of about 1.5 to 1. The result was a bitter two-week battle, in equally bitter cold, ending in a tactical standoff. However, the Russians immediately evacuated Lodz, and pulled their line back about thirty kilometers toward Warsaw. In other words, German forces, outnumbered 3 to 1, had achieved a major strategic victory.

One can only speculate as to what the outcome of World War I would have been had the Schlieffen Plan been carried out faithfully. Even accepting the near certainty that the Battle of the Marne would have been a German victory, this does not necessarily mean that France would have collapsed, or that—given a French collapse—Britain would necessarily have accepted a result less decisive than the outcome of the Napoleonic wars.

In his Foreword to Schlieffen's *Cannae,* General von Freytag-Loringhoven makes clear his own assessment of what would have happened, and also makes an assertion regarding German combat superiority over the Allies which—without the statistics just cited—might seem inconsistent with the outcome of the war:

> Notwithstanding the sharp delineation of the Cannae doctrines Count Schlieffen was no schematist. He knew that in war many means lead to the goal. However broad his knowledge of the achievements of modern war technique and however constantly he had furthered its development in our Army, his opinions remained steadfastly tentative in this domain, because the possibility of testing the technique of new weapons on a large scale was wanting in peace time. Before the war we all could only surmise their actions on the ground and in the air. Reconnaissance, Victory, and Pursuit, the paving of the way for a Cannae, as well as the penetration, all evinced more than ever before, and in a much higher degree, that they depended on the effect of the weapons of the enemy. This explains partly why, except for Tannenberg, a real Cannae did not occur in the World War. That one did not occur in the West at the beginning of the war is the fault, in the first instance, of the Supreme Command. Indeed it was the Schlieffen Plan on which our operations were based, yet in their actual execution it was departed from. His constant exhortation to make the right army flank as strong as possible was not heeded.
>
> As in this respect, so also the apprehensive foreboding of the Field Marshal in his composition, "The War of the Present Time," came true. The long dragged out war ruined world industry. The frontal juxtaposition of the forces excluded a complete decision. The appeal for a stronger war establishment for Germany made by Schlieffen in his "About the Armies of Millions" was heeded too late. . . . In the work: "Benedeck's Leadership of the Army from the Newest Researches" Count Schlieffen's purpose is to point out where an unlucky selection of a Commander in Chief may lead. . . .

The Field Marshal shows in his writings that he always aspired to the ideal, well knowing that one must set up a demand for this to attain anything of high standard. In this, at least, we were successful in the World War. From the publications of our enemies we know now how near we were, several times, to final success, in spite of our numerical inferiority; and this is not a trifle. The annihilation doctrine has not died in the German Army. Count Schlieffen was the one best fitted to further Moltke's art of war. He drew the most pertinent deductions from the constant growth of armies and the enlarged conditions of the present. The fear of mass armies we have overcome, thanks to him, and in the handling of the weapons we have shown ourselves to the last superior to our opponents. If the World War constitutes a high title of honor for us, General Field Marshal Count Schlieffen has a rich share therein.[3]

Schlieffen was an exceptional man, and on the basis of the record it is difficult not to agree with the praise given him by Freytag-Loringhoven. But, significantly, Schlieffen probably would have been unknown had it not been for the institution which he headed, the German General Staff. He was the representative and spokesman of institutionalized military excellence, and thanks to the institution, his own excellence was permitted to make its mark on history.

Yet despite excellence, the institution had now suffered a grievous defeat. By the terms of the Treaty of Versailles, the Allies believed they had destroyed it with a Zama or a Waterloo. As we shall see, however, that defeat, severe though it was, is more comparable to a Metaurus or a Leipzig.*

---

*At the Metaurus, 207 B.C., Hannibal's brother Hasdrubal was defeated and killed by Roman Consul Nero; however Hannibal was able to continue to wage war successfully until his final defeat by Scipio Africanus at Zama, 202 B.C. Similarly, the allied armies inflicted a grievous defeat on Napoleon at Leipzig, in 1813, but he fought two more vigorous campaigns before his final defeat at Waterloo in 1815 by Blücher and Wellington.

NOTES TO CHAPTER ELEVEN

[1] For an interesting discussion of how the new German tactics, which Hutier had not designed but had merely been the first to use in a major operation, became known as the Hutier Tactics, see Dr. Laszlo M. Alfoldi, "The Hutier Legend," *Parameters,* Vol. V, No. 2.

[2] Colonel T. N. Dupuy, *The Quantified Judgment Method of Analysis of Historical Combat Data* (Dunn Loring, Va.: 1976).

[3] Schlieffen, *op. cit.,* pp. viii-ix.

Chapter Twelve

PICKING UP THE PIECES
Groener, Seeckt & the General Staff

 GROENER AS ASSISTANT CHIEF OF STAFF / In the turmoil of demobilization, revolution, and counterrevolution in Germany in the months immediately following the Armistice, the officer corps of the Army remained the one solid element around which a new nation might be constructed. The nucleus of this element was, of course, the General Staff, now ably directed and guided by General Groener, who had replaced Ludendorff as First Quartermaster General in the closing weeks of the war. Combining firmness—which sometimes became ruthlessness—with persuasion and example, Groener and other officers held together a functioning, operational Army which suppressed mutiny and revolt and restored order, despite all-out Bolshevik efforts to extend their influence from Moscow, Leningrad, and the Baltic to Berlin and the Rhine.

In his intellectual, military, and administrative talents, Groener was a true successor of Moltke and Schlieffen. Like Scharnhorst, he had to recreate a new army, in a new social system, from the chaos of defeat. While his personal political views were perhaps closer to those of Clausewitz than to those of Gneisenau, Boyen, or Grolman, his sure instinct for the interrelationship of the Army and society under the guidance and control of a strong but responsible government, warrants favorable comparison to Scharnhorst. As with the concepts of that illustrious predecessor, however, he was only partially successful, and—as in the case of Scharnhorst—the partial success carried with it the seeds of eventual disaster.

Continuing the comparison, Groener was neither a Prussian nor an aristocrat by birth. Also like Scharnhorst his father was a noncommissioned officer in the Württemberg Army which young Wilhelm Groener joined in 1884, at the age of seventeen, as an officer candidate. Commissioned a second lieutenant in 1886, he entered the War Academy in 1893, and in 1897, one year after graduation, was detailed to the Great General Staff in Berlin. From then until 1911 his service alternated between tours with troops in the Württemberg infantry, and General Staff duty. In 1912 he became a department head in the Great General Staff; shortly after the outbreak of the war, in 1914, he was promoted to colonel and appointed Chief of Field Railways. His performance in this demanding position was so outstanding as to win for him the coveted "Pour le Merite" decoration, usually reserved for exceptional battlefield success or for feats of heroism. He was also promoted to the rank of Major General. In 1916 he became Chief of the War Office, in the War Ministry, and as such was responsible for supervising and coordinating Germany's industrial production in support of the war effort. Early in 1918 he was placed in command of an army corps on the inactive Eastern Front, then in March became Chief of Staff of the army group occupying the Russian Ukraine. It was from this post that he was called to replace Ludendorff as First Quartermaster General, in October 1918.

Groener's role as one of the three men who were to collaborate to save Germany (the others were the civilian Socialists, Ebert and Noske) began shortly after he arrived at Spa on October 28, Almost simultaneously the Emperor had also arrived at the Army High Command Headquarters (*Oberste Heeresleitung,* OHL), taking refuge with the Army to escape political pressures in Berlin for his abdication. These pressures were a consequence of President Wilson's October 24 refusal to deal with "the militaristic and monarchical masters" of Germany. William had expected that by sacrificing Ludendorff—who resigned on the twenty-sixth—Wilson would be satisfied, but it was evident to all German political leaders that Wilson was also demanding the Emperor's removal. The *Reichstag* party leaders called for abdication, and when Prince Max also urged it, the Emperor left Berlin to seek the protection of his loyal generals. He received the expected support and sympathy from Hindenburg and Groener. Both loyal soldiers were aghast at the idea of abdication and would not counsel William in that direction. Hindenburg's attitude is revealed by his reverent references in his memoirs to the "Most Gracious Kaiser, King, and Lord."

REVOLUTION IN GERMANY / Soon, however, Groener began to realize that there was revolution afoot within Germany. Long-standing social grievances had been enflamed into revolt by hunger, by the defeat of the armies, and by the propaganda of Bolsheviks and Bolshevik-influenced agitators. Groener also was well acquainted with the moderate Socialist leaders Friedrich Ebert and Philipp Scheidemann through his work on war production earlier in the war. He respected these trade-union leaders, now part of the new government, and was impressed by their urgent demands that the Emperor must abdicate for the good of Germany.

Then on November 4, 1918, came a mutiny of the fleet at Kiel. When ordered to go to sea in search of the British fleet, the sailors refused and seized control of the naval base. Soon they had also taken over Hamburg and Bremen. On November 7 revolution broke out in Munich, and a Bavarian Soviet Republic was proclaimed.

Ebert and Scheidemann had wanted a peaceful, democratic, and gradual Socialist revolution. That revolution was now in danger from more radical groups called Independent Socialists and Spartacists, who were influenced by the ideas and agents of the Russian Bolshevik revolution. The moderate Socialist leaders now urged Groener to obtain William's abdication and save the monarchy. This time Groener tried to persuade Hindenburg, but the loyal old Imperial servant still could not countenance the idea.

ABDICATION OF THE EMPEROR / On November 8 Groener explained to the Field Marshal that revolution was spreading through all of Germany. It was now clear that the Army could not be counted on to put down internal revolution; even if it wished to, it could hardly hold the crumbling Western Front and fight a civil war at the same time. Hindenburg finally realized that his world was falling to pieces. He spent one of the few sleepless nights of his life, and in the morning he was ready to tell William that he must step down. When the Field Marshal and Groener came into the Emperor's presence, however, Hindenburg could not bring himself to break the news. He gestured toward Groener, who haltingly explained that the Emperor must abdicate. Hindenburg then sadly confirmed what Groener said.

While the bitter Emperor was trying to make up his mind, Prince Max took matters into his own hands, announcing that William and the Crown Prince had abdicated the thrones of Germany and Prussia, and that he himself was resigning as Chancellor. Ebert would become Chancellor and would appoint a regent to govern for the young heir to the throne. In this way Prince Max and Ebert hoped to save the monarchy that they both honored. They were too late, however. The Spartacists captured the Imperial Palace and proclaimed a Soviet Republic. The moderate Socialists in response proclaimed a German Socialist Republic from the *Reichstag.* Somehow, in the collapse of its armies and economic life, Germany had almost accidentally become a republic.

Hindenburg now had the hard task of telling the Emperor that he must leave Germany, that he was not safe in his own country. Once more the Field Marshal shifted the thankless task to Groener. After more hours of indecision, William accepted the inevitable. Late on November 9 he appointed Hindenburg his successor as Supreme Commander of the German armed forces. Thus, although there was no change in either his title or his duties, First Quartermaster General Groener automatically became the acting Chief of the General Staff.

HINDENBURG AND STABILITY / That evening Hindenburg also made the crucial decision to serve the new republic. Groener had shown him the Allies' armistice terms. They were very severe, the terms a victor would hand to a vanquished army. Groener and Hindenburg knew that they had no choice but to accept, and had so informed Ebert. They knew also that if Hindenburg, with his great prestige, remained as Supreme Commander there was a chance for orderly demobilization of the Army; the morale of the people might not break altogether, and the new government would stand a good chance of putting down the spreading Communist revolts.

Many German officers were trying to decide where their highest loyalty lay, whether or not to support the republic, so alien to their monarchist traditions. Hindenburg thought, as he wrote later, "that I could help many of the best of them to come to the right decision in that conflict by continuing in the path to which the wish of my Emperor, my love for the Fatherland and Army, and my sense of duty pointed me." His example was decisive. The German officer corps grudgingly decided that loyalty to Germany transcended their dislike of the republic; Hindenburg and the officers held the Army together in defeat. But many of the promonarchist officers held against Groener (though not against Hindenburg) the lese majesty of virtually dismissing their King and Emperor.

That was for the future, however, even though Groener already recognized that he was likely to be the scapegoat. At the moment he had other more pressing matters on his mind. He and the Staff must make plans for withdrawing the German Army from France and Belgium in the almost impossibly short time allowed by the Armistice terms. At the same time, as the acting Chief of the General Staff, Groener had inherited the responsibility for planning for the future security of Germany, and he took the responsibility seriously. A war had been lost, the Empire had disappeared, but the nation remained. And it was now threatened as seriously by internal forces as from the vengeful Allies approaching the frontiers.

THE GROENER-EBERT AGREEMENT / On the evening of November 9, in his office in Spa's Hotel Britannique, Groener picked up a special telephone, a private line, connecting directly with the Chancellor's office in Berlin. This was the line that Ludendorff had used to exercise his virtual dictatorship over Germany for nearly two years, and Groener had already used it on several occasions to talk to Prince Max of Baden, and more recently with Friedrich Ebert, when he advised the government to accept the Armistice terms. Now, with the Emperor gone, a new republic struggling for its existence in Berlin, and Hindenburg the new Supreme Commander of the Army, Groener had another purpose in calling. Germany had suffered enough; it must be preserved from the horrors of revolution and civil war such as was sweeping Russia. This would be possible only if both the legal government and the Army could be preserved, and brought together by a new linkage replacing the personal connection which had heretofore been provided by the officers' oaths to the King and Emperor.

Fortunately Ebert was in his office and immediately answered the phone. Groener wasted no words. He offered the support of the Army to the government and assured the Chancellor that the High Command would bring it back to Germany in good order. Ebert, apparently sensing that this implicit expression of loyalty to the new regime was not unconditional, asked Groener what the Army expected in turn from the government. Groener responded that "the Field Marshal"—in other words the High Command—expected that the government would assist the Army in maintaining discipline, in assuring supplies during the hasty withdrawal from France and Belgium, and—above all—in opposing the threat of Bolshevism to the nation, using the Army as its instrument in this opposition.

Ebert promptly and gladly accepted these veiled conditions for Army loyalty. As Groener requested, the Chancellor sent a telegram to Spa, confirming the understanding, directing the troops to obey their officers and to maintain discipline "under all circumstances," and exhorting the soldiers' councils, as a matter of "their highest duty," to cooperate with their officers and the High Command "to prevent disorder and mutiny."

"THE STAB IN THE BACK" MYTH / One month later, however, the ordinarily level-headed Ebert committed a blunder in his efforts to provide both the German people and the Army with visible signs of ties between the government and the Army, although it is possible that he never recognized the implications for him, Germany, and the world. As part of his skillful campaign to sustain the legitimacy and popularity of his shaky government, on December 11 he ordered a defiant parade in Berlin, as though the Armistice was a mutually agreed ending of the war, and not the virtual surrender instrument which in fact it was. To emphasize his interpretation, after the field-gray columns recently returned from France had marched impressively up Unter den Linden and were assembled in massed formations in front of the reviewing stand at the Brandenburg Gate, Ebert made a short speech, beginning with the fateful words: "I salute you, who return unvanquished from the field of battle."

Ebert thus set the stage for the myth that the Germany Army had not been defeated by the Allies, but had been betrayed—"stabbed in the back"—into an unfavorable peace by disloyal elements at home. While Ebert undoubtedly recognized the implication of his words, and probably assumed that this would merely be attributed in part to pardonable chauvinism and in part to placing the blame on the Spartacists and other Communists, there were other implications as well. Since he was heading the civilian government at the time the Armistice was accepted by Germany, and since he had approved the document, he was taking on himself at least some onus for betraying the "undefeated" Army, and absolving the High Command (and the General Staff) from any responsibility for this peace. This "stab in the back" myth would become a major contribution to Germany's willingness to fight again two short decades later.

THE GENERAL STAFF PICKS UP THE PIECES / While Groener and his General Staff undoubtedly appreciated Ebert's words, it is doubtful if any of them could predict the long-term effects—although many German officers would have welcomed them. They were far too busy making the arrangements that got those parading troops, and the millions of their comrades, back from the fighting fronts. Once the retreat to the Rhine was well under way, the High Command moved from Spa back to Germany, first briefly to Bad Homburg, then to permanent quarters in Kassel. There Groener and the General Staff immediately immersed themselves in the problems of short-term and long-range planning. There were five major problems, of which two were administrative and organizational, two were operational, and one was theoretical.

The organizational problems were to reconstruct an effective Army, even as the war-weary veterans, who had retained their discipline as far as the Rhine, melted away once they were safely in central Germany. The second problem was to assure the continuity and undiminished effectiveness of the General Staff.

The first of the operational problems was to provide the support which the government required, and which Groener had promised, in restoring order and reestablishing fully respected central authority in Germany. The second was to assure the security of the vaguely defined eastern frontiers of the new German Republic in a manner that would protect the nation from the danger of aggression by a resurgent Poland, while at the same time being responsive to the confused and confusing Allied requirements.

The theoretical problem was to assess the recent war experience so that the German Army—whatever it might be—could be employed with the greatest possible effectiveness in its tasks of providing internal and external security.

The operational problems as well as the theoretical were handled by the Operations and Regional divisions of the Staff, with Colonels Wilhelm Heye and Ernst Hasse playing important roles.

For the first of the administrative problems—the retention of an effective military force that could be the basis of a new peacetime Army—Groener established a special working group of some of the most experienced and trusted officers of the General Staff, including Major Werner von Fritsch, Major Kurt von Hammerstein-Equord, Major Baron Ludwig Wilhelm von Willisen, and Captain Kurt von Schleicher.

Groener, who had been an instructor at the War Academy before the war, was particularly interested in the planning for the continuity of the General Staff. While studies of this matter were being conducted by the working group in the Central Branch of the Staff, Groener seems to have given these problems much personal consideration, before he was forced to divert his attention elsewhere.

Despite defeat, the General Staff was proud of its record in World War I in controlling, guiding, and directing the armies that fought with such marked success from the English Channel to the shores of the Red Sea. There was much to be proud of: the performance of the small but remarkably efficient staffs of armies, corps, and divisions; the consistently superior combat effectiveness of German units at all levels; and the exceptionally large number of excellent field commanders who almost invariably outgeneraled their opponents at all levels of command—army, corps, division, regiment, and company. Interestingly, of nearly a hundred German generals (aside from royal Princes) who exercised command of armies, army groups, or comparable independent commands, only one—Kluck—had not been a General Staff officer.

But what had the war done to the institution?

At the outbreak of hostilities, the War Academy had closed down. The students waiting to continue the second and third years of the curriculum were quickly assigned to staff positions in the Great General Staff or to vacant posts in the army and corps general staffs, usually replacing officers who had been hastily plucked out to be given key staff or command assignments in newly mobilized replacement corps and divisions. As more divisions, corps, and armies were created, and as Troop General Staff officers began to suffer their share of casualties, there was an increasingly serious shortage of trained and qualified General Staff officers. This shortage was partially alleviated by assigning to staff positions officers who had graduated from the War Academy, but had not been appointed to the General Staff.

But as the stalemate pervaded the fighting fronts, and as attrition inevitably continued to thin the ranks of the General Staff, a General Staff replacement system had to be devised. Promising young combat officers who gave evidence of having the required qualities of intellect and character were encouraged to apply for the General Staff. Applicants were recommended by their immediate commanders, their records scrutinized by higher staffs, and then given a relatively simple examination. (First priority in consideration were officers who had completed one or two years in the War Academy in 1914). Those who were selected and passed the examination were then assigned to field General Staff positions, where they had to serve a nine-months' apprenticeship. Of these, perhaps half were finally selected—on the basis of a comparison of commanders' reports—for appointment to the General Staff Corps.

Many General Staff officers were concerned by the fact that these new additions to the General Staff were not being trained or evaluated on a basis of common standards, and thus were not being indoctrinated with the common conceptual approach to military problems that had been one of the principal characteristics of General Staff success. Early in 1917 the Chief of Staff of the Crown Prince's Army Group authorized a three-week intensive training course at Sedan for the group's General Staff applicants. The results were so good that a recommendation was sent to the Central Department of OHL that this program should be adopted on an Army-wide basis, under OHL supervision and coordination. The recommendation was promptly and enthusiastically approved, and a total of thirteen such courses, varying in length from three to four weeks, were held between July 1917 and September 1918. Close to five hundred officers went through this course, and by the end of 1917 future successful completion of the Sedan Course—as well as nine months of satisfactory on-the-job training—became a prerequisite for transfer to the General Staff Corps.

In this way, formal education and practical combat staff experience were combined with the traditional examination and selection processes to assure maintenance of the high standards of the General Staff, despite the exigencies of the war. Groener's problem now was to shift back to peacetime procedures without any lowering of the standards.

The pressing demands of the two operational problems—internal security and threats from the East—did not permit Groener to spend as much time as he would have wished either on doctrinal assessment of the war's lessons or on planning for the revitalization of the General Staff. And when later he might have had the time, the provisions of the Versailles Treaty had completely changed the context of Germany's military problems, even though the requirements continued.

NADIR OF THE GERMAN ARMY / The internal-security problem had come to a head shortly after the December 11 parade in Berlin.

Radical and leftist elements—led by the Communist Spartacists and Independent Socialists—were incensed that the government had brought troops into Berlin. Believing that they were supported by a tide of popular indignation, they tried vainly to gain control of the Congress of Workers and Social Councils, meeting in Berlin from December 16 to 20. When this effort failed, the extreme leftists decided to resort to violence. On the afternoon of December 23 a mob, consisting mostly of sailors of the People's Naval Division, seized several public buildings, including the old Imperial Palace, and surrounded the Chancellery. They also seized control of the central government switchboard, cutting off the Chancellery from all outside communications. Or so they thought.

Ebert, however, still had his secret direct line to Groener's office, and called the First Quartermaster General to tell him about the crisis in Berlin. Groener at once sent orders to General Arnold von Lequis, commanding military forces in the Potsdam-Berlin area, to suppress the uprising.

By this time the dissolution of the Army had reduced the number of effective troops under Lequis' command to barely a thousand men. Apparently OHL was not aware of the sad state of readiness of Lequis' command, and he seems to have done nothing to inform Groener of the situation. Whether this was because he did not yet realize the grave deterioration of his command himself, or because he feared to expose his own leadership failures, is not clear. In any event, Lequis sent all the troops he could scrape together to the Imperial Palace. The troops were winning a two-hour battle against the even more disorganized sailors, when a mob of Berliners, hastily assembled by leftist leaders, attacked the soldiers from the rear. At the same time part of the crowd—including many women— dashed out into the square in front of the palace, daring the troops to fire at them. This was too much for the soldiers. Most of them disappeared into the crowd, and only a handful of troops accompanied the disgusted officers back to Potsdam to report the defeat to Lequis.

This was undoubtedly the low point of the history of the German or Prussian Army. But while Groener and his associates were undoubtedly embarrassed by the disgraceful showing of the Army in Berlin on Christmas Eve, the unreliability of their troops was not thereby suddenly revealed to them, as some historians have suggested. In fact, circumstances in the Baltic States had already demonstrated both the unreliability of the existing Army and the urgent need for dependable troops. Either because of unexpected developments in the Baltic area, or as a result of their independent assessment, Groener's special study group had already proposed a temporary measure for quickly obtaining effective and dependable forces. This was to authorize selected individual commanders to form independent units, recruited by voluntary enlistment from hundreds of thousands of unemployed veterans. Equipment, provisions, and pay for these units would be provided by the government.

EMERGENCE OF THE FREE CORPS / Several people have been credited with conceiving the idea for these Free Corps, as they came to be called. It seems likely that the idea was first suggested by Major von Willisen of the special study group in late November. It is possible, however, that Willisen's suggestion had been inspired by the simultaneous and apparently spontaneous establishment of local paramilitary groups of demobilized soldiers throughout Germany. These veterans, on their own initiative, or under the sponsorship of wealthy land-holders or merchants, formed local security groups to protect people and prop-erty from the bands of lawless Communists, which had begun to appear through-out Germany in early and mid-November. Many such local groups were estab-lished in December and later, and whether they inspired or were inspired by the Free Corps phenomenon does not much matter. The first such unit to receive government sponsorship and support was established in mid-December by General Georg Maercker, in Salzkotten. Several other similar units were estab-lished in the Berlin area in late December. These were placed under the com-mand of General Baron Walter von Lüttwitz, who had been appointed Chief of *Generalkommando Berlin* to replace General von Lequis shortly after the Christ-mas Eve debacle in front of the Imperial Palace.

The veterans who enrolled in these Free Corps units were men who either could not get jobs in the depressed economic environment of defeated Germany, or who by preference returned to the military life to which they had become accustomed during the war years. Since they were volunteers, since they were serving under leaders they knew and trusted, they had a far different attitude toward military service from that of the conscripted soldiers who had melted away in the earlier demobilization demoralization. Paradoxically, many of these aggressive Free Corps volunteers had been untrustworthy conscripts in late 1918. A few weeks earlier they would have grumbled against discipline, and would have sought to avoid either training or housekeeping chores. Now they responded cheerfully, like Prussian Guards (which some of them had been), to strict discipline; they trained willingly and eagerly on drill fields, maneuver grounds, and target practice ranges. Not that much training was needed to bring them to a high state of military efficiency. After all, these were the men who had fought so skillfully on battlefields all over Europe until they were over-whelmed by the Allied manpower superiority.

POSTWAR OPERATIONS IN THE BALTIC STATES / Even before the Christ-mas Eve fiasco, Groener's General Staff was planning to enlist Free Corps Units for service in the Baltic States, particularly Latvia. Ironically, these men were being readied for combat service outside Germany as a result of demands placed upon Germany by the victorious Allies. Article XII of the Armistice reads in part as follows: "All German troops presently in territories which formed a part of pre-war Russia shall ... withdraw within the frontiers of Germany as [on August 1, 1914], such withdrawal to take place as soon as the Allies deem proper, depending upon the internal situation in these territories."

One such portion of prewar Russia from which the Allies did not want the Germans to withdraw, until other arrangements could be made for defense, was the Baltic region, the former Russian provinces of Estonia, Latvia, and Lithuania, which had been ceded to Germany by the Treaty of Brest Litovsk. But the Armistice had nullified that treaty, and most of the war-weary German troops stationed in the Baltic provinces, eager to return home to demobilization, mutinied when ordered to remain. The Soviet Government had also denounced the Treaty of Brest Litovsk immediately after the Armistice, and had begun to send troops into the Baltic provinces, although their advance was slowed by local resistance on the part of the Balts.

It was the mutiny of German troops in the Baltic region that had first revealed to Groener and his staff the unreliability of their Army. One of the major stimuli to the adoption of the Free Corps concept was Allied demands that Germany must live up to the terms of Article XII of the Armistice; German troops must prevent Soviet encroachment in the Baltic states until the local governments of the three small states were able to defend themselves.

It is not surprising that this Allied demand that Germany hold the Bolshevik menace out of the Baltic area suggested to some members of the General Staff an opportunity to regain these provinces for Germany. While Groener was too realistic to believe that the Allies would permit this, he too must have been intrigued by the possibility. But, regardless of hopes or motives, the requirement was clear: Germany had to send reliable troops to hold these provinces and, if possible, to eject the Soviet invaders. Early in January Free Corps units began to go to Latvia, and later in the month Groener appointed General Count Rüdiger von der Goltz, who had been the commander of German forces in Finland, to command the new Free Corps Army assembling in southern Latvia and Lithuania near Libau. The chief of staff of this army was Major General Hans von Seeckt, recently returned to Germany from Turkey. Seeckt operated Command North from headquarters in Königsberg, while von der Goltz assumed personal field command of the Free Corps units in Latvia and Lithuania.

By the end of February, von der Goltz had cleared the Soviets out of most of Latvia. Then, taking advantage of the distraction of the German Supreme Command with internal turmoil in Germany, he made a bid to reestablish German control of the Baltic provinces. This, as Groener had foreseen, was unacceptable to the Allies. Upon Allied demand, the German High Command was forced to stop the flow of supplies and reinforcements to von der Goltz, and he was eventually defeated by local forces, with French and British assistance. Finally, late in 1919, the Baltic Free Corps units retreated back to East Prussia, where most of them were demobilized.

Early in the year Groener had moved the High Command from Kassel to

Kolberg, on the Baltic shores of Pomerania, so as to be able to give closer attention and supervision to the Latvian campaign. But events within Germany soon forced the General Staff to focus its attention southward. To understand these events it is necessary to go back to Christmas week of 1918, before OHL moved to Kolberg.

NOSKE AND CIVILIAN AUTHORITY / Following the Army's discomfiture at the Imperial Palace, Berlin remained in a state of limbo, part controlled by the Spartacists and their allies, and part wondering when the next surge of revolution would strike the capital. To deal with this explosive situation Ebert had a happy thought. During the first week of November, after the outbreak of the naval mutinies at Kiel which led to the German collapse, the Chancellor—Prince Max of Baden—had turned to Ebert, who was the Chairman of the Socialist Party and a member of Baden's Cabinet, to seek assistance in finding a Socialist who would have the strength and the patriotism to restore order in Kiel. Ebert had recommended the military specialist of the Party, Gustav Noske, a giant of a man who had good trade-union credentials and was also an ardent and loyal nationalist. Baden appointed Noske as Governor of Kiel, and in a week the tough trade-union leader had used cajolery and ruthless employment of a few loyal units to restore order and discipline in the fleet. His impressive height and bulk had helped him cow obstreperous opponents.

Remembering Noske's success at Kiel, Ebert—after a confirming phone call to Groener—on December 27 again called on his Socialist colleague, appointing him, in effect, Minister of National Defense. Since (thanks to Bismarck) there was no such position in the existing German Constitution, Ebert gave Noske the temporary title of Commander in Chief. It did not matter that there was already a Commander in Chief (Hindenburg). The Army knew and liked Noske, as he knew and liked the Army, and both were happy to have him assume and firmly exercise the command responsibilities of a Minister of Defense; it was not a time for niceties in military protocol or semantics.

Extracting a promise from the sailors' council in Kiel not to interfere in the confused situation in Berlin, Noske left Kiel and assumed his new position. Informed by General von Lüttwitz (who willingly addressed Noske as Commander in Chief in Berlin) of the availability of the new Free Corps units in his Berlin Command, Noske accepted Lüttwitz's invitation to inspect these units, and on January 4, 1919, he and Ebert visited a camp at Zossen, near Berlin. After reviewing Maercker's spic-and-span, goose-stepping troopers, Noske is said to have clapped Ebert on the back, remarking, "Don't worry, everything is going to be all right now."

NOSKE AND THE ARMY RESTORE ORDER IN GERMANY / Noske consulted with Groener, then ordered Lüttwitz to clear the Spartacists from Berlin. This was done during the so-called Bloody Week—January 11-13—when the Free Corps gained revenge in full for the Christmas Eve discomfiture of the Army.

Following these events, OHL had made its move to Kolberg and was concerned with supervising operations in Latvia and also with a brief Free Corps adventure in Posen. That city had been seized (with tacit OHL approval) from the resurgent Poles by several Free Corps units. The Free Corps units had been withdrawn from Posen in late February, however, as a result of Allied demands.

Then, in the expected third spasm of revolution, Spartacist-inspired disorder once again erupted in Berlin, and spread across the country. At this time the National Assembly was meeting in Weimar to create and adopt a new constitution. With Groener's approval, Ebert called Noske back to Berlin from Weimar, and gave him the title of Commander in Chief of Brandenburg. On March 4 Noske ordered Lüttwitz to commit a force of some 42,000 troops to clear Berlin. The job was done by March 9, under Noske's personal supervision. The best and most reliable of the Free Corps—notably Maercker's brigade, which was able to restore order with little bloodshed—were then sent by Groener to other regions in Germany where Communist-inspired unrest was provoking violence. In April it was Braunschweig and Magdeburg; in May it was Munich and Stettin; and in June the last important center of Spartacist resistance was broken in Hamburg.

ARMY REORGANIZATION AND THE VERSAILLES TREATY / It was while the Berlin operation was in full swing that the National Assembly, meeting at Weimar, produced a vague but workable Provisional *Reichswehr* Law. This law, and the government decree to enforce it, finally officially dissolved the old Imperial Army, and for the first time set up a central German Ministry of Defense. This post, of course, had already been virtually established by Ebert when he had called Noske to Berlin, two months earlier. Now Noske had confirmation of his title and responsibilities.

Groener immediately began to put this new law into effect, beginning to transform Free Corps units into *Reichswehr* formations. He expected to have the job done by mid-1920, at which time the new *Reichswehr* was to have a peacetime strength of about 300,000 men, a substantial reduction from the 400,000 men under arms in April and May 1919.

This planning, and the force-development program which was emerging from General Staff studies, were suddenly rendered meaningless by the terms of the peace treaty, which the Allies presented to the German representatives at Versailles on May 7, 1919. Although these terms were harsh, this was not unexpected to the Germans, well aware of how each side presents an extreme position at the beginning of a tough negotiating process. This time, however, the Germans were told that there would be no negotiations—it was "take it or leave it." Unsaid but unmistakable was the consequence of refusal to sign on or before June 20, 1919: The Allied forces occupying the Rhineland would move eastward to occupy all of Germany.

General von Seeckt, now the senior military adviser to the German delegation at Versailles, sent back a copy of the terms to Groener at Kolberg; the

General Staff began an immediate analysis of the most important of those provisions.

The German Army was to be limited to 100,000 officers and men. The men were to serve under twelve-year enlistments; officers were not to be eligible for retirement before twenty-five years of service. The Army was to be reduced to a strength of 200,000 within three months, and was to be down to the 100,000-man strength (including 4,000 officers) by March 3, 1920. There were to be no combat aircraft, heavy artillery, tanks, or other "offensive" weapons as classified by the Allies. The General Staff was to be dissolved, "and may not be reconstituted in any form." Dissolution was also decreed for the War Academy and for all cadet-training schools.

The Allied occupation of the Rhineland would continue; thus a provision for the complete demilitarization of the occupied area was somewhat meaningless. However, there was to be an additional demilitarized strip of territory fifty kilometers deep, just east of the occupation zone. Germany could have only a token navy, with no submarines and no surface vessels of more than 10,000 tons. All of these military provisions were to be enforced by an Allied Control Commission.

Although not directly military in significance, two provisions of the Treaty aroused particular resentment not only in the officer corps, but among the entire population. Germany was to agree to surrender its wartime leaders for trial on the charge of violations of the laws of war. And the German nation was to acknowledge its guilt for having started and waged an aggressive war.

GERMAN REACTION TO VERSAILLES / As far as Germany was concerned, the one positive result of the announcement and publication of the Treaty terms was its unifying effect upon the people. All Germans, whatever their political affiliation, agreed that the terms were unacceptable.

At Kolberg the reaction of the General Staff officers against the Treaty terms was, understandably, even more bitter than among the population at large. However, with typical General Staff objectivity, they undertook a thorough analysis of the Treaty terms and their implications—including the likely consequences of a German refusal to sign the Treaty. Late in May Groener reported the results of that analysis to Hindenburg: no matter how distasteful the Treaty, consequences of refusal to sign would be worse. There was no doubt that the Allied armies would attempt to occupy all of Germany, and there was nothing that the 400,000 men in the new *Reichswehr* and the Free Corps could do about this, save to kill a few Allied soldiers before themselves being crushed in defeat.

Remembering the Wars of Liberation against Napoleon, Groener and the Staff also carefully considered the possibility that the people of Germany would rise in a "people's war" against the Allied invaders. Reluctantly they concluded that not only would there be no mass rising of the war-weary population, the Spartacists would seize the opportunity for a nationwide revolt. The outcome would be disaster, chaos, and dismemberment of Germany. The Allies then would undoubtedly prevent any amalgamation of the fragmented nation in the foreseeable future. There was no recourse but to sign the Treaty and accept its terms, difficult and distasteful though they were. Groener discussed the matter with the Field Marshal, who reluctantly agreed. In late May Groener telephoned Ebert and told him the results of his study.

During June, however, with the June 20 deadline for signing the Treaty rapidly approaching, popular opposition intensified. Ebert himself wanted to reject the Treaty, if this could be done without the risk of renewed war and disaster. And it was now evident to him that most German military men and a majority of his Cabinet were in favor of defying the Allies, no matter what the consequences. After a stormy Cabinet meeting on June 4, Ebert asked Groener for a formal military estimate of the situation.

GROENER AND GERMAN ACCEPTANCE OF VERSAILLES / Groener, who yielded to no one in matters of patriotic pride, and aware of the strong senti- ment against the Treaty among senior Army officers, reviewed the situation again, very carefully, vainly seeking to find at least some basis for hope that the Army—with the support of a majority of the people—could successfully defend Germany against Allied invasion. Regretfully, about June 15 he reported to Ebert that the situation was hopeless; the Allied occupation forces had been alerted and were ready to move if Germany did not accept the Treaty; the *Reichswehr* could delay them and could hurt them, but could not stop them. Although opposed to the Treaty, the German people would not support the Army. The consequences of resistance would be catastrophic, as he had already reported.

Ebert accepted this military opinion philosophically, but in order to con- vince his Cabinet, he insisted that it be put in writing, and approved by Hinden- burg. When Hindenburg sought to find some basis for counseling resistance, Groener again reminded him of the consequences.

"There would be a general outcry against counterrevolution and mili- tarism," he reputedly said.[1] "The result would only be the downfall of the Reich. The Allies, balked of their hopes of peace, would show themselves piti- less. The officer corps would be destroyed and the name of Germany would disappear from the map." Reluctantly the old man accepted the inevitable and in a letter to Ebert of June 17 confirmed Groener's report. He insisted, however, in concluding his letter with the following words:

> In the case of a serious Allied attack we can hardly be successful in view of their numerical superiority and ability to envelop both our flanks. An advantageous result of the operation is therefore very doubtful. But as a soldier I prefer honorable destruction to a disgraceful peace.[2]

Groener knew how difficult it would be for Ebert to withstand the pressures of unthinking chauvinists, who would try to twist or misinterpret the Field

Marshal's final words as a basis for suicidal defiance of the Allies, so he carried the letter personally to Weimar, arriving there that night. During the next two days he participated in a series of meetings with senior military men, and with President Ebert, Prime Minister Scheidemann, and Defense Minister Noske. Scheidemann would not sign the treaty, and would not ask the *Reichstag* to approve it, but neither would he lead the nation to war against the clear recommendations of the General Staff. He resigned. The President even considered resignation, but decided against it. Meanwhile, the Allies extended the deadline to June 23.

Noske assumed that he (Noske) would be called upon to form a government to replace Scheidemann's. He asked Groener if he could count on the loyalty of the Army. Groener, in front of a roomful of other generals, most of whom opposed his views, reiterated the General Staff assessment of the hopelessness of resistance, but assured Noske that if the government decided to defy the Allies, he and the General Staff would loyally direct the military operations, and do everything possible to defend the nation, no matter how hopeless the situation might seem to be. He saw that he had failed to convince the diehard soldiers, but hoped that Noske had recognized the logic of the General Staff assessment. He took a train back to Kolmar. Noske had been careful to hide his personal views, but apparently he accepted Groener's dispassionate General Staff assessment and rejected the emotional chauvinism of the other generals, who assumed the Defense Minister agreed with them. Thus, had he become Prime Minister, it seems likely that he would have recommended a *Reichstag* vote to accept the Treaty. However, Ebert instead chose Gustav Bauer as Prime Minister. Late on June 22 Bauer received a vote of confidence from the *Reichstag* on the basis of a recommendation that Germany sign the Treaty, but without acknowledgment of the provisions for accepting war guilt or for surrendering alleged war criminals for trial. This decision was telegraphed early next morning to the German delegation at the Peace Conference. It was, however, rejected that afternoon by the Allies, who issued an ultimatum, giving Germany until 6:00 P.M. on the twenty-fourth to sign the Treaty unconditionally.

The result was near panic in the Ebert-Bauer government in Weimar. A group of senior officers had already offered Noske the opportunity to be dictator if he would defend the nation's honor by refusing to sign the Treaty. The Spartacists and other left-wing groups had made it clear that failure to sign the Treaty would mean a popular uprising against the government. Thus, no matter what it did, the government seemed to be faced with revolt and civil war.

Meanwhile, in Kolberg, Groener and his staff reviewed the situation while four British destroyers cruised the Baltic waters offshore within easy range of the temporary headquarters of the General Staff. Once again Groener and Hindenburg studied the objective assessment of their subordinates. The result was the same. Hindenburg himself at one point is reputed to have asserted, "You know as well as I do that armed resistance is impossible!"[3]

This was the third time in a little more than seven months that Ebert was faced with a situation in which Germany was on the verge of dissolution into bloody chaos. As on previous occasions, he remembered his private telephone line to the First Quartermaster General. He called a Cabinet meeting for noon, then shortly after 11:00 A.M. on June 24, with less than seven hours remaining before the expiration of the Allied ultimatum, Ebert telephoned Groener.

Hindenburg was with Groener when the call came. The Field Marshal recognized what was happening when he heard Groener speaking for himself and the General Staff, obviously avoiding reference to Hindenburg. To allow Groener to speak more freely, he quietly left the room.

Groener calmly repeated the firm opinion of the General Staff that resistance was hopeless, then added that, "as a German" he felt obliged to advise the President that "peace must therefore be concluded under conditions laid down by the enemy." Knowing full well that on this occasion, as on the previous one, the personal consequence would be the likelihood of accusations of treason, Groener took the personally distasteful action that he knew was essential for the survival of Germany. He continued to avoid the mention of Hindenburg's name, and Ebert, understanding the situation, this time carefully refrained from requesting a confirmation from the Field Marshal. Groener then expressed his opinion that the government could expect loyal Army support if the situation and the implications were clearly and forcefully represented. He suggested that Noske, popular with the Army, should demand such loyalty as an alternative not only to Allied invasion, but to the inevitable civil war that would accompany such an invasion.[4]

Gratefully Ebert followed Groener's suggestions. The Cabinet accepted. The *Reichstag* met and voted to accept the Treaty, and German acceptance was delivered by telegram to the Allies just a few minutes before the expiration of the deadline. Noske made the appeal to the Army that Groener suggested. The Army smoldered, but remained loyal.

Meanwhile, Hindenburg had returned to Groener's office, and in a gesture typical of his relationship with both Ludendorff and Groener, laid his hand upon the shoulder of his First Quartermaster General. He understood what Groener had done and why he had done it. Hindenburg was no coward, but he recognized that he should be disassociated from the unpalatable decision. Gruffly but kindly he said: "You are right. The burden which you have undertaken is a terrible one, and you must again be the black sheep."[5]

Thus the Army General Staff assumed responsibility for Germany's acceptance of the Treaty of Versailles. But Groener, in keeping with tradition, shielded his subordinates from that responsibility, and also deliberately shielded his Commander in Chief, Germany's war hero, from the consequences. As a result, other Army men could, and did, say that neither they as a group, nor Hindenburg as a person, had made that fatal decision; it had been that Württemberger, son of an NCO, Wilhelm Groener.

THE EMERGENCE OF SEECKT / Next day, June 25, Hindenburg resigned from his position as Commander in Chief. At a farewell ceremony on July 2, Groener bid an emotional farewell to the old man in the name of the Army and the General Staff. For the second time in his life Hindenburg retired to private life. Meanwhile, on the thirtieth, Groener also submitted his resignation, to be effective on July 15. He had already submitted to Noske his recommendations for assuring military-command continuity. On July 5 Noske announced the establishment of a Preparatory Commission for a Peace Army, as Groener had suggested. Also, as he had recommended, Lieutenant General von Seeckt was appointed President of that Commission and also the Chief of the Army Command Troop Office, which was to assume all legal jurisdiction allowed within the Versailles Treaty, previously exercised by the now-forbidden General Staff.

Seeckt, born in Schleswig on April 22, 1866, came from a noble Prussian family with a military tradition. His father had been a much-decorated General under William I and the elder Moltke. Young Hans did not attend cadet school, but joined a guards regiment as a subaltern at the age of nineteen. Ten years later he was accepted as a student at the War Academy, and in 1899, less than a year after graduation from that institution, he became a member of the General Staff Corps. In the next fifteen years he had a very active peacetime career, in which brief periods of service with troops were interspersed with coveted staff positions and opportunities to travel abroad as a military observer. At the outbreak of the war, he was a lieutenant colonel, and he soon won distinction as the Chief of Staff of the III Corps in Kluck's First Army. His success in that post caused General von Falkenhayn to promote him to colonel on January 27, 1915, and to appoint him on March 9 the Chief of Staff of the newly established Eleventh Army, under General August von Mackensen.

This was the army that Falkenhayn established to spearhead the planned breakthrough of the Russian lines in Poland in May 1915. Seeckt's plans were crowned with success, in one of the most decisive victories of the war, which resulted in Mackensen's promotion to Field Marshal. To the annoyance of some of his colleagues, Seeckt was also rewarded by promotion on June 26, 1915, to Major General, over the heads of several General Staff officers senior to him.

Early in 1916 Mackensen, appointed to the command of a composite German-Austrian-Bulgarian army group for the Romanian Campaign, asked for Seeckt as his Chief of Staff. Again Seeckt had the opportunity to see his plans crowned with a resounding victory. During most of 1916 and 1917, however, Seeckt was Chief of Staff of the army group of the Austrian Archduke Charles, and continued in that post under the Archduke Joseph when Charles became the last Austrian Emperor. In that position, although he was the virtual army-group commander, Seeckt had little chance to taste success. In Hoffmann's memoirs there are several reports of Seeckt's appeals for German reinforcements, particularly in the grim days of Russia's 1916 Brusilov Offensive.

Seeckt's final appointment during the war was as Chief of Staff of the Turkish Army, a position he held from December 1917 until early November

1918. By this time, of course, he was one of the most experienced Chiefs of Staff in the German Army, and it has sometimes been suggested that he would have been selected as Ludendorff's replacement in October 1918, had he not been so far away. This is possible, although Hoffmann would seem to have been an even more likely choice. However, Groener was selected because his efficiency as Director of Railroads in Berlin had been so directly perceived by the Emperor and Prince Max of Baden, and because he could get to Spa in a few hours.

In any event, Seeckt joined Hindenburg and Groener at Kassel, in December 1918, and early the next month he was sent to Königsberg to replace Hoffmann as Chief of Staff (virtually the Commander in Chief) on the Eastern Front, and to supervise the disorderly retreat of mutinous German troops from the Ukraine and the Baltic. Early in 1919 he organized the movement of the Free Corps back into the Baltic States, and prepared the overall plans that resulted in von der Goltz's recapture of Riga in May.

At that time Seeckt was sent to Versailles to be the military member of the German delegation to the Peace Conference. Thus it was that, at the end of June 1919, Seeckt probably knew and understood the military clauses of the Treaty of Versailles—and their implications—better than any man in Germany. It was this, combined with his exceptionally broad experience and proved ability, that led Groener to select him as President of the Preparatory Commission of the Peace Army, and to recommend him initially as the Chief of the Army Command. Upon Groener's retirement, July 7, Seeckt became Chief of the General Staff for one week, until its formal dissolution on July 15, 1919.

Meanwhile, Noske had come to know and like Colonel Walther Reinhardt, the last War Minister of Prussia, who had worked closely with the new Defense Minister in establishing the ministerial machinery under the Provisional *Reichswehr* Law. Württemberger Groener believed that fellow Württemberger Reinhardt lacked the strength of character and intellectual brilliance of the Prussian Seeckt. But when Noske promoted Reinhardt, and appointed him Chief of the Army Command, Groener urged that Seeckt should head the Troop Office. (In the new War Ministry organization, replacing the staff machinery of the General Staff, the Army Command Office was to exercise administrative control over the units of the Army; under the Army Command Office, the Troop Office was responsible for organizational planning and training supervision.)

During the six weeks between Seeckt's return from Versailles and his assumption of the responsibility of planning for Germany's new, 100,000-man Army, Seeckt and Groener must have had many a talk about the future of Germany, of the German Army, and of the General Staff. (There was a brief interruption in this period, when Seeckt was sent to Latvia to persuade von der Goltz to follow Allied instructions; as a result the Germans reluctantly withdrew from Riga on July 11, by which time Seeckt was back in Berlin, working with the Preparatory Commission in quarters set up in the old General Staff building on Bendlerstrasse.)

DISSOLUTION OF THE GENERAL STAFF / It seems safe to assume that both Groener and Seeckt had already considered the possibility of deliberately evading the provisions of the Versailles Treaty, and equally safe to assume that they had seen no reason why such evasion should conflict with the strict code of honor of a German officer. At the very least it must have been evident to them that the provision for the dissolution of the General Staff was both illogical and unenforceable so long as an army existed at all.

Whatever may have been the conceptual contribution of Groener to the solution of the problem of controlling and directing an army without a formal general staff, and how the resultant organization should be related to, and be a successor of, the old Great General Staff, it now became Seeckt's problem, and Seeckt properly has been given credit (or blame) for the solution.

Germany's acceptance of the Versailles Treaty automatically dissolved the Kolberg Supreme Headquarters—OHL—and the General Staff. Seeckt and his Commission became in fact the successor organization, but only briefly, since Noske was already implementing the new staff and command organization which Groener and the General Staff had planned for the peacetime Army under the Provisional *Reichswehr* Law. Seeckt saw it as the problem of his Commission to adapt the Groener plan and the Groener command organization to the new requirements of the 100,000-man Army, then at leisure to adapt this to a long-term plan and organization which would at some future date permit the reestablishment of an adequate German Army.

NOTES TO CHAPTER TWELVE

[1] John W. Wheeler-Bennett, *The Nemesis of Power* (New York: 1954), p. 52.

[2] Wilhelm Groener, *Lebenserinnerungen* (Göttingen: 1957), p. 501.

[3] Wheeler-Bennett, *op. cit.,* p. 58.

[4] Groener, *op. cit.,* p. 507.

[5] *Ibid.* See also Dorothea Groener-Geyer, *General Groener: Soldat und Staatsmann* (Frankfurt: 1955), p. 162.

Chapter Thirteen

CLANDESTINE RECOVERY
The Seeckt Era

 THE NEW GERMAN ARMY / The new organization, under the revised Groener-Seeckt concept, provided for overall command of the Army to be exercised by the Minister of Defense. Military advice to the Minister would be provided by an Army Command, a staff organization which (under the Seeckt adaptation of the Groener plan as required by the Versailles Treaty) no longer included a General Staff. The senior military officer in this administrative staff organization—Major General Reinhardt—had the somewhat ambiguous title of Chief of the Army Command. Thus, while he was without question the chief of a staff, he was not *the* Chief of *the* General Staff, nor was he a Commander in Chief; he was something less than both.

The staff, or Army Command, itself, consisted of four major branches. First was the Personnel Office, which was of course the lineal descendant of the old Military Cabinet. The Chief of this office was General Johann Ritter und Edler von Braun. Next was the Troop Office, a meaningless title adopted by Groener and Seeckt for an agency which was to perform the planning and coordination functions which had previously been the responsibility of the Great General Staff. Noske approved Groener's recommendation that Seeckt should be the Chief of this staff agency. The third major staff division was the Ordnance Office, initially directed by Colonel Baron Friedrich Kress von Kressenstein, who had distinguished himself as a commander of Turkish troops during the war. The final major staff agency was that of the Army Administrative Service, which at first operated with a civilian chief, directly under the Minister of Defense, and was independent of the Army Command. Noske soon recognized, however, that the administration of the Army required a military officer to transmit and (sometimes) translate civilian directives. He chose for this post General Hans von Feldmann.

The Army itself consisted of two major operational commands, which Groener had originally envisaged as field armies, one for the East and one for the West. Under the Seeckt adaptation, to meet the 100,000-man army limitation of the Versailles treaty, these operational or group commands were now organized as two corps headquarters—each capable of expansion to field army should events permit or require. Under these were seven *Wehrkreise* (regional military districts), with each district supporting an infantry division in the manner in which the prewar districts had supported army corps. Thus the operational unit in District I was the 1st Division; the district commander was also the division commander. Four of these districts, comprising the eastern and central regions of Germany, were under Group Command I, with headquarters at Berlin; three were under Group Command II, located at Kassel.

LÜTTWITZ, SEECKT, AND REINHARDT / With the resignation and retirement of Hindenburg, the senior officer in the Army was General Baron Walther von Lüttwitz, the commanding General of Group Command I. Since there was neither a Commander in Chief nor a Chief of the General Staff, Lüttwitz seems to have considered it to be his responsibility to serve as an unofficial leader of, and spokesman for, the officer corps.

General Reinhardt, however, as the Chief of the Army Command, considered that he held the senior position in the Army, and thus was responsible officially for providing the kind of Army leadership which Lüttwitz was assuming. Noske certainly acted as if Reinhardt were the military leader of the Army. Reinhardt seems to have realized, however, that his title and position were ambiguous, and that a number of the Army's senior officers—particularly most of the district commanders, who were all senior in rank to him—accepted Lüttwitz' nominal leadership. He decided, therefore, to avoid a confrontation until his position and authority were more securely established.

Old customs and traditions do not die easily, particularly in the German Army. The man who held the position closest to that which had been preeminent in the Army for three quarters of a century was General von Seeckt. It was recognized throughout the Army that, even though there was no longer a General Staff Corps, and there was no Great General Staff, Seeckt as Chief of the Troop Office was virtually functioning as the chief of an unofficial general staff, and he was respected as a man of the Moltke-Schlieffen caliber who had the training, background, and experience to serve as their successor. Thus, even the officers who accepted Lüttwitz as the unofficial spokesman for the officer corps, were willing to follow any official instructions they might receive from Seeckt. That officer, typically self-effacing and anonymous in the Schlieffen tradition, made no effort to capitalize on his reputation or his role as unofficial Chief of Staff. His position, too, was ambiguous, and he was further restrained by the provisions of the Versailles Treaty from any attempt to resolve that ambiguity. Single-mindedly he devoted himself to the administrative problems of demobilization, reorganization, and General Staff continuity to the extent possible under the Treaty terms, and to the operational problems of planning for the security of Germany with an Army inadequate in size either to assure government control within the frontiers of a troubled nation, or to protect the eastern frontiers against old and vengeful foes. (The western frontier, of course, was already held by the Allied occupation armies.)

Lüttwitz made his first move to consolidate his position of leadership in the officer corps soon after the new Army organization began to function. On July 21 he held a conference of senior officers of Group Command I to discuss the role of the Army in the shaping of the new *Reich,* and establishing its course within the hated Treaty constraints. Present at the meeting were at least two of the district commanders (General Burghard von Oven of District III, the Berlin region, and General Georg Maercker, of District IV), Major General Paul von Lettow-Vorbeck, commandant of Schwerin, and other commanders of garrisons in the Berlin region, plus senior officers of Lüttwitz' own staff, including his Chief of Staff, Colonel Karl von Stockhausen, and his Operations Officer and son-in-law, Major von Hammerstein-Equord. Also present were at least two distinguished retired officers, General Max Hoffmann and Colonel Max Bauer, who had been Operations Officer under Ludendorff at Spa, and undoubtedly represented Ludendorff at this staff conference.

Lüttwitz presented to the conferees his views on what the Army should do to force the government to adopt policies that were militarily acceptable and consistent with the honor of Germany and its Army. The principal elements in his program were the following: refusal to surrender Army leaders to the Allies for trial as war criminals; insistence upon the maintenance of a military force adequate to preserve Germany from the danger of Bolshevism, either internal or external; retention of the unity of the nation against various separatist movements, particularly in Bavaria; and a demand that members of the Marxist Independent Socialist Party (closely allied to the Communist-Spartacists) be excluded from the government. All of those present seem to have endorsed these goals heartily, but they were sharply divided into three groups on the means whereby these goals were to be achieved.

Lüttwitz boldly proposed that the Army press these demands vigorously, so as to force the government to choose between the alternatives of subservience to the military, and a clear-cut confrontation with the Army's leaders. In the latter event, he would respond by the use of force to establish a military dictatorship. Several of those present, including Colonel Wilhelm Reinhard (not to be confused with General Walther Reinhardt), and the hero of East Africa, Lettow-Vorbeck, fully endorsed Lüttwitz' bold proposals. At least two officers—Oven and Maercker—expressed doubts as to the wisdom of any resort to force, and urged that the goals be achieved by maintaining pressure on Ebert, both directly and through Noske. A third group, which seems to have included Stockhausen and Lüttwitz' son-in-law, Hammerstein-Equord, were appalled by the Lüttwitz proposal for a military dictatorship, but guardedly expressed their opposition to such a course of action on the practical grounds that it would be bound to fail. At least one member of this latter group seems to have informed Seeckt about the meeting.

THE LÜTTWITZ-KAPP PLOT / Despite the lack of enthusiasm of most of his officers for the extreme measures that he advocated, Lüttwitz decided to assert his leadership and to make plans for a takeover of the government. He formed close alliances with ultraconservative political and patriotic associations and consulted frequently with both retired and active officers who shared his views, and who were mostly members of these right-wing associations. Among the retired officers were Ludendorff and Bauer. Among active officers, Lüttwitz' most outspoken supporters were Lettow-Vorbeck, Reinhard, and naval Commander Hermann Ehrhardt (leader of a Free Corps naval brigade). Lüttwitz also continued to cultivate the possible support of more moderate officers, like Oven and Maercker, on the assumption that the logic of his position and their own honor as officers would induce them to support him when the time for action was at hand. He also succeeded in causing the transfer of Stockhausen, who had made clear his opposition to any kind of dictatorship.

Lüttwitz, however, had no intention of becoming a dictator himself. For this role he wanted an experienced civilian government official, who could deal with political and administrative problems, while Lüttwitz provided the power and military expertise in support of policy. For this position he found Dr. Wolfgang Kapp, who had been an East Prussian government official, had gained some reputation during the war as an outspoken member of the Pan-German League, and had provided some assistance to Ludendorff in the intrigue that forced the 1917 resignation of the wartime Chancellor, Bethmann-Hollweg. Kapp thus had administrative experience, and to Lüttwitz he seemed to have the requisite political qualifications. The two men found each other completely agreed on the future of Germany, and in the fall of 1919 began to plan for the establishment of a militarily supported dictatorship.

Despite the clear evidence that many of his subordinates did not share his opinion as to the need for a military dictatorship to save Germany, Lüttwitz seems to have made no efforts to hide his treasonable discussions and slowly maturing coup d'etat plans from his staff. As a result, Seeckt was kept informed of these discussions and plans, even after Lüttwitz had forced the transfer of Stockhausen. On several occasions Seeckt reported these developments to Noske. The Defense Minister, who seems to have obtained some information about these activities from other sources, was also aware that Lüttwitz was not supported by his staff, and at the same time had only amused contempt for Kapp. As a result Noske discounted the danger, and did not take Seeckt's warnings seriously.

The plot was nevertheless serious, and by early 1920 Lüttwitz and Kapp had reached agreement to seize power in the late spring or early summer. Their timetable was suddenly altered, however, by two independent but closely related Allied actions.

On February 3, 1920, the Allies submitted to Germany a list of those military and civilian officials who were to be surrendered to the Allies for trial as war criminals. The list (which the Allies said was "incomplete") contained more than 850 names, and consisted mostly of senior wartime military officers (starting with the Crown Prince and Hindenburg) plus the principal civilian governmental leaders. (The Allies also demanded extradition of the Emperor from the Netherlands; the Dutch refused.) Except for the Independent Socialists and Spartacists, all shades of German opinion were united in outrage at the Allied demand, and even the Marxists were critical of the Allies' inclusion of clearly honorable and responsible officials on the list. Had the government shown any evidence of intention to comply with the Allied demands (which it did not), Lüttwitz was prepared to move to seize power.

It was an unrelated but almost simultaneous action by the Allied Control Commission that forced the hands of Lüttwitz and Kapp. The Commission demanded the immediate demobilization of the Free Corps naval brigades, which had been temporarily incorporated in the *Reichswehr* the previous year. Allied intelligence was aware that these brigades—particularly that of Commander Ehrhardt—were not only extremely well trained and efficient, but were also hotbeds of German nationalism. The Allies also undoubtedly knew something of Lüttwitz' plans and intentions and of the fact that Ehrhardt's brigade was to play a major role in Lüttwitz' plans for seizure of control of Germany.

Seeckt was perhaps even more aware of the importance of Ehrhardt's brigade to Lüttwitz' plans, and thus saw no reason to delay or avoid compliance with the Allied demand for its demobilization. Consequently, the German government reported its willingness to comply, and Noske issued routine orders for the demobilization, to be effective on March 12.

When Lüttwitz' protests against the demobilization order were ignored, he decided to carry out his coup d'etat at once. Again Seeckt warned Noske, and again Noske took no action. On the evening of March 10 Lüttwitz issued an ultimatum in person to President Ebert and Noske, and was taken aback by the vehemence with which the two politicians rejected his terms. The General appeared so discomfited that Noske seems to have been convinced that danger of a coup was slight, and he and Ebert both expected to receive the General's resignation in the morning. When he did not resign, late on the eleventh, Noske ordered Lüttwitz to be placed on leave.

Lüttwitz, however, was no Boulanger.* He telephoned to Ehrhardt, whose garrison was only twenty kilometers from Berlin, and ordered him to march his men to the city. He notified Kapp and the other principal conspirators, who had not expected the putsch to take place for several months, and prepared to take over the government. He was confident that the small garrison in the city would obey his orders, and he had a commitment that the police and Security Policy would also support him.

By evening of the twelfth, Ebert and Noske realized that they had misjudged Lüttwitz. Their amused condescension was changed first to alarm and then—as word came in that Ehrhardt's troops were on the road—to panic.

---

*French General Goerges E. J. M. Boulanger in 1889 led a conspiracy to seize power in France; then, when accused of his conspiracy, he deserted his adherents and fled to Belgium.

"THE TRAGIC CONSEQUENCES . . . IF REICHSWEHR CLUBS REICHS-
WEHR" / Late that night, just before midnight, Noske called a hasty meeting
of the senior officers of the Ministry of Defense and of the Berlin region. Present
were Reinhardt, Seeckt, the other principal division chiefs of the Army Command and of the Ministry, General Burghard von Oven, Commanding General of
District III, and Major General Baron Erich von Oldershausen, Lüttwitz' new
Chief of Staff.

Noske announced to the assemblage, which he called a council of war, his
intention to order the Berlin garrison to resist the naval brigade until other
troops, summoned from more distant garrisons, could arrive to defeat the
putschists. He then asked emotionally if he could count on the loyalty of the
Army. Reinhardt announced his loyalty and his agreement that orders should at
once be issued to defend the city against Ehrhardt's troops.

The next speaker was Seeckt. The story of this dramatic incident has been
told many times and with many embellishments. Often omitted in the telling,
however, are Seeckt's activities both just before and just after the meeting;
without this context his words and attitude in responding to Noske become
ambiguous.

Seeckt was unquestionably furious with Noske for having failed to heed his
repeated warnings of the conspiracy and for having failed to take action that
could have forestalled the putsch. Seeckt put out of his mind—if he ever considered it—the idea of taking the initiative himself of ordering troops from other
areas to Berlin to protect the government. Such an order issued by Noske would
have had all the force of the authority of the state, and Seeckt was certain that
it would have been obeyed by all of the district commanders. But from Seeckt
the order could have been considered a military counter coup by another ambitious general and could even have precipitated the military confrontation, and
probably bloodshed, which he wished at all costs to avoid. He had checked,
however, on the possibility of using the Berlin garrison against Ehrhardt, and
quickly realized that these troops would be no match in numbers, training, or
weaponry for the tough naval brigade veterans. Furthermore, the local commanders all seemed to be committed to Lüttwitz. The local police, and the
Security Police as well, were also in Lüttwitz' pocket. There was nothing in
Berlin that could stop the conspirators.

Thus it was with some bitterness that Seeckt responded to Noske's request
for support: "Troops do not fire on troops, Herr Minister. Are you planning to
arrange a battle at the Brandenburg Gate between troops who a year and a half
ago were fighting shoulder to shoulder against the enemy?" Most accounts then
suggest that Seeckt got up and walked out of the meeting and went on an
indefinite leave of absence; these accounts give the impression that he was wash-
ing his hands of responsibility, and that he did not have the moral courage to
take a definite stand in support of the government against the military rebels.

In fact, an exchange continued between the two men for several more
minutes. The now emotional Noske accused the general of secretly favoring the

insurgents. Seeckt did not bother to remind the Minister of his past warnings; retaining his temper, he calmly denied the accusation, adding: "But I know the tragic consequences, and perhaps I alone know what combat would bring. If *Reichswehr* clubs down *Reichswehr,* then all comradeship in the officer corps is at an end. When that occurs, then the true catastrophe, which was avoided with so much difficulty on November 9, 1918, will really occur."

Noske then announced that he would mobilize the police. Seeckt calmly replied that it was too late, that the police were already controlled by Lüttwitz Finding that all of those present agreed with Seeckt except Reinhardt and his own aide, Major Erich von Gilsa (who had been suspected of being a conspirator), Noske berated the generals for deserting him and threatened suicide. Then, recovering control, he closed the meeting.

Seeckt did not leave the conference room until that moment. He then returned to his office and sent out a message to the chiefs of staff of both group commands and the seven districts, informing them of the pending putsch, and directing them to ignore all orders from any authority other than that of the constituted government. Either then or earlier he had directed Oldershausen to send a similar message to all commanders in Group Command I. He then went home.

Soon after returning home, shortly after dawn that morning, Seeckt sent his written resignation to the Ministry by his aide-de-camp. En route to the Ministry, the aide also gave Seeckt's instructions to Heye, Chief of Staff of the Troop Office. That officer was to go to the Ministry in civilian clothes and to stay there during the putsch to represent Seeckt.

Meanwhile, at Noske's urging, soon after midnight Ebert had called a Cabinet meeting. It was there decided that, since immediate resistance was impossible, the government should abandon the capital and marshal resistance against the rebels from Dresden. At 5:00 A.M. the ministers slipped quietly out of the city in a ragged motorcade. At the same time Ehrhardt's brigade was being fed soup from its rolling kitchens at the Siegsallee, just beyond the Brandenburg Gate, and its commander was chatting quietly with General Ludendorff, who just "happened" to be out taking a very early morning stroll.

THE KAPP PUTSCH / Lüttwitz and Kapp triumphantly took over the government buildings at 7:00 A.M. They soon found out that the triumph was not so complete as they had thought. In the first place, the Socialist Party, presumably by the direction of Ebert, Bauer and Noske (although they later denied it), called a general strike, paralyzing the city. On top of that, of the handful of civil servants that reached their offices that Saturday morning, only a few recognized the authority of the putsch government.

More serious was the attitude of the military officials at the Defense Ministry. Colonel Bauer had been hastily recalled to active duty by Lüttwitz, and appointed Chief of Staff of Group Command I, to replace the "unfaithful" Oldershausen who, (like Seeckt) had submitted his resignation. Lüttwitz, appointing himself Minister of Defense, sent Bauer as his representative to the Ministry. There he found only a handful of officers, all in civilian clothes, under the direction of Colonel Heye. Following his instructions from Seeckt, Heye now informed Bauer that the officers there would accept no orders from anyone except General Reinhardt (who was at home) or General von Seeckt (also at home). Lüttwitz had appointed General von der Goltz to head the Troop Office, in place of Seeckt, but that officer never visited the *Reichswehr* Ministry or the Bendlerstrasse General Staff offices to challenge Seeckt's authority. Lüttwitz, however, after getting Bauer's report, did visit the Army Command offices, to receive the same message from Heye—delivered with full respect—as had Colonel Bauer. Still respectfully, Heye informed Lüttwitz that it was his personal opinion that the conspiratorial government would soon collapse. Lüttwitz stalked out but made no further effort to issue orders to the Army Command staff, using his own Group Command I headquarters to transmit messages to other military headquarters throughout Germany.

One of those orders went to General Maercker, commander of the 4th Division (or District IV) in Dresden, directing him to arrest the members of the Ebert government. Although opposed to the coup, Maercker was aware that Lüttwitz had never been officially relieved of command. Thus he seems to have had difficulty in reconciling the conflicting calls of duty and responsibility. He seems to have accepted this order from his superior commander nominally by informing Ebert and the senior ministers, shortly after their arrival in Dresden, that he had orders to arrest them. Noske responded heatedly that the orders were illegal; Maercker then calmly but ambiguously said that he would interpret his orders as authorizing him to support the legal government. Ebert and Noske, deciding (probably wrongly) that they could not trust Maercker, moved on to Stuttgart, where General Walther von Bergmann, the commander of District V, was not under any vestiges of authority of Lüttwitz. Bergmann and his superior —General Roderich von Schoeler, commander of Command Group II—both issued immediate declarations of loyalty to the legal government.

Meanwhile, in Berlin, Seeckt had put on civilian clothes, then gone to the Ministry of Justice to visit Dr. Eugen Schiffer, the Vice-Chancellor and Minister of Justice of the Ebert-Bauer government. Schiffer had volunteered to remain in Berlin to represent the legitimate government. Embarrassed by his presence, the Lüttwitz-Kapp forces had allowed Schiffer to stay in his office, under protective custody. Seeckt told the Vice-Chancellor that he had submitted his resignation but that until it was accepted he was still Chief of the Troop Office. He thereupon offered his services to Schiffer, whenever these might be needed. Schiffer gratefully accepted, and after a brief but cordial conversation, Seeckt returned home, where he remained for the four remaining days that the Kapp-Lüttwitz government retained control in Berlin.

Sunday afternoon the Socialist Party declared a general strike throughout the nation. The effects of this, beginning Monday morning the fifteenth, were devastating. Even if the bureaucrats had wanted to come to work—and most of them did not—few could have reached their government offices with all transportation paralyzed. The Kapp government debated what to do about this—Commander Ehrhardt recommended taking out all of the union leaders and shooting them, and then began to issue orders to this effect. But Kapp, posing as a friend of labor, got Lüttwitz to countermand Ehrhardt's orders. While Kapp and the handful of civil servants he had recruited attempted to deal with the virtually unsolvable problem of the strike, Lüttwitz and Colonel Bauer somewhat gloomily surveyed the military situation.

The tradition of obedience to orders from a direct superior is rightly strong in any army, and particularly so in the Prussian and German forces. Thus, despite the conflicting orders of March 11 and 12, the four district commanders of Group Command I were used to taking orders from Lüttwitz, and the other three faced the same dilemma as that which was bothering Maercker. Furthermore, all of them, like a large proportion of the officers and men under their command, were at least ideologically sympathetic with Lüttwitz and his anti-Allies, anti-Versailles, ultranationalistic aims. Major General Detlev von Estorff, commander of District I, announced his support of the putsch, as did General von Bernuth, commander of District II, and (with considerable reluctance) General von Oven, of District III. Maercker remained at his post in District IV, without any announcement, and carrying out orders from Lüttwitz with great selectivity. Alone of the Group Command I district commanders, he seems to have remained loyal to the government throughout, and to have considered himself a means for establishing communications between the legitimate and rebel authorities. However, his failure to denounce the Kapp regime was held against him, and he was later dismissed as a result of postputsch investigations by a civil commission.

Since the three district commanders of Group Command II all adhered to General von Schoeler's announced support of the Ebert government, Lüttwitz could count on support from less than half of the senior Army commanders. More serious was the fact that—with a very few exceptions—the chiefs of staff and the general staffs of the district and larger garrison commands were solidly opposed to the putsch regime. In Group Command I and its subordinate headquarters, most of these officers stayed away from their offices during the putsch. They had received their orders from Seeckt, orders which they fully understood and completely respected, even in those few instances where they were personally inclined to the aims of Lüttwitz and Kapp.[1]

Because of the vacillating ineptitude of Kapp, the confused political aims of Lüttwitz and his military adherents, and the unyielding opposition of the workers in the general strike, the Kapp Putsch was probably doomed to failure. This failure was assured, however, by the firm and solid loyalty of the General Staff to the legitimate government, which prevented Lüttwitz from even consolidating the measure of support which many senior officers and important segments of the Army were willing to give him. Seeckt, sitting by the telephone at his study desk in his Berlin home, giving indirect instructions to the stream of visitors who reported to him, was the principal architect of the downfall of Kapp and Lüttwitz.

Early on Wednesday, March 17, the Berlin garrison announced its adherence to the Ebert government. Soon afterward the Security Police called for Kapp's resignation. Kapp, after turning over all "authority" to Lüttwitz, fled. During the afternoon a group of generals and colonels from the Ministry of Defense—all in civilian clothes—called on Lüttwitz. Colonel Heye, in his role as Seeckt's deputy, was their spokesman in urging Lüttwitz to resign. Colonel Bauer called Heye "insubordinate," and some accounts imply that Lüttwitz threatened Heye with drawn sword. In fact, in his rage he apparently shook that weapon—in its scabbard—under the calm nose of the General Staff colonel, but limited his threats to arrest. Heye merely bowed and left the room, followed by the rest of the delegation.

SEECKT TAKES CONTROL / As the rebellion was crumbling, Lüttwitz vainly tried to negotiate with Dr. Schiffer. The Vice-Chancellor refused to accept any message from the general except unconditional resignation. With the telephoned approval of the Ebert government, Schiffer then asked Seeckt to assume command of military forces in the Berlin area. Noske apparently urged that the appointment be given either to Reinhardt or to Oven, who had originally been appointed Lüttwitz' successor on March 12. But Schiffer had no faith in Oven, who had shown too much dexterity in trying to jump from one sinking ship to another, and he was well aware that, despite Reinhardt's firm loyalty, it was Seeckt who had manipulated the military downfall of Lüttwitz.

Immediately after his appointment, using the telephone in Schiffer's office, Seeckt relieved from their commands all of the senior officers of Group Command I who had announced their support of Kapp and Lüttwitz. At almost the same time a two-part drama was taking place in Lüttwitz' Group Command I headquarters. The first brief act was Lüttwitz' resignation. To the last he maintained that his actions had been legal and proper. Accordingly, in his resignation he ironically appointed as his successor, in command of the Army, Hans von Seeckt, the only general he had dismissed during his five days of power.

The next act of the drama had the familiar overtones of a Greek tragedy. At the beginning of the putsch, when Major von Hammerstein-Equord, Lüttwitz' son-in-law and operations officer, had refused to accept Lüttwitz' orders, the old man had ordered him into arrest. Now Hammerstein respectfully but firmly returned the compliment. But when Seeckt learned of this a few hours later, the new Commanding General ordered the immediate release of his predecessor.

It has been suggested that Seeckt was embarrassed by the responsibility of dealing with such a high-ranking prisoner, but technically an officer under arrest is not a prisoner. More likely, the release of Lüttwitz from arrest was the first step in Seeckt's planned program of reconciliation. Save for dismisal, he took no disciplinary action against any of the leading military supporters of the coup, and even in this respect he limited the dismissals to a handful of the most senior officers, as well as to the few General Staff officers who had disobeyed him by supporting Lüttwitz and Kapp.

One reason for Seeckt's quick action to heal the wounds of the putsch was an outbreak of Communist violence in the Ruhr. Expecting that the government and the Army would be paralyzed by the crisis and its aftermath, the Spartacists attempted to seize control of the industries and mines of the Ruhr. But neither government nor Army was paralyzed, and the response was quick and effective.

Noske, still bitter against Seeckt and disappointed that Ebert, Bauer, and Schiffer had overridden him in selecting Seeckt virtually as a new Commander in Chief, resigned on the twenty-fourth, and was replaced by Dr. Otto Gessler. Reinhardt also immediately submitted his resignation, since it was obvious that he no longer enjoyed the confidence of the government as the Chief of the Army Command. Seeckt, appointed to that post on the twenty-seventh, soon recommended to Gessler that the loyalty of Reinhardt be rewarded by appointment to command of District V, to replace General Walther von Bergmann, whose loyalty had also been rewarded by appointment to the command of Group Command I.

Thus, by March 27 the preputsch ambiguity of Army leadership was completely resolved. The Noske-Reinhardt and Lüttwitz foci had disappeared, leaving only Hans von Seeckt as the unquestioned leader of the Army in title and in fact, like the prewar chiefs of the General Staff. His successor as Chief of the Troop Office, newly promoted Major General Heye, functioned in the same fashion as had the First Quartermaster General in the old Imperial Army.

Promptly Seeckt turned to deal with the Ruhr uprising, which had broken out in the demilitarized zone. He pointed out to Ebert that the disorders could not be suppressed so long as the rebels were free to enjoy sanctuary in the demilitarized zone, and recommended that the Allies be requested to permit German troops to operate there for twenty days. He was confident that the disorders could be suppressed in that time. When the Allies unaccountably refused, Seeckt, with Ebert's approval, nevertheless sent in his troops on April 2. They had completed their job and were out of the zone by April 10, and the uprising was elsewhere completely and ruthlessly suppressed by the fifteenth. Meanwhile, in retaliation for this technical Treaty violation, French troops had occupied Frankfurt, Darmstadt, and Duisburg, and did not withdraw from these cities until May 17.

To put down the uprising, Seeckt had been forced to employ some of the Free Corps units which had been scheduled for demobilization. Among these was the Ehrhardt Brigade, after Commander Ehrhardt had given his personal pledge of loyalty to the new Chief of the Army Command. Seeckt accepted the pledge, while warning Ehrhardt that this was in no way to be considered a pardon for his violation of orders in supporting Kapp. If Ehrhardt thought that this reprieve would mean the cancellation of the demobilization order, he was mistaken. True to his word, after the Ruhr rebellion was crushed, Seeckt ordered the postponed demobilization schedule to be resumed, with the Ehrhardt Brigade first on the list.

SEECKT AS UNOFFICIAL CHIEF OF STAFF / For the next six and one half years Seeckt exercised command of the Army and of the General Staff in much the same way as had the two Moltkes and Schlieffen. When his brief period of authority came to a sudden end, late in 1926, for reasons set forth below, the German Army had completely recovered from the defeat of World War I and from the months of turbulence and chaos that had followed that defeat, even though the limiting clauses of the Versailles Treaty were still in effect.

Not that the turbulence ended following the collapse of the Kapp Putsch and the suppression of the Ruhr rebellion. But Seeckt was always the master of events and was able to cope effectively with these while quietly reshaping and strengthening Germany's small army.

Following Poland's victory in the Russo-Polish War of 1920-1921, Seeckt had to plan for possible action to protect East Prussia and Silesia against the threat of resurgent and expansionist Polish nationalism. He did this by reestablishing a kind of Free Corps, under the guise of labor troops, in a so-called Work Command. These units, whose black uniforms soon caused them to be known as the Black *Reichswehr*, were paid and supported partially from *Reichswehr* funds, and partly from donations by the industrial and agrarian organizations to which these battalions were assigned.

The principal commander of these paramilitary organizations was a Colonel von Schwarzkopfen, a former General Staff officer, now nominally a civilian, but actually operating under instructions from Seeckt. Direct official supervision of this organization, soon numbering 20,000 nominal laborers, all veterans and mostly former Free Corps soldiers, was provided by Lieutenant Colonel Feder von Bock, Chief of Staff of District III. General Staff surveillance was provided by a small staff group in the Troop Office, which included Majors von Schleicher and von Hammerstein-Equord.

It has been suggested that this was the first time that Seeckt deliberately evaded the terms of the Versailles Treaty. Other authors, however, have tried to reconcile his clandestine evasions of military terms of the Treaty with his much-vaunted military honor by attributing those terms to the Allied breach of the Treaty implicit in the invasion and occupation of the Ruhr in 1923. In fact, Seeckt's evasions of the Treaty can be traced back to his recommendations and actions after July 5, 1919, as the President of the Preparatory Commission and then as the Chief of the Troop Office.

While Seeckt never bothered to explain his motives or to justify his actions in any respect, it is clear that he did not consider the evasion of the Versailles Treaty terms as being in any way inconsistent with his honor as a German officer. He had taken no oath of allegiance to the Allied governments, or to any of their supervisory agencies. His responsibility was to the government of the Republic, and in the exercise of that responsibility, he was to do his utmost to support the government within Germany, and to secure the frontiers of the nation from foreign invasion. Implicit in this, in the traditions of the German and Prussian armies, was a responsibility to preserve and protect the Army, and to support the comradeship and collective honor of the officer corps. As a General Staff officer, he was convinced that these responsibilites could be properly and efficiently executed only by the perpetuation of the General Staff which was at once, in his eyes (as in the eyes of most German officers for more than a century) both the brains and the heart of the Army.

Thus from the beginning of his assumption of responsibility as a senior official in the Army Command and as the de facto chief of the planning staff of the Army, he had had every intention of deliberately evading that provision of the Versailles Treaty forbidding a German General Staff. So long as there was an Army, Seeckt believed, there had to be a General Staff (no matter what it might be called), and so far as he was concerned, there was only one kind of General Staff—that of Scharnhorst, Moltke, and Schlieffen. As an honored example, he had the clandestine defiance of Napoleon and the Treaty of Paris by Scharnhorst and the Reformers.

Thus the establishment of the Work Commands was not a landmark in the postwar history of the German Army; it was merely an incident within an Army policy already well established and in effect. This evasion, if not direct violation of the Treaty, could not be hidden like the clandestine training and planning activities of the General Staff. There was an outcry in the Allied Control Commission, but the Allies recognized that the Polish threat to Germany was real, and although few of them would have been unhappy if Poland had annexed all or part of Silesia or East Prussia, the result would have been a war, in which German rearmament could have been prevented only by an Allied occupation of the country. France might have been willing, but neither Britain nor the United States was prepared for such drastic action. So the Black *Reichswehr* was tolerated, and Poland was deterred.

ASSESSING THE EXPERIENCE OF THE WORLD WAR / As noted earlier, under General Groener's guidance, the General Staff had begun its assessment of the operational experience of World War I almost immediately after the evacuation of the Rhineland. Colonels Wilhelm Heye and Ernst Hasse had been most actively engaged in this assessment, and in the formulation of defensive plans for Germany's new frontiers. Seeckt did not allow the changed status of the General Staff, now disguised as the Troop Office, to interfere seriously with this assessment, or with the formulation of new tactical-doctrinal concepts.

Following the traditional historical-study approach of Scharnhorst, Müffling, Krauseneck, Reyher, Moltke, and Schlieffen, the undercover General Staff immersed itself in a study of the recent war. There were several major foci of the investigation: the near success but actual failure of the modified Schlieffen Plan in the West; the almost complete success of the Schlieffen doctrine at Tannenberg; the "riddle of the trenches"; the near success but failure of the British use of tanks at the Somme and Cambrai; the near success but failure of their own 1918 Somme, Lys, and Second Marne offensives; and the growing importance of air power in support of the land battle, particularly the British use of air power in helping to slow and then stop the German breakthrough at the Somme in 1918. The German analysts exhaustively compared the many German and Allied breakthrough attempts on the Western Front from 1914 through 1917 with their own initially successful breakthroughs in early 1918, to note significant differences and equally significant similarities.

The assessment of the Schlieffen Plan brought up for consideration all the criticisms that would later be found in the writings of military analysts quoted earlier in this book. On balance, the verdict of the Staff was that the Schlieffen concept had been sound, that it probably would have been successful if the concept of massive right-wing strength had been retained in principle by Moltke, and that the performance of Kluck's First Army in the Battles of the Ourcq and Marne clearly demonstrated that there was no validity in General Walther Bloom's suggestion that insoluble logistical considerations foreordained failure.

Having thus vindicated Schlieffen to the satisfaction of a substantial majority of the General Staff, the analysts then probed to determine the principal causes of failure.

Significantly, they gave less weight to Moltke's shortcomings than to Joffre's accomplishments. The French mobilization had been completed more rapidly than the Germans had anticipated. Particularly important to the actual outcome had been Joffre's magnificent recovery from the initial defeats in the Battles of the Frontiers, and his redeployment of the French Army before the Battle of the Marne. It was obvious to the German critics that, under the circumstances existing in August and early September of 1914, the weakened right wing could not have been completely successful against Joffre's troops under the existing limitations on the speed and endurance of the German infantry.

As to the success of the so-called Hutier Tactics, the postwar German review merely confirmed the analyses of the wartime General Staff. Flexible tactics of fire and movement were seen as logical application of traditional military principles to the new weapons which had brought to fruition the weapons-effects revolution which had begun with the introduction of the rifled musket and conoidal bullet in the mid-nineteenth century. Little more effort was required for this analysis. The key question was "Why, with such tactical successes, had strategic victory eluded Ludendorff's grasp?"

What became evident to the German analysts was that the military technology of the nineteenth and twentieth centuries had vastly increased the power of weaponry, without a comparable enhancement of mobility in its employment. Apparently they recognized that there is a dynamic relationship among firepower, mobility, and dispersion,[2] and that a major change in firepower without comparable change in mobility would have two interrelated effects in the battlefield. To make up for inability to move reserves rapidly, historical trends toward greater dispersion, which usually go hand in hand with augmented firepower, were denied; the only alternative was to mass troops densely, as in earlier wars, while attempting to provide protection from the increased firepower by digging into the ground in trenches and dugouts. Secondly, with this emphasis on field fortification there could be no maneuver until a breakthrough was achieved; but with these fortifications supported by more lethal firepower, a breakthrough took so long to accomplish that the defenders could mass reserves behind the threatened defensive sector before the limited mobility means available to the attacker would permit a rapid exploitation. And so, after a horrible toll of casualties on both sides, a new trench stalemate would come into existence after an advance of a few hundred yards.

The General Staff had, of course, recognized these phenomena during the war and had devised the Hutier Tactics as a response. But despite the success of those new tactics at Riga, Caporetto, and the first few days of the Somme Offensive, victory had eluded the German grasp. Now, in retrospect, it was obvious why. To Seeckt the answer could be given in two words: inadequate mobility.

Just as the limitations on the speed, endurance, and mobility of the German infantry had kept Moltke from success in 1914 with his watered-down Schlieffen Plan, these same limitations had prevented the German Army from reaping the strategic fruits of tactical success in 1918.

This lack of battlefield mobility had had three major effects:

Once the battle groups of the Hutier Tactics had achieved the breakthrough, the Germans found themselves advancing across land that had been devastated by four years of war. Roads and bridges had been pulverized, deep trenches crisscrossed a countryside that had been churned into a mass of overlapping, water-filled shell craters. The Germans did not have the logistical mobility required to keep up a flow of ammunition, food, and other supplies to their troops advancing through a roadless quagmire.

Similarly, they had lacked strategic mobility. Not only were there no fast-moving mobile forces capable of exploiting the gap—a role which cavalry would have performed in earlier wars—they did not even have means to move large numbers of slower-moving infantry close behind the breakthrough troops, nor could they supply adequate reinforcements or replacements to those tiring soldiers.

Finally, once the breakthrough had been made, the frontline infantry soon outran its artillery, which was unable to advance in any significant numbers through the combat-zone morass. Because of this lack of firepower mobility, the advancing Germans lacked sufficient firepower to maintain the momentum of their drive after the British were finally able to move reserves into the gap, or to deal adequately with the British fighter planes strafing them.

Seeckt's intuitive belief that mobility would be the key to success in any future war was fully borne out by these historical studies of the General Staff. To many of the General Staff analysts it seemed evident that a British invention, the tank, would provide at least a partial answer to all three of these mobility deficiencies. The airplane, of course, could contribute to the requirement for mobile supporting firepower. Creating self-propelled artillery by mounting guns on track-laying vehicles and mounting truck bodies on caterpillar tracks would provide means for moving both men and supplies across country as easily as the tanks could move.

One young General Staff officer—Captain Heinz Guderian—was particularly impressed with the potentialities of using a combination of tanks and tractors to create fast-moving motorized infantry units which could gain the kind of victories which had slipped from German grasp on the banks of the Marne and Somme rivers. By 1924 he had earned a reputation as the Army's most ardent and vocal advocate of motorization and mechanization.

COOPERATION WITH RUSSIA / Meanwhile, continuing concern about Poland also led Seeckt to initiate one of his most controversial programs. For reasons that had historically caused Prussia and Russia to accommodate their differences to permit coordinated action against Poland, Seeckt came to the opinion that there must be, and would be, a rapprochement with Russia. While he carefully avoided meddling in political affairs, or in taking action that would force the hand of the German government, as early as mid-1920, when Russian forces were threatening Warsaw, he was sanctioning some clandestine conversations between members of his staff and some of General Michael Tukhachevski's staff, and was planning for possible intervention in Poland. Who took the initiative in the resultant Russo-German military talks is not clear, but it was probably the Germans.

In any event, soon after the Russian Army was finally defeated in the Russo-Polish War, Lenin secretly but officially sought German help in reorganizing the Red Army. Whether or not this request was a fruit of the earlier informal discussions held between Russian and German officers is not known, but Seeckt saw and seized an important opportunity. He established (and may have done so in anticipation of the request) a small planning and coordination group, including Colonel Nicolai, Colonel Hasse, Lieutenant Colonel von Hammerstein-Equord, and Lieutenant Colonel von Schleicher. Secret conversations were held in Berlin and Moscow. (In Berlin, Schleicher's apartment seems to have been the meeting place.)

On May 6, 1921, a German-Russian commercial agreement was signed. The military significance of the nonmilitary agreement was that there was soon thereafter established in Berlin the *Gesellschaft zur Förderung gewerblicher Unternehmungen*, or Company for the Promotion of Industrial Enterprises. A former officer, Major Fritz Tschunke, was its general manager. There followed the establishment of a Junkers aircraft factory near Moscow and the creation of a number of joint firms for the manufacture in Russia of various kinds of military equipment and ammunition. At the same time the Russian Army established several tank and flying schools, in which there were numerous but frequently changing German instructors, as well as some German students. A secret German military mission was established in Moscow, which was visited frequently by officers of the Troop Office planning and coordination group.

There were many results from this clandestine German-Russian military

cooperation. Not least was the political rapprochement, which Seeckt had anticipated, brought about by the Treaty of Rapallo, April 16, 1922. The Allies, who
had obtained some inkling of the military and industrial cooperation already
initiated, assumed that there were secret military clauses to this treaty, but
Seeckt publicly denied this. (After all, in the light of what was already going on,
there was no need for any such secret clauses which might later be made embar-
rassingly public.)

Militarily significant, of course, was the opportunity for German industry to
maintain its expertise in the production of military equipment (forbidden by the
Versailles Treaty), and in particular, to experiment in the development of
improved tanks and military aircraft. At least as important militarily was participation in schooling and military exercises with these forbidden weapons. Not the
least valuable was the opportunity to make some assessment of Russian military
affairs, procedures, and doctrines. Seeckt was satisfied that he was getting everything he had hoped for, as well as everything he had expected, from the clandestine contact with Soviet Russia.

COVERT RECOVERY OF THE GENERAL STAFF / Meanwhile Seeckt had
followed in the footsteps of his predecessors in giving perhaps more attention to
the preservation, improvement, and continuity of the General Staff than to any
other single military matter. There could be no formal courses for prospective
General Staff officers, since there could be neither a War Academy nor any overt
signs of a General Staff. But the same kind of selection process, by a combination of examination and the recommendations of higher commanders, was
carried on as had been the case for more than a century. And while there could
be no formal school, there were War Academy courses, as rigorous and demanding as ever. These were merely decentralized in two-year programs in the
seven district headquarters.

In addition, the most successful students, during the two years of intensive,
secret schooling in the districts, were assembled for a year of selected courses at
the University of Berlin. Close supervision was given by the Troop Office to the
district schools, and to the performance of the selected students at the university. It was not so satisfactory a system as the three-year War Academy had
been, but Seeckt considered that it was a reasonably effective substitute.

Even the repeated crises of 1923 did not keep Seeckt from giving close
personal supervision to these General Staff education activities, as well as to the
intensive training programs that were being carried out by the Army as a whole.
With a small army, Seeckt's aim was to assure a maximum capacity for wartime
expansion by seeing to it that every man could exercise leadership at a level one
or two grades above his peacetime rank. As time would tell, he was fully successful in accomplishing this.

THE CRISES OF 1923 / The year 1923 began ominously. On January 9, the
Allied Reparation Commission declared that Germany was in default on

deliveries of coal and timber, and two days later French and Belgian troops marched through the demilitarized zone to occupy the industrial region of the Ruhr. The German Army did not attempt to prevent the French action, but Seeckt was determined to fight if the French advanced farther into Germany. This seizure of Germany's richest industrial area, combined with French support of separatist movements in Bavaria and the Rhenish provinces, and intensification of threats from Poland—France's ally—led Seeckt to believe that France was attempting to break up Germany without recourse to war. In hopes that the message would reach Paris, he told the American Ambassador: "The distance from Dortmund to Berlin is indeed not great, but it leads through streams of blood." He outspokenly called the French invasion a violation of the Treaty, to justify hastily adopted German preparedness measures in defiance of the military provisions of the Treaty.

Despite his bold words and various overt and barely covert actions in obvious violation of the terms of the Versailles Treaty, Seeckt's estimates to Chancellor Wilhelm Cuno were realistically gloomy. Should war break out, he saw no possibility, even if the newly established and illegal volunteer reserve were to be called up, of ejecting the French from the Ruhr, and doubted if he could keep them from penetrating farther into Germany. If there should be a simultaneous Polish invasion, Silesia and East Prussia would be lost, and it was doubtful if Brandenburg and Berlin could be defended. But this assessment did not keep Seeckt from exerting every effort—within limits that would not bring British or American intervention—to be prepared for war on either or both fronts.

For several months there was a serious possibility that France might achieve the political and economic aims implicit in the Ruhr occupation and French political activities in Germany. The loss of the direct and indirect contribution of the Ruhr to the German economy, combined with the trade stagnation which resulted from German passive resistance to the occupation, brought Germany to the verge of bankruptcy, causing severe social unrest throughout the country and creating a real possibility that Bavaria would secede from the Republic. Germany suffered the most severe inflation in modern history; savings were wiped out; many people were close to starvation. A rash of violence spread across the country, mostly inspired by Communists.

The terrible economic situation brought about the fall of the Cuno government on August 12, 1923. Cuno was replaced by Dr. Gustav Stresemann, probably the most gifted statesman of the Weimar Republic.

Bowing to the inevitable, Stresemann on September 26 made a first move toward reaching an accommodation with France by ending the policy of passive resistance to the occupation of the Ruhr. This action of moderation, however, was castigated by conservatives as a sign of weakness and appeasement. The government of Bavaria, which, since the Kapp Putsch, had been dominated by rightists under the leadership of Gustav von Kahr, declared a state of emergency, and Kahr was appointed virtual dictator.

With Bavaria on the verge of secession, and right-wing unrest elsewhere threatening to become even more dangerous than the recent Communist-inspired troubles, Ebert and Stresemann called an all-night Cabinet session, attended by Seeckt. Early the next morning a state of emergency was declared, with Gessler given semidictatorial powers—exercised, of course, through Seeckt and the Army Command.

Although the principal threat to central authority was in Bavaria, the first challenge faced by Gessler and Seeckt came from an unexpected source. Major Ernst Buchrucker, who was in charge of a Work Command contingent in Silesia, attempted to seize control of Küstrin with his Black *Reichswehr*. His obvious intention was to establish a base for a march on Berlin. He apparently felt certain that he would be joined by most of the *Reichswehr*. After two days of defying national authority, on October 1 Buchrucker's adherents were dispersed with little bloodshed by local military forces, and he and several other ringleaders were arrested. Seeckt at once disbanded the Work Commands.

The Bavarian threat was more serious. The commander of District VII, General Otto Hermann von Lossow, joined Kahr in virtual defiance of central government authority, and in early October refused to obey Seeckt's orders to suppress the hate-spewing newspaper of Adolf Hitler's National Socialists, or Nazis. Seeckt and Gessler moved cautiously, trying to avoid, if possible, precipitation of an open break between Bavaria and the central government. On October 19 Seeckt ordered the dismissal of Lossow. In response, Kahr ordered Lossow to stay at his post as head of the Bavarian 7th Division, and ordered that division to swear allegiance to the Bavarian government, decreeing that the former oath of allegiance to the central government was no longer valid.

THE EMERGENCE OF ADOLF HITLER / While Seeckt and Gessler considered the possible consequences of moving troops into Bavaria to reestablish central authority, a new actor stepped on the national scene. Adolf Hitler, a former corporal of World War days and now leader of the National Socialist Party, had joined forces with General Ludendorff. This unlikely pair saw in the confrontation crisis an opportunity to seize power in Bavaria, and from this base to march on Berlin and overthrow the legal government. The result was the Beer Hall Putsch of November 8, which ended the next day with Hitler cowering on the ground under fire from loyal police, while Ludendorff, with gallant naïveté, ignored the rifle and machine-gun fire and, miraculously unharmed, for all practical purposes marched off the pages of history. At the last minute Lossow, recognizing that his secessionist course had the support of only a handful of his troops, had chosen to reaffirm his loyalty to the central government rather than join forces with Hitler.

Meanwhile, however, the Ebert-Stresemann government, unaware of the belated change of heart of the Bavarian commander, and assuming that Bavaria was in open revolt, had renewed the declared state of emergency, now placing dictatorial powers directly in the hands of General von Seeckt. A few days later, with order and central authority restored in Bavaria, and the Bavarian division completely responsive to Seeckt's directives, the General sought to return his emergency powers to the central government. Ebert and Stresemann, however, feared that more disorders of right or left might break out in other parts of Germany, and insisted that the Army and Seeckt retain executive responsibility throughout the nation. Not until late the following winter, on February 28, when internal peace and a measure of prosperity began to return to the nation, would the civilian leaders reluctantly accept back from an insistent Seeckt the responsibility for governing the nation.

SEECKT AND THE GERMAN ARMY / At the outset of the Bavarian crisis, during the Cabinet meeting of the evening of September 26, Seeckt made a remark which his detractors—and critics of the German General Staff—are fond of quoting as evidence of his dubious loyalty to the government. Ebert is described as turning to Seeckt and asking: "Will the Army stick to us, General?" The apolitical Seeckt is supposed to have replied proudly and condescendingly, "The Army, Herr President, will stick to *me*!"

Those were, approximately, the words spoken between President and General, but they were not all of the words. First Ebert had asked Seeckt about his personal views and attitudes with respect to the issues which had caused the right-wing clamor against the government. Seeckt calmly and firmly assured the President of his complete loyalty to the government. Then, when the President had asked his next question, about the reliability of the Army in this context, Seeckt's response meant that the Army, like its commander, was loyal to the government. He did not imply, or mean to imply, that the Army was loyal to the commander rather than to the government. Nor were his words so interpreted at the time by Ebert, Stresemann, or Gessler. Otherwise they would hardly have left Seeckt in the position of implementer of Gessler's semidictatorship, which was established that evening, nor would they six weeks later have conferred full dictatorial powers upon the General.

Although politically active, the next two years in Germany were otherwise relatively calm, and Seeckt took advantage of the circumstances to perfect still further the *Reichswehr* and its General Staff. During this period, however, his relations with Gessler cooled considerably. The Defense Minister thought he was too often ignored by Seeckt, who nonetheless relied upon him for explaining and protecting Army actions from critics in the *Reichstag* and the Allied Control Commission.

HINDENBURG AS PRESIDENT / On February 28, 1925, Ebert suddenly died, and on April 26 Paul von Hindenburg, now seventy-eight years old, was elected President of the Republic. The relationship between the old soldier and the younger general was cordial, but never close or intimate. Hindenburg apparently chose to forgive but not to forget that Seeckt—a protégé of his rival, Falkenhayn—had gained his fame in World War I as the architect of the Gorlice victory.

This was a Falkenhayn plan, adopted when the Emperor had overruled the plan that Hindenburg and Ludendorff had urged for a different kind of offensive further north.

But no hint of this past unpleasantness was now evident in the relationship between President and General. Hindenburg took a closer personal interest in military affairs than Ebert had, but while this sometimes created frustrations for Seeckt, on balance he found it easier, with Hindenburg's support, to persuade the government to adopt his point of view on policies that affected the *Reichswehr*. This in turn, however, increased the growing friction with Gessler.

Early in 1926 Gessler took a step which was designed to reduce these frictions, while providing him with a base for more effective surveillance of the Army. He established a new Armed Forces Section in the Defense Ministry, to assist him in liaison with the services, and to improve coordination between the Ministry and the Army and Navy Commands. Seeckt does not seem to have had any objection to this action, and probably recommended one of his most efficient subordinates—Colonel Kurt von Schleicher—as the chief of this branch. Seeckt had never had a close relationship with Schleicher—as he did, for instance, with Heye, Hasse, and Fritsch. But he recognized Schleicher's exceptional ability and efficiency, and had given him many important assignments during his period as Chief of the Troop Office and of the Army Command. This new position under Gessler seemed to Seeckt to be ideal for the political talents Schleicher had so clearly demonstrated.

There is no evidence that Seeckt expected Schleicher's appointment would have any purpose other than the liaison and coordination function intended by Gessler. The Chief of the Army Command seems to have made no effort to use Schleicher as his agent within the civilian apparatus of the Ministry. In fact, Schleicher maintained little contact with the Army Command other than his official duties. On the other hand, he seems quickly to have made himself indispensable to Gessler. While this did not bother Seeckt, there is some evidence that he was annoyed by the manner in which Schleicher was cultivating his old association with the President's son, Oskar von Hindenburg, and with Oskar's father, the old Field Marshal-President.

THE DOWNFALL OF SEECKT / Seeckt's leadership of the German Army came to a sudden and abrupt end in the early fall of 1926. During the summer Seeckt had authorized the participation of Prince William of Prussia—son of the former Crown Prince—to attend military maneuvers. While the Hohenzollerns were not banished from Germany, they were expressly forbidden by the Versailles Treaty to have any connection with the government or the Army. In addition, popular sentiment against the Hohenzollerns was strong in republican Germancy, and Germany was at the moment in political negotiations with the Allies about the withdrawal of the Allied Control Commission from Germany. Thus the political implications of the presence of the Prince, in Imperial Army uniform, could be such that Seeckt should have consulted with Defense Minister

Gessler before this was authorized, or should at least have informed the Defense Minister after he made the decision.

Gessler, however, first heard of the matter when a newspaper account of the Prince's attendance appeared on September 25. Already sensitive about the high-handed manner in which Seeckt was directing Army affairs without consulting him, Gessler rebuked the General, who responded with typical icy sarcasm. This led to Gessler's angry demand for Seeckt's resignation. This soon was endorsed by the Cabinet, Gessler receiving the full support of Foreign Minister Stresemann and Chancellor Marx.

Seeckt, however, assumed that Hindenburg would throw the weight of his personal prestige behind his Army commander, particularly on a matter involving the royal family, to which the President still expressed open loyalty. But Hindenburg—possibly influenced by Schleicher, who saw in the fall of Seeckt an opportunity to advance his own personal interests—told Seeckt that as a constitutional president he had no choice but to accept the recommendation of his Chancellor and Cabinet. Whether Hindenburg was sincere, or was motivated either by his long-suppressed jealousy of Seeckt, or by the machinations of increasingly influential Schleicher, will never be known. With some bitterness Seeckt submitted the demanded resignation, which was immediately accepted. General Wilhelm Heye was appointed Chief of the Army Command.

So ended the Seeckt era of the German Army—which might properly be called the Groener-Seeckt era, since Seeckt was the selected successor of Groener, carrying out with brilliance, firmness, and remarkable success policies which had their origins in Groener's brief but important tenure as the acting Chief of the General Staff. In less than eight years, the defeated German Army, on the verge of revolutionary collapse, had recovered its old reputation as the finest army in the world. This had been accomplished by two strong and gifted leaders who, during the process of reconstructing and revitalizing the Army, had also on several occasions saved the nation from political chaos, civil war, and probable dissolution.

These leaders had not appeared miraculously. They were available, and they were prepared to assume responsibility, through their orderly progression through the ranks of the German Army's Great General Staff. It is no criticism of either Groener or Seeckt to suggest that there were among their contemporaries on the Staff others who might have served just as well in their stead. However, through a process which almost invariably brought the finest minds and strongest characters to its leadership, the Staff was directed in these times of great crisis by these two men. Their decisions and actions—strong and personal though they were—reflected the studies, deliberations, and vigorous actions of the anonymous staff officers who continued to function with traditional efficiency, in automatic justification of the selection and training process initiated more than a century earlier by Scharnhorst.

NOTES TO CHAPTER THIRTEEN

[1] See Harold J. Gordon, *The Reichswehr and the German Republic, 1919-1926* (Princeton, N. J.: 1957), for an excellent discussion of the actions and attitudes of the senior officers and the rank and file of the Army during the putsch.

[2] See William G. Stewart, "Interaction of Firepower, Mobility and Dispersion," *Military Review,* March 1960.

Chapter Fourteen

INTO THE NAZI ABYSS

 HITLER AND THE GENERAL STAFF / Possibly more has been written about Adolf Hitler than about any other man of the twentieth century. Some writers attribute his rise primarily to the German generals and General Staff because of their cynical expectation that they could control and "use" him. Others suggest that the only effective center of resistance against Hitler was the Army, as demonstrated by the nearly successful General Staff plot against Hitler on July 20, 1944.

In fact, there was probably more opposition to Hitler in the Army than in any other major segment of German society, and more such opposition among General Staff officers than others. But it would be misleading to suggest that—with a few significant exceptions—this opposition was strong in the years before the war. And even when German defeat was inevitable, and individual General Staff officers were disproportionately numerous among the plotters against Hitler, the General Staff as an institution played no part in the conspiracy. Those who would suggest that the General Staff officers' opposition to Hitler was a belated reaction to his World War II failures in Russia simply ignore the fact that the General Staff as an institution, while opposed to the restrictions of the Versailles Treaty and favoring the rearmament of Germany, was almost continuously in opposition to Hitler on most other issues of military policy and strategy from 1933 onward. On the other hand, those who would suggest that, because of this opposition, the General Staff Corps was blameless in the establishment and maintenance of the Nazi dictatorship ignore the important support that Hitler received at crucial times from people like Werner von Blomberg, Walther von Reichenau, and Alfred Jodl. In particular, they are forced to overlook the fact that the one man most responsible for Hitler's rise—although unintentionally, perhaps even more responsible than Hitler himself—was Kurt von Schleicher, a General Staff officer who himself rose to prominence and power as a protégé of two illustrious leaders of the General Staff, Groener and Seeckt.

Since the story of Hitler's rise to power has been so often described, it will merely be summarized here, to provide the essential context for the

223

role of the General Staff in the rearmament of Germany between 1933 and 1939.

THE RISE OF SCHLEICHER / Schleicher was born on April 7, 1882, at Brandenburg, into an old Prussian-Brandenburg family. After graduation from a cadet school in 1900, he joined the 3rd Foot Guards—Paul von Hindenburg's old regiment—as a second lieutenant. He soon formed a close and significant friendship with his fellow second lieutenant, Oskar von Hindenburg, with whom he frequently visited General von Hindenburg's home. In 1910 Schleicher was selected for attendance at the War Academy, where he was in the same class with Kurt von Hammerstein-Equord. Both of these young men came to the attention of Lieutenant Colonel Wilhelm Groener, then on the General Staff, but a part-time instructor at the War Academy, who considered them the most gifted of the students he encountered while an instructor. Significantly, Groener seems to have thought that they had greater potential than another one of his brilliant students, Werner von Fritsch, two classes ahead of them.

In 1913, after completing his probationary service on the General Staff, Schleicher was appointed to the General Staff Corps, and was promoted to captain on December 18. During most of the war he served in Berlin or at OHL in Spa, as a member of the Great General Staff, although he did win an Iron Cross during a brief period of combat duty on the Eastern Front. He was promoted to major on July 15, 1918. While Schleicher had a reputation for above-average efficiency in a collection of officers of exceptional ability, he seems to have come unfavorably to the attention of Ludendorff, who apparently considered him too much of a dandy. However, when Groener replaced Ludendorff as First Quartermaster General in October 1918, he promptly appointed Major von Schleicher as his personal assistant. During the following winter and spring, Schleicher often carried documents and messages from Groener at Kassel (later Kolberg) to Ebert and Noske in Berlin and Weimar. He was beginning to know, and be known by, the leading military and political figures in Germany. He was a member of the special staff group appointed by Groener to supervise the organization and employment of the Free Corps, and later was a member of a similar group which Seeckt used to supervise and coordinate various clandestine activities of the Troop Office—including the relationship with Russia, and the establishment and operation of the Black *Reichswehr*.

Seeckt, who replaced Groener in 1919, seems to have felt little personal warmth for Schleicher, but, unlike Ludendorff, pragmatically made use of the younger officer's exceptional talents and efficiency. In fact, recognizing Schleicher's particular aptitude for political affairs and for dealing with politicians, Seeckt appointed him his personal assistant during the six-month period when the general was acting dictator of Germany. After that Schleicher, by then a lieutenant colonel, became first Chief of the Political Division of the General Staff, and then, as noted in the previous chapter, Chief of Gessler's new Armed Forces Section, to serve as liaison between the Ministry of Defense and the military services. Exploiting his many contacts throughout the government, and in particular his close friendship with the President, Schleicher's office soon became one of the most influential in Berlin.

There is no conclusive evidence that Schleicher contributed to the downfall of his old mentor, Seeckt. On the other hand, there is no conclusive evidence that he did not, and in the light of his penchant for both intrigue and ingratitude to his benefactors, it is hard to ignore Seeckt's firm belief that Schleicher was responsible.*

Schleicher's personal relations were much better with Seeckt's successor, General Heye, than they had been with "the Sphinx" (as Seeckt was widely known). No longer did Schleicher have to worry about Seeckt's cold, icy scrutiny of his activities, and his intrigues and influence began to grow rapidly.

Then, late in 1927, Defense Minister Gessler became indirectly (and probably innocently) involved in a financial scandal, during which his earlier involvement in Germany's clandestine rearmament became known. Schleicher was in no way involved in the unfortunate publicity, but he persuaded the President to seek Gessler's resignation. Then Schleicher strongly recommended retired General Groener as the new Minister of Defense. Hindenburg, somewhat guiltily aware that Groener had shouldered for him all blame and opprobrium for the General Staff decisions to withdraw army support for the Emperor and to recommend signing of the Treaty of Versailles, was not particularly eager to appoint Groener. However, he did want a military man as Defense Minister, and the only other name seriously recommended was that of Willisen. But Willisen categorically refused to allow himself to be considered as a rival candidate against his old War Academy instructor and General Staff Corps Chief. So the President followed the advice of his young friend, Schleicher, and Groener became Minister of Defense on January 20, 1928.

GROENER AS MINISTER OF DEFENSE / For more than two years there was complete harmony in the administration of German military affairs. Hindenburg —a former Chief of the General Staff—was President, and was extremely cordial to his Minister of Defense—also a former Chief of the General Staff. Groener, while typically vigorous and decisive in his performance as Defense Minister, was always careful to consult both the President and General Heye, the Chief of the Army Command, on all issues of military policy. His right-hand man—whom Groener often referred to as his adopted son—was Major General von Schleicher, who was able to make the wheels of policy turn even more smoothly through his own cordial relations with the President, with Heye and Hammerstein-Equord (who became Chief of the Troop Office in 1929) and with other important figures in the German government. Groener established for him a new section in the Ministry, the *Ministeramt,* or Ministry Office, to be concerned with all policy matters affecting both Army and Navy, and to act as liaison between the services and all other government ministries and political parties.

---

*For a different view of Schleicher, see Appendix D.

During 1929 Chancellor Hermann Müller was frequently ill. At the same time Foreign Minister Stresemann, also in ill health, spent most of his time at the Hague Conference. Thus Groener often found himself the acting Chancellor. Well aware of his own inexperience in both economics and politics, yet forced to deal with complex and serious issues created by the Great Depression, Groener was unhappy about this situation, and leaned more and more heavily on Schleicher—who gloried in this additional power and influence.

The Depression brought with it an increase in political unrest in Germany and led to a return of the kind of violence which had swept the country in the early 1920s. Debate in the *Reichstag* also became more shrill and antimilitary. Schleicher began to think seriously again of an idea which had appealed to him in the earlier period of unrest: the restoration of political and economic peace and stability in Germany through the establishment of a military dictatorship, thus preventing a possible revolutionary takeover by radical extremists of right or left.* Schleicher had been disappointed in 1923 and 1924 when Seeckt had refused to take advantage of his opportunities to seize control. But now, with a military man as President, the situation was even better than it would have been then. The Chancellor of such a government, controlling the nation by virtue of the same constitutional provision which had permitted Ebert to grant power to Seeckt, need not even be military. With Hindenburg as President, Groener as Defense Minister, and Schleicher pulling strings from behind the scenes (because he sought only power, no glory, for himself), it would be best to have a suitably promilitary—and docile—civilian Chancellor.

Schleicher's choice for Chancellor was Heinrich Brüning, who had served gallantly and with distinction as a junior officer during the war, and was known to be generally promilitary. Brüning rejected Schleicher's early overtures, but this did not deter the intriguing general, who consistently underestimated Brüning's strength of character. Schleicher continued to undermine Müller's position and, although it is not clear how much he contributed to it, the Chancellor resigned in March 1930. Groener had no idea of Schleicher's plans, but he admired Brüning, and advised Hindenburg to appoint him Chancellor. Prodded also by the direct urging of Schleicher, Hindenburg asked Brüning to form a Cabinet. However, not long afterward, the new Chancellor failed to receive a vote of confidence from the *Reichstag,* and he called for elections in September.

Through these elections Adolf Hitler again strode onto the stage of history.

HITLER'S ROAD TO POWER / After the suppression of his 1923 Munich putsch attempt, Hitler had been tried and convicted of treason. He was sentenced to prison for five years, but was pardoned after only nine months in detention. In prison he had leisure to think out fully his ideology and plans for creating a Nazi state, which he put down in his book, *Mein Kampf (My Struggle),* which was published after he was released. Although it was dull

---

*For elaboration of this idea, see Appendix D.

reading because of its style and attracted little attention at first, its sales multiplied with the growing strength of the Nazi movement during the next decade.

The chief lesson Hitler drew from the dismal failure of the Munich putsch was that violence, while it had important uses, was not the effective way to seize national power. He decided that he would have to become ruler of Germany by legal means, to avoid any possibility of another confrontation with the Army. His devotion to increasing his strength at the polls, and his avoidance of further putsch attempts, soon won him the nickname "Adolf Legality."

Nazi political strength rose and fell during the late 1920s and early 1930s with the sinking and rising of Germany's economic condition and international position. With increased prosperity and improved relations with Britain and France, as well as some easing of the reparations burden of the Versailles Treaty, in 1928 the Nazis could win only twelve seats out of about 600 in the *Reichstag,* the German parliament.

Hitler's great opportunity was the terrible worldwide Depression that struck Germany in 1930. The prosperity of the late 1920s was swept away, and desperation spread among Germans. Armed bands of Nazis and Communists bloodied and killed each other in the streets. Nazi party membership boomed; Nazi rallies attracted scores of thousands of screaming Germans. In the election of September 1930, supported by 6 million voters, the Nazis won 107 seats and became the second strongest party in the *Reichstag.* Hitler had by this time become a recognized national political leader and was accepted as a colleague by other leaders. Many were disgusted or amused by him, and some felt they could use him for their own purposes. But they respected his political power. So did the powerful industrialists who began to support him and who also thought they could use him.

Despite the Nazi election gains, Brüning was able to put together a coalition government, and so continued as Chancellor. Groener remained Defense Minister, having by this time established a close and cordial personal and working relationship with Brüning.

Groener was particularly alarmed by the Nazi election success. Earlier in the year his growing concern about the dangers of Nazism, and of Hitler's efforts to win support among the officers and men of the Army, had led him on January 22, 1930, to issue a general order warning of the Nazi menace. He pointed out the similarity of Nazism to the threat of Communism, and urged all officers and men to avoid involvement in politics. "The Army," he wrote, "has no other interest and no other task than service to the State. Therein lies the pride of the soldier and the best tradition of the past. . . . To serve the State—far from all party politics, to save and maintain it against the terrible pressure from without and the insane strife at home—is our only goal."

After the election Groener could see that the nationalistic propaganda of the Nazis, combined with Hitler's demagogic oratory, were making inroads into the Army. He recognized that there would be a terrible struggle ahead for the control of Germany and that the role of the Army would be crucial if the country was to be saved from Nazism. He began to prepare.

One of Groener's first moves, in the final months of 1930, was to persuade Heye to retire. Heye had been a loyal and effective deputy to Seeckt. However, he lacked the strong and decisive character which Groener knew would be needed to oppose—and if necessary fight—the Nazis. Heye loyally stepped down, permitting Groener, with Hindenburg's approval, to appoint his old student and faithful follower, Hammerstein-Equord, as the new Chief of the Army Command. General Wilhelm Adam, a division commander, was promoted to become the new Chief of the Troop Command. With this team—including Schleicher, who had always been most outspoken and contemptuous of Hitler and the entire Nazi crew—Groener felt he had the strength he needed in the Ministry and in the Army Command.

At the same time Groener began to realize that, despite his general order ten months earlier, Schleicher had been involved in some of the political maneuvering that had preceded the appointment of Brüning as Chancellor and the disastrous September elections. (Groener, however, did not as yet have any idea that Schleicher had also maneuvered for the fall of the Müller Cabinet.) He began to caution Schleicher against further dabbling in politics.

SCHLEICHER INTRIGUES WITH THE NAZIS / Unknown to Groener, however, Schleicher had already embarked on his most ambitious intrigue. The electoral strength of the Nazis could not be ignored. Some of their nationalistic aims were shared by almost every Army officer, and indeed by a majority of patriotic Germans. Schleicher sought a way, therefore, to turn the recent election results to the Army's advantage. He began to seek secret negotiating contacts with the Nazis.

The first Nazi approached by Schleicher was Ernst Röhm, who had been an infantry captain during the war and had later served in the Free Corps movement. Having become a follower and close friend of Hitler, Röhm had been made the head of the paramilitary force which Hitler had created as early as 1921—the *Sturmabteilungen* (SA), or Storm Troops—and had been able to make good use of his military training and experience in developing this SA into an effective, disciplined force supporting the political aims of the party. Over the years Röhm had retained a personal friendship with an old Army colleague and fellow Bavarian, Lieutenant Colonel Franz Halder, of the General Staff. Halder was no Nazi, and was never in the slightest involved in the rumors and scandals of homosexual activities in which Röhm was implicated. Whether or not Schleicher met Röhm through Halder is not clear; in any event the lieutenant colonel seems to have sat in on some of the secret meetings between the former captain and the lieutenant general.

It soon became evident to Schleicher that Röhm, while unreservedly and fervently loyal to Hitler, retained his love and respect for the Army. It was also clear to Schleicher that Röhm expected that Hitler would soon come to power, and that it was then Röhm's ambition to amalgamate the SA and the Army so that he could eventually become the Commander in Chief of this Nazified army.

The thought of linking their beloved Army with the SA toughs must have been repulsive to both of the Regular Army officers, but Schleicher was able to bring himself to discuss quite seriously with Röhm the possibility of a reserve role for the SA, to be amalgamated with the Army in time of war. In March 1931, the two men reached a formal but secret agreement on this. At that time neither of them dared to tell their superiors—Groener and Hitler—both of whom would have condemned the idea, although for very different reasons.

Meanwhile Schleicher had also been talking directly to Hitler and Goebbels, and to their emissaries, on more political matters. As time went on, Schleicher became more and more convinced that he could use, and then discard, these Nazis. The Goebbels diaries, however, show that the Nazi leaders were never under any illusions as to Schleicher's aims and aspirations. They trusted him even less than he did them, and they were planning to use, and then discard, *him.*

Hitler was at this time preparing for his first bid to take over the government by legal means. He had the temerity to challenge Hindenburg for the Presidency. The Field Marshal probably would not have considered running for reelection had he not been easily (and probably correctly) convinced by Brüning, Schleicher, and others that he was perhaps the only person who could prevent Hitler from being elected President.

In the election of March 13, 1932, Hindenburg received a substantial plurality over Hitler and several other candidates, but failed to get the majority required by the Constitution. After a bitter campaign of vilification, a rerun on April 10 gave Hindenburg approximately 19 million votes over Hitler's 13 million and Communist Ernst Thälmann's 3 million. To Schleicher, satisfied with the clearcut victory of the near-senile Field Marshal, the substantial size of Hitler's vote also confirmed to him the wisdom of his continuing appeasement of the Nazis, at least temporarily. But since the idea of Chancellor Hitler was almost as abhorrent to him as President Hitler, Schleicher knew that, if he was ever to achieve his idea of a military dictatorship under Hindenburg, he did not have much time left—if only because of the Field Marshal's age and failing health.

SCHLEICHER BRINGS DOWN GROENER AND BRÜNING / At the same time Groener had becomed alarmed by preelection activities of Röhm's SA and of Heinrich Himmler's SS (*Schutzstaffel,* Defense Detachment), an elite group of the SA who formed Hitler's bodyguard. Not only had they tried to influence the voting by force and intimidation, but papers confiscated by the police demonstrated that they were prepared to seize physical control of the government if Hitler won the election. On the day after the elections, therefore, Groener and Brüning obtained Hindenburg's approval of the dissolution of the two uniformed Nazi organizations. (To Brüning this action was also valuable in demonstrating to the League of Nations Disarmament Conference the truth of the official German position in refusing to include the Storm Troops in calculations of Germany's military strength.)

Schleicher, for reasons not fully clear, opposed the planned dissolution of the Nazi troopers. Possibly he so overestimated his friendship with Röhm as to believe that he would win the Storm Troopers away from Hitler in a crisis. In any event, Schleicher was able to persuade Hindenburg to change his mind about the dissolution order. Groener, however, was finally able to persuade Hindenburg to take the proper course, but only at the expense—for the third time in their lives—of personally assuming all responsibility for a policy and an action for which Hindenburg should have been responsible.

The order was issued on April 14, and Groener was immediately subjected to a violent campaign of Nazi vilification, supported by many patriotic but naïve Germans who believed Nazi propaganda.

By this time Groener was beginning to realize that Schleicher, with the somewhat reluctant support of Hammerstein, was undercutting him not only in his official relations with the President, but also within the Army. The Defense Minister considered dismissing both of these officers—once the most favored of all of his protégés—but decided against it until the new Brüning Cabinet was more firmly in control. This was a sad mistake, because Schleicher was by this time deep in intrigue with Röhm, Goebbels, and Hitler, and had in fact promised the Nazis that he would get rid of both Groener and Brüning. This conspiracy was unknown to Hammerstein and the other senior officers who had been turned against Groener by Schleicher's misrepresentations. At the same time the Nazis had also secretly decided to get rid of Schleicher after he disposed of Brüning and Groener.

When the *Reichstag* reopened on May 10, Groener was bitterly and cruelly attacked by the Nazis for his dissolution of the SA and SS. In defending himself against the gibes of Goering and his catcalling adherents, without any significant support from the non-Nazi delegates, Groener allowed himself, without adequate preparation, to be trapped into a violent and emotional debate. When he was not being shouted down by the Nazis, his stammering, stumbling appeals to the remainder of the *Reichstag* fell flat. After the embarrassing session, Schleicher brutally told him that he had lost the confidence of the Army, and must resign. Groener assumed that in this showdown with his former "adopted son" he would have the support of Hindenburg, but the Field Marshal blandly protested his inability to intervene. Groener resigned on May 13. Seventeen days later Schleicher achieved his second promised objective: Hindenburg abruptly dismissed Brüning as Chancellor.

By this time the nature of Schleicher's intrigues began to be known and understood by a number of Germans in and out of the Army. A grim joke about him began to circulate in Berlin: the General should have been an admiral, since his military genius consisted of shooting torpedoes under water at his friends. It took months and years, however, before the full scope and implications of Schleicher's duplicity were fully understood within the Army. But by the time Hammerstein ruefully tendered his apologies to Groener, it was too late to close the floodgates Schleicher had opened.

SCHLEICHER BRINGS DOWN THE WEIMAR REPUBLIC / During the next eight months Schleicher was in the middle of the intrigues, conspiracies, and political maneuverings that brought about the downfall of the Weimar Republic. Following his suggestion, Hindenburg chose former Army officer Franz von Papen as Chancellor. Papen had gained notoriety during the war when, as military attaché in Washington, he had ineptly coordinated the German subversive activities that helped bring the United States into the war on the other side. Papen, a clever but shallow aristocrat, had not gained any political maturity in the intervening years. Neither he nor his Defense Minister—Kurt von Schleicher— was able to build any support in the *Reichstag* or in the populace as a whole. Papen was forced to call a new general election.

True to his promise to his Nazi friends, Schleicher was able on June 15 to get President von Hindenburg to rescind the order disbanding the SA and the SS. The methods of persuasion and intimidation of these Nazi bullies undoubtedly contributed to the fact that in the election of July 13 the Nazis won 230 seats out of 608 in the *Reichstag,* giving them the largest representation of any single party—and the largest the Nazis had achieved, or would ever again achieve, in democratic elections.

Hindenburg refused to consider appointing Hitler as Chancellor, and the Nazis would not enter into a coalition under the leadership of any other party. The only possible combination of parties that could form a majority of the *Reichstag* without the Nazis would have had to include the Communists, and this the Social Democrats—with the second largest representation—would not do. In this political stalemate, Papen, like Brüning before him, continued to govern under the emergency provisions Article 38 of the Constitution, while Schleicher entered into complex maneuvering in which he alternated working for and against both Hitler and Papen. The situation was not basically changed by new elections on November 6 in which the Nazis and Social Democrats lost a few seats, while the Communists gained a few. The political stalemate continued.

In an effort to break the deadlock, Hindenburg was finally persuaded by Schleicher to offer the Chancellorship to Hitler, but under terms the Nazi leader would not accept. Meanwhile, Schleicher had been typically undermining Papen's influence with the Field Marshal. Finally, in desperation, Hindenburg offered the Chancellorship to Schleicher. The general had sought to avoid this responsibility, but, unable to wiggle out of it, he accepted on December 2, 1932.

However, as Chancellor, Schleicher was even less successful in conciliating the opposing parties than he had been previously. He was deserted by former friends and political allies, and Papen turned the tables on him by undermining his influence with the President. After one of the shortest and least productive Chancellorships in German history, Schleicher resigned on January 28.

HITLER TO POWER / Two days later Hindenburg again offered the Chancellor-ship to Hitler. This time the Nazi leader accepted, even with Hindenburg's condi-tion that Papen should be his Vice-Chancellor. So it was Schleicher's double-crossing maneuvering that brought to power Hitler—the man he had been attempting to outmaneuver for more than a year—along with the latest enemy he had created by his torpedoing skill. Groener and Brüning, or either man alone, were tough enough and for a while powerful enough to have stopped Hitler. But Hitler had been able to make skillful use of Schleicher to destroy the power and effectiveness of those two major opponents, and then he found it easy to destroy Schleicher's power. Being a man who neither forgave nor forgot, Hitler would soon find the opportunity to destroy Schleicher himself.

As Minister of Defense, Hitler appointed Lieutenant General Werner von Blomberg, a General Staff Corps officer who had become a great Hitler admirer. Blomberg, promoted to General of Infantry on January 30, in turn appointed Walther von Reichenau, another pro-Nazi General Staff Corps officer, as Chief of the *Ministeramt.* Hitler, of course, approved.

A month after Hitler took office, his power was consolidated in a dramatic way. The *Reichstag* building, symbol of German constitutional government, went up in flames on the night of February 27, 1933.

Although the Nazis were never able to make a convincing case for their contention that a Communist conspiracy was back of the fire, Hitler immediately seized upon it as a pretext for complete suppression of the Communist Party. At the same time, he used the suppression of the Communists as a pretext of suppressing all the guarantees of personal liberties in the German Constitution.

Even so Hitler was still not able to get a majority in the elections that spring. By arresting the Communist *Reichstag* members and by skillfully persuading a few others, he was able to gain passage of a law giving him dictatorial powers. This was the beginning of his reign of twelve years as the absolute ruler of Germany, under the title of *Führer,* or Leader.

Hitler at once began an intensive campaign to get the support and loyalty of the Army. It was strikingly successful. While most senior officers seem to have retained their contempt for Hitler as a person, a majority of these approved his openly stated objective of freeing Germany from the shackles of the Versailles Treaty—and were particularly pleased with the emphasis he put upon the necessity for eliminating the constraints on German military power. With the younger officers he was even more successful, since his revolutionary program won the admiration as well as the respect of most of the company-grade officers not already attracted by his ultranationalism.

Hitler soon demonstrated to the Army the seriousness of his determination to remove all restrictions on German rearmament. He approved the Army's plan for a covert expansion to twenty or twenty-one divisions over three years. When the League of Nations Disarmament Conference would not accept Germany's demand for equal consideration with the World War I Allies, Hitler withdrew German representation from the conference, and withdrew from the League of Nations on October 14, 1933.

BECK AS CHIEF OF STAFF / It was about this time that Blomberg, with Hitler's approval, made two major appointments in the Army High Command.

On October 1 he appointed Lieutenant General Ludwig Beck to be the new Chief of the Troop Office—in other words, Chief of the General Staff. Beck, then fifty-three years old, was widely regarded in the Army as one of the most brilliant officers of the General Staff Corps. He had also won the favor of the Nazi Party because, a few years earlier when he was an artillery regimental commander, he had testified sympathetically in favor of two of his younger officers who had been court-martialed as Nazi propagandists. Actually he had no strong feeling for or against the Nazis; he had merely wanted to assure a fair trial for his officers.

A few weeks after Beck's appointment to the Troop Office, Blomberg appointed youthful (forty-five years old) Colonel Friedrich (Fritz) Fromm as Chief of the newly established General Army Office. Fromm was a General Staff officer who had demonstrated great efficiency while serving under Schleicher in the *Ministeramt,* and had then been assigned to the General Army Office when it was created to coordinate a 50,000 man secret Army expansion that had been planned by Brüning and Schleicher.

Thus Beck and Fromm were the two men who would have the major responsibility for the resurrection of the German Army in the next few years. Significantly, Hammerstein had not been consulted about either of these appointments, even though they were the two most important positions in his Army Command.

By January 1934, Hammerstein recognized his own impotence in the new command arrangements, and also began to realize the extent of his own personal responsibility for the results of his failure to back Groener and his blind support of Schleicher. He resigned. A man of great intelligence, honesty, and nobility, Hammerstein was the victim of minor flaws in his character, compounded by circumstances over which he had no control. He was extremely lazy and thus failed to make full use of his exceptional talents; he was for more than a year the blind and willing follower of the less intelligent but more energetic Schleicher. Later—perhaps to a greater degree than any other German general and earlier than most—he had the strength of character and will to act against Hitler; but by then (1934) it was too late, and he never again had the opportunity which he had let slip.

Blomberg decided that Reichenau—who had been promoted to Major General on January 1—should replace Hammerstein as Chief of the Army Command, but the appointment of such a junior general was strongly opposed by most of the senior officers of the Army. They were also suspicious of Reichenau's ardent advocacy of National Socialism, and were embarrassed by his over-eagerness to project a nonconformist, "one of the boys" personality. This was not the kind of man most German generals wanted as the senior officer of the German Army. Hindenburg, in fact, needed no prodding to reach the same conclusion.

FRITSCH AS ARMY CHIEF / Reichenau's name was not approved. Instead, the new Chief of the Army Command, appointed February 1, 1934, was

Lieutenant General Baron Werner von Fritsch, a brilliant, intellectual staff officer and one of Seeckt's favorite assistants. As future events would demonstrate, Fritsch was one of those competent staff officers who lack the decisive strength of character needed for strong leadership in times of crisis. Like most other German Army officers, he shared the anti-Versailles, rearmament aims of the Nazis, and was willing to go along with Hitler—retaining the view, still cherishing by most of the German generals, that they had it in their power to terminate Hitler's regime, should they ever deem it necessary. He was also confident that he and his hardheaded, clear-sighted subordinates in the General Staff could restrain what he sometimes called the "youthful exuberance" of Hitler and his henchmen.

Fritsch's principal concern about the Nazis at this time was Röhm's persistent effort to carry out the scheme he had so often discussed with Schleicher: to amalgamate the Army and the SA into a new German Army, which Röhm would dominate. Aside from the dangerous dilution which such a merger would cause in the superb quality of the small Army Fritsch had inherited from Seeckt and Hammerstein, the idea of Röhm and his gangster and blatantly homosexual associates as participating members of the Army High Command was totally unacceptable to Fritsch—and even to such pro-Nazi alumni of the General Staff as Blomberg and Reichenau.

Hitler was aware of these strong Army views about the SA. Since he was anxious to continue his own partially successful efforts to win the ungrudging support of the Army and since (assisted by constant reminder from Himmler) he had never forgiven Röhm for his secret negotiations with the hated Schleicher, Hitler decided to sacrifice Röhm and the SA for the sake of expediency as well as harmony with the Army. And this, Hitler decided, would be no nominal political sacrifice; it would be a literal blood offering.

HITLER'S BLOOD PURGE, DEATH OF SCHLEICHER / To what extent Fritsch or any of his close associates were aware of the plans of Hitler and Himmler is not known. It is almost certain that they did not realize the enormity of what was about to happen. On the other hand, Fritsch must at least have had some inkling, since on Monday, June 25, he placed the Army on alert. At dawn on Saturday, June 30, there began two days of cold-blooded, officially instigated murder worthy of comparison with the Massacre of St. Bartholomew's Day. Among the first to be gunned down—although hundreds of miles apart at the time—were Röhm and General and Mrs. von Schleicher. In Röhm's case, in Munich, it was Hitler himself who made the arrest and ordered the execution. In Berlin, Goering, with a smirk, told reporters that he had ordered Schleicher's arrest and that the general was killed in resisting. The exact number killed in those thirty-six hours of horror will never be known, but at a postwar trial of some of the SS murderers in 1957, it was established that there were more than 1,000 victims,* including another

---

*Other sources, however, insist that there were no more than 100 victims.

retired general and General Staff officer, Kurt von Bredow, who had been associated with Schleicher.

During this time of officially sponsored lawlessness, Army units remained on alert in their barracks, paying no attention to the sounds of gunfire, interspersed with occasional bomb explosions, that could be heard in every city and a number of rural regions throughout Germany. In a General Order issued on Monday, July 2, Defense Minister von Blomberg "congratulated the Führer [who] has personally attacked and wiped out the mutineers and traitors with soldierly decision and exemplary courage."

If December 24, 1918, had been the low point in the operational history of the German Army, the days of the weekend of June 30-July 2, 1934, when it literally condoned mass murder, were the most shameful—thus far. Whatever one may think of Schleicher, he was neither a mutineer nor a traitor (a charge repeated by Hitler in a speech to the *Reichstag* on July 13). During and immediately after the carnage, aged Field Marshal von Mackensen, and former Chief of the Army Command General von Hammerstein-Equord, were the only military men to speak out boldly. On June 30 Mackensen had tried to reach Hindenburg to get him to stop the slaughter, but under orders from Hitler, the dying President was well shielded from reality. Soon after the purge Hammerstein boldly initiated a movement, which had the enthusiastic but muted support of many other Army officers, to clear the names of Schleicher and Bredow from the false charges of treason. Hammerstein eventually succeeded in this, but ironically it was a success that also—as we shall see—cleared from equally false charges the name of Fritsch, the soldier who more than any other had cause to be ashamed of the accusations against Schleicher and Bredow.

It must be noted, however, that there were a number of active officers who strongly felt that shame, and who would probably have acted if they had had the opportunity to do so. Perhaps most important among these was General Ludwig Beck, the new Chief of the General Staff.

DEATH OF HINDENBURG, HITLER AS FÜHRER / On August 2, 1934, one month after Hitler's blood purge, aged President von Hindenburg finally died. Hitler at once announced that, as "Führer and Chancellor," he was assuming all of the functions and authority of the Presidency. Next day Blomberg had every officer in the armed forces swear a new oath of allegiance—to Hitler personally rather than to the office of the Presidency or to the State. It has been suggested by later writers that this was Blomberg's idea. However, Hindenburg's death had long been foreseen. It would be surprising if Hitler, recognizing the mystical significance of such an oath to the tradition-conscious German officer corps, had not already planted this idea in Blomberg's head.

But if Hitler understood the potential implications of the oath, few did among the officers who took it. Possibly Beck was beginning to recognize that the interests of Hitler and the Army did not coincide, as so many other Army officers were assuming. But if he did, the demands on his time were such that he gave it little thought.

By this time Beck was already beginning to raise the position of Chief of the Troop Office from the obscurity into which it had fallen when Seeckt had moved to the position of Chief of the Army Command and had virtually taken with him the traditional role of Chief of the General Staff. Fritsch, for all of his General Staff experience and technical competence, was not a Seeckt. And in Beck he had a subordinate who understood and took seriously the responsibilities which Seeckt had originally given to the Chief of the Troop Office. Fritsch had no objection to this, nor did he ever have reason to feel that Beck was trying to usurp his responsibility. The two men worked closely and well together in the task of building a new German Army.

THE REARMAMENT OF GERMANY / By this time the rearmament of Germany was real and undisguised, with only occasional lip service to the Treaty limitations. The Allies protested, but did nothing—other than a British invitation to Germany to send representatives to London early in February 1935 for a fruitless discussion of German rearmament. On March 16, 1935, Hitler repudiated the disarmament clauses of the Versailles Treaty. At once the fiction of "Troop Office" was discarded. Beck assumed the title of his true position—Chief of the General Staff—and the name of his staff organization was changed accordingly.

Beck was a Rhinelander who—with typical General Staff objectivity—carefully selected his subordinates and approved new additions to the General Staff Corps with no consideration to their geographic origins. He was an austere intellectual in the Schlieffen-Seeckt tradition. Like a high percentage of German General Staff Corps officers who reached top command and staff positions in the twentieth century, he was an artilleryman.

When he became the Chief of the General Staff, Beck was glad to join Fritsch in the development of plans for a threefold expansion of the German Army, in defiance of the Treaty, and to begin to put those plans into action in the late months of 1933 and early 1934. He was particularly interested in the new *Offizierlehrgange,* or officer courses, which Hammerstein and Adam had established in Berlin, to centralize the hitherto-dispersed General Staff training in the districts. Beck began to transform this training into a true revival of the old War Academy.

On March 16, 1935, when Hitler denounced the Versailles Treaty's armament limitations, he announced that the Army would immediately be increased to 550,000 men in thirty-six divisions. Beck strongly opposed these new force goals. He favored an initial increase of the Army to a strength of some 300,000 men in about twenty or twenty-one divisions over a period of two or three years, with a slow and gradual increase after that to a maximum strength of about 500,000 in the early 1940s. In this way the conscripts could be well trained while the quality of the Army could be maintained by an intensive but orderly expansion of the officer corps. Like Seeckt, Beck felt that large numbers of men were merely cannon fodder if they were not well led, and he wanted to maintain the same high leadership standards that Seeckt had established.

Hitler did not understand the problems of providing leadership, facilities, and support services for an increased army. Germany had the manpower; as far as he was concerned, all that was necessary to make a larger army was to put these men in uniform and give them weapons. He made it very clear to Blomberg, Fritsch, and Beck that he considered their arguments about the time-consuming training of officers to be military pedantry. Any good Nazi, he insisted, would automatically be a good combat leader through his fanatic, patriotic zeal. Beck could not get Hitler to reduce the announced force goals, but he dug in his heels on the issue of the time required to train an officer. With Blomberg and Fritsch in full support of Beck on this issue, Hitler gave in, but he continually harassed the Army leaders, demanding greater speed in the military buildup.

In 1935, with the need for subterfuge ended, Beck could announce the reestablishment of the War Academy. This announcement, however, did not ease the problem of assembling an adequate staff of instructors, which had plagued the *Offizierlehrgange*. The multitudinous requirements for well-qualified officers in the rapidly expanding Army had already strained the resources of the General Staff to the breaking point. Beck solved the problem by using mostly retired General Staff Corps officers in the permanent faculty, with active-duty officers coopted for frequent lectures and seminars. As in the past, major emphasis was put on the study of military history, with retired Colonel Kurt Hesse a principal instructor. Under Hesse, for the first time, the War Academy paid serious attention to the campaigns of the American Civil War. Hesse believed that the fast-moving campaigns of Stonewall Jackson and Ulysses S. Grant were particularly appropriate subjects for study by the leadership of an increasingly mobility-conscious German Army.

FROMM OF THE GENERAL ARMY OFFICE / Meanwhile, the administrative base for the Army's buildup was being developed by one of modern Germany's most efficient and unsung leaders: Colonel Friedrich Fromm (who preferred to sign his name as Fritz).

When Fromm became Chief of the General Army Office he stepped into the third most important position in the German Army, after Fritsch and Beck. The General Army Office had, in fact, been quite recently created for the purpose of coordinating the anticipated expansion of the Army, with responsibilities for force development, organization, and armament. (Schleicher and Brüning had been planning an Army expansion of 50,000 men.) The new office was at least theoretically coequal with the other four principal divisions of the Army Command: the Troop Office (or General Staff), the Personnel Office, the Ordnance Office, and the Administrative Office. Before World War I such a staff agency would have been a division within the General Staff, but apparently Schleicher and Hammerstein, who were responsible for creating the office, were reluctant to offend the Allies doubly by putting an organization created to defy many of the Treaty provisions within an agency that was in itself such defiance. So Blomberg appointed a competent, experienced, but relatively youthful General Staff Corps officer—who in other times would have been a fourth or fifth Quartermaster General—to head this new agency, and his relatively junior rank indicated his relative junior status among the five divisions of the Army Command.

Fromm, however, soon demonstrated that he considered himself subordinate only to the Chief of the Army Command, and on matters affecting his areas of responsibility he insisted on being consulted, or taking the lead, even when the Chief of the General Staff was involved.

Fromm's experience in serving under Schleicher in the *Ministeramt*, combined with his General Staff training and experience, and his routine service in combat and low-level staff units during the war, had given him an exceptionally broad background ideally suited for his present duties. He was, incidentally, a product of the General Staff selection and experience program of the war, and had gone through the Sedan Course of General Staff instruction. Thus, to an exceptional intelligence he added varied troop experience in peace and combat, staff experience from the lowest to highest levels of the Army, and a period of service in the *Ministeramt* where he had dealt successfully with interrelated budgetary, fiscal, and political matters. It was his skillful performance in this office, in fact, which had led Schleicher to help arrange for his appointment as Chief of the General Army Office.

To this skill, experience, and intelligence were added a forceful, tough, but pleasing and diplomatic personality. Fromm soon demonstrated that he had that important but rare quality of being able to delegate authority without losing control. Like many of his contemporaries who had survived the bloodbath of World War I, he was skeptical of old methods of warfare and eager to experiment with any product of new technology that gave promise of avoiding the trench stalemate of 1914-1918. Also, like members of that relatively small generation, he had an open mind about National Socialism. That generation was small because the war experience had imprinted a unique outlook on young men who had been born between 1885 and 1895. The generation was made even smaller because it had sustained most of the losses of the war.

By the end of 1933, very soon after his appointment to his new post, Fromm had reached some definite conclusions about how the Army expansion, which Hitler had already secretly directed, should be carried out. These views were far from identical with those then held by General Beck. Fromm understood and shared Beck's concern about the dangers of too rapid expansion, which would so dilute the carefully created quality of the 100,000-man Army that all of the results of Seeckt's careful plans and preparations would be washed out. He particularly understood why Beck insisted that the combat effectiveness of the Army had to be preserved at all cost during the period of expansion when the Allies might feel impelled to intervene before that expansion went too far; a small but powerful army would be a greater deterrent to Allied invasion than a large but helpless force.

But Fromm pointed out that there were other considerations. Perhaps the most important of these was the chaotic and totally disorganized and unprogrammed relationship of the government and industry at a time when major military expansion was planned. While Beck and the General Staff were slowly developing plans and requirements for a gradually phased Army increase, the Navy and the Air Force were rushing to industry with plans long made in anticipation of the lifting of the Versailles limitations. And Goering, who was the Commander in Chief of the still-secret *Luftwaffe,* was also the second man in the Nazi Party, and the coordinator of a four-year plan of industrial development that Hitler had decreed. Thus he had already identified and alerted a number of industrial firms to gear themselves for air-force production. If the Army did not soon place its orders for its needed new weapons, the other services would exhaust the limited capacity of German industry (of which only a few firms had been involved in small-scale clandestine armament production).

With typical General Staff thoroughness and imagination, Fromm and the handful of General Staff officers who had been assigned to the General Army Office, developed a plan, which he submitted early in 1934 to Fritsch—with a copy to Beck. For a number of administrative reasons—with the question of industrial capacity foremost—Fromm urged the Army Command to take advantage of Hitler's desire for massive expansion, by "stretching the frame of the Army" as far as possible. This would assure the establishment of industrial, technological, and economic requirements which the Army could justify as consistent with long-range expansion and mobilization plans. There was, as he pointed out, a substantial stock of World War I weapons available for equipping such a hastily raised mass Army. But, recognizing the problems that worried Beck, he recommended that expansion be carried out in two simultaneous, parallel programs. One of these, using the majority of the 100,000-man Army as its base, would be a relatively slow expansion of the quality Army demanded by Beck, limited in its growth by the combined availabilities of well-trained junior officers and of the new mobile equipment and weapons which then existed only in prototypes or on drawing boards. The other would be less an expansion than it was the creation of a wholly new mass army, using small cadres from the 100,000 man Army and the old, obsolescent weapons still in storage.

Beck was at first completely opposed to this idea, and this resulted in friction and arguments with Fromm that were to persist to the day of Beck's tragic death and Fromm's downfall. However, the Organizational Branch of the General Staff was very favorably impressed with the Fromm plan, and was able to muster logical arguments which caused the objective and capable Chief to change his mind. Still furious with what he considered to be the brash insolence of a relatively junior General Staff officer, Beck nevertheless finally adopted the Fromm plan, and jointly presented it with him to Fritsch. The Chief of the

Army Command had, of course, been aware of Fromm's ideas from the beginning, and he also had come to the conclusion that it should be adopted.

BEGINNING OF THE PANZER FORCE / Accordingly, in June 1934, a new Motorized Troops Command was created, under General Oswald Lutz. Upon Fromm's strong recommendation, the Chief of Staff of this new command was his old friend and contemporary, Colonel Heinz Guderian.

Guderian, who had briefly attended the War Academy just before the war (1913-1914), was also a product of the General Staff's Sedan Course. In the years immediately after the war, he had made himself the German Army's leading specialist in, and champion of, armored warfare. His staff and command appointments in motorized commands and offices were covers for clandestine work in developing an organization, doctrine, and techniques for tank forces and tank warfare.

During the next year, despite the coolness between Fromm and Beck, there was close coordination among Guderian, Fromm, and Colonel Georg von Soderstern, Chief of the Organization Branch of the General Staff, in the preparation of requirements for tanks, light-artillery pieces, antitank guns, trucks, weapons carriers, field radios, and other new equipment for the Motorized Command. Prototypes were tested, modified, or rejected, and orders were placed with industry when the models were finally approved and accepted.

By the late summer of 1935 a provisional armored—or panzer—training division was operational, and after four weeks of intensive training, went through a series of tactical exercises under the watchful eyes of Generals von Blomberg, von Fritsch, and Beck. Also present were Fromm, Sodenstern, and the newly appointed Chief of the Operations Division of the General Staff, Colonel Erich von Manstein, who had been recommended for this post by Fritsch, his former commanding officer.

Soon after these maneuvers, the name of the Motorized Troops Command was changed to Armored Troops Command, with Lutz still in command and Guderian his Chief of Staff. A few days later, on October 15, 1935, three new panzer divisions were established and Guderian, still only a colonel, was given command of one of these.

This was the beginning of the new elite component of the Army as visualized in Fromm's plan. By this time it was evident that Britain and France would not take any action in response to the German rearmament in defiance of the Versailles Treaty. Thus there was no longer any reason to hide the existence of a German armored service, or the creation of new armored divisions. And both France and Britain were reassured when Hitler solemnly promised that Germany would strictly observe all of the other provisions of the Versailles Treaty. In fact, he had already ordered Beck to prepare plans for German occupation of the Rhineland.

OCCUPATION OF THE RHINELAND / The Treaty specifically stated that the entry of German troops into the Rhineland would be considered a "hostile act" by the Allies. But while France and Britain were preoccupied in 1936 with the threat to international peace posed by Mussolini's attack on Ethiopia, Hitler saw an opportunity to carry out the next step of his program. He ordered the Army to seize control of the Rhineland. Both Fritsch and Beck urged Hitler to postpone this move until the new Army buildup was complete. However, Hitler insisted, promising that the occupying troops could be withdrawn if France responded with force.

When the German troops marched in, on March 7, 1936, France and Britain protested. But the closest thing to forceful action was the massing of thirteen French divisions near the German border, in a defensive posture. For a while, however, the French intentions were unclear, and Blomberg, upon Beck's recommendation, urged withdrawal. Hitler refused. He later said that the forty-eight hours after the march into the Rhineland were the most nerve-racking of his life, but he stood firmly and successfully by his bold bluff. He understood that the psychological irresolution of France and Britain would count for more than the great superiority of their armed forces.

Hitler's timing was perfect. Without firing a shot, Germany gained the military base from which France would be attacked four years later. In celebration of his triumph and also his birthday, on April 20, 1936, Hitler promoted Blomberg to the rank of Field Marshal, Fritsch to Colonel General. Hermann Goering also became a Colonel General in the *Luftwaffe* and Erich Raeder a General Admiral in the Navy.

Beck and several other Army generals (possibly including Fritsch) were prepared to overthrow Hitler if France invaded the Rhineland. But the complete success of the occupation was hailed throughout Germany. Even the General Staff officers, who knew how risky the move had been, could not help respecting Hitler's judgment and nerve.

Hitler had always, since *Mein Kampf* days, seen Fascist Italy as a potential ally in his plans for European domination. For that reason he had excluded the German minority group in northern Italy from his plans for gathering in the *Volksdeutsche,* all the German-speaking peoples of Europe. Mussolini, however, had some ambitions for gaining territory in the Danube area that conflicted with Hitler's plans, and had shown that he regarded any union of Germany and Austria as a threat to his own security in Italy. A brief and brutal attempt by Austrian Nazis to take over Austria's government in 1934 had ended when Mussolini massed Italian troops at the Austrian border. Hitler had been forced to disclaim any responsibility for the putsch attempt. Despite this, however, the Nazi and Fascist governments became more friendly.

The Spanish revolt of 1936, led by General Francisco Franco, caused Hitler and Mussolini to work still more closely together. German and Italian forces were sent to Spain to assist Franco against the left-wing republican government, which was supported by the Soviet Union. There Hitler and Mussolini tested their new armed forces and laid the basis for future collaboration. Italy meanwhile had become isolated from France and Britain by the Italian invasion of Ethiopia and by the economic sanctions the League of Nations had then ordered against Italy. These economic pressures were halfhearted and did little harm to Italy, but the gesture was deeply resented by the Italian people.

THE ROME-BERLIN AXIS / The time was ripe for a formal alliance between Fascist Italy and Nazi Germany. In October 1936, a secret treaty setting up joint foreign-policy aims was signed. The alliance was announced to the world as the Rome-Berlin Axis. The "axis" image suggested a central core around which the rest of Europe would revolve.

Germany's alliance pattern was extended in November 1936 by the signing of an Anti-Comintern Pact—against international Communism—with the militarist regime of Japan. Italy signed the Anti-Comintern Pact the following September, thus joining all three powers in a loose association, which came to be called the Rome-Berlin-Tokyo Axis.

Meanwhile Fromm continued his tireless efforts to coordinate the parallel development of the old-style infantry-artillery Army, largely equipped with World War I weapons, and the new motorized-mechanized mobile units that were to comprise the main striking force of the new German Army. On November 1, 1935, he was promoted to Major General. His personal relations with Beck remained cool, but coordination between the General Staff and the General Army Office was facilitated in October of 1936 when newly promoted Major General von Manstein became Beck's deputy as First Senior Quartermaster.

It was also in 1936 that an earlier clandestine program of summer and weekend training for the intermediate age groups—who had missed conscript service because of the Versailles Treaty—began to bear fruit. These men were incorporated into twenty-one *Landwehr* (reserve) divisions, to create a new mobilization base.

HITLER'S PLAN FOR CONQUEST / On November 5, 1937, an event occurred that was soon destined to disrupt the productive cooperation of the General Staff and the General Army Office. On that day Hitler announced to five of his chief subordinates his plans for a dramatic expansion of Germany over the next few years. The five officials attending that meeting were Foreign Minister Baron Konstantin von Neurath, Defense Minister Blomberg, and the three service Commanders in Chief, Colonel General von Fritsch of the Army, General Admiral Raeder of the Navy, and Colonel General Goering of the Air Force. These were the senior officials who would have to carry out these plans.

Hitler still held to the program he had laid down in *Mein Kampf* many years earlier. The expanding German population must have *Lebensraum* in central and eastern Europe. He seems not to have specifically mentioned either Poland or Russia, but his listeners had no doubt that these were the ultimate targets. First, however, Austria and Czechoslovakia must be occupied to secure better strategic frontiers for Germany and to bring more Germans into the Reich.

Ernst Hasse (*German National Archives*)

Heinrich Brüning, center (*Keystone Service*)

Wilhelm Wetzell
(*German National Archives*)

Baron Werner von Fritsch
(*German National Archives*)

Werner von Blomberg
(*U.S. National Archives*)

Wilhelm Adam
(*German National Archives*)

Baron Kurt von Hammerstein-Equord
(*Military History Institute,
East German People's Army*)

Kurt von Schleicher
(*U.S. National Archives*)

Franz von Papen
(*U.S. National Archives*)

Ludwig Beck (*Keystone Service*)

Ernst Roehm (*U.S. National Archives*)

Walter von Brauchitsch
(*German National Archives*)

Fridolin von Senger and Etterlin
(*Library of Congress*)

Kurt Student (*U.S. National Archives*)

Kurt Zeitzler, with Hitler
(*U.S. National Archives*)

Erwin Rommel (*U.S. National Archives*)

Heinz Guderian (*U.S. National Archives*)

Erich von Manstein
(*U.S. National Archives*)

Friedrich Fromm (*Keystone Service*)

Hans Krebs (*Keystone Service*)

Franz Halder

Adolf Hitler, with Goebbels, Roehm,
Goering, Himmler, Hess, Frick (seated),
et al. (*Keystone Service*)

Force would obviously have to be used, and at some stage it was possible that France and Britain would intervene and would have to be dealt with. The period 1943-1945 was the latest time Hitler gave for the carrying out of his program, but he said the armed forces must be prepared before then because opportunities allowing attack on Austria could arise during 1938, just two months away.

The risk of disaster for Germany seemed so great to three of the five leaders who heard Hitler that after consultation with General Beck they—Neurath, Blomberg, and Fritsch—dared to urge that Hitler reconsider his plans. Hitler was furious, and a few days later Blomberg informed the Führer that he now supported the program of aggression. As to the other two, Hitler decided that because they had dared to oppose him, he would have them removed from power as soon as possible.

DOWNFALL OF BLOMBERG AND FRITSCH / As it turned out, fate decreed that Blomberg would lose his position before the others. His marriage to a woman of bad moral reputation scandalized the Army, and Hitler demanded his resignation. Soon after this Neurath was replaced by Joachim von Ribbentrop, whose aristocratic-sounding "von" was of dubious authenticity and who was lazy and little respected by the other chief Nazis.

Fritsch was treated in the cruelest fashion of the three; he was framed on a humiliating charge of homosexual immorality, removed from office, and then not restored to his position even after a military court proved beyond doubt that he was completely innocent. Beck had urged him to refuse the demand for resignation, to arrest Hitler, and establish a military dictatorship. Beck told Fritsch that the General Staff and the senior officers of the Army would support this action, despite their oath to Hitler, if Fritsch gave the order. But Fritsch was unwilling to take the responsibility, and Beck could not expect the Army to act without orders from the Chief of the Army Command.

On February 4, 1938, Hitler assembled the senior officers of the Army, and announced the dismissals of Blomberg and Fritsch. Manstein, who was known to be a particularly close and loyal friend of Fritsch, was ordered out of Berlin and placed in command of an infantry division in Silesia. Nevertheless the fruitful cooperation between the General Army Office and the General Staff continued, even though Fromm did not establish the same rapport with Beck's new deputy, Major General Franz Halder.

Beck, however, while retaining a personal dislike for Fromm, had come to respect him as an extremely competent and imaginative administrator, and to accept him as a worthy colleague. Fromm, for his part, recognized the intellectual brilliance and sterling military qualities of Beck. Fromm still thought that the Chief of the General Staff was not sufficiently forward-looking in his outlook, and was somewhat impatient of Beck's cautious agonizing before making decisions on major issues. On the other hand, Beck had demonstrated a willingness to adapt, to accept proved experiments, and to act promptly and forcefully once decisions were made.

When Hitler announced the dismissal of Blomberg and Fritsch, he informed his generals that he was assuming the position of Commander in Chief of the Armed Forces. He did not appoint a new Minister of Defense, and in the absence of a minister, General Wilhelm Keitel, the new Chief of the *Ministeramt,* apparently with Hitler's approval, simply transformed the *Ministeramt* into a virtual Armed Forces Staff, thus becoming a sort of Chief of Staff to Hitler. At the same time the Führer decided that his old favorite, Reichenau—who had recently taken over an area command at Munich—should be promoted and made Chief of the Army Command—as he had intended to do in 1933, before the Army generals and Hindenburg had intervened.

At this point, however, a small delegation of senior generals, with General Gerd von Rundstedt as spokesman, moved again to block Reichenau's appointment. Hitler refused to accept Beck—who was recommended by Rundstedt—and, most reluctantly, compromised with the generals by appointing General Walther von Brauchitsch as the new Chief of the Army Command, and promoting him to Colonel General. Reichenau was rewarded with the command of Group Command IV, which was in reality a field army command. As soon as these appointments were made, Hitler purged most of the Army's senior generals—including Rundstedt. Among others sent off to retirement at this same time were Generals Wilhelm J. F. von Leeb, Gunther von Kluge, Maxmilian von Weichs, and Erwin von Witzleben. Soon, however, Hitler realized that he could not dispense with the collective experience and talent of these commanders, all of whom were destined to become field marshals. He called them all back to active duty.

HITLER REORGANIZES THE COMMAND STRUCTURE / Under the new command arrangement, without a Minister of Defense, there was a serious gap in the administration of the civilian-military coordination machinery of Germany. Recognizing this, Hitler ordered that the General Army Office should assume many of the administrative functions that had previously been the responsibility of the Ministry. Fromm would operate under the direction of the new Armed Forces Staff, reporting to Hitler through Keitel. Thus the painfully and carefully achieved teamwork between the General Staff and the General Army Office was brutally shattered. Keitel either could not or dared not act as a coordinator for the armed services, yet he carefully avoided bothering Hitler with administrative decisions. There was no coordination except for what Fromm could establish on a voluntary basis with the Navy and Air Force staffs, and with the Army General Staff. Nevertheless, because of the coordination which had earlier been achieved under Fritsch, this continued, although somewhat haltingly, under the new arrangement.

Before the new Army command team had had a chance to settle down and to establish the critically important new relationship with the General Army Office, Hitler issued instructions for the occupation of Austria.

ANSCHLUSS / Mussolini had prevented *Anschluss*—meaning "union," but in this case specifying the annexation of Austria by Germany—in 1934. By 1938, however, the Italian dictator was more cooperative with his new ally. Hitler could move ahead to fulfill his early, romantic Pan-German dream, which was also a step in his cold-blooded program of conquest.

There was a strong Nazi party in Austria, lavishly supported by German funds and working in close collaboration with the German Nazi government. Rumors of plans for another Nazi coup attempt created a tense atmosphere throughout Austria during 1937 and early 1938. Terrorist bomb attacks and huge Nazi demonstrations were staged. On February 11 the moderate Austrian Chancellor, Dr. Kurt von Schuschnigg, accepted an invitation to discuss Austrian-German problems with Hitler at his mountain estate in Berchtesgaden, Bavaria.

Schuschnigg was greeted by Hitler with extreme rudeness. The German dictator handed the Austrian an ultimatum demanding that Austria become a virtual protectorate of Germany. Under these terms, Austria would remain nominally independent but would really be dominated by Germany and governed by Hitler.

For reasons that still are not entirely clear, Schuschnigg signed the paper and began to carry out its provisions. Then Hitler delivered a speech in which he made clear his opinion that the German population of Austria rightly belonged in the German *Reich* (state) and that Austria as an independent nation should cease to exist.

Schuschnigg now realized that Hitler was about to double-cross him. On March 9 he defiantly called for a popular vote on the question of independence or joining Germany. He believed that—despite their strong sentiment for *Anschluss*—the Austrians would under these circumstances vote to remain independent. He doubted if Hitler would do anything against such an expression of Austrian popular opinion. Possibly he also knew that the German generals had strongly advised Hitler not to risk a European war by invading Austria.

Hitler, however, was sure that the Allies would not go to war for Austria and was sufficiently doubtful of the outcome of Schuschnigg's proposed plebiscite to decide to prevent it. Two days before the plebiscite was to be held, he threatened to send the German Army into Austria unless Schuschnigg resigned and appointed the Austrian Nazi leader, Arthur Seyss-Inquart, to take charge of the government. German troops were massed along the frontier ready to move; in Vienna mobs of Nazis demonstrated. Schuschnigg looked in vain for support from Italy, Britain, or France. When he received no encouragement from any of them, he resigned. But first he ordered the Austrian troops not to resist the German invasion that he now knew was inevitable.

The invasion came the next day, as German troops poured into Austria. In a few hours the little nation was completely occupied. The sincere rejoicing of a majority of the Austrians suggest that both Schuschnigg and Hitler had misread the likely outcome of the plebiscite. The Allies again protested and again did nothing.

Hitler had defied his generals and had won Austria without war. He made a triumphal journey through the country, with many emotional speeches about the land of his birth and youth. He then declared Austria to be a province of Germany and soon even the name of Austria disappeared from maps in Germany.

The first step of Hitler's expansionist program had been completely successful. However, despite Hitler's remarkable successes and luck since 1934, German military leaders knew that a time would come when the Western Powers would back down no longer. They knew how unprepared the German Army still was. To risk war was to risk disaster. On the other hand, Hitler's popularity was such that they did not act against him.

CZECHOSLOVAKIA AND MUNICH / Czechoslovakia was Hitler's next target. At the fateful meeting of November 5, 1937, he had said that Austria and Czechoslovakia should be seized simultaneously. When his military leaders had protested against such a risk, however, he had decided to take Austria first and then Czechoslovakia.

Hitler wanted and expected to seize Czechoslovakia by force and began military preparations in March 1938, immediately after Austria was occupied. The German Army leaders were sure that this action would finally force France and Britain to intervene and were fearful of the consequences. Yet because of what had happened to Neurath, Blomberg, and Fritsch, they avoided open opposition. Some of them, nevertheless, inspired by Beck, planned to stage a coup d'etat and replace Hitler when the order to attack Czechoslovakia was given.

Beck's plan for resistance was dependent upon General von Brauchitsch exercising true leadership as the senior officer of the Army. Without such leadership from the top, Beck was fearful of the kind of division which had caused the failure of the Kapp Putsch. He knew that Brauchitsch agreed with him that Germany was not ready for a new major war, and so he actually wrote a statement for Brauchitsch to deliver at the appropriate moment. But the new Chief of the Army Command revealed that he was even weaker as a leader than Fritsch had been. Beck, like Seeckt at the time of the Kapp Putsch, was reluctant to take action which might result in armed conflict within the Army, and so on August 18, 1938, he submitted his resignation, thinking that Brauchitsch would resign with him and that they could then jointly lead an insurrection against Hitler when the order for the Czechoslovak invasion was issued.

But Beck was doubly frustrated. First Brauchitsch refused to resign, covering his embarrassment with the bold words: "I am a soldier; it is my duty to obey." Even so, Beck thought that the chances of overthrowing Hitler were still good and felt that the issue was so important that it should be attempted, though Brauchitsch's attitude meant that bloodshed in the Army could not be avoided. Now, however, it was the Allies who frustrated Beck.

The British and French leaders were so eager to appease the German dictator that, when the time came, their capitulation temporarily robbed Hitler of his hopes for war—and at the same time robbed Beck and his adherents of their opportunity for a coup attempt.

Hitler's excuse for threatening Czechoslovakia was the existence of a large German population in areas of Czechoslovakia near the German borders—an area called Sudetenland. The Sudeten Germans had been organized by a local Nazi party that was directed from Germany and had been worked up to a pitch of anti-Czech emotion, despite their generally fair treatment by the Czech state.

Prime Minister Neville Chamberlain of Britain, an especially determined appeaser, was fearful that a German invasion of Czechoslovakia would precipitate a new world war. The Czech Army was well trained, well equipped, and determined to fight if the Germans invaded. In such an event Britain and France would be forced by their treaty obligations* to come to the aid of Czechoslovakia, and Chamberlain was determined to do anything he could to prevent this. While Europe trembled at the brink of war, Chamberlain, with the help of Mussolini, arranged for a four-power conference at Munich. It was held September 29 and 30, and attended by Hitler, Mussolini, Chamberlain, and Prime Minister Edouard Daladier of France. Czechoslovakia was not represented. Chamberlain and Daladier accepted all of Hitler's demands. The four great European powers then signed an agreement that virtually forced Czechoslovakia to give Hitler the Sudeten areas. In return, Hitler promised that he would make no further claims of territory in Czechoslovakia or elsewhere. He declared that his desires were now completely satisfied.

Chamberlain felt he had brought "peace with honor" back to England from Munich. Soon, however, it became clear to everyone that Hitler had not been appeased and had no intention of honoring his pledges at Munich. Chamberlain and the other appeasement advocates tried to believe that, since France and Britain had not been ready for war at the time of Munich, their appeasement had at least bought time for preparation. The truth was, however, that at the time of Munich, Germany had been even less ready for war. The Western Allies, with the help of the substantial and well-trained Czech Army.** could probably have blocked Hitler's military moves in 1938 more successfully than in 1939. More important, German Army leaders were prepared to depose Hitler if he ordered an invasion.

Hitler had been well aware of the risks that were involved, and although it is doubtful that he knew the extent of Beck's plans against him, his Gestapo had given him enough information for him to realize that the Army might refuse to invade Czechoslovakia. Thus, when Beck resigned on August 18, this was a

---

*The French obligation under the 1925 Locarno Treaty and subsequent formal guarantee was clear and specific. The British obligation as a Locarno signatory was more ambiguous, but was of course undeniable as an ally of France.
**Doubts have been expressed about the reliability of this Army in the event of war with Germany, since some 25 percent of its personnel were Germans, and about 10 percent Poles and Hungarians. No one knows.

carefully kept secret from the German people and in particular from the Allies—who might otherwise have been able to recognize not only Germany's military weakness but the division of opinion among Germany's military leaders.

On October 1, howeve, the day after the Allied surrender of Munich, Beck's resignation was announced. By that time there was no possibility of a coup against Hitler. The dictator had reached the height of his popularity among the German people—and also with the Army—by the skill with which he had achieved this great bloodless, diplomatic victory over Britain and France.

The Sudeten areas surrendered by Czechoslovakia at Munich had been given to that little country at Versailles so that it would have strategically defensible mountain frontiers. Without these frontiers, and the excellent fortifications system it had built for them, Czechoslovakia was helpless. On March 15, 1939, less than six months after Hitler's assurances at Munich, German troops marched into Prague, the Czech capital, in a lightninglike surprise move. Bohemia and Moravia were annexed by Germany; tiny Slovakia became nominally independent but actually was under German control.

As a result of this ruthless violation of the Munich accord, Chamberlain finally had to recognize reality. He pledged Britain to support Poland if that country was invaded by Germany. That same day Daladier gave a similar French guarantee of support for Poland. But neither did anything about Czechoslovakia.

Hitler was not much concerned with the Anglo-French guarantees to Poland. In seventeen months he had completed the first steps of the program he had presented to his senior subordinates on November 5, 1937, without the loss of a man or weapon. He was now ready to move into the *Lebensraum* lands of Poland. He recognized that this might lead to war with Britain and France, but he now had such contempt for the leadership of those two countries that he thought they might even renege on their pledges to Poland. Even if they did honor their obligations, he was certain that they would not fight vigorously and would soon seek a negotiated peace.

HALDER AS CHIEF OF STAFF / When Beck resigned on August 18, his place was taken by the First Quartermaster General, Franz Halder, then holding the rank of General of Artillery. Halder, a Bavarian, was universally respected in the General Staff and among the senior officers of the Army, but he was almost unknown to the Army as a whole and to the nation. He had been born in Würzburg on June 30, 1884, into a family with a long tradition of service in the Bavarian Army. In 1902 he entered that Army as an officer candidate, and became a second lieutenant in March 1904. Early in his career he was selected for the Bavarian General Staff, and so in World War II, when the Bavarian Army became fully incorporated into the German Army, he found himself serving in OHL as an officer of the Great General Staff.

After the war Halder was one of the select group of officers chosen by General Hans von Seeckt as the nucleus of the new 100,000-man Army. In the years after the war Halder alternated troop duty with staff appointments, but by

1930 he was clearly marked for high command, and most of the rest of his active career was to be spent in senior staff or command positions.

It was in 1930 that Halder—then a lieutenant colonel—played his slightly mysterious, and apparently innocent, part in Adolf Hitler's rise to power, by introducing General von Schleicher to Ernst Röhm, the chief of the Nazi SA Brown Shirts. About the time Hitler became Chancellor, in early 1933, Halder had been assigned as Chief of Staff of the Ninth Military District, and soon afterward was promoted to colonel. Meanwhile, Röhm had been actively laying the groundwork for accomplishing his ambition of taking command of the German armed forces. Despite the strong opposition of German military leaders, Röhm seems to have been confident that, as Hitler's most powerful lieutenant, he could achieve his ambition and create a "people's army" for Hitler. Possibly because Röhm remembered Halder's part in bringing him together with Schleicher, early in 1934 one or more of Röhm's subordinates sought Halder's help in training SA leaders in General Staff procedures. Halder, at once and in person, reported this to General von Fritsch. This was one of a number of incidents that led Fritsch to complain directly to Hitler about the SA, and that also led him secretly to prepare the Army to take immediate action against any possible SA effort to seize power by violence.

Hitler, aware of what was going on, recognized that if the Army was provoked into direct action against the SA, it would probably also remove him as Chancellor. He saw in this state of affairs an opportunity to gain the support and confidence of the Army, at the expense of Röhm and the Brown Shirts. The result was the brutal blood purge of June 30-July 1, 1934.

By 1936 Halder was back on the General Staff as a Major General, and by late 1937 he had been promoted to Lieutenant General and was a division chief in the General Staff. When Hitler dismissed Blomberg and Fritsch in early 1938, he also gave consideration to dismissing the Chief of the General Staff, General Beck, whom he now recognized to be a dangerous anti-Nazi. But he had already decided to transfer from the Staff Beck's deputy—General Erich von Manstein—who was a close friend of Fritsch and was reluctant to strip the General Staff of its two top leaders. For a while, apparently, he considered promoting Halder to Chief of Staff but is said to have decided against it because he thought Halder was a Catholic, and Hitler hated Catholics almost as much as he hated generals. If that was his decision, it was based on error. Although Halder was a Bavarian, he was a devout Protestant. In any event, Hitler kept Beck on as Chief of the General Staff, and somewhat reluctantly promoted Halder to Manstein's former position—First Quartermaster General, or Deputy Chief of Staff for Plans and Operations—with the increased rank of General of Artillery.

When Beck resigned, Hitler once again had to decide what to do about Halder. By this time he had learned not only that Halder was a Protestant and a man of great ability, but that he was also seemingly apolitical. Hitler therefore decided to put him in Beck's place as Chief of the General Staff.

PLANNING AGAINST POLAND / Halder's first task as Chief of the General Staff was to initiate planning for war with Poland. Two and a half years earlier, at the time of the occupation of the Rhineland, Halder had agreed with Beck that a war with the Western Powers would be disastrous, and he joined Beck and the small group of generals who were secretly prepared to overthrow Hitler if France declared war. But France had not declared war, and in the subsequent thirty months the German Army had become much stronger. Halder and most of his senior General Staff subordinates nevertheless believed that Britain and France would go to war if Germany invaded Poland. Unlike Hitler, they believed that the Allies would fight vigorously, and that a German victory was highly unlikely. But they had their orders, and after Munich they knew that a majority of the German people and a majority of the Army were solidly behind Hitler. The chances of a successful coup d'etat had passed when Brauchitsch had refused to act with Beck. The plan for war against Poland—Case Green—was prepared with typical General Staff efficiency.

As a result of the incorporation of the Austrian Army into the *Reichswehr* and the reluctant acquiescence of Fritsch and Beck (and later Brauchitsch and Halder) to Hitler's prodding for continuing expansion of the Army, the strength had grown by April 1, 1939, to about a million men in fifty-one active divisions. (There were about 750,000 reservists in a mobilization base of fifty-two reserve and *Landwehr* divisions.) The officer corps had reached a strength of slightly more than 25,000 active-duty officers; 500 of these were in the General Staff Corps. While this was less than half the number of leaders an army that size required, Halder knew that the quality of the officers in the General Staff Corps was as good as it had ever been. Even though the quality of the officer corps in general was far below the desirable standards—since the junior officers still lacked sufficient training and experience—at least it was passable. The promotion to officer rank of a substantial number of noncommissioned officers of the old 100,000-man Army had helped.

There were twelve armored and motorized divisions in the mobile echelon of the Army with sufficient training and equipment to be called combat ready—and four more were almost ready. But this was only about one fourth of the Army. What worried Halder was the fact that the inadequate number of officers —combined with an even greater shortage of reliable, experienced noncommissioned officers in the rapidly expanding traditional echelon of the Army— meant that few of the divisions of this portion of the Army had been through satisfactory training programs. On top of this, there were simply not enough modern weapons and military equipment for these divisions. The seizure of the Czechoslovak Army's equipment had somewhat alleviated this shortage, but it had also greatly complicated the supply problem by adding many different kinds and calibers of ammunition and making even more complicated a spare-parts supply problem that was already taxing an inexperienced, expanding supply system. Halder's forecast was that a satisfactory state of training for leaders and units for the Army as a whole could be achieved by about 1943 at the earliest.

And yet Halder was aware from intelligence reports that the Polish Army, while almost as large as that of Germany, was not very efficient. If there were no outside interference, Halder believed, Poland could readily be defeated by the much more mobile German Army. But Britain, France, and Soviet Russia all had treaties with Poland, and the two Western Powers had recently reaffirmed their determination to fight if Poland was attacked by Germany. The Russian Army was about twice the size of the newly expanded German Army. Recent experience of German officers training clandestinely in Russia, combined with intelligence estimates, suggested that the quality of the Soviet Army was substantially below that which Halder considered satisfactory for German troops. But if the Red Army were to march to the support of Poland, chances of German victory were not good. Instead of gaining *Lebensraum* for Hitler, the Germans would be hard pressed to save Brandenburg and Silesia from invasion, and East Prussia would probably be lost.

If to the combination of Poland and Russia there should be added Britain and France, Halder saw only the possibility of disaster. The combined numerical strength of the armies of the two Western Powers was less than that of the new German Army, and their quality was estimated to be lower. Although they had both recently begun programs to modernize their armies, they were still generally equipped with outmoded World War I weapons, considered to be inferior to the new weapons of the mobile German divisions. But the Allies had almost inexhaustible supplies of those weapons, while German industrial production had barely been able to supply twelve divisions, with no war reserves. Also, the Western Allies (like Russia) had vast numbers of trained men in their reserve forces, while effective German reserves were limited mostly to aging veterans of the previous war.

Hitler, however, was confident that by agile diplomacy he would be able to divide Britain and France from Russia. He did not think that any of those powers would interfere, but in the worst event, he assured the Army, Poland would be supported only by Russia or by the Western Powers, not both. Halder gave little credence to assurances from Hitler, but he recognized that political realities might bring about the situation as seen by Hitler. In that case, a lightning victory over Poland might be possible, and subsequent stubborn defense against either Russian or Western intervention might lead to a negotiated peace. Such a strategy would be favored in the East by the slowness of Russian mobilization, in the West by the existence of a new line of fortifications along the frontiers of Western Germany, the so-called West Wall, or Siegfried Line, which was being rushed to completion by the Nazi Organization Todt in accordance with Hitler's orders.

While making detailed plans for a defensive strategy should the worst occur, Halder was able to focus the principal planning of the General Staff on the possibly successful strategy of Conquer (Poland) and Divide (the Allies). Such a strategy was favored by the geographical results of the bloodless conquests of Austria and Czechoslovakia. One reason for the quick collapse of Czechoslovakia had been the ability of the Germans to invade that country across its unfortified southern frontier with Austria. Now, with German troops in Slovakia, all of Western Poland was similarly threatened with encirclement.

While the operational planning was going on, administrative and organizational preparations were also being pushed with urgency.

Despite the obstacles to cooperation and coordination created by the peculiar new administrative arrangements for the armed forces, Fromm and Halder nonetheless succeeded in establishing an adequate working relationship between themselves and for their staffs. After all, Fromm and his principal assistants were themselves General Staff officers.

By the end of August 1939, the Army's expansion program, conceived by Fromm and carried through primarily by the efforts of General Staff Corps officers of the Great General Staff and the General Army Office, had given Germany an elite, modern core for its new Army. This now comprised some 200,000 officers and men in sixteen armored, motorized, or light divisions, equipped mostly with new weapons and equipment and highly mobile. Behind this elite successor to the 100,000-man Army was the mass conscript Army, mostly equipped with World War I weapons or captured Czech equipment, its transport and artillery mostly horse drawn. The total strength of the Army was almost 1.1 million men. It was an Army with many deficiencies and fell far short of the standards sought by Groener, Seeckt, Beck, Halder, or even Fromm. Most serious, it lacked the reserves of weapons and trained manpower possessed by the Western Allies and Russia. Nonetheless, thanks to the contributions of these five men and their many anonymous associates in the General Staff Corps, it had become the finest Army in the world and was steadily improving and growing.

Chapter Fifteen

VICTORIES & DEFEAT

 GERMAN COMBAT EXCELLENCE IN WORLD WAR II /
The literature on World War II already far exceeds in volume
that of World War I, and in English alone the bibliographies
have more entries than for either the American Civil War or
the Napoleonic wars. And save for a relative handful of books
on the war in the Pacific or East Asia, a major theme of this
steadily growing literature has been the reputation or performance of the German armed forces, praised by some writers, denigrated by others.

The record of the war very quickly shows the reason for this focus on
German performance. Except for the careers of a handful of the great captains
of history, there is nothing in history—not even the exceptional performance of
the German Army in World War I—to match the size, scope, or completeness of
the early German victories, or the brilliance, versatility, or stubbornness of their
performance on defense.*

A statistical summary of the record of German military performance in
World War II can be found in Appendix E. In essence, that record shows that the
Germans consistently outfought the far more numerous Allied armies that eventually defeated them. In 1943-1944 the German combat effectiveness superiority over the Western Allies (Americans and British) was in the order of 20-30
percent. On a man-for-man basis, the German ground soldiers consistently
inflicted casualties at about a 50 percent higher rate than they incurred from the
opposing British and American troops under all circumstances. This was true

---

*These words are written most reluctantly. The author yields to no one in contempt for the
despicable Nazi regime, for the horrible treatment of the Jews of Germany and other
European countries, or for the regimes of terror which Hitler's lieutenants imposed on the
nations overrun by his armies. In large part, the German Army as an institution has nothing
to do with this frightfulness, but it had considerable indirect responsibility and some
instances of direct involvement in unpardonable brutality. (For instance, Field Marshal
Keitel and General Jodl were convicted at Nürnburg and executed for war crimes, including
the signing of orders directing summary execution of prisoners of war.) The extent of that
involvement is at least indirectly considered in subsequent pages. But the fact remains—
regardless of what we may think of the performance of Germany as a twentieth-century
nation during World War II—that the German armed forces, and particularly the Army,
achieved the standard of military excellence which is the principal subject of this chapter.

when they were attacking and when they were defending, when they had a local numerical superiority and when, as was usually the case, they were outnumbered, when they had air superiority and when they did not, when they won and when they lost.

On the Eastern Front, during those same bitter years of defeat, the German superiority over the Russians was even more marked, although—perhaps significantly—the margin of superiority was less than that of World War I. German combat effectiveness superiority over the Russians in the early days of the war was close to 200 percent; this means that, on the average, one German division was at least a match for three Russian divisions of comparable size and firepower, and that under favorable circumstance of defense, one German division theoretically could—and often actually did—hold off as many as seven comparable Russian divisions. In 1944 this superiority was still nearly 100 percent and the average German frontline soldier inflicted 7.78 Russian casualties for each German lost. This figure, however, has to be adjusted to allow for the fact that the Germans were usually on the defensive, that they had greater proportional mobility in terms of armor and supporting motor vehicles, and that their weapons were, on the average, better than those of the Russians.* But even allowing for these considerations, the casualty trade-off was more than 4 to 1 in favor of the Germans; in other words, under all circumstances of combat, the Germans on a man-for-man basis inflicted more than 300 percent more casualties than they incurred from the opposing Russians.

This record of combat superiority over Germany's enemies was the result of the Army-building efforts of Groener, Seeckt, Hammerstein-Equord, Fritsch, Beck, Fromm, Halder, and their anonymous, equally dedicated colleagues of the German General Staff Corps. The nature of revived German military excellence was first manifested to a startled world in the Polish campaign of September 1939. This lightninglike demonstration of military versatility, in a war totally unlike the trench warfare of World War I, led foreign correspondents to manufacture the descriptive term "blitzkrieg" for an apparently new method of warfare.

There was, of course, much that was new in the German battlefield performance. In fact, the ingredients, the concepts, and the fundamental principles had been available and understood by leading soldiers on both sides in the final year of World War I. The difference between 1918 and 1939 was the manner in which the Germans had restructured these ingredients and had then applied them, with only slightly improved technical equipment, in traditional doctrine and battle plans that would have been well understood and approved by Napoleon. The nature of this performance is objectively described by the greatest historian-participant of World War II, Winston Churchill:

The superiority of the Germans in design, management, and energy [in

---

*There were some exceptions of course, such as the excellent Soviet T-34 tank, the Joseph Stalin I tank, and possibly their 76.2 mm antitank gun and their infantry submachine gun.

the 1940 Norway Campaign] were plain. They put into ruthless execution a carefully prepared plan of action. They comprehended perfectly the use of the air arm on a great scale in all its aspects. Moreover, their individual ascendancy was marked, especially in small parties. At Narvik a mixed and improvised German force, barely six thousand strong, held at bay for six weeks some twenty thousand Allied troops, and though driven out of the town lived to see them depart. . . . The Germans traversed in seven days the road from Namsos to Mosjøen, which the British and French had declared impassable. At Bodø and Mo, during the retreat of Gubbins' force to the north, we were each time just too late, and the enemy, although they had to overcome hundreds of miles of rugged, snow-clogged country, drove us back in spite of gallant episodes, We, who had the command of the sea and could pounce anywhere on an undefended coast, were outpaced by the enemy moving by land across very large distances in the face of every obstacle. In this Norweigan encounter, our finest troops, the Scots and Irish Guards, were baffled by the vigour, enterprise, and training of Hitler's young men.[1]

THE GENESIS OF BLITZKRIEG / In one of the most perceptive of his many wise aphorisms, Clausewitz wrote that "everything is simple in war but the simplest thing is difficult." Like qualified observers and critics of the Allies, the Germans observed the obvious "lessons" of World War I. Unlike the others, however, they had an institution available to make the much more difficult analyses of these observations, to include assessments of the characteristics, limitations, and capabilities of weapons, and the implications of trends in weapons and technology. Following analytical concepts initiated by Scharnhorst and continued by his successors, that institution almost automatically made the even more difficult translation of the analytical results into doctrine, organization, the establishment of requirements for new or modified weapons and equipment, and development of new and revised operational and administrative techniques.

Returning to the Clausewitz simple-difficult aphorism, it was easy—after the appalling demonstrations of power in Poland, Norway, the Low Countries, and France—for Germany's enemies to see what the German Army and *Luftwaffe* had done, and during the course of the war to copy doctrine, organization, matériel, and techniques—and even in some instances to improve on these. But, as the 1943-1944 record shows, it was difficult, and in fact impossible, for these successfully imitative foes to match the German performance, even after that performance had become degraded by shortages of manpower and matériel.

It is also easy for the historian, years after the fact, to observe that the Germans merely adapted long-existing and long-understood fundamental military principles to the modern developments of technology to produce a war machine and a modified method of warfare following the aberrations of World War I. But easy though it is to see this in retrospect, it was plainly difficult at the time, since only the Germans did it, setting the example for the others.

Although Seeckt's agreements with Russia permitted some German military men to gain experience and familiarity with tanks, the limitations of the Versailles Treaty for a long time prevented practical experimentation on a large scale. As a result, German officers in the Motorized Corps avidly read the writings of British tank officers and enthusiasts like G. le Q. Martel, J. F. C. Fuller, and Basil Liddell Hart, as well as those by French armored force specialists like Charles de Gaulle. While the Germans recognized their indebtedness to these early heralds of armored warfare,[2] they soon moved past the French and British in the development of concepts and doctrine for coordinated infantry-armor and air-armor operations, which emerged logically from their continuing analyses of World War I experience.*

As in Britain, France, and the United States, the German tank enthusiasts found that there was much professional military opposition to the idea of adopting tanks and tank warfare on a large scale. There were many reasons for this: the innate conservatism of thoughtful soldiers who realize that serious doctrinal mistakes could jeopardize their nation's security; a widespread dislike of dirty, noisy internal-combustion machines with their rattling caterpillar tracks; a nostalgic devotion to the largely mythical and mystical chivalric ideals of horse cavalry. It was almost as difficult to overcome these traditionalist concepts in Germany as it was in other countries.

But not quite.

For all of the complaints in Guderian's memoirs about the lack of perception among higher commanders and senior General Staff officers, he nevertheless writes about steady progress toward the creation of tank organizations, tank doctrines, and armored-force techniques in the 1920s and early 1930s. Despite Guderian's criticism of the failure of the Chief of the General Staff, Beck, to recognize the potentialities of mobile armored warfare, the fact remains that under Beck's guidance Germany steadily created within its large conscript Army an elite mobile army as rapidly as German industry could provide weapons and equipment. Beck, like Seeckt before him, could see how armor and air power could provide the mobility that was so elusive in World War I. Guderian was undoubtedly the leader of the movement toward armored-warfare doctrine, but it is evident that there were a number of other young General Staff officers with comparable opinions and similar capability, who could readily have provided the leadership in his stead. How different from Britain and France, where Martel, Fuller, and de Gaulle remained prophets without honor.**

THE SPECIFICS OF BLITZKRIEG / The new armored mobile doctrine developed by Guderian and his fellow General Staff Corps officers of the new corps of panzer troops was essentially the incorporation of armored and other track-

---

*See p. 184.
**This was less true of Liddell Hart, since he compromised with the offensive warfare ideals of Fuller and Martel, and attempted to fit armored warfare concepts into a more popularly acceptable doctrine of defensive combat.

laying vehicles into the fundamental concepts of the Hutier Tactics. Perhaps the most important ingredient of the doctrine—just as it had been in 1917 and 1918—was to seek an opportunity for surprise. Small teams, or battle groups, of tanks and tractor-borne armored infantry advanced rapidly under the cover of their own considerable firepower, supported by self-propelled artillery and close-support aircraft, both fighter-bombers and dive-bombers.

Once a penetration was achieved, the battle groups dashed ahead in rapid exploitation, attempting to destroy or disperse any hostile forces they encountered. Making maximum use of radio communications, local commanders immediately supported such penetrations with all the resources at their command, while at the same time reporting the opportunity to higher headquarters. At all echelons the emphasis was on boldness, speed, shock action, and firepower. The enemy was to be allowed no time to recover or to shift reserves to block the gap. Air power was called upon to hammer any stubborn resistance or to reinforce any success. A well-prepared, flexible cross-country logistical system kept a steady supply of fuel, ammunition, and food moving up to join the onrushing spearheads.

In the broadest sense, this was warfare as it had been waged by Alexander the Great, Genghis Khan, and Napoleon, modified only to make use of the latest products of science and technology. It was a concept of warfare that would have been well understood, and undoubtedly approved, by Schlieffen. The question was: Would the concept work as well in practice as in theory, or would some unforeseen events prevent success as had happened in 1914 and 1918?

The answer seemed clear to the new Chief of the Army Command, Brauchitsch, and the new Chief of the General Staff, Halder, within hours of the initial attack on Poland, on September 1, 1939. The answer was confirmed within two weeks. The Polish Army, which had mobilized approximately 800,000 men, was utterly destroyed by a German Army of about 1.25 million men in sixty divisions, of which nine were armored or mechanized—the elite army within the Army. Total German casualties were 44,000 men, killed, wounded, and missing. Polish military losses in killed and wounded—not counting prisoners—were 266,000. Most of these casualties were incurred in the first two weeks.

These statistics can be analyzed in the same way as those for World War I combat performance. Using the same factor of 1.3 to allow for the generally defensive posture of the Poles, every 100 Poles inflicted .4 casualties per day, upon the Germans. Meanwhile, each 100 Germans was inflicting 1.52 casualties per day upon the Poles. This was a German casualty-inflicting superiority of nearly 4 to 1, suggesting (on the basis of other World War II statistical research) a German combat-effectiveness superiority of close to 2 to 1.*

---

*This also suggests that the performance of the Polish Army was statistically better than that of the Russian Army later in the war. But the Poles suffered from two disadvantages that did not affect the Russians two years later. In the first place, Poland did not provide

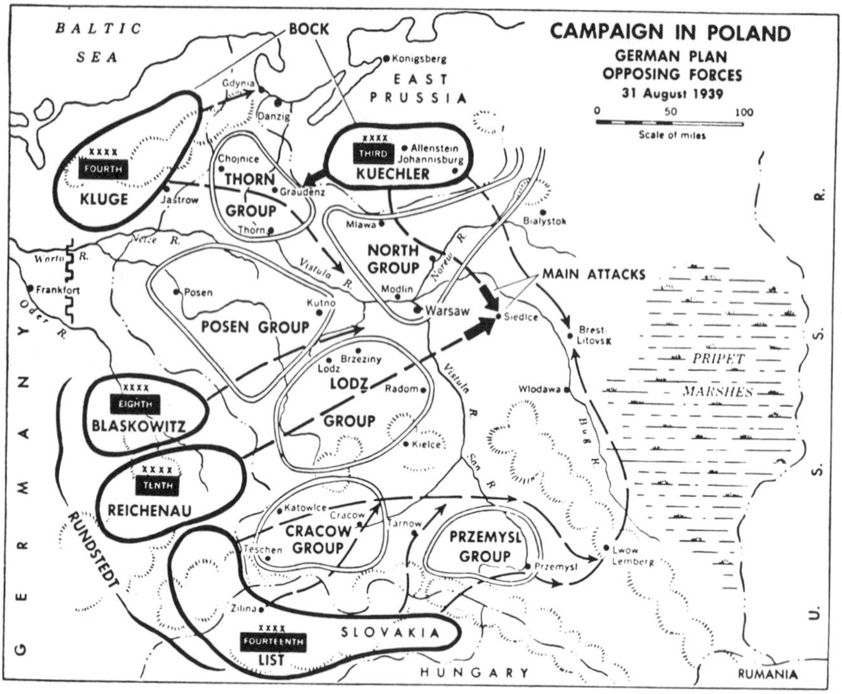
CAMPAIGN IN POLAND
GERMAN PLAN
OPPOSING FORCES
31 August 1939
0 50 100
Scale of miles
BALTIC SEA
BOCK
EAST PRUSSIA
Konigsberg
Gdynia
Danzig
FOURTH
KLUGE
THIRD
KUECHLER
Allenstein
Johannisburg
Chojnice
THORN GROUP
Graudenz
Jastrow
Thorn
Mlawa
Bialystok
NORTH GROUP
Modlin
Warsaw
Siedlce
MAIN ATTACKS
Brest-Litovsk
PRIPET MARSHES
Frankfort
Posen
POSEN GROUP
Kutno
Brzeziny
Lodz
LODZ GROUP
Radom
Kielce
Wlodawa
EIGHTH
BLASKOWITZ
TENTH
REICHENAU
RUNDSTEDT
Katowice
Cracow
CRACOW GROUP
Tarnow
PRZEMYSL GROUP
Przemysl
Teschen
Lwow
Lemberg
Zilina
FOURTEENTH
LIST
SLOVAKIA
HUNGARY
RUMANIA
GERMANY
U. S. S. R.

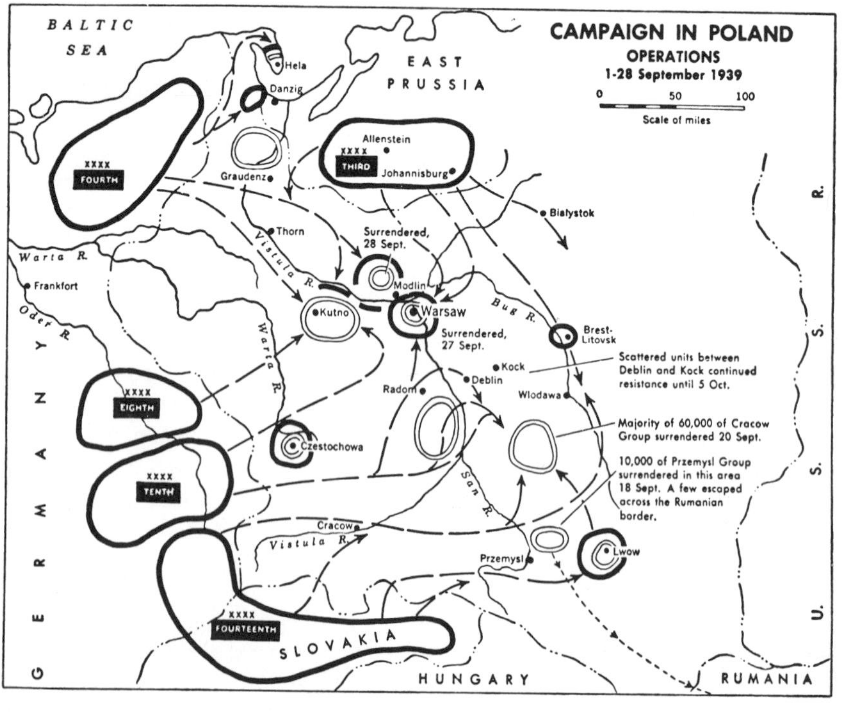
CAMPAIGN IN POLAND
OPERATIONS
1-28 September 1939
0 50 100
Scale of miles
BALTIC SEA
EAST PRUSSIA
Hela
Danzig
FOURTH
THIRD
Allenstein
Johannisburg
Graudenz
Bialystok
Thorn
Surrendered, 28 Sept.
Modlin
Kutno
Warsaw
Surrendered, 27 Sept.
Brest-Litovsk
Kock
Deblin
Scattered units between Deblin and Kock continued resistance until 5 Oct.
Radom
Wlodawa
EIGHTH
Czestochowa
Majority of 60,000 of Cracow Group surrendered 20 Sept.
TENTH
10,000 of Przemysl Group surrendered in this area 18 Sept. A few escaped across the Rumanian border.
Cracow
Przemysl
Lwow
FOURTEENTH
SLOVAKIA
HUNGARY
RUMANIA
Frankfort
GERMANY
U. S. S. R.

Too much has been written about the operations of World War II to make it worthwhile even to attempt to summarize those campaigns in these pages. Instead, as with World War I, a few operational vignettes will highlight some of the qualities of the German Army, and the exceptional performance of its leaders—most of whom had risen through the General Staff Corps—and of the General Staff itself in both victory and defeat.

EBEN EMAEL / There was, for instance, the bold and spectacular seizure of Fort Eben Emael, a vital element in the success of the surprise invasion of the Low Countries and France on May 10, 1940. An American Army officer who later analyzed this aspect of the German offensive of 1940 estimated that in a standard offensive it should have taken substantially more than 4,000 Germans probably a week or more to smash their way through the southern Netherlands, cross the Albert Canal, and overwhelm the fort.[3] Meanwhile the entire German offensive would have been stalled, the Allies would have had time to complete their planned occupation of the Dyle Line in central Belgium, and the course of World War II would have been much different. As it was, he wrote, "Seventy-seven boldly led men, 10 gliders costing about 77,000 [Reichsmarks], and 56 hollow-charge explosives defeated 780 men defending the world's strongest fort . . . in somewhat more than a day, but the decisive struggle took place during the first 20 minutes."[4]

It has been asserted that the idea for the glider assault on Fort Eben Emael was solely Hitler's. This is hard to believe, since it was an essential element of a large and complex plan developed by General Halder's General Staff and was elaborated in its details by the subordinate general staffs of lower echelons, but the origin of the idea is less important than how the attack was planned and the actual operation carried out.

The mission was given in late October 1939 to Lieutenant General Kurt Student, a former Army officer who had served with the Army General Staff and had been a member of the original *Luftwaffe* General Staff when the *Luftwaffe* was established in 1933. Now he was a *Luftwaffe* General, commanding the newly activated 7th Airborne Division. He and his staff were provided the results of Army General Staff studies of attacks on World War I fortresses and were introduced to new attack possibilities created by the postwar invention by German scientists of hollow-charge explosives.* The rest was up to Student.

Student created a task force of less than a hundred men, who for six months devoted themselves exclusively to the problems of reaching the fort by glider,

---

the vast space for retreat which was all that saved the Red Army in 1941. Second, while the Polish Army was valiantly trying to make the best possible use of the limited space available, it was struck in the back by a nominal ally, with whom it had a nonaggression treaty, Soviet Russia.

*This was an adaptation of the so-called Munro effect or focused explosive blast that could penetrate heavy armor plate on warships, on tanks, and on the massive steel cupolas of modern fortifications.

and then destroying its six massive steel cupolas—each with two 120 mm guns—as well as twelve casemates with 75 mm guns, and a number of smaller machine-gun and antiaircraft concrete pillboxes. During the winter and the early spring of 1940, the attack was repeatedly rehearsed on a field near Hildesheim, Germany, on which was constructed a mock-up of the top of the fortress, based on air-photo analysis.

When the attack was actually launched during the night of May 9-10, 1940, as in most complex human endeavors, things went wrong. Two of the ten gliders failed to arrive, one belonging to the assault-force commander (who later was able to get there during the middle of the battle). Some key men were injured in the dawn landings on the top of the fort; others were wounded by defense fire. But the plans had taken into account the possibilities of such mishaps, and the men went calmly about their tasks, quickly destroying the fort's armament and driving away attempted counterattacks. They held the top of the fort until the arrival of German assault columns at the edge of the canal, a few hours later, forced a formal Belgian surrender.

Almost as interesting as the success was the reaction of the men in the two gliders which failed to arrive on time. The glider of Lieutenant Rudolf Witzig, the assault-force commander, had landed a few miles from Köln (Cologne), after its tow rope parted. He commandeered a car and at a nearby airbase was able to persuade a *Luftwaffe* transport-plane pilot to pick up his glider from the field where it had fallen. A few hours later, in midmorning, Witzig and his crew of eight men arrived on top of the fort while the fight was still hot.

Another squad, released prematurely, landed in southern Holland. They attempted to reach the fort overland but encountered opposition as they neared the bridges over the canal. The squad leader was killed; the assistant squad leader, a Corporal Meier, and his seven men captured forty Belgian prisoners. Meier, however, was still intent upon getting to the fort. Leaving his men and their prisoners in a sheltered location on the banks of the canal, he tried to clamber across the twisted girders of a destroyed bridge. Soon he came under intense fire from Belgians in and around the fort, as well as from his comrades on top of the fort. Meanwhile, he had lost contact with the remainder of the squad, which had been attacked and forced to move, herding its prisoners. Meier accompanied the first waves of the German ground assault across the canal and joined his comrades at the fort the next morning. His squad, now with 121 prisoners, then joined another part of the assault force.

This was the spirit, dedication, and combat skill—the products of intensive training—which not only won Fort Eben Emael but soon smashed all Dutch, Belgian, and French resistance.

CRETE / A year later, General Student was the commander of a much larger, equally successful, but far more costly operation. By that time he was commander of the XI Airborne Corps, consisting of his 7th Airborne Division and the 5th Mountain Division. After the German conquest of Yugoslavia and

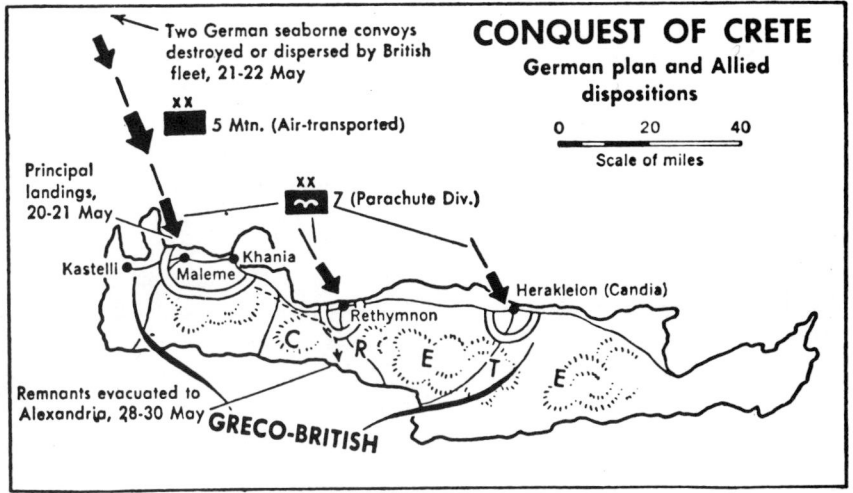

Greece—an operation brilliantly planned and mounted by Halder and his General Staff with ten days' notice—Student and his corps were given the mission of capturing the island of Crete. The 7th Division—including most of the veterans of Eben Emael—was to make an airborne assault on the island's key airports, to be followed by the 5th Division, lifted to the captured airports by transport planes. Some attached infantry units and the vehicles of the 7th and 5th Divisions were to follow in a flotilla of small vessels from southern Greece, making a night crossing of the Sea of Crete to avoid possible interference from British Admiral Sir Andrew Cunningham's Mediterranean Fleet.

Crete was defended by about 25,000 British troops (about half of whom had recently been badly battered in the Greek Campaign) and a Greek garrison of 14,000. The overall commander was New Zealand Major General Bernard C. Freyberg. Although the total force available to Student (counting the attached units to come by sea) was only slightly more than 20,000 troops, the German high command knew that the defenders were short of artillery and heavy weapons, and believed that the operation could succeed with intensive support from the *Luftwaffe*.

On May 20, after a week of *Luftwaffe* attacks had destroyed most of the RAF planes on Crete, and driven the remainder to Egypt, Student's paratroopers landed near the principal airports of Maleme (Khania), Réthimnon, and Herakleion (Iraklion, or Candia). Despite rigorous British counterattacks, the paratroopers were able to establish small landing grounds for their glider-borne comrades, and then the Germans attacked the three airports. The British and

Greek defenders drove them back, however. So the Germans dug in, and waited for reinforcements to arrive by sea.

The seaborne reinforcements never arrived. Despite terrible losses from German air attacks, Admiral Cunningham's ships retained control of the sea around Crete, and destroyed two small German convoys on the nights of May 20-21 and 21-22.

Recognizing that the only hope of success was his airborne assault, on the twenty-first Student committed most of the remainder of his 7th Division by gliders, landing near Maleme. The paratroopers and glidermen then succeeded in seizing part of the runway. Immediately transport planes began to bring in the remaining elements of the 7th Division and the 5th Mountain Division. Of the first transports that landed, few were able to take off again. Some were shot down by the British as they approached the field; some crash-landed; others were hit by artillery and small arms while they were unloading their passengers. But enough reinforcements arrived in this costly fashion to enable the Germans to seize the remainder of the field by dark. On the twenty-second, they pushed out far enough so that the British infantry weapons could no longer reach the runway. By evening of the twenty-third, all of the 5th Division had arrived, and Student could start an offensive to seize the island. By evening of the twenty-sixth, Freyberg reported by radio to Cairo that he could no longer hold Crete. During the next four days about 17,000 British and Greek troops were evacuated to Egypt, under heavy German bombardment.

The British and Greek defenders had the advantage of numbers and of well-prepared defenses on and overlooking the airfields, plus the magnificent support of the Royal Navy. The Germans had the advantage of air superiority and overwhelming air support. Nonetheless General Student's feat of capturing the island with an airborne force never greater than 15,000 men—initially without any artillery, heavy weapons, or vehicles—defeating a force nearly three times as large as his own, was one of the great feats of military history.

Fortunately for the Allies, however, Hitler seems to have been appalled by the losses suffered by the airborne troops—5,670, mostly in the 7th Parachute Division—and by the loss of 151 of the 650 German transport planes in the operation (120 more were badly damaged but repairable). In any event, the Germans did not undertake another major airborne operation during the war.

The British and Greek ground-force defenders suffered 3,480 casualties, and 11,835 were captured. Perhaps 6,000 Greeks took refuge in the hills of Crete or put on civilian clothes and became lost in the population. Admiral Cunningham's fleet lost four cruisers and six destroyers sunk by German aircraft and several other vessels were badly damaged; 2,011 British sailors were killed or drowned, and nearly 1,000 more were wounded.

Less than a month later the German General Staff had redeployed the troops that had conquered Yugoslavia and Greece, and committed them to the tremendous invasion of Russia—Operation "Barbarossa"—that began on June 22. In the early weeks of that invasion there were many extraordinary exploits by

German troops. One of the outstanding performances was that of the LVI Army Corps, part of Field Marshal von Leeb's Army Group North. The commander of the LVI Army Corps was General Erich von Manstein. Since Manstein was later assessed by his fellow German generals as probably the outstanding commander of the war, it is well to review his career up to this time, and particularly a major controversy in which he had been involved a few months earlier.

ERICH VON MANSTEIN / Erich von Manstein was born in Berlin on November 24, 1887, into an old Prussian military family.* After graduating from cadet school in 1906, he became a lieutenant in the 3d Regiment of Footguards. Six years later he was selected for attendance at the War Academy, and completed the first year of the three-year course in 1913-1914. He served with great distinction in France, East Prussia, Poland, and Serbia; he was badly wounded in November 1914, but by May 1915 was again serving near the front as an army staff officer. By this time he had been selected for the General Staff Corps, and he served as an operations officer on several army and division staffs until the end of the war. After the war he was one of the General Staff Corps officers selected by Seeckt for the 100,000 man Army, and served both with the Great General Staff and with troops.

In 1934, as Chief of Staff of District III, in the Berlin region, Colonel von Manstein had become extremely interested in the experimental work of General Lutz and Colonel Guderian with the Motorized Troop Command; he and Guderian established a firm bond of personal friendship and mutual professional respect. This continued after Manstein became Chief of the Operations Branch of the Great General Staff in 1935. In October 1936 he was promoted to Major General—considerably ahead of most of his contemporaries—and became the First Quartermaster General and deputy to General Beck.

In February 1938 he was relieved of his duties on the General Staff, since Hitler and the Nazis were suspicious of his close friendship with General von Fritsch. At first he was given command of a division in Silesia, and then he became an army chief of staff for the occupation of Czechoslovakia. In August 1939 Manstein became chief of staff to General von Rundstedt, who commanded the Eastern Army Group in the invasion of Poland. When Rundstedt was shifted to the West in October 1939 to command Army Group A in the projected invasion of Western Europe, Manstein accompanied him. During that winter, as plans for the invasion were revised and refined, Manstein became involved in a professional argument with General Halder, Chief of the General Staff, about the details of those plans.

PLAN "YELLOW"—HALDER VS. MANSTEIN / The General Staff plan for the invasion of France—known as *Fall Gelb*, Case (or Plan) "Yellow"—was based

---

*His father was General Eduard von Lewinski, who died while Erich was a child. He was adopted by Lieutenant General George von Manstein, his mother's brother-in-law, member of another well-known Prussian military family.

mainly upon an assessment of the difficulties of breaching the Maginot Line in northeastern France. That line of fortifications, built between 1930 and 1934, extended along the entire Franco-German frontier from Switzerland in the south to Montmédy in the north. There were no comparable fortifications along most of the Franco-Belgian frontier, because the French intended—in the event of a German invasion of Belgium—to move most of their field forces into Belgium to prevent any possibility of success by an improved German Schlieffen Plan.

The German General Staff agreed with the French General Staff that the Maginot Line fortifications were too formidable for an assault as long as there was any possible alternative strategy. So Halder and his subordinates explored the possibility of an updated Schlieffen Plan. They came to the conclusion that such a plan had a greater possibility of success than the French realized. If they could break rapidly through the eastern defenses of the Netherlands and Belgium, they hoped to be able to meet the advancing French and British armies in central Belgium, before they had a chance to complete their deployment. (The capture of Eben Emael was an important element of this concept.) Under these circumstances, by rapidly massing great forces in Holland and Belgium, the Germans thought they could defeat the Allies, drive them back across the frontier into France, and thus bypass the Maginot Line. Continuing to maintain overwhelming strength on the right wing, Halder hoped to be able to carry to a successful conclusion the concept of Schlieffen, which the younger Moltke had botched.

Manstein was unhappy with this plan, which provided for massing most of the German armored divisions and the bulk of the infantry divisions opposite the Netherlands frontier under General von Bock's Army Group B. Rundstedt's smaller Group A, consisting mostly of a lesser number of infantry divisions, was deployed opposite Belgium and Luxembourg. It would serve mainly as the connecting link between Bock's striking force and the still smaller Army Group C, under General von Leeb, deployed in defensive positions opposite the Maginot Line. Manstein thought the French, remembering how close to success the Schlieffen Plan had come in 1914, would be expecting this very plan, and that the Germans would lose the key advantage of surprise. Since the Allied armies, even without the Belgians and Dutch, were about as large and as well equipped as the Germans, he feared that there was little chance of success. But when he expressed his views to the General Staff, Halder responded, in effect: We understand all of this as well as you do; the only alternative is a costly attack against the Maginot Line.

Manstein, who had been discussing the problem with Guderian, now commanding an armored corps, insisted that there was another alternative. He pointed out that both the French and the Belgians had concentrated only small forces in and behind the rugged Ardennes Forest region of eastern Belgium and northern Luxembourg. They apparently believed that this mountainous, wooded region was not suitable for the fast-moving armored columns of the German

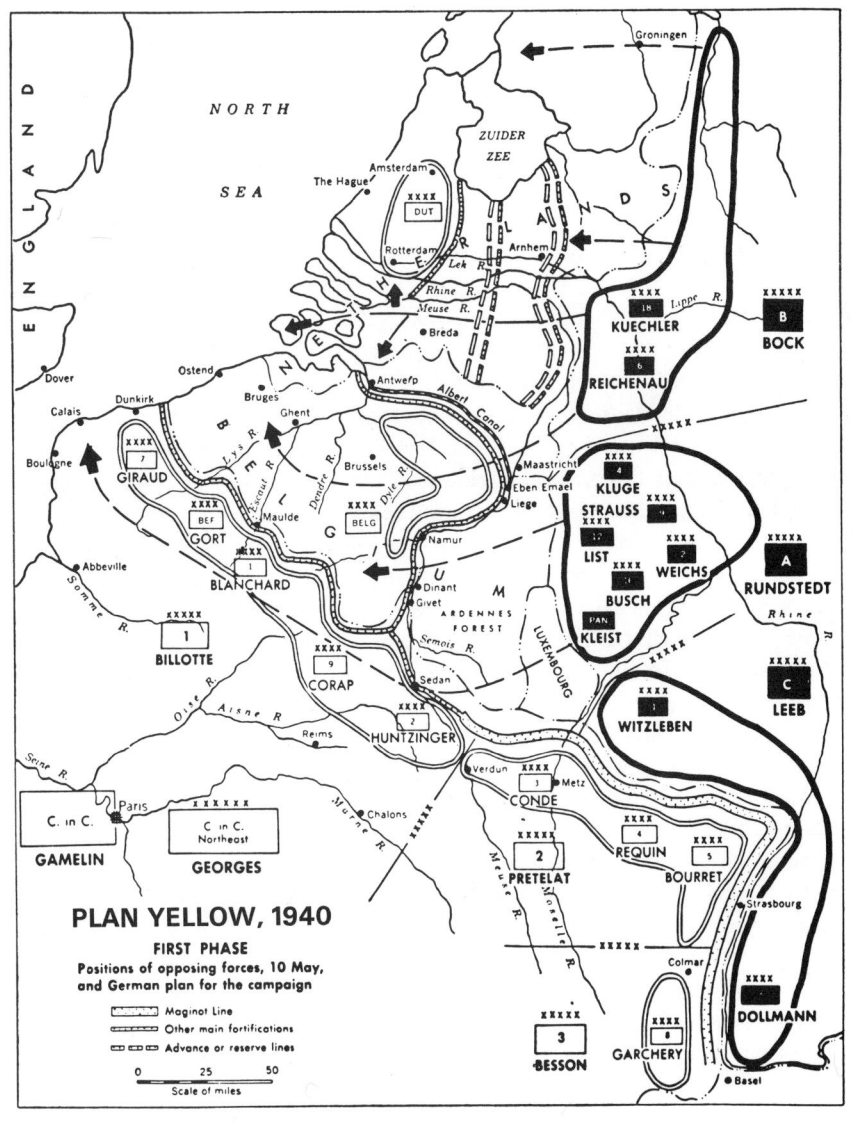

PLAN YELLOW, 1940

FIRST PHASE

Positions of opposing forces, 10 May, and German plan for the campaign

Maginot Line
Other main fortifications
Advance or reserve lines

0   25   50
Scale of miles

blitzkrieg. Manstein assumed that it was the opinion of Allied planners that if the Germans were shortsighted enough to attempt a major movement through the Ardennes, they could be delayed until reserves could be brought up to hold the easily defended line of the Meuse River.

Manstein and Guderian believed, however, that a surprise armored blow through the Ardennes could move so quickly that the Allies would not have time to organize a solid defense on the Meuse, and that a complete breakthrough could be made. If the attack were then pressed vigorously, they believed, the onrushing German armored forces could reach the English Channel near Boulogne and Calais, cutting off the Allied armies in Belgium. Such an unexpected operation would have the advantage of surprise. Moreover, the plan would actually take advantage of the Allied expectation of a new Schlieffen Plan, by enticing them into a trap in Belgium and Holland.

Halder was not at first very much impressed with the Manstein plan. Quite independently Hitler had made similar suggestions in the late fall of 1939, and Halder had been put to considerable trouble to "prove" such an operation was "impossible." He doubted that the German armor could get through the Ardennes as rapidly as Manstein believed and Guderian promised. Also there would be very serious problems of supply and reinforcement through the narrow, easily blocked roads of the Ardennes. However, with typical objective thoroughness, he and the General Staff again undertook a new study of this possibility.

Meanwhile Rundstedt had become completely convinced of the feasibility of Manstein's plan, and insisted that it be given more consideration by Brauchitsch and Halder. At Rundstedt's insistence, on February 7, 1941, a war game was held at his headquarters at Koblenz to test the feasibility of the Manstein plan. To Rundstedt, Manstein, and Guderian the outcome of the war game completely demonstrated the feasibility of their plan.

Though Brauchitsch and Halder continued to express doubts, Halder's earlier opposition had been shaken by the results of the games, which he and the General Staff reviewed in great detail. When a second game was held on February 14, Halder became convinced that Manstein was right, and recommended to Brauchitsch that they adopt the Manstein concept and that most of the armored and mechanized divisions be shifted from Bock's army group to Rundstedt's. This was done.

By early February, however, Brauchitsch had become so annoyed by Manstein's vigorous support of his proposal, that he ordered the obstreperous younger general away from Rundstedt's army group and sent him to command a new corps headquarters in Silesia. Manstein, unaware that he had finally convinced Halder, was summoned on February 17 to an interview with Hitler in Berlin, while he was on his way to his new command. He had an opportunity to express his ideas on the coming operations in some detail to Hitler. He was unaware of the similarity of Hitler's earlier suggestions to Halder and was pleased that Hitler agreed with him. Thus when the new operation order was issued on February 20, making most of the changes Manstein had recommended, he assumed that this was a result of his conversation with Hitler, without realizing that his plan had already been adopted by Halder.

OPPOSING FORCES AND CONCEPTS IN THE WEST / Manstein's plan proved to be an ideal operational concept for a German Field Army that had by this time grown to a strength of nearly 2.5 million men in 136 divisions. As a result of the experience in Poland, the four light mechanized divisions had been converted to full-strength armored divisions, and a new armored division had been formed, giving the mobile element of the Army a total strength of ten armored and seven motorized divisions. Concentrated in these ten armored divisions were 2,547 tanks, of which 1,478 were light tanks, armed only with machine guns or 20 mm machine cannon; 687 were medium tanks, with 50 mm guns, and 278 "heavy" tanks had 75 mm guns. The remaining 135 were specially equipped command tanks.

The opposing Anglo-French Field Army was slightly smaller in numbers—a little more than 2 million men—organized in 112 divisions.[5] When joined by 600,000 Belgians and 400,000 Dutch, the Allies had a significant numerical superiority. The French and British also had substantially more tanks than the Germans—some 3,600—at least equal in quality, and many better armed and armored. There was, however, a substantial difference in the organization of the Allied armored units, and in the concept of their employment. The French had three armored divisions and three light-cavalry mechanized divisions. But more than half of the French armor was parceled out among the infantry divisions or in reserve battalions and regiments. And even the armored and cavalry mechanized divisions were distributed among several French armies.

The German doctrine, on the other hand, emphasized the principle of mass by the concentration of tanks in armored divisions, and the massing of armored divisions into corps and groups. Infantry and artillery closely supported the tanks, with the artillery often right behind the line of contact, firing over open sights. Light armored ground forces and air observation units were integrated into reconnaissance teams to support each army group. Engineers were readily available for mining and stream crossing. Antiaircraft was well forward and successfully protected river-crossing sites and choke points from Allied air attacks. The availability of 88 mm antiaircraft guns was frequently useful in another respect, in that they were the only weapons effective against the most heavily armored Allied tanks. By use of radio communications, German commanders could exercise much greater control over subordinate units than could their Allied counterparts. The whole was a closely integrated, highly articulated team which had been well trained under appropriate tactics and doctrine, received combat experience in Poland, and had trained intensively again in the winter 1939-1940 to assimilate that experience.

THE BATTLE OF FLANDERS / When the German attack came on May 10, the operations went just as Manstein had foreseen, resulting in German victory in one of the most decisive and momentous campaigns in military history.

Beginning with the fall of Fort Eben Emael, the German plans were carried out as though controlled by clockwork. Of course, it was not as easy as it seemed, and there was much drama, much gallantry, and extremely hard fighting on both sides. But whenever things seemed to go wrong or to deviate from their plans, the Germans called upon *Auftragstaktik* to carry them through to their objectives in dazzling displays of boldness, initiative, and imagination.

Just as the war games in Koblenz had predicted, the armored spearhead of Army Group A reached the Meuse late on D+2–May 12. That evening, Major Walther Wenck, operations officer of the 1st Panzer Division of Guderian's corps, noted the remarkable similarity of the actual course of operations to the war game. The division's units had reached the river in the same places, and none of the missions had been changed. From his files he pulled out the order he had issued in the *Kriegsspiel* operation at Koblenz on February 14. Changing only the date, he issued the same order to the division. Next morning, with massive close air support from the *Luftwaffe,* the 1st Panzer Division smashed its way across the river near Sedan. At the same time, further north near Dinant, the 7th Panzer Division, commanded by General Erwin Rommel, was making a similar and equally successful assault crossing.

The bridgeheads were quickly expanded by follow-up units, as the rampaging panzers continued their drive to the West. By May 15 the French Seventh

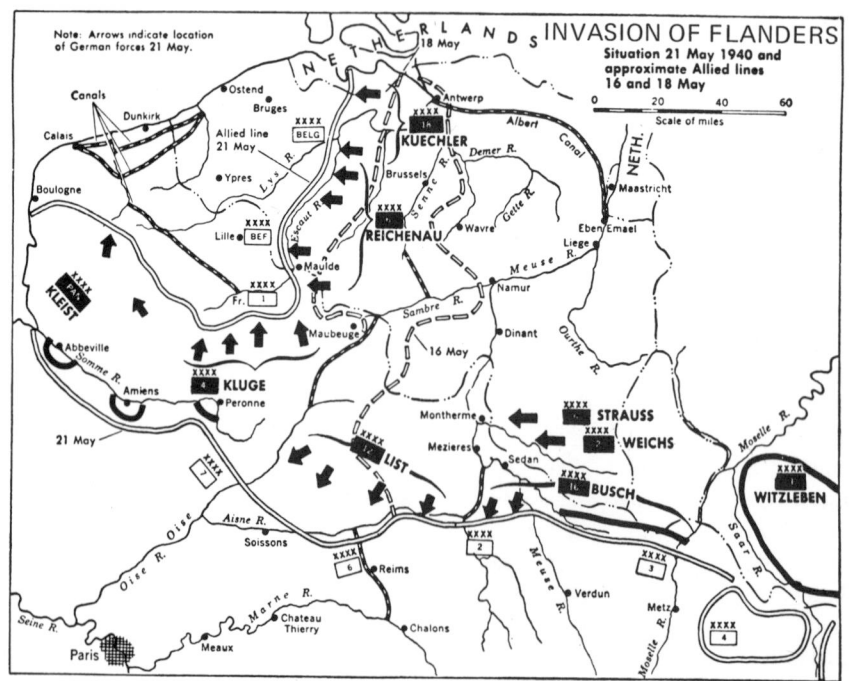

Army had been shattered, and the left wing of the Second Army had been pulverized.

That morning the newly appointed British Prime Minister, Winston Churchill, received a telephone call from his French counterpart, Paul Reynaud. "We have been defeated; we have lost the battle," the French premier told him. Later that morning the Dutch Army surrendered. As Churchill wrote in his memoirs, "I did not comprehend the violence of the revolution effected since the last war by the incursion of a mass of fast-moving heavy armour."[6] In fact, with the possible exception of Charles de Gaulle, it is doubtful if anyone outside Germany—and conquered Poland—had really comprehended this revolution until it overwhelmed them.

That afternoon Churchill flew to Paris, and there he and Premier Reynaud received a briefing from General Gamelin, the French Commander in Chief, about the German breakthrough at the Meuse. "Presently I asked General Gamelin," Churchill wrote later, "when and where he proposed to attack the flanks of the [German penetration]. His reply was: 'Inferiority of numbers, inferiority of equipment, inferiority of method'—and then a hopeless shrug of the shoulders."[7]

The mass of German infantry, on foot with animal transport, followed in the wake of the armored and motorized spearhead to mop up, consolidate, widen, and defend the penetration. It soon developed that these units were unable to keep up with the twenty-to-eighty miles-per-day of the armored advance, and there was thus always an undefended vacuum behind the spearhead. While this worried the German command, the Allies were never able to flow into this zone to cut off the spearhead, because their reconnaissance means were inadequate to find it, and their mobile counterattack means were both inadequate and improperly handled.

Manstein's infantry corps—recently arrived from Silesia—was one of these follow-up units. He participated in the closing operations of the Battle of Flanders, and in the final defeat of France the following month. Early in 1941 he was given command of the LVI Army Corps (an armored formation) concentrating in East Prussia, in preparation for war with Russia.

MANSTEIN IN OPERATION "BARBAROSSA" / The plan for the invasion of the Soviet Union was code named Operation "Barbarossa." Despite delays caused by the unanticipated invasion of the Balkans, by mid-June Halder's General Staff had assembled in East Prussia, Poland, Slovakia, and Hungary the largest field force in German history: 149 divisions (of these 135 were German, the others Romanian and Hungarian) comprised of more than 3 million men, 3,350 tanks, 600,000 motor vehicles, and 625,000 horses. (Interestingly, this continued reliance upon horse-drawn transportation can be compared with the 726,670 horses that were included in Germany's mobilized army in 1914.)[8]

When Operation "Barbarossa" began on June 22, 1941, Manstein's LVI Panzer Corps spearheaded the northeastern drive of Army Group North into

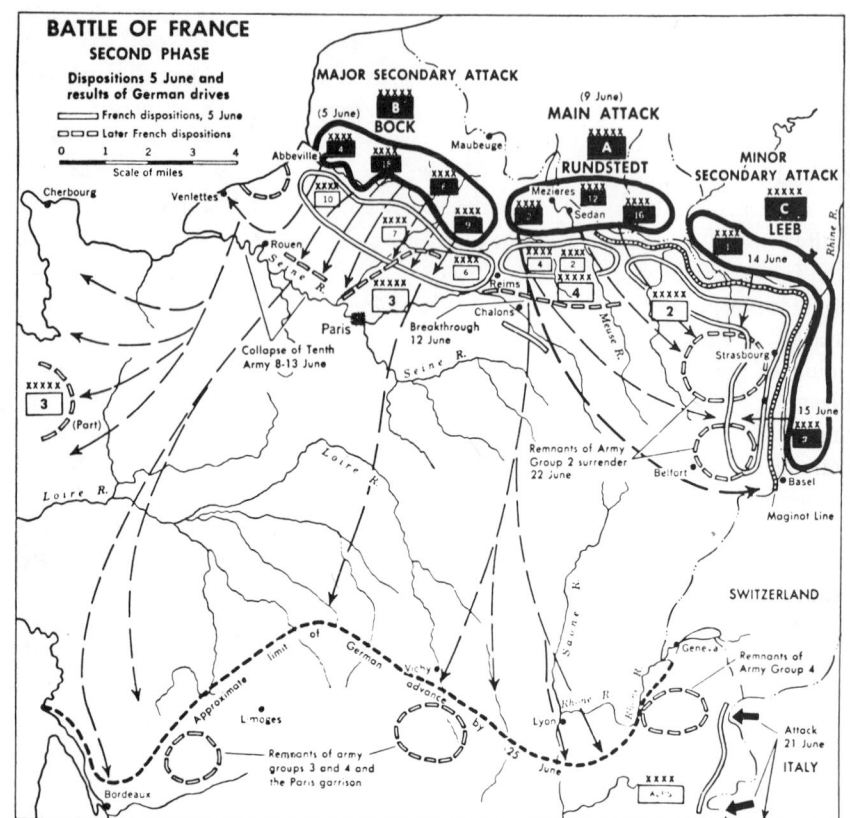

BATTLE OF FRANCE
SECOND PHASE
Dispositions 5 June and
results of German drives

Lithuania, in the general direction of Leningrad. Four days later, after advancing at the amazing rate of fifty miles per day, his spearheads made surprise assault crossings of the Dvina River, and occupied the city of Dvinsk, after capturing two major bridges before the astonished defenders had time to set off their prepared demolitions. By July 2, when the remainder of the German army had caught up, Manstein was authorized to renew the drive to the northeast. By July 15 his advanced elements had moved forward another 250 miles to Lake Ilmen—a rate still in excess of twenty miles per day—where Manstein and his corps had to fight off Soviet encirclement until, once more, the rest of the army caught up with him, four days later.

These accomplishments, in an area unsuitable for tank and motorized operations, were followed by a series of successful battles against Soviet counterattacks, winning particularly favorable attention for Manstein. Thus, when Colonel General Eugen Ritter von Schobert, commander of the German Eleventh Army in the Crimea, was killed by a Russian mine, Manstein was immediately selected to take his place. During September Manstein (who also commanded the Third Romanian Army) occupied most of the Crimean Peninsula against determined Russian resistance and blockaded the remaining Russians in Sevastopol and the Kerch Peninsula. He held his ground during the Russian winter counteroffensive, and in July 1942 finally captured Sevastopol, and cleared the Kerch Peninsula. For this he was promoted to Field Marshal.

While the German summer offensive of 1942 was approaching Stalingrad and the Caucasus, Manstein was shifted to command on the Leningrad front. Despite inadequate forces, he was expected to take Leningrad. Like Halder—who was on increasingly bad terms with Hitler—Manstein was appalled by a directive to undertake a major offensive that was in no way linked to the German main effort further south. It was in fact directed in almost the opposite direction. Loyally, however, he attempted the impossible. Although he failed, he was nevertheless able in September to destroy the Soviet Second Shock Army, which had counterattacked near Lake Ladoga.

On November 19, 1942, Hitler reaped the consequences of his centrifugal offensives with grossly inadequate forces and a ridiculous command structure. Soviet counteroffensives north and south of Stalingrad broke through the attenuated German and Romanian armies, and on November 21 succeeded in encircling the German Sixth Army in and around Stalingrad. That day Manstein was ordered to take his Army headquarters from the Leningrad front to establish a new Don Army Group, which would consist of the surrounded Sixth Army, the badly battered Fourth Panzer Army, the Third Romanian Army (which was also surrounded), and the Fourth Romanian Army. In the following weeks Manstein succeeded in creating a new front with a few reinforcements and the shattered remnants that had been placed under his command. If Hitler had permitted the Sixth Army to fight its way out of the encirclement, as its commander, General Friedrich Paulus, and Manstein both wanted, the result would still have been a German defeat, but might well have been followed by at least a local

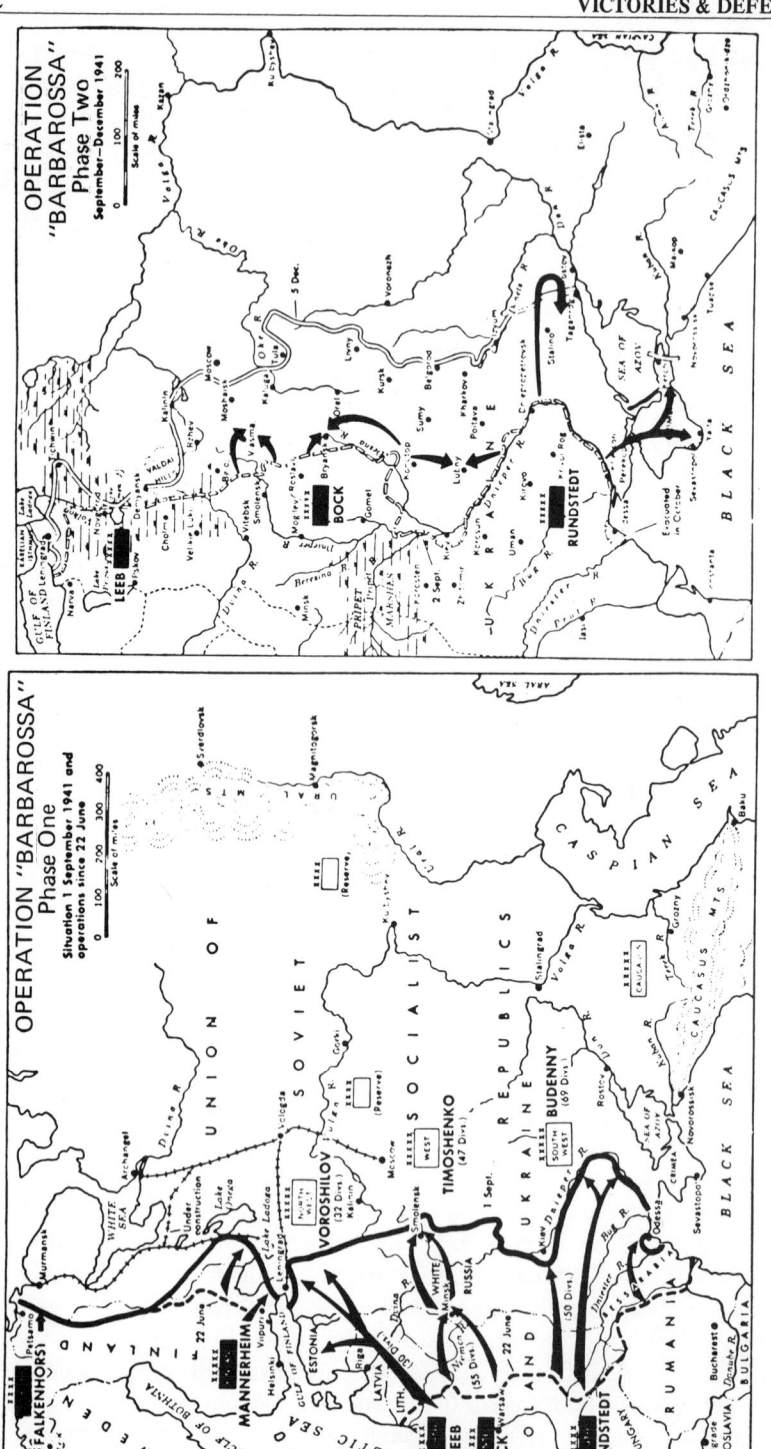

counteroffensive victory. As it was, because of Hitler's obstinacy, Germany suffered its most decisive military defeat since November 1918, ending forever any hope of victory over Russia.

Nevertheless, a little more than six months later, Manstein might have won for Hitler a local success of sufficient magnitude to permit a stabilized, stalemated front, and even the possibility of a negotiated peace. To set the stage, in March 1943 in a surprise offensive at Kharkov, Manstein won Germany's last major victory on the Eastern Front.

THE BATTLE OF KURSK / Manstein urged a prompt exploitation of this success by cutting off a bulge around Kursk, a result of the Kharkov victory. OKH agreed, Hitler at first approved, then postponed the operation for two months, because he wanted to wait until Panther tanks and the newly developed German Tiger tanks could be available in large numbers. (He completely ignored the fact, pointed out to him by his General Staff, that the Soviet tank production rate was substantially greater than that of Germany.) Had Operation "Citadel" gone as Manstein planned in early May, it might have been successful. In the interval, however, the Soviets made the Kursk salient one of the most thoroughly fortified areas in the history of modern warfare, and assembled vast reserves behind the front.

When the Germans finally did attack, on July 5, they had a total force of more than 900,000 troops around the Kursk salient, of which about one third, opposite the northern side of the salient, were part of Field Marshal von Kluge's Central Army Group, and about two thirds, concentrated on the south, were in Manstein's Southern Army Group. Opposing them were some 1.3 million Russian troops, with at least 300,000 more in reserve, available to be committed.

On the northern face of the salient the Central Army Group's Ninth Army was soon halted. On the southern face, after seven days of vicious fighting, Manstein's two armies—Fourth Panzer and Detachment Kempf—advanced more than thirty-five kilometers toward Oboyan and broke through the Soviet defensive zone, about halfway to Kursk. This was an incredible accomplishment, in the light of the strength of the defenses, the tenacity of the Russian resistance, and the Soviet numerical superiority. On July 11, however, the Soviet committed a reserve tank army on this front, halting the German advance, and bringing to a climax the greatest tank battle in history. In following days more Russian reserves were committed, forcing the Germans back.

In his memoirs Manstein states his conviction that his troops could have repulsed this counteroffensive and gone on to capture Kursk. The only reason this did not happen, he insists, is that on July 13 Hitler, worried by the Allied invasion of Sicily, ordered a halt to the offensive so that reserves could be sent to the West. Because of this, Manstein writes, "The assault groups . . . had to be withdrawn to their original start lines." He then concludes: "And so the last German offensive in the East ended in a fiasco, even though the enemy opposite

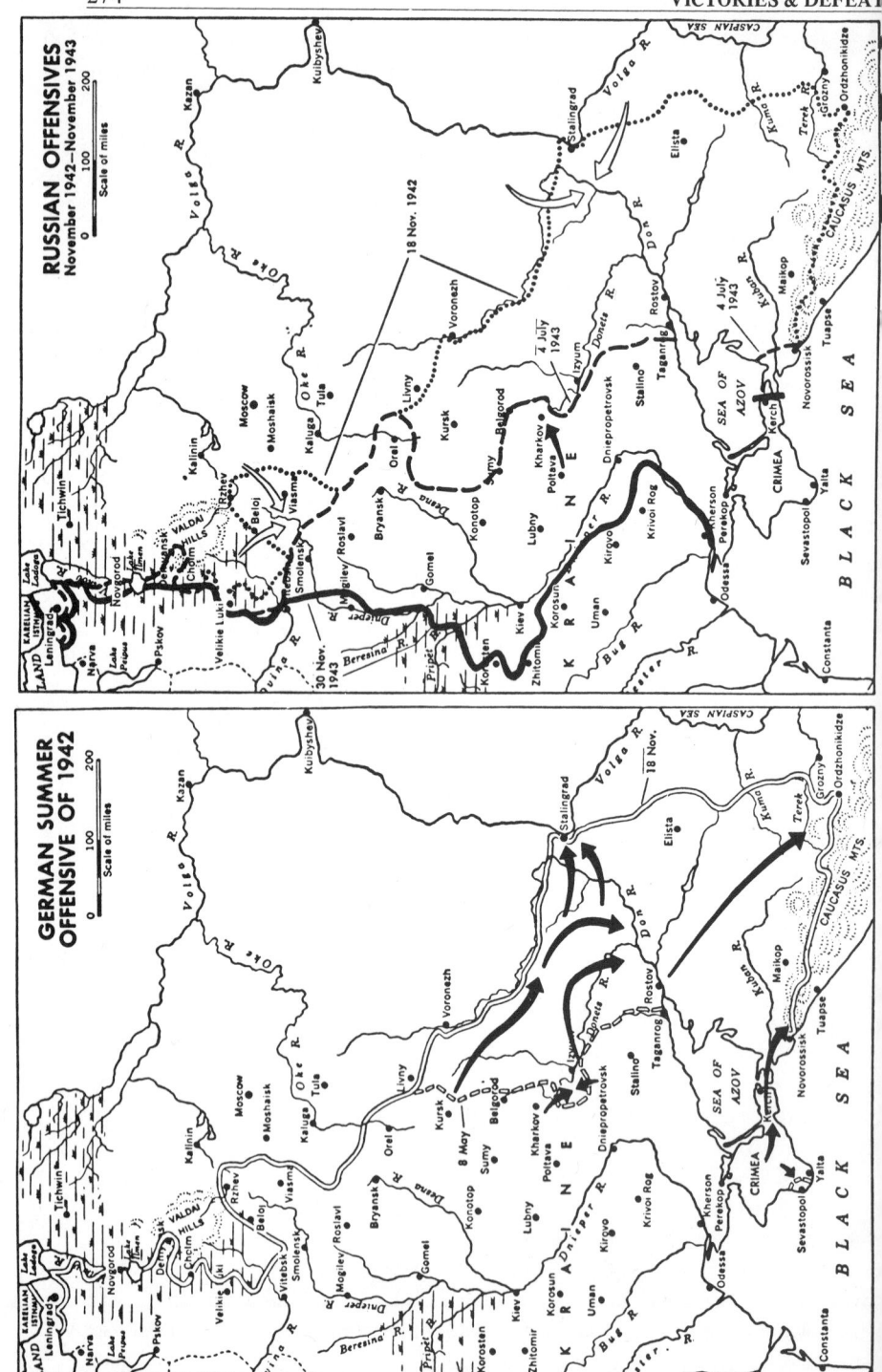

the two attacking armies of Southern Army Group had suffered four times their losses in prisoners, dead and wounded."[9]

Manstein did not exaggerate either the facts or the magnitude of the German accomplishment in inflicting such losses upon the powerfully fortified Russian armies. An objective assessment, however, leads to the conclusion that, even without Hitler's interference, the exhausted German divisions, all reserves committed, would not have been able to defeat the Soviet counteroffensive.

"PRINCIPLES AND OUTLOOK OF THE GENERAL STAFF" ON THE DEFENSIVE / For the next eight months Manstein fought a series of brilliant defensive, delaying battles against Soviet armies outnumbering his own by margins of 3 or 4 or sometimes as much as 7 to 1. At the same time he was endlessly arguing with Hitler, whose refusal to face reality and whose repeated prohibitions against further withdrawals threatened innumerable new disasters like Stalingrad. On March 30, 1944, Hitler—as a result of the conniving of Goering, Himmler, and Keitel, all of whom feared and hated Manstein—relieved Manstein of his command.

In the final pages of his memoirs,[10] Manstein has some interesting observations about "the perpetual struggle we had had to wage with the Supreme Commander to get operational necessities recognized."

> Our repeated demands for the establishment of a *clear focal point of effort at the decisive spot* . . . and for *operational freedom of movement* in general . . . were merely outward manifestations of the struggle. The basic issue was between two incompatible conceptions of strategy and grand tactics:
>
> (i) *Hitler's,* which arose from the personal characteristics and opinions . . . of a dictator who believed in the power of his will not only to nail down his armies wherever they might be but even to hold the enemy at bay. The same dictator, however, who fought shy of risks because of their inherent threat to his prestige and who, for all his talent, lacked the groundwork of real military ability. . . .
>
> (ii) That of *Southern Army Group Headquarters* [i.e., Manstein] , which was based on the traditional principles and outlook of the German General Staff . . . the views of military leaders who by virtue of their education and training still firmly believed that war was an *art* in which clarity of appreciation and boldness of decision constituted the essential elements. An art which could find success only in mobile operations, because it was only in these that the superiority of German leadership and German fighting troops could attain full effect.

As Manstein suggests, "the principles and outlook of the German General Staff" were still major factors in the performance of the German Army, factors that would continue to exert remarkable influence on every officer and man until the final German collapse, over a year later. The General Staff itself, however, was no longer a major element in the formulation of either German military policy or German strategy.

THE DECLINE OF THE GENERAL STAFF / The decline of the General Staff as the key military institution in Germany had begun when Hitler assumed the position of Defense Minister and Commander in Chief of the Armed Forces in early 1938. At that time he had established his own personal command staff—the Armed Forces High Command (*Oberkommando der Wehrmacht,* or OKW) under General Keitel. To offset Keitel's toadying ineptitude, OKW included a number of competent officers with General Staff background and experience, including General Alfred Jodl, who was chief of the OKW Operations Staff. Although it was not organized or manned for the responsibility, OKW increasingly assumed the advisory role traditionally held by the Army General Staff (for all practical purposes the Army High Command: *Oberkommando des Heeres,* or OKH). The decline of OKH accelerated at the time of Munich, when Hitler dismissed General Beck as Chief of the General Staff. Nonetheless, under Beck's successor, Colonel General Franz Halder, OKH at least played its traditional role with respect to the Army and the Army Commander in Chief, Field Marshal von Brauchitsch, in the preparations for and the conduct of the operations in Poland, in the Low Countries and France, and in the first six months of the Russian Campaign.

The declining influence and prestige of the General Staff were obvious, however, when Hitler interfered with the operations in that campaign by ordering the encirclement of the Kiev Pocket, in August and September 1941. This halted the main thrusts toward Moscow, the economic, political, and railroad center of Russia, and allowed the Russians breathing time to reorganize and to improve their defenses of that vital point. This diversion of effort meant that a victory in Russia could not be achieved before winter. Yet earlier Hitler had overruled Fromm and Halder when they had requested resources to equip the Army for winter operations, on the grounds that this would not be necessary.

When the exhausted German armies, unprepared for a winter campaign, were finally halted by Russian counterattacks on December 6, 1941, Hitler would not admit that the failure was due to his own many errors of judgment; rather he blamed the Army Commander in Chief—Brauchitsch—and the principal army group and army commanders for not having been sufficiently aggressive. He relieved all of them, and assumed the title and responsibility of Army Commander in Chief himself.

HALDER VS. HITLER / Although he did not relieve Halder, Hitler still further diminished the importance of the General Staff by taking away from the Chief of the General Staff his traditional responsibility for assignment and employment of General Staff Corps officers; this was transferred to the Army Personnel Office—which was now directly under Hitler as Army Commander in Chief.

From this time on, also, Hitler limited all operational responsibility of the General Staff—or OKH—to the Russian front, assigning operational responsibility for other theaters to Keitel's OKW. This created near hopeless confusion in all German planning, since OKH remained responsible for supervising the nonoperational activities of the Army as a whole, and for coordinating the activities of the field armies with General Fromm's Replacement Army. Thanks, however, to the personal efficiency of Halder, Fromm, and Jodl (rather than the inept Kietel), and their principal General Staff Corps subordinates, the system still operated with amazing efficiency, despite the confusing staff relationships.

Halder was not prepared, however, to surrender the last traditional responsibility of the General Staff, which had in fact been its raison d'etre in the eyes of its founders, Scharnhorst and his Reformers. This was to preclude or offset inept meddling of nonmilitary kings (or dictators) by sound advice or offsetting counteractions. Relations between Hitler and Halder had grown steadily worse, and Halder made no effort to hide his contempt for Hitler's military ignorance. He protested with especial vigor Hitler's plan for a three-directional offensive in the summer of 1942. It made no sense to him to disperse the outnumbered German forces by simultaneous thrusts eastward toward the Don and Stalingrad, southeastward into the Caucasus, and northward toward Leningrad, leaving vastly larger Russian forces to strike one or more of the exposed flanks of these offensives. Hitler angrily overruled Halder's undiplomatic protests. Halder thought of resigning—as many of his colleagues thought he should—but feared that if he did he would be followed by someone who would not have the courage even to dispute unsound decisions with Hitler. In August and September, as the German drives toward Stalingrad and the Caucasus exposed the thinly held flanks of the attacking units to possible Soviet counterattack, he protested again, with increasing acerbity. Finally, on September 25, 1942, Hitler could stand it no longer. Curtly and brutally he dismissed Halder, replacing him with a much younger, competent, but unimaginative officer, Major General Kurt Zeitzler.

ZEITZLER AS CHIEF OF THE GENERAL STAFF / Zeitzler, in fact, did not turn out to be the yes-man Hitler had anticipated. But he lacked the intellectual brilliance of most of his predecessors in the office of Chief of the General Staff, and became virtually Hitler's military executive officer, rather than a true Chief of the General Staff in the Prussian-German tradition. For all practical purposes Scharnhorst's General Staff died when Halder was relieved.

Zeitzler, of course, inherited the situation about which Halder had protested, and which on November 19 collapsed as Halder had predicted. Zeitzler endeavored, in every way that he possibly could, to get Hitler to issue orders that would allow General Paulus' Sixth Army to fight its way out of the Stalingrad encirclement. But the arguments he and Manstein presented to Hitler seemed to become meaningless when Goering promised to keep the Sixth Army supplied by air. Although Goering quickly demonstrated that he did not have the ability to direct such an operation—which could never possibly have succeeded—Hitler ignored all evidence that the Sixth Army was doomed. Symbolically Zeitzler tried to dramatize the Stalingrad situation by limiting his own meals and those of the entire Staff to the amount of food available to each of the surrounded

FINAL RUSSIAN OFFENSIVES
0 100 200
Scale of miles
BALTIC SEA
GULF OF FINLAND
GULF OF RIGA
Helsinki
Leningrad
Narva
Pskov
Lake Peipus
Velikie Luki
ESTONIA
LATVIA
Riga
LITHUANIA
Kovno
Vilna
Grodno
Minsk
Memel
Konigsberg
EAST PRUSSIA
Niemen R.
16 Dec. 1944
Danzig
Warsaw
Vistula R.
Brest-Litovsk
PRIPET MARSHES
Pripet R.
Beresina R.
Dnieper R.
Duina R.
Korosten
Kiev
Zhitomir
Rowne
Dubno
Lwow
Tarnopol
Cernauti
Iasi
Uman
Bug R.
Dniester R.
Prut R.
UKRAINE
POLAND
Cracow
Posen
Oder R.
Breslau
Stettin
Berlin
Hamburg
Elbe R.
Magdenburg
Leipzig
Torgau
Dresden
Prague
7 May 1945
GERMANY
DENMARK
Nurnberg
Munich
Ulm
Danube R.
Linz
AUSTRIA
Graz
Zagreb
Trieste
Zara
ADRIATIC SEA
Rimini
Budapest
HUNGARY
Belgrade
Sarajevo
YUGOSLAVIA
CARPATHIAN MTS.
RUMANIA
Ploesti
Bucharest
Danube R.
BULGARIA
Constanta
BLACK SEA

RUSSIAN OFFENSIVES
December 1943—December 1944
0 100 200
Scale of miles
BALTIC SEA
GULF OF FINLAND
GULF OF RIGA
Helsinki
Lake Ladoga
Leningrad
Novgorod
Lake Ilmen
Demyansk
Cholm
Narva
Pskov
Lake Peipus
Velikie Luki
Vitebsk
Smolensk
Mogilev
Gomel
ESTONIA
LATVIA
Riga
LITHUANIA
Kovno
Vilna
Grodno
Minsk
Memel
Konigsberg
EAST PRUSSIA
Danzig
Warsaw
Vistula R.
Brest-Litovsk
PRIPET MARSHES
Korosten
Kiev
Zhitomir
1 Dec. 1943
22 June 1944
Rowne
Dubno
Lwow
Tarnopol
Cernauti
Iasi
Uman
Kirovo
Odessa
UKRAINE
POLAND
Cracow
Posen
Oder R.
Breslau
Stettin
Berlin
Dresden
Prague
GERMANY
Vienna
Graz
Zagreb
Zara
Budapest
HUNGARY
13 Dec. 1944
Belgrade
Sarajevo
YUGOSLAVIA
CARPATHIAN MTS.
RUMANIA
Ploesti
Bucharest
Danube R.
BULGARIA
Constanta
BLACK SEA

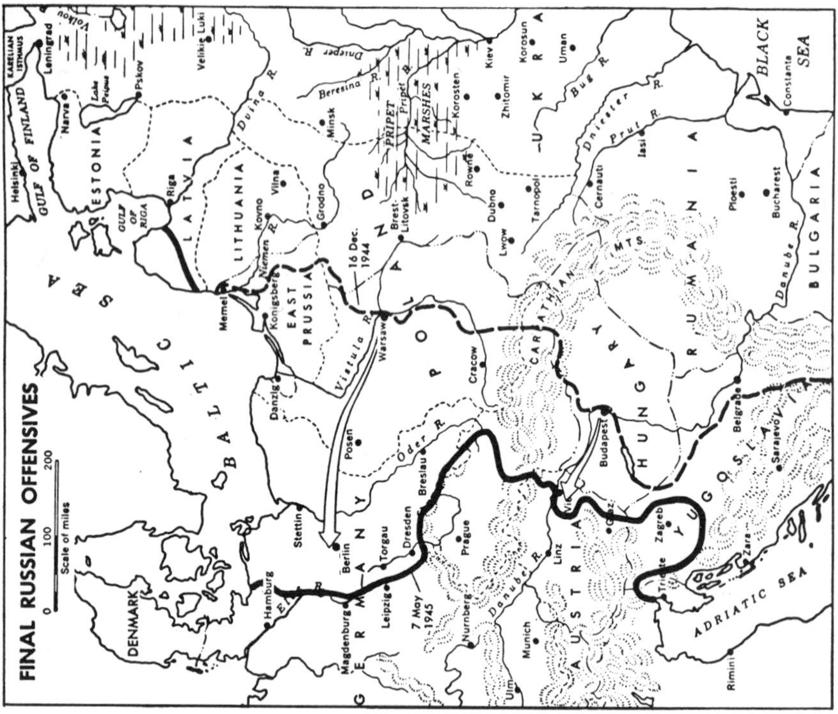

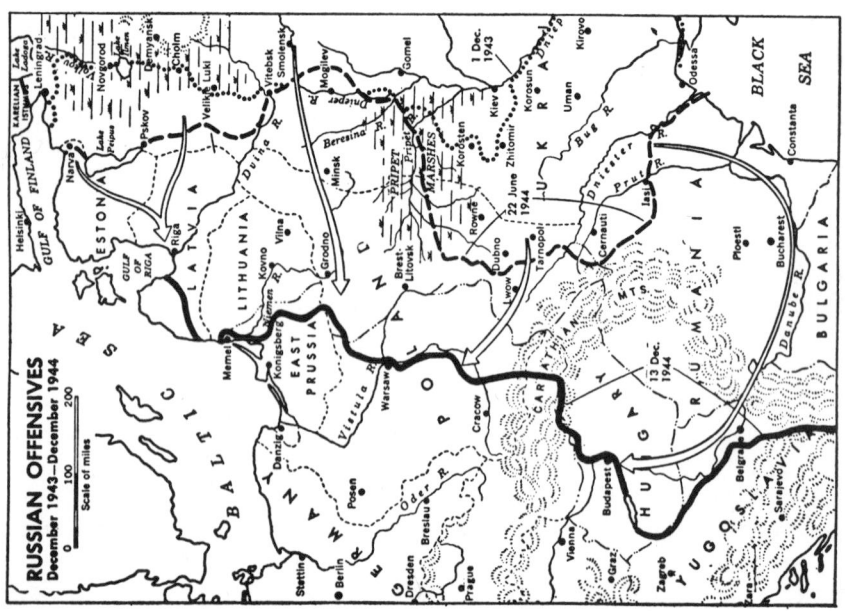

soldiers in Stalingrad. But as Zeitzler became thin and haggard, Hitler ordered him to resume full meals and then refused to accept his resignation.

This was the first of five times in the twenty-two months of his service as Chief of OKH that Zeitzler tried to resign. The last two times were when Manstein was dismissed, but Hitler refused to accept either his oral or written resignations. On September 24, 1943, Hitler promoted him to General of Infantry, then on January 30, 1944, to Colonel General.

THE PLOT AGAINST HITLER / On July 20, 1944, Hitler suspected almost every General Staff Corps officer of being in the conspiracy to assassinate him; he dismissed Zeitzler, who was for a time imprisoned. Armaments Minister Albert Speer (who had been under some unfounded suspicion himself) was finally able to persuade Hitler that Zeitzler had not been aware of the plot.

Possibly the greatest personal tragedy of the July 20 assassination plot against Hitler was that of Colonel General Fromm. While he never suffered the humiliations and tortures of many of the convicted conspirators, they had at least taken part in the conspiracy, which Fromm had refused to do. No one knew better than he how Hitler's policies were leading Germany to inevitable defeat and ruin, but like many other senior German officers, he felt that his personal oath of loyalty to Hitler precluded him from taking part in any effort to overthrow the dictator. Whenever any of the conspirators had attempted diplomatically to sound him out, he had pointedly changed the subject. Yet the conspirators believed that if Hitler were once dead, Fromm would join them. This was certainly the view of Colonel Count Klaus von Stauffenberg, one of the ringleaders, who was Fromm's chief of staff. Stauffenberg was the man who actually carried and placed the bomb that was intended to kill Hitler.

On July 20, when the conspirators thought Hitler had been killed by the bomb, they asked Fromm to join them. However, he soon discovered that Hitler had survived, and tried to arrest the rebel leaders. He was therefore quickly locked up in his office by Stauffenberg, who placed a guard on the door. When the conspiracy collapsed, Fromm was able to escape from his office, assumed command in Berlin, and quickly ordered summary trials and executions of several of the ringleaders, including Stauffenberg. He also seized General Beck, one of the principal leaders, but gave his old rival the opportunity to shoot himself. When Beck did not succeed in killing himself and was found lying on the floor, writhing in a pool of blood, Fromm ordered a soldier to shoot him.

But Hitler would not believe that Fromm had not been a conspirator, and saw in his actions of the evening of July 20 the efforts of a guilty man to cover up his guilt. Also, he could not forgive Fromm for preventing him from having the sadistic pleasure of seeing movies of Stauffenberg and Beck slowly tortured to death—as was the case with some other conspirators like Field Marshal von Witzleben and General Karl Heinrich von Stulpnagel. In any event, the evidence proved that Fromm had been well aware of the conspiracy and had failed to report it. He was kept in prison for several months and, despite the efforts of

Speer to have him released, was executed in March 1945. His actions and motivations in the closing hours of the putsch attempt are difficult to assess.

Fromm's place as the Chief of Equipment and Commander of the Replacement Army was taken by Reichsführer Heinrich Himmler, Chief of the Gestapo and the SS. By this time, however, there was little that even the crude and inept Nazi chieftain could do either to postpone or to hasten the now inevitable collapse of Germany.

GUDERIAN AS CHIEF OF THE GENERAL STAFF / Although inevitable, the collapse was prolonged, and this was due to the effects of the "traditional principles and outlook of the German General Staff," about which Manstein wrote.

To replace Zeitzler, Hitler appointed Colonel General Guderian, who was known not to have been implicated in the plot. Guderian, one of the most brilliant mobile-combat-force commanders in history, was a competent but unexceptional staff officer. Like Zeitzler, he lacked the intellectual capacity for high command in the tradition of the German General Staff. Under the circumstances this had little effect, positive or negative, on the outcome of the war. Guderian strove mightily to retrieve the situation on the Eastern Front, which he characterized as "appalling." But even if Hitler had been willing to accept his advice, the situation was now hopeless.

Guderian was one of the army commanders whom Hitler had relieved in his wholesale housecleaning after the German failure to take Moscow, in December 1941. Following a year of inactivity, he had been appointed Inspector General of Armored Troops on March 1, 1943. By this time Guderian seemed to have regained Hitler's confidence, but he almost lost it when he tried to persuade the dictator that he should appoint a Commanding General of the Army. He and Fromm and Speer had all agreed that until a full-time military commander replaced Hitler's part-time, uneducated, and obstinate performance of that role, there could be no real improvement in the military situation. By coincidence, however, both Field Marshals von Manstein and von Kluge made similar recommendations to Hitler at about the same time, and he wrongly suspected a General Staff conspiracy. Soon after this, Guderian suffered a serious heart attack, but he had fully recovered when Hitler appointed him Chief of the General Staff.

FRIDOLIN VON SENGER UND ETTERLIN / Among the many who understood, admired, and adhered to the "traditional principles and outlook of the German General Staff" was an officer who was fully qualified for membership in the General Staff Corps but who had been denied the opportunity by fate: Fridolin (Frido) Rudolf Theodore von Senger und Etterlin.

The career of this man provides an insight into the thinking and attitudes of a deeply religious, highly individualistic, fervently anti-Nazi German officer who could and did adapt himself to the doctrines, "principles and outlook" of the General Staff, and fight stalwartly and effectively for his country, even when it was controlled by a dictatorship that he hated. The answer to this apparent paradox can be found in his thoughtful war memoirs,[11] one of the most fascinating military writings to emerge from World War II. Among his many exploits of combat leadership on three fronts during the war was a corps operation that ranks with that of Scheffer-Boyadel at Lodz as one of the great feats of modern military history.

Frido von Senger und Etterlin was born into an aristocratic Baden family at Waldshut on September 4, 1891. He was a Rhodes Scholar at Oxford from 1912 to 1914, and, as he later wrote, "became a career officer by a mere chance." When World War I broke out, he still had one more year of schooling before qualifying for the degree of doctor of philosophy. He was called up for service in his reserve regiment on the outbreak of the war, was soon commissioned an officer, and served throughout the war on the Western Front as a field artilleryman. After the war he was one of the few nonregular officers who were selected for retention in Seeckt's 100,000-man Army. After two years at the Cavalry School at Hanover, in 1921 he was recommended for the General Staff, and passed the required examinations. He was not selected for General Staff Corps training, however, because he was over thirty years of age, and so served as a troop officer for the next eleven years at Göttingen with his cavalry regiment.

Early in 1934, as the German Army was beginning to expand and the General Staff was being stretched thin, Senger, then a major, was ordered to Berlin and detailed to the General Staff. During the next four years he was a member of the Operations Division of the Great General Staff, and developed a great admiration for Generals Beck, Hammerstein-Equord, and Fritsch. Although, as he later wrote, he recognized that horse cavalry was "an anachronism in war," like so many other horse-cavalry soldiers of armies around the world in the decades between the wars, his affection for horses and fellow horsemen was such that he was content to return to Göttingen in 1938, to assume command of his old cavalry regiment.

It was as the commander of an increasingly motorized cavalry regiment, and then brigade, that he fought in 1940 in the forefront of the invasions of Holland, Belgium, and France. On June 19 his brigade outraced General Erwin Rommel's 7th Panzer Division to gain the honor of capturing Cherbourg.

After service as a liaison officer in Rome, Senger was selected for promotion to Major General, and in late 1942, just after the collapse of the German front north and south of Stalingrad, was sent to the Eastern Front to take command of a panzer division. Assigned to the Fourth Panzer Army of Manstein's newly created Don Army Group, Senger's 17th Panzer Division spearheaded the vain effort to break through to relieve Stalingrad, and then was almost constantly engaged in more successful operations culminating in Manstein's Kharkov counteroffensive in the spring of 1943.

SENGER IN SICILY AND CORSICA / Senger's exceptional performance as a panzer-division commander led in the summer of 1943 to his promotion to lieutenant general and to his appointment to a new position. The Anglo-American victory in Tunisia had been followed by ominous Allied preparations for an offensive across the Mediterranean against Italy. Despite the elaborate Allied cover plan, which attempted to convince the Germans that an Allied invasion of Sardinia was intended, the operations staff of OKW calculated that Sicily must be the Allied objective. Field Marshal Albert Kesselring, commanding Axis forces in the Southern Theater, needed a senior German officer who combined both General Staff and combat experience to command German forces in Sicily and to act as his representative and liaison officer with the Italian Army commander on the island. Senger, now due for a corps command but not yet assigned, was the logical man.

Senger was unable to stop the inevitable Allied conquest of Sicily, but he planned and coordinated the beginning of the remarkable withdrawal of the battered German and Italian divisions from the island. He was not present to take part in the actual withdrawal, brilliantly conducted by General Hans Hube, commanding the XIV Panzer Corps. Kesselring had selected Senger to command the German Army, Navy, and Air Force units on the islands of Sardinia and Corsica. Nominally Senger's task was to coordinate German support of the Italian defense of those islands, in anticipation of an early Allied amphibious assault. More important, however, were his secret instructions from Kesselring to be prepared to evacuate the German units in the event of the likely defection of Italy from the Axis alliance.

The defection occurred on September 8, and by a combination of bluff, diplomacy, and hard fighting against Italian troops and French guerrillas, Senger concentrated his troops in southern Corsica, meanwhile pulling all German detachments out of Sardinia. On September 14 Senger received orders transmitting Hitler's directive to execute all of the captured Italian officers—some two hundred. By radiotelephone Senger notified Kesselring that he would not obey the order. This was neither the first nor the last time that Senger refused to obey Nazi instructions contrary to the laws of war. If he had ever been defeated, he himself would probably have been executed at Hitler's order. But since he was invariably successful, he got away with his disobedience.

On October 3—despite Allied control of sea and air—Senger completed the difficult and dangerous evacuation of Corsica. In fact he got a personal commendation from Hitler for his masterful handling of "a movement whose fulfillment in such completeness could not have been expected." Senger was told after the war that there had been a debate in OKW as to whether he should be commended for his success, or thrown into jail for disobedience, but that "his supporters had won the day." In fact, Hitler and OKW approved Kesselring's decision to reward Senger with the command of the XIV Panzer Corps whose former commander—General Hube—had just been ordered to Russia to take command of an army.

SENGER AND THE XIV PANZER CORPS / The XIV Panzer Corps held much of the western and central region of the peninsula-wide front of the Tenth Army

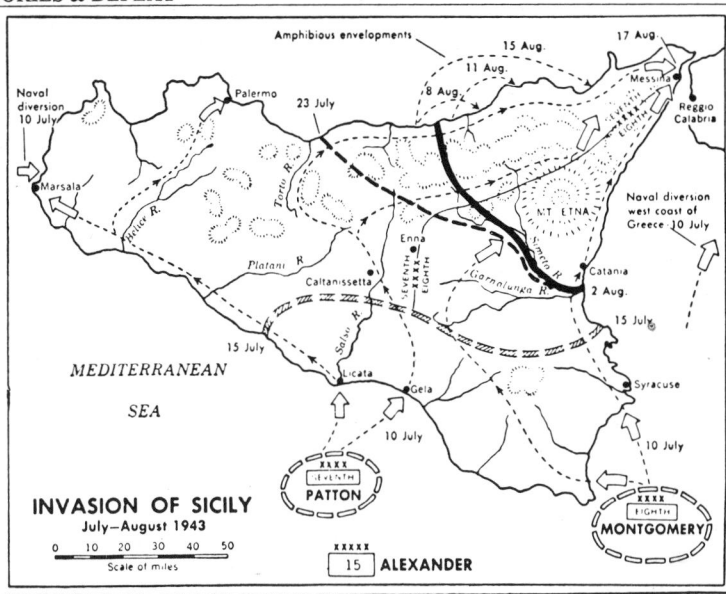

INVASION OF SICILY
July–August 1943
0 10 20 30 40 50
Scale of miles
Amphibious envelopments
15 Aug.
17 Aug.
11 Aug.
8 Aug.
Messina
Reggio Calabria
Palermo
23 July
Naval diversion 10 July
Marsala
Torto R.
Belice R.
MT. ETNA
Naval diversion west coast of Greece 10 July
Enna
SEVENTH
EIGHTH
Simeto R.
Platani R.
Caltanissetta
Catania
2 Aug.
Gornalunga R.
15 July
Salso R.
15 July
MEDITERRANEAN
SEA
Licata
Gela
Syracuse
10 July
10 July
XXXX
SEVENTH
PATTON
XXXX
EIGHTH
MONTGOMERY
XXXXX
15
ALEXANDER

Tiber R.
Rome
Sangro R.
Trigno R.
Termoli
ADRIATIC
SEA
Anzio
8 Oct. 1943
Foggia
Gulf of Gaeta
Volturno
Bari
Naval diversion
Naples
Salerno
Brindisi
Gulf of Salerno
Taranto
XXXX
FIFTH
CLARK
Main attack, 9 Sept.
TYRRHENIAN
SEA
9 Sept.
XXXXX
15
ALEXANDER
Secondary attack
3 Sept.
Messina
Palermo
Reggio Calabria
XXXX
EIGHTH
MONTGOMERY
Marsala
Catania
Licata
Gela
Syracuse
SICILIAN
STRAIT
INVASION OF ITALY
Situation 8 October 1943 and Operations since 3 September
0 50 100
Scale of miles

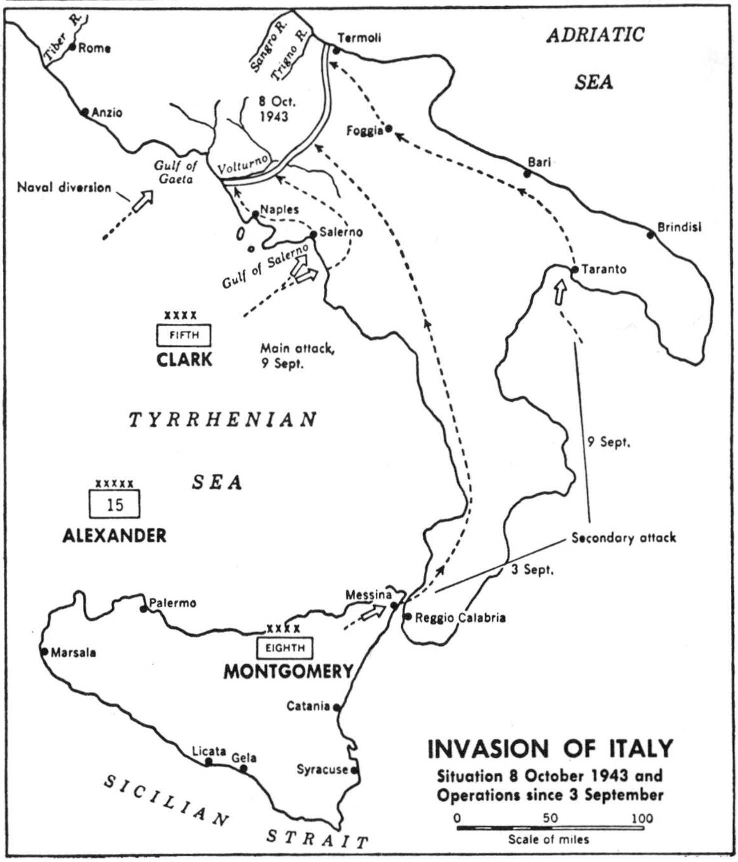

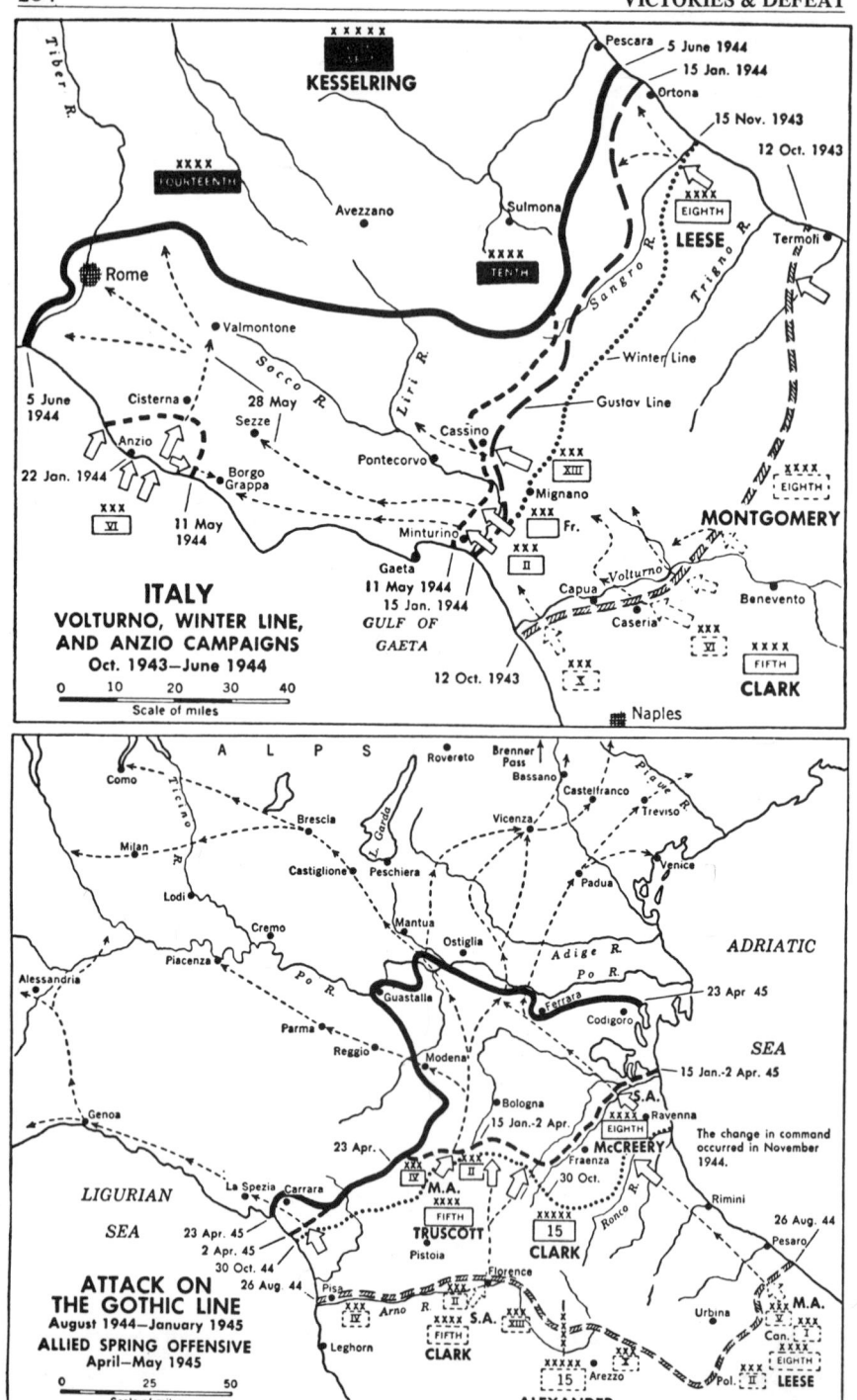

ITALY
VOLTURNO, WINTER LINE,
AND ANZIO CAMPAIGNS
Oct. 1943—June 1944

Scale of miles
0   10   20   30   40

ATTACK ON
THE GOTHIC LINE
August 1944—January 1945
ALLIED SPRING OFFENSIVE
April—May 1945

Scale of miles
0   25   50

of General Heinrich von Vietinghoff-Scheel. Against its front in the Volturno River Valley, the American Fifth Army made repeated assaults, forcing a slow German withdrawal. By mid-January the XIV Corps had fallen back to the previously prepared positions of the so-called Gustav Line, behind the Garigliano and Rapido rivers, the focal point being the small city of Cassino, where the main Rome-Naples road and railroad crossed the Rapido River.

On this line for the next five months Senger and his XIV Corps threw back repeated Allied attacks, of which the three most strenuous are known in history as the Battles of Cassino. One result of this success was that thereafter through the war Senger, although a corps commander, usually was assigned five or more divisions—virtually a small army—even though the usual corps command was two or three divisions. Kesselring, knowing that Hitler would never approve the promotion of this vigorously anti-Nazi Catholic general to army command, nevertheless used him as virtually the equivalent of an army commander. At least he got Hitler to approve Senger's promotion to General of Panzer Troops after his first defensive victory at Cassino.

Senger's tribute to his subordinate commanders after his three Cassino victories is significant in what it says both about the man and about the German Army:

> Our success at Cassino reflects the numerous examples in the history of war where results depend on the personality of the commander in the field. It is widely known that the main credit for the outcome of the first battle of Cassino goes to Major-General Baade, also that in the second battle the laurels for holding on to the town go to Lieut. General Heidrich. These two divisional commanders were at the same time paragons for their troops. But here I must put in a word for the young company commanders, the battalion commanders and the commanders of regiments, most of whom must remain anonymous. For it is they who bear the brunt of the close-in fighting, whose merit and courage and devotion determine the value of the troops. Many of them carry the Knight's Cross or the Iron Cross, many others rest in eternal peace among the adamantine rocks. Your steadfast bearing in the hour of greatest crisis and your loyalty to your commanding general will not be forgotten. If I mention one of the best by name, let him represent all of you. For I would like to take this opportunity to lower my sword before the grave of Major Knuth, the defender of Cassino in the first battle, who while leading his regiment into action found a hero's death on the day after I had decorated him with the Knight's Cross. As this leader fought, so did the soldiers fight, especially the infantry, but also the pioneers, the gunners, the rocket-launcher men, and not least, the medical orderlies, the mine-detectors, the truck-drivers and the mule-drivers on supply roads that were constantly under fire.

GREINER AND SENSFUSS, REPRESENTATIVE GENERALS / Perhaps the most remarkable thing about the command exploits of men like Senger, and like

Student and Manstein, is that such performances were not unusual. Close examination of German combat operations in World War II reveals—with occasional lapses and exceptions—the same kind of cool, competent, bold, imaginative, opportunistic leadership on the part of practically all German division, corps, army, and army-group commanders, in success as well as in adversity, in defense as well as in attack.

There was, for instance, Lieutenant General Heinz Greiner, commander of the 362nd Infantry Division when the Allies burst out of the Anzio beachhead. Greiner (who had earlier won praise from Manstein for his performance as a regimental commander and staff officer) was just returning from leave when his division was literally overrun by the massive air-supported assault of the U.S. 3rd Infantry and 1st Armored Divisions on May 23 and 24. Allied intelligence reported that the 362nd was "destroyed." Thus when the 1st Armored Division began its exploitation of the breakthrough on May 26 through Velletri, in the zone of the 362nd Division, no serious resistance was expected. But in one of the most intensive one-day battles of the war, under Greiner's inspiring leadership, the 362nd not only held, its counterattacks drove the surprised American tankmen back to their starting positions.

Another man worth mentioning is General Franz Sensfus of the 312th Volks Grenadier Division, which attacked across the Sauer River on December 16, 1944, to secure the left flank of the Ardennes Offensive (known to most Americans as the Battle of the Bulge). The division's objective was limited: to pin down as many American units as possible, to prevent the transfer of reserves northward against the German main effort. Most of the men were young, inadequately trained recruits, or elderly reservists called to service as the Allied armies closed in on Germany. Not only was the division's task complicated by the necessity of making an attack across a river, it was opposed by a more numerous force of experienced Americans in the battle-seasoned 4th Infantry Division. Achieving complete surprise, the Germans drove back the 4th Division for two days, until the arrival of American reinforcements finally brought their advance to a halt. The 312th then dug in and held its newly won ground against repeated counterattacks by the much more numerous Americans.

General Sensfuss' leadership was, of course, a major factor in this amazing feat of arms. But the General Staff of Halder, Zeitzler, and Guderian also deserves considerable credit. They had steadfastly refused to allow any curtailment in the training time and training schedules for young officers and noncommissioned officers, despite Hitler's repeated efforts to force a change. Convinced that poor leadership meant not only poor performance, but also high casualties, they stuck to their guns, and Hitler was forced to back down. That was why Sensfuss could expect and receive first-rate performance from units made up of men otherwise inadequately trained.

The list of German generals who could and did demonstrate such combat command virtuosity is almost as long as the roster of generals. At the higher command levels such names as Rundstedt, Kesselring, Rommel, Bock, Leeb,

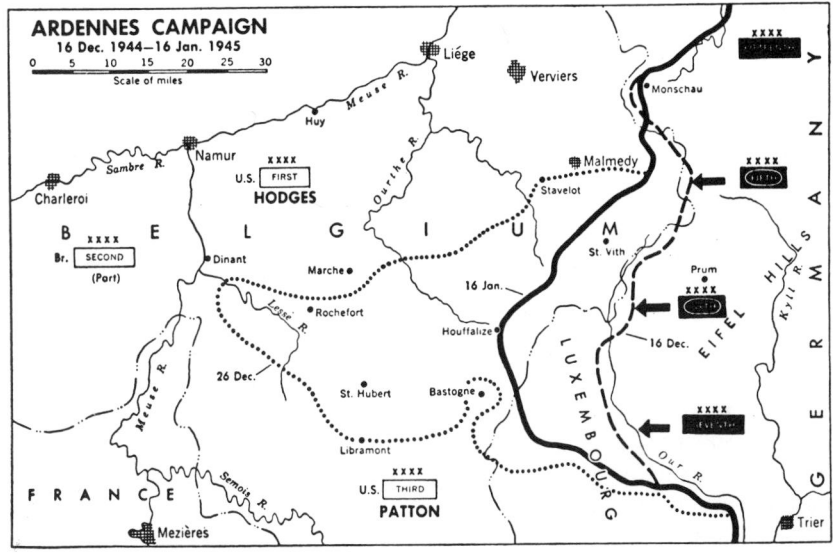

Kluge, Kleist, and many others come to mind. It is doubtful if any army has ever had such a vast number of consistently competent high-level leaders.

SENGER'S SHIFT ACROSS THE ITALIAN FRONT / It is peculiarly fitting to return to General von Senger und Etterlin for a final example of the superb combat leadership provided by the German officer corps in World War II. Senger was a unique individualist; neither by birth, appearance, nor actions did he fit into any mold of "Prussian militarism." Yet, like so many other unorthodox individuals who rose to the top in the German Army, he adapted and disciplined himself to perform with undeviating loyalty and cooperation, in accordance with a well-defined—even though flexible—doctrine, and did so without any loss of his personal individuality. Thus he was both unique and typical.

Possibly the most outstanding feat of arms by any corps commander in World War II was performed by Senger not long after Greiner's magnificent defense of Velletri had won a brief respite for the German Fourteenth Army, which had been encircling Anzio. At that time Senger's XIV Panzer Corps was slowly withdrawing from Cassino because the American Fifth Army had broken through the LI Corps to its right, holding the right wing of the battered Tenth Army. When the Fourteenth Army line collapsed, Senger pulled back two divisions to the Alban Hills, and was virtually fighting on two fronts in an effort to extract the remainder of his own corps as well as the even more seriously threatened LI Corps. However, with the collapse of the Fourteenth Army there seemed to be no way to prevent the American VI and II Corps from driving northeastward into the Tiber River Valley.

Field Marshal Kesselring had just about written off the extreme westward divisions of the Tenth Army, when the pressure suddenly relaxed. Instead of going up the Tiber Valley, as Kesselring feared, General Mark Clark had turned his Fifth Army northward toward Rome. Clark gained fame as the liberator of Rome but lost his opportunity to end the Italian Campaign in the summer of 1944, because Kesselring, with his Tenth Army still intact even though battered, now saw an opportunity also to save the remnants of his Fourteenth Army.

Kesselring ordered the XIV Panzer Corps (still an interior corps of the Tenth Army) to join the Fourteenth Army, now streaming to the rear in considerable confusion to the west. General von Vietinghoff, Tenth Army commander, protested because he did not want to lose Senger, his most able subordinate. This, of course, was the very reason that Kesselring wanted him with the Fourteenth Army. Kesselring had just relieved the commander of the Fourteenth Army, General von Mackensen, son of the venerable Field Marshal of World War I fame. He undoubtedly wanted to put Senger in command of the Fourteenth Army, but knew he could not since Hitler would never accept such a confirmed anti-Nazi as the commander of an army. But with Senger and his army-sized corps with the Fourteenth Army, it might have a chance to recover.

The mission given to Senger was unusual. His XIV Panzer Corps was to shift westward—keeping some divisions, dropping others, and picking up still others as he moved—across the front of the Tenth Army's rescued right-wing corps to establish a link between the Tenth and the shattered Fourteenth Army. Then he was to continue westward across the entire two-corps front of the Fourteenth Army. When he reached the sea, he was to anchor himself, dig in, and halt the Allied pursuit up the coastal roads from Rome to Pisa and Florence. But—and here is the significant aspect of this operation—in the disastrous situation that existed, Kesselring could not afford to withdraw either the XIV Panzer Corps or its divisions from the line. This movement of a panzer corps of five to seven frontline divisions had to be made across the front of two armies while fighting a combat withdrawal under severe pursuit and pressure from the Allies.

The movement took two weeks. And when Senger's right-flank division reached the coast, near Grosetto, the XIV Panzer Corps (which by this time was most of what remained of the Fourteenth Army) carried out the theater commander's orders, dug in, and brought the Allied pursuit to a halt. Thanks to the partly unintentional collaboration of three men—General Clark, Field Marshal Kesselring, and particularly General von Senger und Etterlin—the Italian Campaign was destined to continue for ten more bitter months.

One assessment of the accomplishment was made by Vietinghoff, commanding the Tenth Army, in a message sent as a final tribute to the corps and commander taken away from him during the battle:

XIV Panzer Corps has been able to withdraw the panzer and panzer grenadier divisions engaged on its front and to apply them to their new task of protecting the right flank with such speed that at the very last moment the enemy's northward breakthrough and the concomitant disruption of the German front were frustrated. Exceptional difficulties were involved in the execution of this movement. That they were overcome constitutes a masterpiece in the art of military leadership and is in line with the corps' previous high achievements.[12]

This, however, was only one of many masterpieces of military leadership in the German Army in that disastrous year.

NOTES TO CHAPTER FIFTEEN

[1] Winston Churchill, *The Gathering Storm,* Vol. I of *The Second World War* (Boston: 1948), pp. 648-649.

[2] See, for instance, Heinz Guderian, *Panzer Leader* (New York: 1952), p. 20.

[3] Colonel James E. Mrazek, *The Fall of Eben Emael* (Washington, D.C.: 1970), p. 187.

[4] *Ibid.,* p. 183.

[5] It is surprising that precise figures on manpower, divisions, and tanks are not available. The numbers given here are based upon analysis of various sources, including German records in the U.S. National Archives, William L. Shirer, *Collapse of the Third Republic* (New York: 1969); A. Goutard, *The Battle of France, 1940;* and T. D. Stamps and V. J. Esposito, *A Military History of World War II* (West Point: 1953).

[6] Winston Churchill, *Their Finest Hour,* Vol. II of *The Second World War* (Boston: 1949), p. 43.

[7] *Ibid.,* p. 49.

[8] Ropp, *op. cit.,* p. 184.

[9] Erich von Manstein, *Lost Victories* (Chicago: 1958), 449.

[10] *Ibid.,* pp. 547-548; the emphasis is Manstein's.

[11] F. R. T. von Senger und Etterlin, *Neither Fear nor Hope* (New York: 1964).

[12] *Ibid.*

Chapter Sixteen

LESS THAN SUPERMEN

 A DIFFERENT VIEWPOINT / Although I have been stressing the excellence of German military performance in the two World Wars, it is, to be fair, possible to assess that performance in a much more negative way. Let us therefore pause for a moment and see how such a "negative assessment" might be framed and how well it meets the facts.

The Germans lost World War I, and they also lost World War II. These simple truths would seem to provide prima-facie evidence that German military "genius"—whether personalized or institutionalized—was not performing very well during those wars. It has been suggested that by concentrating on the undoubted technical competence of the Prusso-German military system, its admirers have overlooked its structural weaknesses.

If the Germans were so good, why did so many of them die in the Falaise-Argentan Pocket? Why did so many surrender in Tunisia? Why did they not drive the Anglo-Americans into the sea at Salerno or Anzio or Normandy? Why were they unable to capture surrounded Leningrad?

Do the events of 1944—when the Germans were being consistently beaten—represent either a "riddle" or a German "miracle" in staving off defeat? In the West, after all, the Germans were aided by the fact that the Allies had outrun their supply lines; this was an Allied problem (not necessarily a failure), but hardly a German achievement. Furthermore, it has been suggested that the Allied advance (once the supply problem had been alleviated) was slow because of bad weather and terrain unsuitable for offensive operations. And so, since the Germans had technical skills, it was no problem for them to develop an effective defense under such circumstances.

As to Italy, in 1944, terrain and weather, combined with the declining importance of the theater and Anglo-American tactical disagreement, also permitted the Germans to construct an effective defense line across the peninsula. This defense was skillful but hardly a "miracle."

In the East, of course, the Russians, who had not yet recovered from Stalin's purges of the 1930s, were slowed down because they also outran their supply lines. In fact, the ability of the Germans to remain in the war through

1944 was more due to the noteworthy achievements of Albert Speer in war production than to any questionably superior fighting ability of the German Army.

To those who see little of value to learn from German military institutions, the principal failure of those institutions in World War II, as in World War I, was a failure in strategic conceptualization. And what good is mere technical competence if the strategic planning is incompetent or inadequate?

World War I, it is similarly asserted, was also marked by a variety of German strategic blunders. There was, for instance, diversion of forces on many fronts: France, Russia, Italy, Turkey, the Balkans, Africa. There was inadequate coordination with Austria-Hungary and with Turkey—which was hardly a valuable ally anyway. The General Staff based its plans and preparations on the assumption that the war would be short. On top of this Schlieffen's plan to invade the Low Countries assured the entry of England—and British seapower—into the war. This, however, was possibly to be expected, because land-minded German generals had no understanding of the strategic significance of sea power. Nor did they have any understanding of the potential military power of the United States.

It has been suggested that at the beginning of the war the outcome of the Marne Campaign revealed serious weaknesses in the German system of command. Among the specific failures were the lack of communications between GHQ and the field armies, virtually complete abdication of command by Moltke to Lieutenant Colonel Richard Hentsch, who conferred only with the army chiefs of staff and not with their commanding generals, and too many unwarranted deviations from the prewar plan. One critic has averred, in fact, that the German command in the early months of the war could be better characterized as a tragicomedy of errors, rather than an institutionalization of either ability or excellence.

Also, as attested from many Allied diaries and reminiscences, one of the most characteristic aspects of German troop action was its predictable regularity, such as invariable hours for harassing or interdiction artillery fires.

Another major failure of the German General Staff was its inability to effect a satisfactory relationship with civilian authority. OHL dictated to the Emperor's government, and assuredly its greatest mistake was to throw its weight into the scales in support of unrestricted submarine warfare. Had it not done so, there was some possibility of a negotiated peace in 1917.

The story was similar for World War II. The multifront diversion of forces was repeated. So, too, was the predictable regularity of German troop activity. Again sea power was ignored, as was the potential power of the United States, and again a short war was expected. A major failure was the lack of German-Japanese strategic coordination against Russia.

Perhaps even more significant was the World War II inability of the Germans to grasp the strategic implications of air power. The *Luftwaffe* was organized by former ground soldiers like Milch and Kesselring to serve efficiently as flying artillery over the battlefield. The failure of the Germans to grasp the long-range strategic potentialities of air power—as had Italy's Douhet, Britain's Trenchard, and America's Mitchell—demonstrated a fatal error in German military thinking.

As in World War I, the General Staff was never able to achieve a satisfactory relationship with Germany's civilian authority. This was particularly significant after the war was plainly lost. Although in June 1944 Rundstedt could tell Hitler—through Keitel—"Make peace, you fool," the officers of the General Staff, spellbound by their oath of allegiance to Hitler, let him continue to direct the government until the entire country had been occupied by enemy forces.

Critics also point to another major respect in which the German General Staff compares unfavorably with the Allied command machinery in World War II. After the fall of France in mid-1940, the Germans had an excellent opportunity to invade Britain. Although they had a plan—Operation Sea Lion—they were never able to bring it off. The Allies, on the other hand, not only were successful in their main landing on the coast of France in 1944, they also conducted a number of other successful amphibious operations, far more widely scattered than the fronts with which the Germans were concerned.

Finally, in the light of the battlefield outcomes of World Wars I and II, what basis is there for suggesting that the German generals were better than those they opposed? The fact that talent knows no national boundaries is seen in such names as Foch, Pershing, and Allenby; Slim, Montgomery, and Alexander; LeClerc and de Lattre de Tassighy; Zhukov and Koniev; Marshall, Eisenhower, MacArthur, Bradley, and Patton. Having studied war and prepared for it, the Germans had an initial advantage over their opponents, who were less ready at the outset. But as those opponents mobilized their strength, that temporary German advantage was lost.

Thus, in essence, Prusso-German military successes were based upon a transitory technical mastery of war. The ultimate failure in both conflicts came because the German military system—unlike those of the Allies—was too narrowly specialized.

A BALANCED ASSESSMENT / It is useful to give some thought to German failures and the many successes of enemies over German military forces, if only to provide perspective on the objectives of Scharnhorst and his fellow-Reformers and on the extent to which these objectives were met and not met in the later Prussian and German armies.

In the Jena and Friedland campaigns the Reformers had seen undeniable evidence that Prussia's former military ascendancy in Europe had been transitory, that Prussians had no inherent military qualities surpassing those of the French or Russians, that a military tradition meant nothing if it were entrusted to the care of inept or unmilitary leaders, and that the days of personal royal armies had ended forever.

Thus the reforms which they instituted, and which were perpetuated and refined by their successors as chiefs of the General Staff, were based upon the premise that Prussians, as soldiers or leaders, had the same human frailties of body and weaknesses of mind as their actual and potential enemies. Their solution to the problem of Prussia's security, therefore, was to establish a system that would make the most out of normal human strengths and abilities and minimize the human weaknesses of the average Prussian—weaknesses of which they were all too aware.

Proud though they were of Prussia and Prussia's military accomplishment, they could have been under no illusions that any system could eliminate all human error or create human beings with greater than human attributes.

With this in mind, there can be no better way to assess the extent to which the Reformers succeeded in their objective of institutionalizing military proficiency, than to explore subsequent Prusso-German military failures under this institutionalized system. Let's review them one by one.

German losses in the Falaise-Argentan Pocket were substantial. The Germans lost about 10,000 dead, at least 30,000 wounded, and about 50,000 captured. Allied casualties were about 40,000 in these same operations. While not negligible, these losses in no way impaired the ability of the Allies to pursue the defeated Germans in one of the great victories of British and American arms.

German military men, in their postwar memoirs, assert that the Falaise Pocket would never have occurred if Hitler had not ordered his generals not only to stand and fight in untenable positions, but had actually caused them to poke their heads into the trap by a counteroffensive. This happens to be true, but in the light of the Scharnhorst objective, it is more useful to see how the Germans performed when they were so misused by their civilian leader. German forces totaling about 200,000 men were virtually surrounded in central Normandy by Allied forces totaling nearly 1 million ground troops, and were under almost incessant, unopposed attacks from the air by the most powerful tactical air forces the world has ever seen. What is most remarkable about the Falaise Pocket is that the Germans, being in this situation for whatever reason, fought their way out, and saved more than half of the troops that would have been lost had the Allies been equally alert and skillful. In this sense, the Germans, although defeated, clearly outfought the encircling Americans and British.

In Tunisia, in May 1943, there were perhaps 100,000 Germans in the Axis armies that surrendered to the victorious Allies. It is somewhat difficult to understand why this should be a black mark against the Germans, since—like the Americans on Bataan and Corregidor, or the British in Singapore—they had the choice of surrendering to overwhelming force or being annihilated for no worthwhile purpose. They had held off the superior Allied forces for six months, though at the outset of the campaign those Allies had been closer to their final objective, Tunis, than had the Germans. These are the same Germans whose performance in North Africa was somewhat ruefully assessed by a British officer in writing about the "bitter lessons" of this experience:

There is no doubt that the Germans, of all ranks, were more highly

> professional as soldiers than the British. Their knowledge and practical application of the weapons available to them was in almost all cases superior. . . . They were tough, skilful, determined, and well-disciplined soldiers. . . . Their standard was reached, in a few cases excelled, by some of the British; but a large proportion of the 8th Army's troops never attained it.[1]

There is an equally good answer to the question why the Germans did not drive the British and Americans into the sea at Salerno, Anzio, and Normandy. The Allies had overwhelming military power that the Germans had no possibility of matching. Two very different examples cited in recent American publications—one on a grand strategic scale, the other at the lowest possible tactical level—demonstrate the effect of this material superiority.

In its issue of April 5, 1976, *Time* magazine, reporting on the death of British Field Marshal Montgomery, commented as follows on Monty's great victory at El Alamein: "When his painstakingly prepared attack came on October 23, 1942, Montgomery had 230,000 men and 1,100 tanks facing Rommel's 80,000 men and 260 tanks. Yet when the battle was over, the British losses were triple those of the enemy's." Nonetheless, Montgomery, when elevated to the peerage, was proud enough of his costly victory to call himself Viscount Montgomery of Alamein.

A recent book by Stuart H. Loory quotes retired U.S. Army Colonel David H. Hackworth telling about the time that he learned something about German combat excellence.

> I remember a German lieutenant captured at Salerno who I was guarding in 1946 in a prisoner-of-war camp. He was a real toughlooking kraut and I was a young punk, a pimply-faced kid. He could speak perfect English, and I was riding him. I said, "Well, if you're so tough, if you're all supermen, how come you're here captured and I'm guarding you?"
>
> And he looked at me and said, "Well, it's like this. I was on this hill as a battery commander with six 88-millimeter antitank guns, and the Americans kept sending tanks down this road. We kept knocking them out. Every time they sent a tank we knocked it out.
>
> "Finally, we ran out of ammunition and the Americans didn't run out of tanks."
>
> And that's it in a nutshell.[2]

No better indication of what the Germans could do under difficult circumstances, when both surprised and outnumbered, is to be found a year later, in September 1944, in the Arnhem-Nijmegen operation—code-named "Market Garden" by the Allies. With the odds less one-sided (although still against them numerically), the Germans rallied and drove the Allies back.

The evidence is quite conclusive, in fact, that, even when their world was collapsing around them, German soldiers in World War II continued to fight tenaciously and skillfully so long as there was any possibility of successful resistance. Two American psychologists, who served in the Psychological Warfare Division of General Eisenhower's headquarters, have commented on this German military steadfastness as follows:

> Although distinctly outnumbered and in a strategic sense quantitatively inferior in equipment, the German Army on all fronts, maintained a high degree of organizational integrity and fighting effectiveness through a series of almost unbroken retreats over a period of several years. In the final phase, the German armies were broken into unconnected segments, and the remnants were overrun as the major lines of communcation and command were broken. Nevertheless, resistance which was more than token resistance on the part of most divisions continued until they were overpowered or overrun in a way which, by breaking communication lines, prevented individual battalions and companies from operating in a coherent fashion. Disintegration through desertion was insignificant, while active surrender, individually or in groups, remained extremely limited throughout the entire Western campaign.[3]

The German failure to take Leningrad is simply one more example of the multitude to be found in World War II where the German reach exceeded the grasp. As at Stalingrad, they were opposed by a much more numerous, grimly determined foe, and lacked the resources to complete the job. This is, of course, a further indictment of German strategy and strategic aims. But again the objective historian is obliged to credit the answer provided so unanimously in German postwar military memoirs: Had Hitler not overruled the General Staff in ordering such rash and dispersed offensives, these disasters would not have occurred.

As to the German recovery from the disasters of mid-1944, it is difficult to find many other military accomplishments more worthy of being called a "miracle." Granted that the primary explanation is relatively prosaic: It was not the Germans who engineered the miracle; it was the Allies, whose overcaution and slowness gave the Germans the opportunity to recover. But rarely have armies so totally defeated shown such amazing qualities of recuperation, once the opportunity was offered. No comparable historical example comes to mind.

Albert Speer unquestionably deserves credit for the production "miracle" that provided the equipment employed by the rejuvenated German armies in their amazing December counteroffensive. But it should be realized that he merely put into effect the production concepts and plans which had long before been recommended by the General Staff and which Hitler had hitherto turned down. Speer's miracle, in fact, would not have been possible without the close cooperation of a product of the German General Staff, General Fritz Fromm.

To criticize the German General Staff for the inadequacies of the Austrian, Turkish, or Bulgarian armies in World War I fails to recognize the brilliance of the German accomplishments in making good use of inferior troops in coalition warfare. To criticize the Germans for failure to coordinate their strategy with

Japan in World War II is no more realistic than to blame the Allied Combined Chiefs of Staff for failure to coordinate strategy with the Russians. Just as it takes two to tango, it takes two to cooperate.

Twice Germany mistakenly failed to prepare for a long war, but, in both cases, once it was evident that they were in such a war, German military leadership at least had more realistic views of what needed to be done than did other elements in German society. From that point on, their long-range planning—as distinct from their war-making potential—was not inferior to that of the Allies.

The criticisms of the Schlieffen Plan have been dealt with elsewhere. But to attribute to the Schlieffen Plan the British decision to go to war is unrealistic. The Germans knew that Britain and France were allies; they assumed that Britain was committed to the war. The planned thrust across the Low Countries was, at least in part, designed to minimize the effectiveness of that participation.

There is, however, considerably more validity to the assertion that the German General Staff underestimated the importance of sea power and the military potential of the United States. The Hindenburg-Ludendorff approval of unrestricted submarine warfare was a blunder—even though the submarine campaign came perilously close to success. But the main reason for the blunder lies in another criticism of the General Staff—its failure to establish a satisfactory relationship with civilian governmental authority. This, of course, was the fatal flaw of the General Staff system to which so much attention has been devoted in earlier pages of this book: the inability of Scharnhorst and the Reformers to establish a system in which the Army would be responsive to the will of the people or the people's representatives in government.

As to the failures of the Marne Campaign, these are easy to see in retrospect. An all-too-human general, who had doubts about his own capabilities but who had been personally selected by the Emperor against the recommendations of the prior Chief of Staff, failed in a time of extreme crisis. The criticism of the Hentsch mission is unfounded. Hentsch performed in accordance with the system and made the right decisions for and in the name of the Chief of Staff. The system functioned perfectly, despite the prior failure of the Chief of Staff, and this was one reason the defeat was not a disaster. Had things gone the other way—and they came very close to doing so—even more damning criticism, no matter how unjustified, would have been leveled at Joffre.

The criticism of German predictable regularity unquestionably has some basis. But we could and did make similar criticisms of the Japanese, and the German memoirs are replete with comparable remarks about their enemies—including us. Such criticism, no matter how well-founded, cannot detract from the fact that it was in military innovation and improvisation that the "methodical" Germans consistently excelled their enemies.

One of the most justifiable military criticisms of Germany in World War II was its neglect of strategic air power. Yet there are many Americans who believe that our concentration on strategic air power resulted in some serious deficiencies in American and British tactical air support. The Germans almost certainly were wrong; but—as with the Americans—it was a question of the allocation of resources, and they opted to develop the best possible integration of air-ground military forces and doctrines.

The greatest failure of the General Staff in World War II was its ultimately disastrous underestimation of the Russians. Admittedly, if Hitler had treated the White Russians and the Ukrainians as liberated peoples instead of slaves, and if he had not interfered with military plans during the summers of 1941 and 1942, the outcome might well have been different. But his attitude had undoubtedly been influenced by overoptimistic General Staff opinions, such as that expressed by Halder in his diary, twelve days after the campaign started: "The war has been won; we only have to finish it. . . ." It is no credit to the German General Staff that their evaluation of Russian military capabilities was no better than that of the staffs of Britain, France, or the United States.

Whether the General Staff or its members could or should have taken more initiative in overthrowing Hitler is debatable. The issue has been sufficiently discussed on earlier pages to demonstrate that there is no obviously easy answer. Related to this is the question of what the German generals and General Staff should have done about the brutal Nazi excesses in Poland and Russia— particularly about the horrors of the campaign of extermination against the Jews. Would American or British officers have done better under similar circumstances? We must hope so.

It is not very constructive, on the other hand, to criticize the German General Staff for having failed to develop the amphibious competence of the Western Allies. In fact, their one major amphibious plan, for Operation Sea Lion, seems to have been sound enough. But Allied amphibious operations were dependent upon control of both the air and the sea. The Germans were bold and innovative enough to develop a plan which would work if only they could achieve temporary control of the air. This the *Luftwaffe* could not do—and probably could not have done even had it been organized for strategic air warfare. Thus the plan was never attempted.

As to commander-to-commander comparisons, these also are not very helpful. It is, of course, possible to prepare long lists of competent Allied generals. It is also possible to prepare long lists of Allied examples of command failure or hesitation or indecision. Comparison in terms of army groups, armies, corps, and divisions, in each war, reveals longer lists of proven, qualified, successful German commanders at each level than for the total of their opponents and allies. And although the Allies had no monopoly on blunders, indecision, or hesitation, a list of such German failures is much shorter than such a list for the Allies. No serious, authoritative student or practitioner of modern war has been able to make a comparison of German forces and their enemies in any terms other than those quoted earlier from Churchill, Carver, Rousset, and others, all testifying to the great battlefield superiority of the Germans. We might like to think that these advantages accruing from earlier and better preparation declined after Allied mobilization and the early acclimatization of battle, but the facts demonstrate that this was not the case. The Germans retained their battlefield superiority in both wars right up to the end, despite effects of attrition and war-weariness.

Two American soldier-scholars have noted and commented on this phenomenon in the following words:

> Despite repeated catastrophes, the Wehrmacht remained so cohesive that it fought effectively until overrun. . . . German battlefield cohesion related directly to the individual soldier's . . . perceptions of his immediate officers and NCOs as men of honor eminently deserving of respect, who in turn cared for their men. German Army officers were very carefully selected and virtually all had education superior to the average German. Moreover, the high selection standards for German officers were maintained throughout the war. . . . The fighting qualities of the German Army in large measure can be attributed to the quality of its leadership. . . . The German historical model during World War II emerges as one of high military professionalism and cohesion."[4]

In the mid-1970s two widely read books have told the world about British success (with considerable American assistance) in breaking the most secret German codes of World War II.[5] As a result, Allied intelligence and the British and American war leaders and senior field commanders were aware of the most closely guarded German operational plans. It is hard to estimate just how valuable this capability was to the Allies, but it is certain that it was *extremely* valuable. As the two authors clearly demonstrate, this ability "to read the Germans' mail" on numerous occasions meant the difference between Allied victory and defeat, and certainly had a significant effect upon the overall war outcome.

Two observations come immediately to mind.

It was fortunate for the Allies that they had this essentially technical and technological superiority over the Germans—as they did also in the field of industrial war production—to help offset the purely military German combat superiority. At the same time, this fact of intelligence advantage gives a fresh insight into the German military accomplishment. How much more remarkable it was that they were able to perform so well on the battlefield even though they had unwittingly surrendered most of their opportunities for surprise, while the Allies were able to plan and prepare for every important German military operation.*

Napoleon and Hannibal are generally conceded to have been geniuses of the art of war. Both had their human failings, and in each case those failings contributed to their ultimate defeat at the hands of more numerous, more powerful, enemies. But few responsible historians or military critics would suggest that

---

*The only important exception appears to have been the Germans' December 1944 Ardennes Offensive, the details of which seem never to have been communicated by radio.

they were not geniuses because they were finally defeated, or that their victorious opponents were better generals. In fact both Blücher and Wellington freely admitted the superior ability of Napoleon, and Scipio Africanus gave at least indirect testimony of comparable respect for the genius of Hannibal.

The German General Staff was a human institution, and it, too, had human frailties and weaknesses, which contributed, at least in part, to its two major defeats in this century. Yet the performance of that General Staff, and of the Army it designed and built in both of those disastrous wars, was comparable in terms of military excellence to Napoleon and Hannibal at their best. Perhaps, in this sense, it is not too much to say that in striving to institutionalize excellence in military affairs, the German General Staff can be said to have institutionalized military genius itself.

NOTES TO CHAPTER SIXTEEN

[1] Michael Carver, *Tobruk* (London: 1964), p. 255.

[2] Stuart H. Loory, *Defeated: Inside American's Military Machine* (New York), p. 39.

[3] Edward A. Shils and Morris Janowitz, "Cohesion and Disintegration in the Wehrmacht in World War II," *The Public Opinion Quarterly,* Vol. 12, No. 2 (Summer, 1948), p. 280.

[4] Paul L. Savage and Richard A. Gabriel, "Cohesion and Disintegration in the American Army," *Armed Forces and Society*, Vol. II, No. 3 (Spring, 1976), p. 40. This thoughtful, carefully researched article makes a distressingly powerful argument that the American Army "disintegrated" in Vietnam and in the process compares that Army and its leadership most unfavorably to the performance of the German Army and its leaders in World War II.

[5] F. W. Winterbottom, *The Ultra Secret* (New York: 1974), and Anthony Cave Brown, *Bodyguard of Lies* (New York: 1976).

Chapter Seventeen

THE INSTITUTION OF EXCELLENCE

 *Why* was Germany able in the early twentieth century to produce so many generals like Hindenburg, Ludendorff, Hutier, Hoffmann, Scheffer-Boyadel, Rundstedt, Kesselring, Manstein, Model, Rommel, Student, and Senger und Etterlin—to name only a few? Why did German junior leaders and the individual private soldiers, perform so well under such leadership in two world wars? Why did they consistently inflict more casualties on us than we did on them? And why was this German combat superiority usually manifested by greater imagination and bolder initiative—at all levels, from top to bottom, performance just the opposite of the stereotype of German soldiers that we see in American motion pictures and TV shows?

There seem to be five possible alternative hypothetical explanations:

1. German genetic superiority validated Hitler's Master Race thesis;

2. Germans are inherently adaptable to military life and warmaking, to an extent greater than other nationalities;

3. The Germans, with defeat and invasion of their homeland staring them in the face in both world wars, simply fought harder and more desperately than the Allies;

4. Historically German culture created a society which encourages methodical efficiency and a military tradition attracting their best minds and best efforts;

5. The Germans have created more effective military institutions than have other countries.

Let me deal briefly with each of these.

There is no scientific evidence to support any assertion of German genetic superiority. Geneticists point out that there *is* no German race, and the Aryan, or Indo-European peoples include many nationalities and pigmentations that could not have fitted the artificial Nazi concept of the blonde Nordic as a typical Aryan. Furthermore, the blonde Nordics are a minority among Germans. Think, for a moment, of pictures of Hitler and others among the Nazi leadership; other than Goering—hardly an inspiring figure of a man—not a blonde Nordic among them.

Those who offer this thesis are confusing cultural and environmental influences with inborn characteristics. And this is the fundamental fallacy of the second hypothesis, even though it may be made to appear superficially plausible by carefully selected historical examples. However, despite the amazing record of German combat experience since the middle of the nineteenth century, and despite some instances of German military brilliance before then, an objective survey of the historical record will not demonstrate any exceptional German adaptability to military affairs before the early nineteenth century.

As to the second thesis, it would be rash to assert that there is nothing in the German character which might make Germans more adaptable to soldiering than other nations. Yet it would be equally rash to make a contrary assertion. (One need only think of the reputation of the German divisions of the Union XI Corps in the Civil War.) I agree with Gordon Craig, who has written: "To assign national characteristics to a people is at best a chancy business, and arguments based on such attribution are apt to fall of their own weight."[1] The case for this hypothesis simply cannot be proven.

This brings us to the hypothesis that German performance in the world wars was outstanding because defense of their homeland spurred them to exceptional efforts. It is undoubtedly true that the Germans' performance was enhanced by their desire to preserve the Fatherland from invasion. But then, if that is offered as the major explanation of their superiority, how can we account for the fact that the Germans demonstrated the same kind of superiority over the Allies when they were marching on Paris, or Warsaw, or Kiev? The hypothesis does not provide an answer to the question.

As to the fourth hypothesis, like all peoples, the Germans have been shaped historically by societal, cultural, and particularly geographic influences. Lack of easily defensible frontiers has made Germany a battleground since the Roman era. Concern about the protection of these frontiers has certainly been a significant factor in German military affairs for the past two centuries and more. It has also been a major influence in generating public respect and support for the military and in encouraging many of the best and brightest German minds to seek military careers. It has also been important in making civilians readily adaptable to military life and mobilization.

German people and their organizations do seem to be methodical and efficient, and to show a tendency toward regimentation. Nevertheless, that efficiency and regimentation, which have certainly contributed to Germany's military capability, have also led to the kind of stultification which resulted in disastrous defeat by Napoleon at Jena in 1806. Furthermore, the Germans have no corner on cultural traits contributing to efficiency. It has already been indicated that the Allies, particularly the British, outperformed the Germans in the related fields of intelligence and spying. And, despite the genius that both Fromm and Speer eventually brought to the task, it is doubtful if German industrial production management in either world war was as efficient as those of the United States or the United Kingdom. So, clearly, cultural traits can at best provide only part of the answer.

This leaves us with the last hypothesis—that of some sort of organizational phenomenon. Only this one provides consistent answers to the questions which arise when trying to correlate cultural influences with German military performance. The organization responsible for this phenomenon is, of course, the Prussian General Staff, which later became the German General Staff.

The fundamental explanation of German combat ability, and of the quality of German military power as demonstrated in two world wars, lay in the organization and operation of the Prussian/German General Staff. In military history, consistent performance comparable to that of the German armies in World Wars I and II can be found only in armies led by such military geniuses as Alexander, Hannibal, Caesar, Gustavus Adolphus, Genghis Khan, and Napoleon. Such a comparison automatically suggests that through the General Staff the Germans had institutionalized military excellence.

Here is most of the answer to the question of why and how the Germans performed so well. The corps and division commanders of the Prussian Army of 1814 and 1815 had understood military principles, but Blücher and Gneisenau could not count on performance in accordance with those principles except under their direct supervision. Half a century later Moltke's corps and division commanders were soldiers so dedicated to military excellence that sound performance in accordance with sound principles and doctrines had become second nature, and Moltke could rely on this, wherever he himself might be. This assured kind of performance marked what is probably the most significant distinction between the German armies of the two world wars on the one hand and their opponents on the other. The Germans had no monopoly on an understanding of military theory, or an ability to analyze operational experience. Nor did they have a monopoly on military competence. But what they did have was a monopoly on consistently reliable and excellent performance throughout the army in accordance with doctrine and theory.

There was nothing inherent in the Prussian soldiers and leaders of 1815 to assure that their descendents would be supersoldiers such as those that fought the Allies of World Wars I and II. There was nothing about their performance in the Napoleonic wars to suggest that they were any more suitable for such a transformation than were British, French, American, or Russian soldiers of the same era, or of the twentieth century, for that matter.

In the intervening century the *only* significant military professional development in Prussia and Germany that was not matched in these other countries was the creation of the Prussian, later German, General Staff, and the special qualities of professionalism that differentiated that General Staff from imitations in all other nations. This matter of professionalization is important, because Germany's involvement in, and loss of, the World Wars was in no way connected with the professional organization, indoctrination, or performance of the German General Staff. The General Staff was not simply a symptom of German military proficiency, but the primary cause of it.

The role of the General Staff in German politics has been thoroughly surveyed by a number of historians, among whom Walter Goerlitz, John Wheeler-Bennett, and Gordon Craig are outstanding. The political role of a supposedly apolitical institution should neither be ignored nor forgotten, but it is irrelevant to the basic military question: How did the German General Staff manage to create an army of average human beings which could consistently outfight other armies of equally average human beings?

At least a major part—if not all—of the answer lies in the success with which the General Staff fulfilled the essential purpose for which it was created: the institution of excellence. More specifically, the way the General Staff accomplished its objective may be summed up under ten overlapping headings:

Selection
Examination
Specialized training
Historical study emphasis
Inculcation of the initiative
Responsibility
Goal of technical-tactical perfection
Objectivity in analysis
Regeneration
Leavening process

The officers of the German General Staff were the elite of the Army, carefully selected through a process far more rigorous and deliberate than that of any other army. Since cultural influences unquestionably attracted a substantial proportion of Germany's best men to the Army, this selection process brought to the German General Staff a very high proportion of the finest minds of the nation.

Examination was necessarily an essential part of the selection process, as well as a prerequisite for promotion, even among officers not selected for the General Staff. The examinations required all officers to study their profession seriously, thus contributing to improved professional understanding and performance throughout the entire Army.*

Specialized training has of course been an ingredient in the preparation and development of General Staff officers in all armies. But the Germans had more intensive schooling and practical staff training and exercises than is, or has ever been, the case in any other modern army, with the possible exception of the Soviet Russian Army since World War II. It is at least noteworthy that the current Soviet military educational and training system seems to be largely modeled on that of the Germans.

The German General Staff always placed great emphasis on the study of military history. (Even though few people have read them, the writings of

---

*It has been pointedly suggested that one of the greatest weaknesses of the modern United States Army is failure to use examinations as a basis for promotion or for selection for its General Staff.

Clausewitz come to mind.) In his rise to the top, Field Marshal von Moltke headed up the Military History Division of the General Staff, and his published historical studies have caused him to be recognized as one of Germany's better historians, civilian or military. Schlieffen based his famous and frequently mis-understood plan upon studies which are included in his well-known military history text, *Cannae.* While the organization of the General Staff was often modified over the years, a Military History Division was always one of its principal components. Many General Staff officers wrote about the significance of military history, and while most noted the danger of seeking immutable tactical or technical lessons from historical study, they invariably emphasized the importance of history for acquiring the theoretical foundations of military science, and for gaining an understanding of human performance in conflict situations.

If any one aspect of military performance was emphasized more than any other in the General Staff and in all German military training, it was en-couragement of individual initiative. American General Albert C. Wedemeyer, the last American officer who attended the War Academy before World War II, remembers this emphasis. It was summarized, he recalls, in the concept: "When in doubt, attack!"* This, of course, was how Gronau saved the German First Army at the Ourcq.

There is no direct evidence that German military emphasis on imagination and initiative has been due to a conscious effort to offset any traditional German cultural trait of regimentation. If not conscious, however, this may well have been an unconscious motivation of German General Staff theorists. That these efforts to encourage initiative and imagination were successful is evident from the fact that it was in this area, probably more than any other, that the German, at all levels, excelled in both world wars.

Responsibility, as a characteristic of the General Staff, was a concept similar to, but not quite the same thing as, initiative. It was partly the willingness to accept responsibility that goes with initiative, but even more, it was a realiza-tion that any German soldier or officer was, to some extent, his brother's keeper. If something was going wrong nearby, a German officer or soldier would feel a responsibility to do something about it, regardless of personal risk or physical danger. In most armies we can find similar instances of personal commitment, but almost never so pervasively as in the German Army. And unfortunately, in other armies, one can find over the course of history an off-setting general willingness, often eagerness, not to get involved in someone else's problems.

Anyone who has reviewed German staff documents cannot fail to marvel at the objectivity of their staff analyses and estimates. This was true not only when they attempted to analyze the causes of defeat or failure, but also in their evaluation of technical or tactical performance of other nationalities, in peace

---

*Discussion with the author, 1973.

and war. There was no NIH—"not invented here"—syndrome in the German General Staff.

The goal of tactical-technical perfection was characterized by unceasing efforts to improve conceptual doctrine and tactics as well as practical training and performance. Up to the time of the First World War, the General Staff did not have responsibility for the general organization or training of the German Army; that was the duty of the War Ministry, of which the General Staff was only a semiautonomous part. But the War Minister was always a general and always a former member of the General Staff, completely imbued with all of the General Staff's special concerns and characteristics. And of course, the War Minister received, and always gave careful consideration to, General Staff studies that related to organization and training. Anyone who suggests that the pre-World War I General Staff was responsible only for doctrine and planning, and not for the practical implementation of that doctrine and the organization to carry out plans, fails to understand how the German military system actually worked, regardless of organization charts. Beginning with Seeckt, this General Staff responsibility became explicit.

There was a conscious, continuing effort by General Staff officers—and not just the Chiefs of the General Staff—to assure not only that the institution would survive, but that it would not become obsolescent through overemphasis on tradition and custom. Regeneration was in part assured by the careful selection process, which brought fresh, bright minds into the institution. But it was also assured by deliberate and effective efforts to avoid the ruts of convention, practice, and custom, while at the same time encouraging high standards by judicious emphasis on tradition.

The leavening process, whereby the influence of the General Staff was made effective throughout the entire German Army, was accomplished in several ways. In the first place, those officers who went to staff schools and colleges but failed to be selected for General Staff positions, had at least been exposed to much of the specialized training received by General Staff officers. Second, military journals, which included writings of General Staff officers on military history and modern military theory, were read eagerly by all German officers and the reputation of the General Staff encouraged these officers to conform to the ideas and concepts presented in what they read. Certainly everyone benefited from the training methods devised or suggested by the General Staff, with emphasis on perfection in battle-drill performance, combined with encouragement of initiative. Finally, there were at least one or two General Staff officers in each division—usually the commander and his operations staff officer—and other General Staff officers were assigned to all senior operational or regional command headquarters. These officers gave the orders, set the example, supervised and commented on training, and gave frequent lectures. The process was very effective, as shown by performance of corporals and even privates, as well as generals, in both world wars.

Throughout this book I have tried, through a process of historical examination, to suggest precisely how the General Staff influenced both the German military establishment and German performance in war. In some cases, that influence was obvious and direct; in others, subtle and indirect. Doubtless much more remains to be learned about the subject. Yet to me, the present evidence seems sufficient to support conclusively the proposition that the General Staff had more to do with German military excellence in the nineteenth and twentieth centuries than any other single factor.

This thesis will probably be challenged on several grounds by both soldiers and scholars.

Some Americans, veterans of one or both of the world wars, might even challenge the basic premise and insist that their units were not only as good as their German opponents but actually outperformed them. It is obvious that such individuals must have been extremely fortunate in having served in units with combat effectiveness so much higher than that of the average American unit, as shown in Figure E-3 of Appendix E. They were more fortunate, for instance, than British Field Marshal Sir Michael Carver, in light of his comments about the superior professionalism of the German soldiers against whom he fought.

It is possible, of course, to accept the evidence of German military excellence in the world wars and still not be convinced that this was due to the German General Staff or any kind of institutionalized excellence or genius. For instance, German emphasis on the soldierly qualities of courage, energy, and athletic prowess, and the national adherence to the concepts of discipline and obedience may seem to some people to provide a more convincing basis for German military preeminence than does the emphasis on bookish learning found in this thesis. Such a challenge will make the point that the Germans were good fighters because of their soldierly qualities not their scholarship.

It is well to remember that the Germans had no monopoly on such soldierly qualities as devotion to duty, gallantry, and disregard for danger and death. Examples of these qualities can be found in the American, British, and Russian records in as much profusion as in those of the German Army. The records of other armies will also demonstrate that intellectual attainments could be combined with soldierly qualities in those armies as in German armies, and in fact most of the top leaders in those other armies have combined these characteristics. The difference, however, lies in the manner in which the Germans deliberately and systematically sought to combine these qualities. A German officer was never selected for the General Staff unless he was perceived to have demonstrated vigor, courage, and a strong character—as well as above-average intelligence. A unique trait of the German Army was its systematic efforts to make first-rate soldiers as well as independent-minded scholars out of any man who gave evidence that he could combine these characteristics.

In most armies, intellectual individuality is viewed with some suspicion and even hostility; it is an automatic challenge to authority and the Party Line. In the German Army this natural human reaction also existed—but was offset by the General Staff's deliberate efforts to encourage and reward intellectual individualists.

As to the military virtues of discipline and obedience, these were obviously well-understood by German soldiers in both world wars. But, to remind themselves that these qualities must be tempered by intelligence and common sense, German officers never allowed themselves to forget Prince Frederick Charles' statement to the blundering major: "His majesty made you a major because he believed that you would know when *not* to obey his orders." The importance of the Prince's dictum was, in World War II, ignored by Hitler—who would not brook disobedience—and by his generals who adapted themselves to his rigidity. The consequence was some of Germany's worst defeats.

Some Germans—even some German General Staff officers—might use this issue of selective disobedience of orders as a basis for questioning whether sweeping responsibility for German military excellence should be attributed to the General Staff. They are fond, for instance, of linking Prince Frederick Charles's quotation with their concept of *Auftragstaktik,* which they rightly consider to be a major element in historical German combat performance. It will be recalled that this concept was one upon which Moltke relied so heavily. A precise translation means "mission tactics," and the essence of this doctrine is that the subordinate commander is responsible for endeavoring at all times to carry out the mission concept of his superior, whether he has orders or not, or whether his latest orders apply to a changing situation. In fact, *Auftragstaktik* was a concept pioneered by Scharnhorst, fostered by his successors, and brought to perfection by Moltke. It was a deliberate creation of the General Staff and is in fact very close to the heart of what the General Staff was all about.

The record of the German General Staff demonstrates any number of instances of human frailties such as shortsightedness, self-satisfaction, errors of judgment, jealousy, indecision, lack of imagination, and battles unnecessarily lost. Yet each of these failings can be found to some extent in the record even of an Alexander or a Napoleon. We call them geniuses because they displayed these frailties less often than their enemies, because through attention to detail and intellectual attainments, they were consistently ahead of their opponents. It was the essential quality of the General Staff, as it seems originally to have been envisaged by Scharnhorst, that it enabled men who individually lacked the qualities of a genius to perform institutionally in a manner that would provide results ordinarily achievable only by genius.

NOTES TO CHAPTER SEVENTEEN

[1] Craig, *op. cit.,* p. XIII.

Epilogue

SOME IMPLICATIONS

When, in 1954, the governments of the victorious Western Allies of World War II agreed to allow Germany to begin a limited rearmament, there was an understandable outcry from many people in Britain, France, the United States, Belgium, and the Netherlands. Not a few patriotic Germans, recalling the military and militaristic history of their nation and in particular the uses to which German military power was put in World Wars I and II, were also appalled at the prospect of a new German *Wehrmacht*. How was it possible to forget so soon the terrors of Auschwitz, Belsen, Buchenwald, and Dachau? How could the Allies rearm a nation that had last used its military power not only in an effort to exterminate the Jews, but also to subdue and enslave the rest of Europe in a policy of brutal decimation calculated to wipe out the potential leadership of any uprising against German domination?

As the new German Army grew in strength after 1955, the West German government was obviously sincere in its efforts to avoid the autonomous militarism of Imperial Germany and also to prevent any recourse to the subterfuges employed by Seeckt and his successors in evading Allied controls imposed by the Treaty of Versailles. Nevertheless, strong opposition to the idea of German rearmament continued. While some polemics, misrepresentations, distortions, and out-of-context quotations[1] were self-defeating—making it hard for either scholars or statesmen to take them seriously—nonetheless, thoughtful people could not and cannot ignore the manner in which Germany has, several times in the past century, used its military might to bring tragedy to Europe and much of the world.

It is clear, however, that the American, British, and French statesmen who agreed to the rearmament of Germany had not forgotten recent history. They were simply acutely aware of other more recent historical facts that made them recognize the dire threat to Europe and the world posed by the expansionist and subversive policies of the government which was responsible for the Katyn Massacre, and for the ruthless enslavement of much of Eastern Europe: Stalin's Soviet Union. Therefore, the possible dangers of German rearmament had to be weighed against the possible dangers of Soviet and Communist expansion without that rearmament. In this context the policymakers of the Western Allies had little choice but to allow the rearmament of Western Germany and even, in fact, to encourage this rearmament for the common good of the free world.

One factor influencing this decision was the distinction which the Allied policymakers could perceive—or at least thought they could perceive—between military strength and its misuse. In the so-called peace-loving countries of the Western Alliance, military strength has always been at least tolerated—although often ignored—as the means for gaining security against aggressive or expansionist neighbors. And, lest our memories be too short, these peace-loving countries have in the past been known to use military strength to expand frontiers from London to Cape Town and Tasmania, from Paris to Casablanca and Tahiti, and from New York to San Francisco and Manila.

It is possible to argue that it was German military strategy—the Schlieffen Plan—which led to the German invasion of neutral Belgium, that German naval leaders were at least partly responsible for the arms race with Britain, which contributed to the drift toward war before 1914. And it is undeniable that German Army leaders—in other words the German General Staff—were quite willing in 1914 to accept the war as an opportunity to end the dangerous converging threat of the Franco-Russian alliance. As for World War II, the point can also be made that military opposition to Hitler's bold and ruthless course to war was not because of opposition to his policies but was merely a manifestation that the soldiers either did not believe that Germany was yet ready for war or doubted that their nation could overcome the coalition that Hitler's policies were creating.

Nevertheless, even granting these facts, it was clearly demonstrable to Allied military leaders in the 1950s that the German armed forces of the two world wars were the instruments of policy and not the creators of the aggressive aims of their government. Even more significant in the eyes of Western policymaking, before those wars the German military forces had been controlled by militaristic, authoritarian regimes, and the German people had had no control over the armed forces, or over their employment. Thus, if more realistic controls could be established over the employment of German armed forces than those of the Versailles Treaty, and if the antimilitaristic elements of Germany itself could be encouraged to develop their own constitutional system assuring democratic control of the armed forces, then it seemed that the undoubted dangers of German rearmament would be acceptable, particularly in the light of the alternative danger.

It would be gross disregard of history in general, and German history in particular, to assume that all risk of future German militarism has disappeared either because West Germany has a democratic government or because apparently realistic controls permit Germany to have combat formations larger than a corps only within the context of NATO military organization. Furthermore, the fact that the West German government has established procedures and policies for assurance of civilian control over the armed forces does not in itself assure either the German people or the peoples of the rest of the world that this army will always remain responsible to popular, democratic control. After all, Germany's one previous experience in democratic popular government was not very successful or long-lasting.

Moreover, some of the most chauvinistic and expansionist activities in history took place in democracies, from Pericles' Athens, through Cicero's Rome, to Britain, France, and the United States in the nineteenth century. History shows that democracy and nationalism are not inconsistent with chauvinism and expansionism. Thus it is not necessarily astonishing, or the basis for indicting a people, that the rise of Hitler and German rearmament in the 1930s were facilitated by popular support of the Nazis and many of their aims.

Another matter for concern is that East Germany is certainly not a democracy, and there is evidence that the East German armed forces, although largely modeled on those of Moscow, have incorporated many features—including military doctrine and control mechanisms—from past German history. As long as two separate Germanys exist, there is a danger that hopes of eventual reunification may inspire one or both to policies of military adventurism reminiscent of the past. On the other hand, would a reunification of Germany, under either of the two governments, pose a greater threat to the peace of Europe and the world?

These are only some of the most important reasons why the people of the so-called free world must retain doubts about a rearmed Germany and about the reestablishment of a high order of military efficiency in both the currently democratized forces of West Germany and the totalitarian controlled forces of East Germany. Yet from the viewpoint of the NATO alliance, the carefully considered decision having been taken to rearm Germany, it would be self-defeating to impose controls on the new West German armed forces for the deliberate purpose of impairing their efficiency.

Experience to date of the West German armed forces—happily never tested in battle—suggests that the strong efforts to ensure a measure of civilization and democratization within the Army, as well as the continuation of strong civilian controls, have not resulted in an inefficient, ineffective Army. Superficial evidence suggests that the units of that Army are functioning within the NATO framework with efficiency at least comparable to that of the two other major military NATO partners, the United States and Great Britain. The Germans—using a British gun for firepower—in the 1960s developed the Leopard tank, probably then the best in the world, and have been in the forefront in designing other excellent items of military equipment and weaponry for themselves and the other NATO armed forced.

To those who are concerned about the future of a remilitarized Germany—and this should embrace all thinking people of the free world, including the Germans—there is at least one encouraging historical fact. Until the reappearance of a new German armed force in 1956, the most determined previous German effort to assure popular, civilian authority over the Prussian-German armed forces, through a responsible, democratic government, had been made by the very men who created the control institution which assured Prussian-German military excellence. Scharnhorst and his fellow-Reformers were primarily concerned with this aim of a true peoples' army for reasons of Prussian national security, which remains a valid and proper objective. But they were also influenced by the example of military despotism in neighboring Napoleonic France.

This encouraging fact in German military history and in the origins of the German General Staff should also be noted by Americans wondering about the possible incompatibility of democracy and military excellence, or wondering whether some features of the German General Staff system might improve American military efficiency. It is clear that the people who established the German General Staff system saw no incompatibility between military efficiency and popular, constitutional control of armed forces. The record also shows clearly that their failure to achieve the kind of constitutional control that they wanted was due to political causes and not to the military effectiveness of their new staff system.

American officers who have seen West German training and maneuvers have commented with respect and admiration on the efficiency of German performance, and the capability of German troops to react quickly, flexibly, and effectively to unforeseen maneuver circumstances. West German General Staff officers have demonstrated outstanding capabilities on the various NATO staffs. True democracy and traditional German military excellence appear to be as compatible in practice as they were in Scharnhorst's imagination.

Interestingly, for more than a century there have been occasional efforts by some American military men, impressed by the efficiency of the German General Staff, to get that system, or some of its features, adopted by the United States Army. Among the first of these admirers of German General Staff efficiency was Emory Upton, one of the most illustrious of American military thinkers. His views (posthumously) and those of Arthur L. Wagner eventually came to the attention of a civilian Secretary of War seeking ways to improve a military organization that had proved itself quite inefficient in the Spanish-American War. It was quickly evident to the logical mind of Secretary Elihu Root that a General Staff system was the answer to that inefficiency. Yet in his efforts to create an American General Staff, Mr. Root was at the outset opposed by none other than the illustrious Commanding General of the Army, Lieutenant General Nelson A. Miles, who denounced the proposed system as an effort to create an alien, Teutonic militarism in the United States.

Although Mr. Root was at least partly successful in his efforts to establish an American General Staff, the United States has never had a system as well-organized, as efficient, or as militarily effective as that of Germany. A major reason for this has been the vocal, emotional opposition of individuals who, like General Miles, see a General Staff as essentially totalitarian and incompatible with American democratic ideals.

The United States Army General Staff was probably at its most effective during and just after World War I, when it was based in very large part on the quite efficient French copy of the German original. It was that staff, and the military training and educational system which it created and supervised, which was perhaps the major ingredient in the rapid and comparatively efficient expansion of the United States Army in World War II. Today, however, the General Staff, as envisaged by Elihu Root and as directed by such Chiefs of Staff as March, Pershing, Summerall, MacArthur, Craig, and Marshall, has virtually disappeared. The United States has neither a true Army General Staff nor an Armed Forces General Staff.

Does the United States need such a General Staff, or can we achieve the very best possible military efficiency through the adaptation of traditional American free-enterprise business efficiency to the armed forces? It may even be asked whether the General Staff system, even if not inconsistent with American democracy, is still relevant. After all, the world has changed greatly since the time of Moltke and Schlieffen, even since the time of Seeckt and Beck. Modern technology and modern organizational theory may very well have made the General Staff system as outmoded as the steam locomotive. Finally, there is still no assurance that the system that worked so well in the army of totalitarian Germany is truly adaptable to the armed forces of a democratic America.

There are at present no assured answers to these questions. There are, however, two general reasons for nagging concern about the failure of the United States to have such a system and for urging as soon as possible a truly responsible study to seek answers to the key questions.

In the first place, there are a number of reasons to believe that American military efficiency today is not of the same high order as was that of Germany under its General Staff system.* There is also some evidence that, despite high standards of conduct and operational efficiency, individual and combined military performance of members of the U.S. Armed Forces officers corps is not uniformly up to those standards and fails to match the consistently high levels of performance of the German officer corps in peace and war under the influence of the German General Staff.[2]

Second, although the United States has generally ignored (rather than rejected) the example of the German General Staff, the only significant potential military opponent of the United States—Soviet Russia—has been assiduously studying and borrowing from the German example. The General Staff of the Soviet Armed Forces is similar in its organization and in its method of operation to that of the prewar German Army. The military educational system of the Soviet Armed Forces is patterned on that created for Prussia by Scharnhorst and

---

*J. A. Stockfisch, an economist, operations research analyst, and student of American and German defense policies, attributes the difference in efficiency in part to the fact that, at least in Imperial Germany, the German Army was shielded from involvement in the hurly-burly of parliamentary budgetary politics both by constitutional lines of authority (responsibility only to the monarch) and by Bismarck's policy of a five-to-seven year budget cycle. See J. A. Stockfisch, *Plowshares into Swords* (New York: 1973), p. 85.

Clausewitz, and adapted by such men as Moltke, Schlieffen, Seeckt, and Beck. The Russians seem to believe that it was because of this control system and its related educational system that their armies were so consistently outperformed by the Germans in the two World Wars.

Simply because the Soviet Union has adopted a system that may not be desirable or ideal or relevant to the United States is no reason for us to rush to follow their example. Modern Soviet leaders have not demonstrated either political or military infallibility or a record of consistent efficiency. Yet in the light of the historical facts, and in the light of the Soviet reaction to at least some of those historical facts, it would be dangerous for the United States to continue blithely to ignore either the current Soviet example or that of the German General Staff, which for more than a century, on many a bloody field repeatedly demonstrated its special genius for war.

NOTES TO EPILOGUE

[1] See, for instance, Charles R. Allen, Jr., *Heusinger of the Fourth Reich* (New York: 1963).

[2] See, for instance, Savage and Gabriel, *op. cit.*, p. 344.

Appendix A

CHRONOLOGY

1806	October 14	Battle of Jena-Auerstadt
1807	June 14	Battle of Friedland
1807	July 7-9	Treaties of Tilsit
1807	July 25	Formation of military reorganization commission under Scharnhorst
1808	March 1	Reestablishment of the War Department (War Ministry) in Prussia
1808	September 8	Treaty of Paris
1809	July 5-6	Battle of Wagram
1812	September 7	Battle of Borodino
1812	October 19-November 30	Napoleon's retreat from Moscow
1812	December 30	Convention of Tauroggen
1813	March 11	Scharnhorst appointed Quartermaster General, Chief of Staff
1813	May 2	Battle of Lützen (Gross Görschen)
1813	June 28	Scharnhorst's death in Prague
1813	July 21	Gneisenau temporarily assigned as Quartermaster General of the Army
1813	October 16-19	Battle of Leipzig
1814	April 11	Abdication of Napoleon
1814-1815		Congress of Vienna
1814	June 3	Boyen named first Prussian War Minister
1814	September 1	War Department reorganized as War Ministry
1814	September 3	Prussian law for general conscription
1815	June 18	Battle of Waterloo
1815	June 22	Second abdication of Napoleon
1815	November 20	Peace of Paris
1816	January 31	Reorganization of Quartermaster General Staff as General Staff
1819	July	Carlsbad Decrees
1819	November	Boyen resigns
1821	January 11	Müffling appointed Chief of Army General Staff
1824/25 Winter		General Staff autonomous from War Ministry
1829	January 29	Krauseneck appointed Chief of the General Staff
1836		Introduction of two-year active compulsory military service in Prussia
1841		Boyen reappointed War Minister
1848-1849		First Danish-Prussian War

1848		Prussian national assembly attempts to purge officer corps
1848	May 13	Reyher appointed Chief of the General Staff
1857	October 7	Moltke assumes duties as Chief of the General Staff
1859	April-July	Austro-French War
1859	December 5	General von Roon appointed Prussian War Minister
1859	December	Beginning of army reform crisis in Prussia
1860	May 5	House of Deputies rejects draft law on army reform
1862	September 23	House of Deputies definitively refuses to fund army reform
1862	September 24	Bismarck appointed Prussian Prime Minister
1864		Second Danish-Prussian War
1866	June 2	Chief of Army General Staff given right to issue orders directly to field troops
1866	June-August	Seven Weeks' War
1866	July 3	Battle of Königgrätz (Sadowa or Hradec Králové)
1867	January 31	Reorganization of General Staff into Main Establishment (*Hauptetat*) and Supporting Establishment (*Nebenetat*)
1867	April	Luxembourg crisis between France and Prussia
1867	November 9	Compulsory military service law in North German League
1870-1871		Franco-Prussian (Franco-German) War
1870	August 16-18	Battles of Mars La Tour and Gravelotte
1870	September 1	Battle of Sedan
1871	January 18	Foundation of the German Empire
1871	January 28	Surrender of Paris
1871	April 27	Prussian-German General Staff issues first memorandum on two-front war against France and Russia
1883	May 24	Chief of Prussian-German General Staff gets right of direct access to the sovereign
1887	November 30	General Staff memorandum on preventive war against Russia
1889	April 8	Waldersee appointed Chief of the General Staff
1890	March 18	Resignation of Bismarck
1891	February 7	Schlieffen appointed Chief of the General Staff
1894	July	New strategic plan of General Staff for two-front war
1895	June	Opening of Kiel Canal
1897	January 22	Waldersee's memorandum on coup d'etat for William II
1905	December	Schlieffen Plan
1913	October 1	Greatest German Army increase since 1871: peace strength increased by 136,000 to 760,908 noncommissioned officers and men
1914-1918		World War I
1914	August 13	Formation of War Matériel Department in Prussian War Ministry

1914	August 26-30	Battle of Tannenberg
1914	September 5-12	Battle of the Marne
1914	September 6-15	Battle of the Masurian Lakes
1914	September 14	Change in Army High Command (OHL): Moltke replaced by Falkenhayn
1914	November 1	Hindenburg appointed Commander in Chief for the East (*Oberost*) with Ludendorff his Chief of General Staff
1914	November 16-25	Battle of Lodz
1915	February 4-22	Winter Battle
1915	May-June	Gorlice-Tarnow Breakthrough
1915	May 7	Sinking of the *Lusitania*
1916	February-December	Battle of Verdun
1916	July-November	Battle of the Somme
1916	August 29	Change in OHL: Hindenburg appointed Chief of the General Staff; Ludendorff First Quartermaster General
1916	September 2	Centralization of military command of the Central Powers in the OHL
1916	September - December	Conquest of Romania
1917	September 3-5	Battle of Riga
1917	October-December	Battle of Caporetto
1918	March-April	German Somme and Lys offensives
1918	July	Second Battle of the Marne
1918	July 18	Allied counteroffensive begins
1918	August 8	"Black Day of the German Army"
1918	October 26	Ludendorff resigns; succeeded by General Groener
1918	October 28	Naval mutiny at Kiel
1918	November 9	Abdication of William II; Hindenburg Supreme Commander of Armed Forces
1918	November 11	The Armistice
1918	November 24	Secret order of OHL to set up voluntary organizations (Free Corps)
1918	December 24	Spartacists rout Army in Berlin
1919	January 5-15	Spartacist revolt crushed in Berlin
1919	March 6	Provisional *Reichswehr* Law
1919	June 28	Treaty of Versailles
1919	June 30	OHL transformed into *Kommandostelle* Kolberg
1919	July 3	Hindenburg resigns; succeeded by Groener
1919	July 7	Germany ratifies Treaty of Versailles; Groener resigns, succeeded by Seeckt
1919	July 15	Dissolution of the General Staff
1919	October 1	Reich Defense Ministry established; Reinhardt appointed Chief of Army Command
1919	October 11	Seeckt appointed Chief of Troop office (General Staff)

1920	March 13-17	Kapp Putsch
1920	March 26	Seeckt appointed Chief of Army Command
1920	April 2-10	Suppression of Ruhr disorders
1920	May 11	Secret decree on training of part-time volunteers
1921	January	Seeckt memorandum on possible tripling of *Reichswehr*
1921	March 8	Allied occupation of Düsseldorf, Duisburg, and Ruhrhort because of reparations payment default
1921	March 23	Defense Law passed by *Reichstag*
1921	May 6	German-Russian commercial agreement
1923	January 11	Allied occupation of Ruhr
1923	September 27	Ebert transfers executive powers to the Reich Defense Ministry; start of Seeckt "dictatorship" (ended March 1, 1924)
1923	November 8-11	Hitler's Beer Hall Putsch
1925	April 26	Hindenburg elected President
1925	October 16	Locarno Treaties
1926	February 1	*Wehrmacht* Department (*Abteilung*) formed under Colonel von Schleicher
1926	October 8	Seeckt's resignation
1928	January 20	Groener appointed Defense Minister
1929	March 1	Formation of Ministry Office (*Ministeramt*); General von Schleicher permanent deputy of Reich Defense Minister Groener
1931	October 8	Defense Minister Groener also takes over the Ministry of the Interior
1932	March 13	Hindenburg reelected President, over Hitler
1932	April 14	Groener orders dissolution of Nazi SA and SS paramilitary organizations
1932	May 13	Groener resigns
1932	May 30	Hindenburg dismisses Brüning
1932	June 2	Schleicher becomes Defense Minister under Papen
1932	December 1	*Reichswehr* war game in event of civil war
1932	December 3	Schleicher appointed Chancellor
1933	January 30	Hitler appointed Chancellor
1933	February 27	*Reichstag* Fire
1933	March	Formation of the *Luftwaffe* as the third branch of the armed forces
1934	June 30-July 1	Blood Purge
1934	August 2	Death of Hindenburg; Hitler assumes combined offices of Reich Chancellor and Reich President
1935	March 16	Hitler denounces Versailles Treaty prohibiting German armament; obligatory military service reintroduced; start of open rearmament
1936	March 7	Reoccupation of the Rhineland
1937	November 5	Hitler discusses future program of aggression in conference with Foreign Minister and Commanders in Chief

1937	December 21	War Ministry directive for Green Case (possible war against Czechoslovakia)
1938	February 4	Dismissal of Blomberg and Fritsch; Hitler becomes War Minister; formation of the OKW (High Command of the *Wehrmacht*) with Keitel as Chief
1938	March 12-13	Annexation of Austria
1938	September 29-30	Munich conference
1938	October 1	Occupation of Sudeten areas of Czechoslovakia
1939	March 14	Annexation of the rest of Czechoslovakia and establishment of the Slovak state
1939	April 3	OKW Directive White Case, for attack on Poland
1939	September 1	Start of World War II with the attack on Poland
1940	April 9	Attack on Denmark and Norway
1940	May 10	Start of attack in the west; Battle of Flanders begins
1940	June 5	Battle of France begins
1940	June 10	Italy enters the war
1940	June 22	France surrenders; armistice signed at Compiègne
1940	June 23	Beginning of preparations for the attack on the U.S.S.R.
1940	June-August	Battle of Britain
1940	August-September	Plans for landing in Britain (Operation "Sea Lion")
1941	April-May	Balkans Campaign
1941	May 20-31	Battle of Crete
1941	June 22	Attack on the U.S.S.R.–Operation "Barbarossa"
1941	December 5-6	Start of Soviet counteroffensive
1942	June 28	Start of German summer offensive in Russia
1942	August 24	Battle of Stalingrad begins
1943	January 31-February 2	Capitulation of German troops in Stalingrad
1943	February 18	Total war proclaimed in Germany
1943	July-August	Battles at Kursk
1943	September 8	Italy withdraws from Axis
1943	September 11	Allied Salerno landing
1944	June 4	Allies capture Rome
1944	June 6	Allied landings in Normandy
1944	June-July	Annihilation of Army Group Center in White Russia
1944	July 20	Abortive coup against Hitler
1944	December 16	Beginning of German Ardennes Offensive
1945	April 16	Beginning of Soviet Berlin Offensive
1945	April 30	Hitler's suicide
1945	May 8	Surrender signed

Appendix B

THE POLITICAL & MILITARY LEADERSHIP OF PRUSSIA-GERMANY, 1808-1945

Date	Chief of State	Senior Minister, Prime Minister or Chancellor	Minister of War	Chief of General
1808, March 1	Frederick William III (since Nov 16, 1797, to June 7, 1840)	Baron Carl vom Stein (since Oct 1807)	*Maj. Gen. Gerhard v Scharnhorst (to June 17, 1810)	*Maj. Gen. Gerhar Scharnhorst (to June 17, 1810)
November	. . . .	Count Alexander Dohna & Baron Carl Altenstein (to Dec 1809)		
1810, January	. . . .	Pr. Charles August v Hardenberg (to Nov 1822)		
June 17	. . . .		*Maj. Gen. K. Ernst v Hake (to Aug 1813)	*Gen. K. Ernst v Hake (to Mar 181
1812, March	. . . .			*Col. Gen. Gustav Rauch (to Mar 18
1813, March 11	. . . .			Gen. Gerhard v Scharnhorst (to J 28, 1813)
July 21	. . . .			Gen. A. N. v Gneis (to June 1814)
1814, June 3	. . . .		Gen. L. G. Hermann v Boyen (to Nov 1819)	Gen. Karl v Grolma (to Nov 1819)
1819, November	. . . .		Gen. K. Ernst v Hake (to Oct 1833)	*L. Gen. J. J. O. A. Rühl v Lilienstern (to Jan 11, 1821)
1821, January 11	. . . .			L. Gen. Baron J. F. W. v Müffling (Jan 29, 1829)
1822, November 26	. . . .	Office of Prime Minister vacant; King acted as own Prime Minister		
1829, January 29	. . . .			L. Gen. J. W. v Krauseneck (to Ma 13, 1849)
1833, October	. . . .		Gen. Job v Witzleben (to 1837)	
1837	. . . .		Gen. J. G. Gustav v Rauch (to Mar 1, 1841)	

*Acting

3

THE POLITICAL AND MILITARY LEADERSHIP OF PRUSSIA-GERMANY,
1808-1945 (continued)

Date	Chief of State	Senior Minister, Prime Minister or Chancellor	Minister of War	Chief of General Staff
1840, June 7	Frederick William IV (to Jan 2, 1861)			
1841, March 1		. . . .	Gen. L. G. Hermann v Boyen (to Oct 6, 1847)	
1847, October 7		. . . .	Gen. Ferdinand v Rohr (to Apr 2, 1848)	
1848, March 14		. . . . Count Adolf H. v Arnim-Boytzenburg (to Mar 24, 1848)		
April 2		. . . . Ludolf Camphausen (to June 1848)	*L. Gen. K. F. v Reyher (to Apr 26, 1848)	
April 26		. . . .	Gen. Count August v Kanitz (to June 16, 1848)	Gen. Karl F. v Reyher (to Oct 7, 1857)
May 13		. . . .		
June 27		. . . . David Hansemann & Rudolf v Auerswald (to Sep 10, 1848)	Gen. Baron L. Roth v Schreckenstein (to Sep 7, 1848)	
September 7		. . . .	Gen. Ernst v Pfuel (to Nov 2, 1848)	
September 21		. . . . Gen. Ernst v Pfuel (to Nov 2, 1848)		
November 2		. . . . Gen. Freidrich W. v Brandenburg (to Nov 6, 1850)		
November 8		. . . .	Gen. Karl A. v Strotha (to Feb 27, 1850)	
1850, February 27		. . . .	Gen. August v Stockhausen (to Dec 31, 1851)	
November 6		. . . . Baron Otto v Manteuffel (to 1858)		
1852, January 1		. . . .	Gen. Eduard v Bonin (to 1854)	
1854		. . . .	Gen. Count Friedrich v Waldersee (to Nov 6, 1858)	
1857, October	Prince Regent William (to Jan 2, 1861)			
October 29		. . . .		Maj. Gen. Helmuth v Moltke (to Aug 10, 1888)
1858		. . . . Pr. Charles Hohenzollern-Sigmaringen (to Mar 1862)		
November 6		. . . .	Gen. Eduard v Bonin (to Nov 28, 1859)	

THE POLITICAL AND MILITARY LEADERSHIP OF PRUSSIA-GERMANY, 1808-1945 (continued)

Date	Chief of State	Senior Minister, Prime Minister or Chancellor	Minister of War	Chief of General Staff
1859, December 5	. . . .	. . . .	Gen. Albrecht v Roon (to Nov 9, 1873)	
1861, January 2	William I (to Mar 9, 1888)			
1863, September 24		. . . . Otto Eduard L. v Bismarck (to Mar 18, 1890) (Chancellor in 1871)		
1873, November 9		. . . .	Maj. Gen. Georg v Kameke (to Mar 3, 1883)	
1883, March 3		. . . .	Maj. Gen. Paul Bronsart v Schellendorf (to Apr 8, 1889)	
1888, March 9 June 15	Frederick III (to June 15, 1888) William II (to Nov 9, 1918)			
August 10		. . . .		Gen. Count Alfred v Waldersee (to Feb 1891)
1889, April 8		. . . .	Gen. Julius v Verdy du Vernois (to Oct 4, 1890)	
1890, March 4		. . . . Lt. Gen. Leo v Caprivi (to Oct 28, 1894)		
October 4		. . . .	Gen. Hans C. G. v Kaltenborn-Stachau (to Oct 19, 1893)	
1891, February 7		. . . .		Col. Gen. Count Alfred v Schlieffen (to Jan 1, 1906)
1893, October 19		. . . .	Gen. Walther Bronsart v Schellendorf (to Aug 14, 1896)	
1894, October		. . . . Pr. Chlodwig v Hohenlohe (to Oct 1900)		
1896, August 14		. . . .	Gen. Heinrich v Gossler (to Aug 15, 1903)	
1900, October		. . . . Count Bernhard v Bülow (to July 14, 1909)		
1903, August 15		. . . .	Gen. Karl v Einem (to Aug 11, 1909)	
1906, January 1		. . . .		Col. Gen. Helmuth v Moltke (to Sep 14, 1914)

THE POLITICAL AND MILITARY LEADERSHIP OF PRUSSIA-GERMANY, 1808-1945 (continued)

Date	Chief of State	Senior Minister, Prime Minister or Chancellor	Minister of War	Chief of General Staff
1909		Theobald v Bethmann-Hollweg (to July 1917)		
August 11			Gen. Josias v Heeringen (to June 7, 1913)	
1913, June 7			Gen. Erich v Falkenhayn (to Jan 21, 1915)	
1914, September 14				Gen. Erich v Falkenhayn (to Aug 29, 1916)
1915, January 15			Lt. Gen. Adolf Wild v Hohenborn (to Oct 29, 1916)	
1916, August 29				Field Marshal Paul v Hindenburg (to July 3, 1919)
October 21			Gen. Hermann v Stein (to Oct 9, 1918)	
1917, July		Georg Michaelis (to Oct 1917)		
October		Count Georg v Hertling (to Oct 1918)		
1918, October		Prince Max v Baden (to Nov 10, 1918)		
October 9			Lt. Gen. Heinrich Scheuch (to Nov 9, 1918)	
October 30				
November 9	No head of State (to Feb 11, 1919)	Friedrich Ebert (to Feb 11, 1919)	No Minister of War* (to Jan 1919)	*
1919, January 2			Col. Walther Reinhardt (to Feb 13, 1919)	
February 11	Friedrich Ebert (to May 28, 1925)	Philipp Scheidemann (to June 19, 1919)		
February 13				
June 22		Gustav Bauer		
July 3				Lt. Gen. Wilhelm Groener (to July 7, 1919)
July 7				Maj. Gen. Hans v Seeckt (to July 15, 1919)

*Hindenburg appointed Supreme Commander of the Armed Forces; Groener became Acting Chief of the General Staff.
†First Minister of Defense

322

THE POLITICAL AND MILITARY LEADERSHIP OF PRUSSIA-GERMANY, 1808-1945 (continued)

First Quartermaster General (Deputy & Acting Chief of Staff)	Minister of Defense	Chief of Army Command (C-in-C, Army)	Chief of Troop Office (Chief of Gen. Staff)
Gen. Erich Ludendorff (to Oct 26, 1918)			
Maj. Gen. Wilhelm Groener (to July 3, 1919)			
. . . .	Gustav Noske† (to Mar 25, 1920)		
No First Quartermaster appointed			

Date	Chief of State	Senior Minister, Prime Minister or Chancellor	Minister of War	Chief of General Staff
July 15				General Staff disbanded
1919, October 1				
October 11				
1920, March 26		Hermann Müller (to June 25, 1920)		
March 28				
June 25		Konstantine Fehrenbach		
1921, May 10		Joseph Werth		
1922, November 14		William Cuno (to (Aug 12, 1923)		
1923, February				
August 12		Gustav Stresemann (to Nov 23, 1923)		
November 23		Wilhelm Marx		
1925, January 15		Hans Luther (to May 12, 1926)		
February 21	Death of Pres. Ebert			
May 12	F. M. Paul v Hindenburg (to Aug 1, 1934)			
October				
1926, May 14		Wilhelm Marx		
October 7				
1927, January 27				
1928, January 20				
June 13		Hermann Müller (to Mar 27, 1930)		
1929, October 1				
1930, March 30		Heinrich Brüning (to May 30, 1932)		
November 1				

First Quartermaster General (Deputy & Acting Chief of Staff)	Minister of Defense	Chief of Army Command (C-in-C, Army)	Chief of Troop Office (Chief of Gen. Staff)
. . . .		Maj. Gen. Walther Reinhardt (to Mar 26, 1920)	
. . . .			Lt. Gen. Hans v Seeckt (to Mar 26, 1920)
	Otto Gessler (to Jan 19, 1928)	Lt. Gen. Hans v Seeckt (to Oct 6, 1926)	
. . . .			Maj. Gen. Wilhelm Heye (to Feb 1923)
. . . .			Maj. Gen. Otto Hasse (to Oct 1925)
. . . .			Maj. Gen. Wilhelm Wetzell
. . . .		Gen. Wilhelm Heye (to Oct 31, 1930)	
. . . .			Maj. Gen. Werner v Blomberg (to Sep 30, 1929)
. . . .	Lt. Gen. Wilhelm Groener (to May 13, 1932)		
. . . .			Maj. Gen. Baron Kurt v Hammerstein-Equord (to Oct 31, 1930)
. . . .		Col. Gen. Baron Kurt v Hammerstein-Equord (to Jan 31, 1934)	Maj. Gen. Wilhelm Adam (to Sep 30, 1933)

THE POLITICAL AND MILITARY LEADERSHIP OF PRUSSIA-GERMANY,
1808-1945 (continued)

Date	Chief of State	Senior Minister Prime Minister or Chancellor	Minister of War	Chief of General Staff
1932, June 1	. . . .	Franz v Papen (to (Nov 17, 1932)		
December 2	. . . .	Gen. Kurt v Schleicher (to Jan 28, 1933)		
1933, January 30	. . . .	Adolf Hitler (to Apr 30, 1945)		
October 1	. . . .			
1934, February 1	. . . .			
August 2	Adolf Hitler (to Apr 30, 1945)			
1938, February 4	. . . .			
October 31	. . . .			
1941, December 19	. . . .			
1942, September 24	. . . .			
1944, July 21	. . . .			
1945, March 29	. . . .			
April 30	. . . . Suicide of Adolf Hitler			

THE POLITICAL AND MILITARY LEADERSHIP OF PRUSSIA-GERMANY,
1808-1945 (continued)

First Quartermaster General (Deputy & Acting Chief of Staff)	Minister of Defense	Chief of Army Command (C-in-C, Army)	Chief of General Staff
	Gen. Kurt v Schleicher (to Jan 28, 1933)		
	Col. Gen. Werner v Blomberg (to Jan 27, 1938)		
. . . .			Gen. Ludwig Beck (to Oct 31, 1938)
. . . .		Col. Gen. Werner v Fritsch (to Feb 3, 1938)	
. . . .	Adolf Hitler (to Apr 30, 1945)	Col. Gen. Walther v Brauchitsch (to Dec 19, 1941)	
. . . .			Gen. Franz Halder (to Sep 24, 1942)
. . . .		Adolf Hitler (to Apr 30, 1945)	
. . . .			Lt. Gen. Kurt Zeitzler (to July 20, 1944)
. . . .			Col. Gen. Heinz Guderian (to Mar 28, 1945)
. . . .			Gen. Hans Krebs (to May 7, 1945)

Appendix C

GERMAN PERFORMANCE
IN WORLD WAR I

AGGREGATED STATISTICS, FIFTEEN WWI BATTLES / Shown below (Figure C-1) are the highly aggregated, approximate statistics of fifteen World War I battles, ten on the Western Front and five on the Eastern Front, against Russia. Of the ten on the Western Front, four were battles primarily against the French, five primarily against the British, and one against the Americans. The battles are identified by commonly known names, dates, duration, major forces involved, and the operational posture (attack or one of the three varieties of defense) in relation to success or failure.

The first statistical column gives the approximate strengths of the opposing forces.

The next column gives, in round numbers, the generally accepted casualties to each side. In four battles on the Eastern Front which resulted in German capture of exceptional numbers of Russian prisoners, the casualty figures are shown *with* (underlined) these prisoners included and without (not underlined) the prisoners.

The next column breaks down the casualty figures to casualties per day.

The next column shows percentage of casualties per day, as related to the starting, or overall, strength figure shown three columns to the left.

The next column provides a value which is termed "Score" to represent the casualties per day as a percentage of the force inflicting the casualties, derived by applying the casualties of one side to the starting or overall strength figure of the other side; i.e., the casualties inflicted per day per 100 men.

The last column, "Score Effectiveness," adjusts the Score value to reflect approximately the known operational advantage which is conferred by defensive posture. Using factors for defensive advantage which have been derived from extensive World War II research (see Appendix E), but which have not been intensively tested against World War I experience, these advantages are 1.3 for Hasty Defense, 1.5 for Prepared Defense, and 1.6 for Fortified Defense. In instances in early battles of the war where both sides were attacking (and thus at least partially also involved in hasty defense), the factor is estimated at 1.2. The resulting Score Effectiveness value is thus an approximate reflection of "normalized" casualty-inflicting capability of the opposing sides in each of the battles. The low values for long battles are a clear reflection of a phenomenon noted in detailed World War II analyses—namely that the Score Effectiveness value of any military force declines steadily in prolonged combat

SCORE EFFECTIVENESS STATISTICAL COMPARISON / The next chart (Figure C-2) presents a simple statistical analysis of the data in the statistical summary of the fifteen battles.

Part I, Overall, shows summaries for the fifteen battles, and for the ten battles on the Western Front and the five battles on the Eastern Front.

Part II shows an average Score Effectiveness comparison by nation.

In both instances calculations for the Eastern Front show results both with and without the exceptional German hauls of Russian prisoners.

The consistent German superiority in inflicting casualties against all Allied opponents is clearly demonstrated, even when war-weary Germans were pitted against fresh Americans.

FIGURE C-1 / AGGREGATED STATISTICS OF FIFTEEN WORLD WAR I BATTLES

	Date	Battle	Duration (Days)	Opposing Forces
1.	1914, Aug 14-23	The Frontiers	10	German Armies, West French Armies
2.	1914, Aug 26-29	Tannenberg†	4	German Eighth Army Russian Second Army
3.	1914, Sep 5-10	The Marne	6	German Armies, West French Armies
4.	1914, Sep 9-14	Masurian Lakes†	5	German Eighth Army Russian First Army
5.	1914, Nov 11-25	Lodz	15	German Ninth Army Russian Army Group, N.W.
6.	1915, Feb 7-21	Winter Battle†	15	German Eighth & Tenth Armies Russian Tenth Army
7.	1915, May 2-4	Gorlice-Tarnow†	3	German Eleventh Army Russian Third Army
8.	1915, Sep 25-Nov 8	Champagne II	45	German Third Army French Second Army (+)
9.	1916, July 1-Oct 31	Somme I	123	German Second Army British Fourth & French Sixth Armies
10.	1917, April 9-24	Arras	15	German Sixth Army British Third Army
11.	1917, April 16-30	Aisne II (Nivelle offensive)	15	German Seventh Army (+) French Fifth & Sixth Armies (+)
12.	1917, July 31-Nov 6	Ypres III	98	German Fourth Army British Fifth & Second Armies
13.	1918, Mar 21-Apr 9	Somme II	20	German Ruprecht Group British Fifth, Third & Fourth Armies
14.	1918, Apr 9-30	Lys	22	German Sixth & Fourth Armies British First Army
15.	1918, Sep 26-Nov 11	Meuse-Argonne	47	German Gallwitz Group U.S. First & Second Armies

Posture* Suc./Fail		Strength	Casualties	Casualties Per Day	Percent Cas/Day	Score	Score Effectiveness
A		1,200,000	200,000	20,000	1.67	2.50	2.08
	A	1,390,000	300,000	30,000	2.16	1.44	1.20
A		187,000	13,212	3,303	1.77	16.04 / 4.68	13.37 / 3.90
	A	160,000	120,000 / 35,000	30,000 / 8,750	18.75 / 5.47	2.06	1.72
	A	900,000	300,000	50,000	5.56	4.63	3.86
A		1,200,000	250,000	41,666	3.47	4.17	3.48
A		288,600	40,000	8,000	2.77	8.66 / 3.47	7.22 / 2.89
	A	273,000	125,000 / 50,000	25,000 / 10,000	9.16 / 3.66	2.93	2.44
A	A	260,000	60,000	4,000	1.54	2.44	2.03
A	A	400,000	95,000	6,333	1.58	1.00	0.83
A		250,000	40,000	2,667	1.67	5.60 / 2.67	
	HD	300,000	210,000 / 100,000	14,000 / 6,667	4.67 / 2.22	0.89	
A		175,000	25,000	8,333	4.76	38.10 / 11.43	38.10 / 11.43
	PD	300,000	200,000 / 60,000	66,667 / 20,000	22.22 / 6.67	2.78	1.85
FD		190,000	60,000	1,333	0.70	1.70	1.06
	A	500,000	145,000	3,222	0.64	0.27	0.27
FD		250,000	500,000	4,065	1.63	2.18	1.36
	A	600,000	670,000	5,447	0.91	0.68	0.68
FD		120,000	75,000	5,000	4.17	4.67	2.92
	A	276,000	84,000	5,600	2.03	1.81	1.81
FD		480,000	40,000	2.667	0.56	1.64	1.03
	A	1,000,000	118,000	7,867	0.79	0.27	0.27
FD		200,000	200,000	2,041	1.02	1.53	0.96
	A	380,000	300,000	3,061	0.81	0.54	0.54
A	A	870,000	190,000	9,500	1.09	1.15	1.15
FD	FD	550,000	200,000	10,000	1.82	1.73	1.08
A	A	500,000	175,000	7,955	1.59	1.39	1.39
FD	FD	400,000	152,500	6,932	1.73	1.99	1.24
	FD	380,000	126,000	2,681	0.71	0.73	0.46
A		600,000	130,000	2,766	0.46	0.45	0.45

*Postures: A - Attack; HD - Hasty Defense; PD - Prepared Defense; FD - Fortified Defense. Drawn battles are shown by indicating both success and failure.
†Russian casualties are shown *including* prisoners (*underlined*), and without prisoners (not underlined).

Figure C-2 / WORLD WAR I SCORE EFFECTIVENESS STATISTICAL COMPARISON

I. OVERALL

	No. of Battles	Total Engaged	Total Casualties	Average % Casualties /day	Average Score Effectiveness
Allies	15	8,329,000	3,099,000*	4.86	1.24
Germans		6,250,000	2,044,000	2.04	5.51 (or 2.61*)
W. Allies	10	6,896,000	2,349,000	1.48	1.10
Germans		5,090,000	1,866,000	1.87	1.63
Russians	5	1,433,000	750,000*	1.50	1.50
Germans		1,160,000	178,000	13.26 (or 4.58†)	5.75 (average of averages)

II. BY NATION

	Battles	Average Score Effectiveness
French	4	1.31
Germans		2.01 or $1/1.54$
British	6	1.07
Germans		1.56 or $1/1.45$
Americans	1†	0.45
Germans		0.46 or $1/1.02$
Russians	5	1.50
Germans		13.26 or $1/8.84$ (or $1/3.05$‡) (or 4.58†)

*Omitting Russian prisoners in four battles.
†Meuse-Argonne.
‡410,000 of these were Russian prisoners at Tannenberg, Masurian Lakes, Winter Battle, and Gorlice.

Appendix D
A DEFENSE OF SCHLEICHER*

Schleicher is usually reproached for his love of intrigue. This is reminiscent of some historians' choice of words for bravery: They credit friendly troops with "heroism," whereas the enemy fights, at best, "fanatically." In the context of a positive overall assessment of Schleicher's activities, many if not all of his "intrigues" would be called "skillful maneuvers" had he been ultimately successful. Lest we forget it, once the constitutional system of a country disintegrates, backstage figures and the horse holders of the mighty gain even more power than they normally hold. Whosoever desires to achieve any purpose has to use back doors, even if he dislikes it.

Schleicher has never had an opportunity to defend himself against his critics, since Hitler had him killed, whereas Groener, Papen, Brüning, and many others could write their memoirs. Even Goebbels had his diaries published. The only Schleicher biography available is a very slender volume written by Thilo Vogelsang.[1] Thus we should start from a few evident facts to establish a reasonable basis for some questions and analysis.

1. The agony of the Weimar Republic began in the summer of 1930, when the parliament became paralyzed. Thenceforth, in all important matters, the government operated by decree, under Article 48 of the Constitution. The political system of the country disintegrated, with the economy—barely recovered from history's worst inflation—soon to follow. This left the Army as one of the few solid national institutions, and gave it a political role which it had to accept whether its leaders liked it or not. Even refusal to accept a political role would have been a political act of primary importance. Since the Army commander (Hammerstein) was inactive, the obvious man to exert the political role was Schleicher. He probably accepted that role with delight. What were his motives? Vanity? Ambition? Desire to help his country? Sense of duty? I do not know. My guess: a combination of all four of these motives. Which was paramount? Who knows?

2. Schleicher was intelligent enough to know that open political involvement would inevitably mean involvement in party politics and therefore would be detrimental to his influence and to the Army. Thus he remained in the background, pulling the strings. This was unusual for a politician, although perhaps pardonable for an officer whom the disintegration of the political system forces to assume a political role and who risks ruin of his instrument, of the Army, if it becomes too deeply involved in party politics.

3. The conditions under which Schleicher worked were determined by one fact: Since the country was starving, the majority of the voters believed that

*From a letter to the author by Dr. Franz Uhle-Wettler.

democracy had failed and that only a dictator could solve the problems. Harzburger Front, Communists, *Deutschnationale,* and National Socialists certainly disagreed as to where the strong man should come from. But they were unanimous in their rejection of the existing system, and between them they controlled about 60 percent of the votes.

4. Given the role of the Army under these conditions, Schleicher had to face one question only: How can a dictatorship of the radicals be avoided, even though a majority of the electorate is desperate enough to want it?

As far as I can see, Schleicher was one of the very few politicians and officers in Germany at that time who faced that problem squarely and without any illusions. Obviously, democratic rule could not be preserved indefinitely once the parliament is paralyzed and once the people vote for parties promising to do away with democracy. In the long run a dictatorship was inevitable, based on the remaining reasonable elements in the nation, and designed for a threefold purpose:
  —to solve the problems which a paralyzed parliament is unable to solve;
  —to keep the door open for reintroduction of democratic government;
  —and, foremost, to keep the radicals from power.
This is what Schleicher tried. He knew that a radical dictator could only be avoided by disregarding the apparent desire of the majority of the voters, i.e., by a strong man taken from the more moderates. Since the Social Democrats had ostracized Noske long ago, only the Army could furnish such a man.

Under the circumstances Schleicher had two options:

1. He could make advances to the National Socialists with the ultimate aim of splitting their party and ruling with the support of their more reasonable elements. He came close to success in this—Hitler's deputy, Strasser, broke loose. Unfortunately he did not succeed in carrying along a major proportion of the party.

2. Thus the only alternative left was a military dictatorship based on the tacit or, preferably, open support of the trade unions. This was certainly not a very agreeable solution, but what other solution was there? And interestingly enough, again Schleicher came close to success. The unions (Theodor Leipart) vacillated. Then the Social Democrats (Otto Wels) called them back.

From that moment Schleicher was dead, first politically and soon physically as well. The road was open for Hitler. Schleicher's performance as Chancellor was one of the most ineffective in German history. But does this show his inability? Or does it show the shortsightedness of the unions, which were soon disbanded, and the shortsightedness of the Social Democrats, who were soon proscribed?

Possibly Schleicher was not a very sympathetic personality, although we do well to remember that we see him mainly through the glasses of his opponents— from Groener via Brüning and Papen to Goebbels. But I believe Schleicher was the only major personality of the later Weimar Republic who had a clear idea of the situation and who faced it squarely. Moreover, he was the only one with a workable plan to prevent a radical dictatorship, despite the apparent desire of a majority of the electorate for such a dictatorship.

This, to my mind, makes him one of the most interesting, possibly even one of the most appealing, personalities of the late, dying republic. The clearness of his perception, the absence of illusions, the logical consequence of his plans and his abhorrence of Communist and Nazi radicalism alike may have been enhanced by his service in the Army and by his General Staff education. There is no gainsaying that he failed. But did he fail dishonorably? He failed primarily because a majority of the voters believed the problems of the country could only be cured by a medicine that he would not accept—and that later proved to be lethal. Last, not least, he failed because the unions and the Social Democrats could not overcome their traditional, outdated attitude toward the military, which has never been criticized more aptly and devastatingly than by a recent Hitler biography.[2] This is all the more astonishing since probably most of the generals, and certainly Schleicher, had long since overcome the traditional attitude of the military aristocracy toward the working class.

Sometimes I wonder what would have happened if Schleicher had not been an aristocrat but like Hitler of humble birth, not been a general but a corporal turned politician. Possibly he would have succeeded in persuading the unions to tolerate a dictatorship of his, based on the Army and designed to keep the radicals from power. The fate of Germany and of Europe would have been different and certainly not worse. A few weeks after they refused even to negotiate with Schleicher, the unions did nothing to keep another strong man, a civilian of humble birth, from power. They were soon to learn that they and their country had not chosen the lesser evil.

NOTES TO APPENDIX D

[1] Thilo Vogelsang, *Kurt von Schleicher* (Göttingen: 1965).

[2] Joachim Fest, *Hitler* (Frankfurt: 1974), p. 499.

GERMAN PERFORMANCE IN WORLD WAR II

PERFORMANCE AGAINST WESTERN ALLIES / In the process of developing and refining the Quantified Judgment Method of Analysis of Historical Combat (QJMA),[1] the Historical Evaluation and Research Organization (HERO) has compiled a data base of more than a hundred World War II engagements, plus additional data on the Korean and Middle East wars. Listed below from that data base (Fig. E-1) are some seventy-eight divisions and corps engagements between German forces and those of the Western Allies. Fig. E-2 is a summary of some of the data for each of these engagements (related to Figure E-1 by identification number) providing further information as to Allied and German units, and their postures, as related to success and failure, their percentage of casualties per day, and their score effectiveness. The column N_f/N_e gives the relative numerical manpower ratio of the opposing forces.

Figure E-3 presents a statistical comparison of German and Western Allies Score Effectiveness in these seventy-eight engagements, similar to that shown for World War I in Appendix C. (The reader is cautioned that the averages shown in Part II of that figure reflect overall averages from the entire data base, and not from the summaries by four categories of posture, success, and failure.) The German score effectiveness superiority over the Western Allies in these seventy-eight engagements is almost identical to that found in the ten samples examined for World War I.

Figure E-4 lists the relative combat effectiveness and relative average score effectiveness of the divisions which participated in three or more of the seventy-eight engagements listed in Figure E-1. Note that the average combat effectiveness of German units is about 23 percent greater than that of the Allied units.

PERFORMANCE AGAINST RUSSIA / HERO's data base for the Eastern Front in World War II is less comprehensive than that for the Western Fronts. However, the next two figures demonstrate that the German combat effectiveness and score effectiveness superiorities over the Russians was much greater than over the Western Allies, although not so lopsided as in World War I.

Figure E-5 presents some statistics of the Oboyan Sector of the Battle of Kursk, where in July 1943 the German XLVIII Panzer Corps attacked for seven days against the Soviet Sixth Guards and First Tank Armies. During those seven days the Germans, with a numerical inferiority of 2 to 3, advanced about thirty-five kilometers through the most heavily fortified area the world had seen since November 1918. They were stopped only when an additional Soviet tank army and other reserves were introduced into the battle, completely changing the force ratios shown. This German advance was possible only if the Germans had a combat effectiveness superiority over the Russians of at least 168 percent, or a relative combat effectiveness value (CEV) of 2.68. In most of the examples studied by HERO, the Score Effectiveness (SE) value has been greater than the CEV; usually about the square of the CEV; in this instance it was somewhat less, presumably because of the decrease in Soviet vulnerability due to the massive fortifications.

Figure E-6 presents some general statistics for the Eastern Front for 1944. During most of that year the Germans were on the verge of collapse, but they did not collapse. In the light of the force disparity between the two sides, this was possible only if 2.5 million Germans (with the advantage of defensive posture) had a combat effectiveness superiority over the Russians of close to 88 percent, or a CEV of 1.88. It will be noted that the German score effectiveness superiority over the Russians was almost 6 to 1, probably reflecting the Soviet penchant for mass attacks without regard to casualties.

Figure E-1 / SELECTED ENGAGEMENTS, WORLD WAR II

Salerno Campaign, September 9-18, 1943

Engagement   1. Port of Salerno, September 9-11, 1943
           2. Amphitheater, September 9-11, 1943
           3. Sele-Calore corridor, September 11, 1943
           4. Tobacco factory, September 13-14, 1943
           5. Vietri I, September 12-14, 1943
           6. Battipaglia, September 12-15, 1943
           7. Vietri II, September 17-18, 1943
           8. Battipaglia II, September 17-18, 1943
           9. Eboli, September 17-18, 1943

Volturno Campaign, October 12-December 8, 1943

Engagement   10. Grazzanise, October 12-14, 1943
           11. Capua, October 13, 1943
           12. Triflisco, October 13-14, 1943
           13. Monte Acero, October 13-14, 1943
           14. Caiazzo, October 13-14, 1943
           15. Castel Volturno, October 13-15, 1943
           16. Dragoni, October 15-17, 1943
           17. Canal I, October 15-20, 1943
           18. Canal II, October 17-18, 1943
           19. Francolise, October 20-22, 1943
           20. Monte Grande, October 16-17, 1943
           21. Santa Maria Oliveto, November 4-5, 1943
           22. Monte Lungo, November 6-7, 1943
           23. Pozzilli, November 6-7, 1943
           24. Monte Camino I, November 5-7, 1943
           25. Monte Camino II, November 8-12, 1943
           26. Monte Rotondo, November 8-10, 1943
           27. Monte Camino III, December 2-6, 1943
           28. Calabritto, December 1-2, 1943
           29. Monte Maggiore, December 2-3, 1943

Anzio Campaign, January 22-February 29, 1944

Engagement   30. Aprilia I, January 25-26, 1944
           31. The Factory, January 27, 1944

SELECTED ENGAGEMENTS, WORLD WAR II (continued)

    32. Campoleone, January 29-31, 1944
    33. Campoleone counterattack, February 3-5, 1944
    34. Carroceto, February 7-8, 1944
    35. Moletta River defense, February 7-9, 1944
    36. Aprilia II, February 9, 1944
    37. Factory Counterattack, February 11-12, 1944
    38. Bowling Alley, February 16-19, 1944
    39. Moletta River II, February 16-19, 1944
    40. Fioccia, February 21-23, 1944

Rome Campaign, May 11-June 4, 1944

Engagement 41. Santa Maria Infante, May 12-13, 1944
            42. San Martino, May 12-13, 1944
            43. Spigno, May 14-15, 1944
            44. Castellonorato, May 14-15, 1944
            45. Monte Grande, May 17-19, 1944
            46. Formia, May 16-18, 1944
            47. Itri-Fondi, May 20-22, 1944
            48. Terracina, May 22-24, 1944
            49. Moletta Offensive, May 23-24, 1944
            50. Anzio-Albano Road, May 23-24, 1944
            51. Anzio Breakout, May 23-25, 1944
            52. Cisterna, May 23-25, 1944
            53. Sezze, May 25-27, 1944
            54. Velletri, May 26, 1944
            55. Villa Crocetta, May 27-28, 1944
            56. Campoleone station, May 26-28, 1944
            57. Ardea, May 28-30, 1944
            58. Lanuvio, May 29-June 1, 1944
            59. Campoleone, May 29-31, 1944
            60. Tarto-Tiber, June 3-4, 1944

Le Mans to Metz, August 14-September 14, 1944

Engagement 501. Seine River, August 23-25, 1944
           502. Moselle-Metz, September 6-11, 1944
           503. Metz, September 13, 1944
           504. Chartres, August 16, 1944
           505. Melun, August 23-25, 1944

Saar Campaign, November 8-December 7, 1944

Engagement 601. Château Salins, November 10-11, 1944
           602. Morhange-Conthil, November 13-15, 1944
           603. Bourgaltroff, November 14-15, 1944
           604. Baerendorf I, November 24-25, 1944
           605. Baerendorf II, November 26, 1944
           606. Burbach-Durstel, November 27-30, 1944
           607. Sarre Union, December 1-2, 1944
           608. Singling-Bining, December 6-7, 1944
           609. Seille River, November 8-12, 1944
           610. Morhange-Faulquemont, November 13-16, 1944
           611. Francaltroff-St. Avold, November 20-27, 1944
           612. Durstil-Farebersviller, November 28-29, 1944
           613. Sarre River, December 5-7, 1944

Engage-ment	Allied Units	Allied Data Posture/Success S	F	Percent Cas/Day	Score Effect	German Units	German Data Posture/Success S	F	Percent Cas/Day	Score Effect
1	B 46 ID	—	A	3.95	1.02	16 Pz	PD	—	0.94	3.85
2	B 56 ID	—	A	2.98	0.99	16 Pz	PD	—	0.78	2.75
3	US 45 ID	—	A	2.01	1.12	16 Pz	HD	—	0.71	2.45
4	US 45 ID	HD	—	1.58	1.96	16 & 29 Pz	—	A	2.38	2.51
5	B 46 ID	HD	—	2.25	1.78	HG Pz	—	A	1.50	2.30
6	B 56 ID	HD	—	3.65	1.61	16 Pz +	—	A	1.89	3.86
7	B 46 ID	HD	—	0.67	1.59	H G Pz	—	A	1.50	1.74
8	B 56 ID	A	—	1.02	0.98	16 Pz	—	Del	0.79	2.02
9	US 45 ID	A	—	1.24	0.96	16 & 26 Pz	—	Del	0.90	2.44
10	B 7 AD	A	—	0.85	0.68	15 Pz Gr	—	PD	0.33	2.05
11	B 56 ID	—	A	2.49	1.08	H G Pz	PD	—	1.18	3.94
12	US 3 ID	A	—	0.72	0.75	H G Pz	—	PD	0.52	2.50
13	US 45 ID	A	A	0.31	1.26	3 & 26 Pz	Del	Del	1.01	1.22
14	US 34 ID	A	—	0.36	0.58	3 Pz Gr	—	Del	0.40	1.66
15	B 46 ID	A	—	1.13	0.51	15 Pz Gr	—	PD	0.25	2.94
16	US 34 ID	A	—	0.13	0.89	3 Pz Gr	—	Del	0.33	1.33
17	B 46 ID	A	—	0.42	0.93	15 Pz Gr	—	PD	0.57	1.73
18	B 7 AD	A	—	0.43	0.75	15 Pz Gr	—	PD	0.28	1.60
19	B 7 AD	A	A	0.18	0.96	15 Pz Gr	PD	PD	0.18	1.06
20	B 56 ID	A	—	0.61	0.76	H G Pz	—	PD	0.46	2.20
21	US 34 ID	A	—	1.23	1.28	3 Pz Gr +	—	PD	1.69	3.28
22	US 3 ID	—	A	1.09	1.34	3 Pz Gr	FD	—	1.41	2.82
23	US 45 ID	—	A	0.37	0.54	3 Pz Gr	FD	—	0.20	1.59
24	B 56 ID	—	A	0.41	0.81	15 Pz Gr	FD	—	0.10	2.06
25	B 56 ID	—	HD	1.98	0.42	15 Pz Gr	A	—	0.14	2.24
26	US 3 ID	—	A	0.34	0.66	3 Pz Gr	FD	—	0.25	1.36
27	B 56 ID	A	A	0.67	1.25	15 Pz Gr	FD	FD	1.06	3.27
28	B 46 ID	A	A	0.70	0.84	15 Pz Gr	FD	FD	0.13	2.95
29	US 36 ID	A	—	0.72	0.59	15 & 29 Pz	—	FD	0.30	1.82
30	B 1 ID	A	—	2.99	0.81	3 Pz Gr	—	HD	0.74	4.60
31	B 1 ID	HD	—	0.34	0.73	3 Pz Gr	—	A	0.46	1.10
32	B 1 ID	—	A	1.39	0.87	3 Pz Gr	PD	—	0.49	1.71
33	B 1 ID	HPD	—	7.45	3.14	C C G	—	A	2.53	3.11
34	B 1 ID	HPD	—	4.09	1.56	3 Pz Gr	—	A	0.64	1.47
35	US 45 ID	HPD	—	0.81	1.40	65 ID	—	A	1.13	1.33
36	B 1 ID	—	HPD	1.75	1.35	C C G	A	—	0.98	2.08
37	US 45 ID	—	A	0.43	1.77	715 Lt I	HPD	—	1.46	1.50
38	US 45 ID	HPD	—	1.60	1.88	4 Divs	—	A	1.33	1.26
39	B 56 ID	HPD	HPD	4.34	1.88	65 ID & 4 Para	A	A	1.69	4.56
40	US 45 ID	PD	—	0.97	0.78	114 Lt I	—	A	0.56	1.28
41	US 88 ID	A	—	1.48	3.09	94 & 71	—	FD	5.59	2.33
42	US 85 ID	A	A	3.19	2.62	94 ID	FD	FD	4.42	4.46
43	US 88 ID	A	—	0.94	2.89	94 & 71	—	Del	4.44	1.95
44	US 85 ID	A	—	1.63	1.98	94 ID	—	FD	2.95	3.04
45	US 88 ID	A	—	0.76	2.10	94 ID	—	HD	3.64	2.33
46	US 85 ID	A	—	0.58	2.06	94 ID	—	Del	3.15	2.77
47	US 88 ID	A	—	0.53	1.50	94 ID	—	Del	1.90	3.14
48	US 85 ID	A	—	0.49	1.64	94 ID	—	HD	1.90	4.34
49	B 5 ID	A	—	0.67	2.43	4 Para	—	FD	1.86	1.92
50	B 1 ID	A	—	0.56	2.48	65 ID	—	FD	2.16	1.58
51	US 1 AD	A	—	1.46	2.04	3 & 362	—	FD	3.52	1.74
52	US 3 ID	A	—	2.54	2.48	362 ID	—	FD	4.52	2.94
53	US 85 ID	A	—	0.30	1.43	29 Pz	—	W/d	1.34	1.47
54	US 1 AD	—	A	5.25	3.84	362 ID	FD	—	10.70	3.54
55	US 34 ID	—	A	0.87	2.29	3 Pz Gr	FD	—	2.18	1.45
56	US 45 ID	A	—	0.93	2.34	65 ID	—	FD	2.74	1.76
57	B 5 ID	A	—	0.52	1.81	4 Para	—	FD	1.63	1.60

RESULTS OF QJM ENGAGEMENT CALCULATIONS, WORLD WAR II (continued)

	Allied Data					German Data				Anal
Allied Units	Posture/ Success S	F	Percent Cas/Day	Score Effect	German Units	Posture Success S	F	Percent Cas/Day	Score Effect	Nf/N
S 34 ID	–	A	1.19	1.97	3 Pz Gr	FD	–	2.86	2.24	2.83
S 1 AD & 45 ID	A	A	1.46	2.02	3 & 65	FD	FD	2.91	2.16	1.88
1 & 5 ID	A	–	0.75	2.36	4 Para	–	FD	3.92	2.44	3.50
S XX Corps	A	–	0.19	1.20	First Army	–	PD	2.01	1.48	2.71
S XX Corps	A	–	0.46	1.09	First Army	–	Del	0.68	1.60	1.44
S XX Corps	–	A	0.59	1.11	First Army	FD	–	0.53	1.76	1.54
S 7 AD	A	–	0.72	1.97	First Army	–	HD	6.95	2.24	1.88
S 7 AD	A	–	0.19	1.03	48 ID + 11 Pz & elem	–	PD-W	2.02	2.13	2.87
& 4 AD	A-HD	A-HD	0.82	1.14	XIII SS Corps	FD-A	FD-A	1.99	3.21	3.90
S 4 AD & elem 35	A	–	1.54	0.87	11 Pz & 361 ID	–	Del	0.87	3.54	3.43
S 4 AD & elem 26	–	A	0.89	1.27	Elem 11 Pz & 361 ID	Del	–	1.08	1.98	1.59
S 4 AD	A-HD	–	0.37	1.41	PzLehr & 361 ID	–	HD-A	2.09	1.26	1.48
S 4 AD	A	–	0.35	1.54	Pz Lehr Div	–	HD	3.33	1.17	2.27
S 4 AD	–	A	0.16	1.01	Pz Lehr Div	Del	–	1.07	0.76	2.42
S 4 AD	A	–	0.70	0.73	11 Pz, Pz Lehr, & 25 Pz Gr D	–	PD	1.08	1.93	3.27
S 4 AD	–	A	0.51	0.92	25 PzGr & 11 Pz	FD	–	1.21	1.52	3.02
S XII Corps	A	–	0.86	1.69	XIII SS & LXXXIX Corps	–	FD	4.14	2.79	4.22
S XII Corps	A	A	0.87	1.74	XIII SS & LXXXIX Corps	Del	Del	3.23	2.54	3.26
S XII Corps	A	–	0.46	1.45	XIII SS & LXXXIX Corps	–	Del	1.91	1.82	2.75
S XII Corps	–	A	0.27	1.13	XIII SS & LXXXIX Corps	Del	–	1.32	1.29	2.93
S XII Corps	A	–	0.42	1.39	XIII SS & XC Corps	–	Del	1.88	1.47	2.86

Figure E-3 / WORLD WAR II SCORE EFFECTIVENESS STATISTICAL COMPARISON

I. OVERALL, GERMANS VS. WESTERN ALLIES
(78 Engagements)

	Total Numbers Engaged	Total Casualties	Average % Casualties /day	Average Score Effectiveness
W. Allies	1,783,237	47,743	1.25	1.45
Germans	940,198	48,585	1.83	2.25

II. BY POSTURE, VS. WESTERN ALLIES
(78 Engagements)

	Allies	Germans	German Preponderance
Attack: Successful	1.47	3.02	2.05
Failure	1.20	2.28	1.90
Defense: Successful	1.60	2.24	1.40
Failure	1.37	2.29	1.67
Average*	1.45	2.31	1.59

*Averages based on total battles.

Figure E-4 / TENTATIVE ESTIMATES, AVERAGE DIVISION COMBAT EFFECTIVENESS (78-Engagement Data Base)

Divisions/ Corps	No. of Eng.	Average Intensity	Average Differential from Normal	Average Score Effectiveness	Assessed Combat Effectiveness	Remarks
US						
1st Armored	3	6.77	-0.08	2.63	86.60	Rome campaign only; value seems high
3d Infantry	4	4.80	-0.87	1.31	66.17	Value seems low
4th Armored	8	3.95	-1.47	1.11	61.59	
34th Infantry	5	4.14	-1.52	1.40	65.28	
45th Infantry	9	4.29	-1.30	1.40	64.50	
85th Infantry	5	5.28	-1.73	1.95	71.95	Rome campaign only
88th Infantry	4	5.02	0.28	2.40	84.64	Rome campaign only
XII Corps	5	4.78	-0.48	1.48	69.69	
XX Corps	3	3.93	-1.93	1.13	<u>60.09</u>	
		Average Effectiveness, US			70.06	
British						
1st Infantry	8	5.71	...	1.66	70.37	
5th Infantry	3	4.47	...	2.13	74.92	Value seems high
7th Armored	3	2.97	...	1.11	64.50	
46th Infantry	6	5.27	...	1.11	65.76	Value seems low
56th Infantry	9	5.56	...	1.08	<u>54.14</u>	
		Average Effectiveness, British			65.94	
		Allies Average Effectiveness			68.59%	
German						
H. Goering Pz	5	3.52	0.57	2.54	87.43	
Pz Lehr	4	4.70	0.57	1.28	70.63	Value seems low
3d Pz Gren	16	4.24	0.65	2.10	81.83	Value seems low
4th Para Div	4	6.03	1.25	2.63	90.90	
11th Pz	5	3.88	1.18	2.44	88.13	
15th Pz Gren	9	1.52	0.11	2.09	79.90	
16th Pz	7	3.50	-0.38	2.84	88.62	
65th Infantry	5	5.82	0.54	2.28	83.87	
94th Infantry	8	6.46	-0.09	3.05	92.03	
362d Infantry	3	9.10	-1.16	2.74	84.33	
XIII SS Corps	5	7.08	0.76	1.98	<u>80.60</u>	
		Average Effectiveness, German			84.36%	Exceeds Allied average by 23%

Figure E-5 / KURSK STATISTICAL COMPARISONS
Oboyan Sector, July 5-11, 1943

	Soviet	German	Ratio
Manpower	98,000	62,000	1.58 - 1.00
Tanks and Assault Guns	817	650	1.26 - 1.00
Artillery and Mortars			
(75mm & over)	1,675	1,014	1.65 - 1.00
Air Support Sorties (est.)	3,150	3,150	1.00 - 1.00
Casualties	22,000	13,600	1.62 - 1.00
Casualties/Day	2,444	1,511	1.62 - 1.00
% Casualties/Day	2.49	2.49	1.02 - 1.00
Tank Losses	450	350	1.29 - 1.00
Relative Combat Effectiveness			
(approx.)	1.0	2.35	1.00 - 2.35
Score Effectiveness	1.39	2.55	1.00 - 1.83

Figure E-6 / SOVIET-GERMAN FORCE
COMPARISONS EASTERN FRONT, 1944

	Russian	German	Ratios
Field Force Strength	6,100,000	3,500,000	1.74/1 - 2.44/1
		2,500,000	
Relative Combat			
Effectiveness*			1.34/1 - 1.88/1*
Total Battle and			
Non-Battle Casualties	7,000,000	1,800,000	
Non-Battle Casualties	2,000,000 (est)	700,000	
Battle Losses	5,000,000 (min)	1,100,000	4.55/1.00
Battlefield Exchange Ratio			
Per man (3.5 mil Germans)	0.18	1.4	1.00/7.78
Relative Score			
Effectiveness*			1.00/5.98

*Defensive posture factor applied: 1.3

NOTES TO APPENDIX E

[1] Dupuy, *op. cit.*,

Appendix F
HALDER THE ENIGMA

General von Seeckt was known in the German Army as the Sphinx. General Franz Halder, the last true Chief of the German General Staff, was fully as uncommunicative and inscrutable as Seeckt. His role as leader of the Army's resistance to Hitler throughout World War II is still not fully known and may never be.

Hitler had selected Halder as Chief of the General Staff in September 1938 to replace anti-Nazi General Ludwig Beck, because he was convinced that Halder was a totally apolitical soldier. Usually a good judge of men, in this case Hitler was deceived by Halder's enigmatic personality. It is true that Halder seems to have had no interest in political affairs and that he was determined to remain aloof from politics. But he was also strongly anti-Nazi and had in fact been conspiring with Beck to overthrow Hitler when the British and French surrender at Munich made this impossible. Apparently he saw no contradiction between avoidance of politics and the overthrow of an evil dictator.

After the war Halder discussed with Allied military men and with a number of German and American historians the basic outlines of his secret role as one of the leaders of the anti-Nazi resistance from 1939 through July 20, 1944, as well as the tortures and interrogations to which he was subjected in prison from July 1944 until he was liberated from Dachau in May 1945. But he has never revealed the details of his resistance activities, nor has he seriously defended himself against charges that he failed to seize opportunities to overthrow Hitler in 1939 and later. He has hinted, however, that someday there will be more "information concerning the small resistance group within OKH, centered around myself."[1]

Equally enigmatic is the following comment: "I personally have proof that my Bavarian origin would have caused at least a silent opposition among the commanders, who in many instances came from the old Prussian military families; and for this reason, it would have made doubtful the direct implementation of any orders issued by me."[2]

As it was, Halder successfully concealed from Hitler and the Gestapo all of his conspiratorial activities (even though he was strongly suspected after the July 20, 1944, assassination attempt). And in the four years he served as Chief of the General Staff, he endeavored to serve Germany faithfully, in the process carrying out the orders of Germany's supreme leader, as had his fifteen predecessors. Like them, also, he was evidently at first confident that the institutionalized genius of the General Staff could make up in peace and war for the military shortcomings of the current political leader.

Halder knew that Hitler was unlike any of the kings, emperors, or

---

*Adapted from the Introduction to *The War Diaries of Franz Halder*, Colorado Springs, 1976.

presidents with whom his predecessors had had to deal, and in those four years he was to learn that institutionalized military genius had its limitations. During those years, Hitler virtually destroyed the General Staff. Thus Halder, although he had three successors before the war ended, was the last true Chief of the General Staff established by Scharnhorst.

In cryptic notes, largely written in shorthand, Halder kept a personal journal of the important events of the last three of those years, recording events leading to his own downfall, the ruin of his beloved General Staff, and the destruction of Germany. Those notes were to become known as the *War Diaries* (or *War Journal*) *of Colonel General Franz Halder.*

Unfortunately, the private journal only partially reveals Halder—as a man, as a soldier, and as the director of what was perhaps the finest war machine in all military history. Nevertheless, some hints can be found in his sparse entries. Additional insights may be gained by comparing what appears in other records and documents about events discussed by Halder in his journal.[3] Also, after the war, Halder cooperated with the United States Army's military history effort to compile a series of monographs about the war by former German senior officers; one can learn much about Halder's military attitudes and strategic thinking by reading his introductions and commentaries on the monographs prepared by his colleagues.

All of the chiefs of the General Staff, from Scharnhorst through Halder, were extremely intelligent men and exceptionally capable soldiers. With the possible exception of Scharnhorst himself, however, and also possibly of Schlieffen,* none of these brilliant soldiers could be considered a genius of the caliber of Napoleon or Frederick the Great; however, with their General Staff colleagues, they all epitomized institutionalized military excellence.

As men, despite their great individuality, they fall into two general categories. There were the politically conscious intellectuals, like Scharnhorst himself, who understood and cared about the relationship of the Army to the State, and about their own responsibility to the State and to history, but who were always careful to subordinate their personal opinions completely to the decisions of established authority. Then there were the equally intellectual military concentrators, who were not interested in—or did not have time for, or feared—politics and political affairs. Of these Moltke was the prime example; fortunately for his place in history, he was teamed with a political genius, Bismarck.

Beck was the last of the line of politically conscious chiefs of staff, running from Scharnhorst and Gneisenau through Wilhelm Groener and Hans von Seeckt. Halder (if we ignore—as we may—his three successors) was apparently the last of the military concentrators, from Karl von Müffling through Moltke and Hindenburg-Ludendorff. Unfortunately for their places in history, Paul von Hindenburg and Erich Ludendorff lacked a Bismarck with whom to collaborate; so did Halder.

After the war, some German generals and nonmilitary scholars of several nations criticized Halder for not having defied Hitler, and for having subserviently carried out Hitler's orders to wage wars of aggression. General Frederick Hossbach wrote that Halder "placed the reputation of the High Command at the

---

*Neither of these men had an opportunity to exercise high command in war.

disposal of an immoral political leadership and weakly gambled it away.... In respect to the security of the nation, [he] failed to exert . . . political, military, and moral responsibility."[4]

Gordon Craig, in his *Politics of the Prussian Army*, compares Halder unfavorably to Beck, because Halder was not, Craig says, "so easily moved by moral issues."[5] This may be unfair to Beck as well as to Halder. Yet Hossbach and Craig are both probably right in principle, and with the benefit of objective hindsight. But—at the time and in the circumstances—what was a man with Halder's background and training to do? And what, in fact, did Beck accomplish by taking another course?*

Halder was a conscientious soldier, who performed with his very best military efforts in patriotic devotion to duty as he saw it. His best was very good indeed and of a technical competence truly worthy of comparison with Moltke. But the odds were too great, and his best was not good enough to accomplish the miracles that Hitler needed for victory.

---

*General Friedrich Fromm—an old rival—allowed Beck to commit suicide when the assassination plot failed on July 20, 1944. For that act of mercy Fromm later was tortured and executed by a Nazi firing squad.

NOTES TO APPENDIX F

[1] "Command & Commanders in Modern Military History," *Proceedings,* Second Military History Symposium, U.S. Air Force Academy, Colorado Springs, Colo., 1971, p. 191. This was an excellent opportunity for Halder to present himself and his wartime activities in the most favorable possible light. He deliberately passed it up.

[2] *Ibid.,* p. 197.

[3] See, for instance, Earl F. Ziemke, "Franz Halder at Orsha: The German General Staff Seeks a Consensus," *Military Affairs,* December 1975, p. 173.

[4] Hossbach, *Zwischen Wehrmacht und Hitler,* as quoted in Craig, *op. cit.,* p. 497.

[5] Craig, *op. cit.,* p. 499.

BIBLIOGRAPHY

Addington, Larry H., *The Blitzkrieg Era and the German General Staff, 1865-1941.* New Brunswick, N.J.: 1971.

Allen, Charles R., Jr., *Heusinger of the Fourth Reich.* New York: 1963.

Arenz, Wilhelm, *et al.*, *Rückzug und Verfolgung-Zwei Kampfarten, 1757-1944. Beiträge zur Militär-und Kriegsgeschichte,* Vol. 1. Stuttgart: 1960.

Aschenbrandt, Heinrich, *Kriegsgeschichtsschreibung und Kriegsgeschichtsstudium im Deutschen Heere.* Monograph, Historical Division, U.S. European Command, 1953.

Balck, William, *Development of Tactics—World War* Translated by Harry Bell. Fort Leavenworth: 1922.

Barnett, Correlli, *The Swordbearers.* New York: 1964.

Benoist-Mechin, Jacques, *Sixty Days That Shook the World; the Fall of France: 1940.* Translated by Peter Wiles. New York: 1963.

—— *Histoire de l'Armee Allemande.* 10 vols. Paris: 1938-1964.

Bloem, Walter, *The Advance from Mons, 1914.* Translated by G. C. Wynne. London: 1930.

Blumenson, Martin, *The Duel for France.* Boston: 1963.

Bretnor, Reginald, *Decisive Warfare.* Harrisburg: 1969.

Bronsart von Schellendorf, Paul, *The German General Staff,* London: 1908.

Bryant, Arthur, *The Turn of the Tide.* Alanbrooke diaries. New York: 1957.

Caidin, Martin, *The Tigers Are Burning.* New York: 1974.

Carver, Michael, *Tobruk.* London: 1964.

Cave Brown, Anthony, *Bodyguard of Lies.* New York: 1976.

Chandler, David, *The Campaigns of Napoleon.* New York: 1966.

Churchill, Winston S., *The Second World War.* 6 vols. Boston: 1948-1953.

—— *The World Crisis.* 6 vols. New York, 1931.

Clausewitz, Karl von, *On War.* Translated by O. J. Matthis Jolles. Washington: 1950.

—— *Principles of War.* Translated by Hans W. Gatzke. Harrisburg: 1942.

Cole, Hugh, *The Lorraine Campaign. U.S. Army in World War II.* Washington: 1950.

—— *The Ardennes: Battle of the Bulge. U.S. Army in World War II.* Washington: 1965.

Craig, Gordon, *The Politics of the Prussian Army, 1640-1945.* New York: 1956.

De Gaulle, Charles, *The Call to Honor, 1940-1942.* Translated by Jonathan Griffin. London: 1955.

Degener, Hermann, *Wer Ists.* Berlin: 1928.

---

*Major portions of all German-language books listed here have been translated for the author by Lucille M. Petterson.

Demeter, K., *The German Officer Corps, 1650-1945.* London: 1965.

Deutsch, Harold C., Charles v. P. von Luttichau, Peter Paret, Walter Warlimont, Leo Freiherr Geyr von Schweppenburg, Hasso von Manteuffel, Erich von Manstein, Franz Halder, Adolf Heusinger. "The End of the Prussian Military Tradition in Germany." *Proceedings,* Second Military History Symposium, U.S. Air Force Academy, Colorado Springs: 1971.

De Weerd, H. A., ed., *Studies on War.* Washington: 1943.

Dupuy, R. Ernest, *St. Vith: Lion in the Way.* Washington: 1949.

—— and T. N. Dupuy, *Military Heritage of America.* New York: 1956.

—— *The Encyclopedia of Military History.* New York: 1970.

Dupuy, T. N., *A Military History of World War II.* 19 vols. New York: 1962-1965.

—— *The Military Life of Frederick the Great of Prussia.* New York: 1969.

—— *The Military Lives of Hindenburg and Ludendorff of Imperial Germany.* New York: 1970.

—— *The Military Life of Adolf Hitler: Fuhrer of Germany.* New York: 1969.

—— *The Military Life of Napoleon, Emperor of the French.* New York: 1969.

—— et al. *A Military History of World War I.* 12 vols. New York: 1967.

Earle, Edward Mead, ed., *Makers of Modern Strategy.* Princeton: 1943.

Erfurth, Waldeman, *Surprise.* Translated by Stefan T. Possony and Daniel Vilfroy. Harrisburg: 1943.

—— *Training and Development of German General Staff Officers.* Monograph. Historical Division, U.S. European Command, 1948.

Ergang, Robert, *The Potsdam Fuhrer: Frederick William I.* New York:1941.

Falkenhayn, Erich von, *The German General Staff and Its Decisions, 1914-1916.* New York: 1920.

Falls, Cyril, *The Art of War from the Age of Napoleon to the Present Day.* New York: 1961.

—— *A Hundred Years of War.* London: 1953.

Foertsch, Hermann, *The Art of Modern Warfare.* Translated by Theodore W. Knauth. New York: 1940.

Förster, Gerhard, *et al., Der Preussisch-deutsche Generalstab, 1640-1965.* East Berlin: 1966.

Frederick II, *Instructions of Frederick the Great for his Generals. Roots of Strategy.* Edited by Thomas R. Phillips. Harrisburg: 1941.

Fried, Hans E., *The Guilt of the German Army.* New York: 1942.

Fry, James C., *Combat Soldier.* Washington: 1968.

Fuller, J. F. C., *The Conduct of War, 1789-1961.* New Brunswick, N.J.: 1961.

—— *A Military History of the Western World.* 3 vols. New York: 1954.

Germany, Reichswehrministerium, *Troop Command.* Translated by U.S. War Department. Washington: 1933.

Goerlitz, Walter, *History of the German General Staff.* Translated by Brian Battershaw.* New York: 1961.

—— *Der Deutsche Generalstab.* Frankfurt, 1952.*

---

*There are substantial and relevant portions of the original version not included in the 1961 Battershaw translation.

Gordon, Harold J., Jr. *The Reichswehr and the German Republic,* 1919-1926. Princeton: 1957.

Goutard, A. *The Battle of France, 1940.* Translated by A. R. P. Burgess, New York: 1959.

Greiner, Heinz, *Kampf um Rom Inferno am Po.* Neckargemünd: 1967.

Groener-Geyer, Dorothea, *General Groener: Soldat und Staatsmann.* Frankfurt: 1955.

Groener, Wilhelm, *Lebenserinnerungen [Memoirs],* Göttingen: 1957.

Guderian, Heinz, *Panzer Leader.* New York: 1952.

Halder, Franz. *The Private War Journal of Franz Halder.* Colorado Springs: 1976.

Hermann, Carl-Hans, *Deutsche Militärgeschichte−Einführung.* Frankfurt: 1968.

Hindenburg, Paul von, *Out of My Life.* 2 vols. New York: 1919.

Historical Evaluation and Research Organization, *Historical Trends Related to Weapon Lethality.* 4 vols. Washington: 1964.

—— *Historical Data on Tactical Air Operations; The Volturno Campaign, 13 October-15 November 1943.* McLean, Va.: 1969.

—— *German Evaluation of Allied Air Interdiction in World War II.* McLean, Va.: 1969.

—— *Historical Data on Tactical Air Operations; the Rome Campaign, 11 May-17 June, 1944.* McLean, Va.: 1970.

—— *Historical Data Research on Tactical Air Operations−Interdiction from Falaise to Westwall.* Dunn Loring, Va.: 1970.

—— *Use of Historical Data in Evaluating Military Effectiveness.* Dunn Loring, Va.: 1970.

—— *Historical Data Research on Air Interdiction in World War II.* 2 vols. Dunn Loring, Va.: 1971, 1972.

—— *A Study of the Relationship of Tactical Air Support Operations in Land Combat.* Dunn Loring, Va.: 1971.

—— *Opposed Rates of Advance of Large Forces in Europe.* Dunn Loring, Va.: 1972.

—— *Historical Evaluation of Barrier Effectiveness.* Dunn Loring, Va.: 1973.

—— *German and Soviet Replacement Systems in World War II.* Dunn Loring, Va.: 1975.

Hitler, Adolf, *Mein Kampf.* Harrisburg: 1939.

Hittle, F. D., *The Military Staff, Its History and Development.* Harrisburg: 1949.

Hohenlohe-Ingelfingen, Prince Kraft zu, *Letters on Artillery.* Translated by N. L. Walford. London: 1898.

Höhn, Reinhard, *Scharnhorsts Vermächtnis.* Bonn: 1952.

Holborn, Hajo, *A History of Modern Germany, 1648-1945.* 2 vols. New York: 1969.

Holder, L.D., "Seeckt and the *Führeheer,*" *Military Review,* October 1976, p. 71.

Howard, Michael, *The Franco-Prussian War.* New York: 1962.

——, ed., *Soldiers and Governments.* Bloomington, Ind.: 1959.

Huzar, Elias, *The Purse and the Sword,* Ithaca, N.Y.: 1950.

Irvine, Dallas, "The French and Prussian Staff Systems Before 1870." *Journal of the American History Foundation,* ii, 1938.

—— "The Origin of Capital Staffs." *Journal of Modern History,* June, 1938.

Jany, Curt, *Geschichte der Preussischen Armee vom 15, Jahrhundert bis 1914.* Osnabrück: 1967.

Jukes, Geoffrey, *Kursk: The Clash of Armor.* New York: 1969.

Kessel, Eberhard, *Moltke.* Stuttgart: 1957.

Kesselring, Albert, *A Soldier's Record.* New York: 1952.

Kitchen, Martin, *A Military History of Germany, from the Eighteenth Century to the Present Day.* Bloomington, Ind.: 1975.

Klein, Burton H., *Germany's Economic Preparedness for War.* Cambridge, Mass.: 1959.

Kluck, Alexander von, *The March on Paris and the Battle of the Marne, 1914.* London: 1923.

Koehler, Erik, and Helmuth Reinhardt. *The Chief of Army Equipment and Commander of the Replacement Army, OKH.* Monograph, Historical Division, U.S. European Command.

Kohler, Eric, *The Germans.* Princeton: 1974.

Kohn, Hans. *The Mind of Germany.* New York: 1960.

Kosch, Wilhelm, *Biographisches Staatshandbuch.* Bern: 1963.

Kuhl, Hermann J. von, *The Marne Campaign, 1914.* Ft. Leavenworth, Kan.: 1936.

—— and Walter F. A. von Bergmann. *Movements and Supply of the German First Army During August and September 1914.* Translated by U.S. Army War College. Washington: 1929.

Leach, Barry A. *German Strategy Against Russia, 1939-1941.* Oxford: 1973.

Liddell Hart, Basil H., ed. *The German Generals Talk.* New York: 1948.

Liman von Sanders, Otto V. K., *My Five Years in Turkey.* Annapolis: 1927.

Ludendorff, Erich, *Ludendorff's Own Story.* 2 vols. New York: 1919.

—— *The General Staff and its Problems,* translated by F. A. Holt. New York, undated, c. 1921.

McElwee, William, *The Art of War: Waterloo to Mons.* Bloomington, Ind.: 1974.

Mackesy, Kenneth, *Guderian, Creator of the Blitzkrieg.* New York: 1976.

Manchester, William, *The Arms of Krupp.* Boston: 1968.

Manstein, Erich von, *Lost Victories.* Chicago: 1958.

Mason, Herbert Molloy, Jr., *The Rise of the Luftwaffe, 1918-1940.* New York: 1973.

Maude, Frederick N., *The Jena Campaign, 1806.* London: 1909.

Meier-Welker, Hans, ed., *Untersuchungen zur Geschichte des Offizierkorps. Beiträge zur Militär-und Kriegsgeschichte.* vol. 4. Stuttgart: 1962.

Mellenthin, F. W., von, *Panzer Battles, 1939-1945.* London: 1955.

Melville, C. F., *The Russian Face of Germany.* London: 1932.

Menne, Bernhard, *Blood and Steel: the Rise of the House of Krupp.* New York: 1938.

Model, Hansgeorg, *Der deutsche Generalstaboffizier.* Frankfurt: 1968.

Moltke, Helmuth K. B. von, *Strategy: Its Theory and Application: The Wars for German Unification, 1866-1871.* Translated by the British War Office. London: 1907.

—— *The Franco-German War.* London: 1914.

Morgan, John H., *Assize of Arms: The Disarmament of Germany and Her Rearmament, 1919-1939.* New York: 1946.

Mrazek, James, *The Art of Winning Wars.* New York: 1968.
—— *The Fall of Eben Emael.* Washington: 1970.
Murphy, Robert, *Diplomat Among Warriors.* New York: 1964.
Nickerson, Hoffman, *The Armed Horde, 1793-1939.* New York: 1940.
Paret, Peter, *Yorck and the Era of Prussian Reform, 1807-1815.* Princeton: 1966.
Parkinson, Roger, *Clausewitz.* New York: 1971.
Post, Gaines, Jr., *The Civil-Military Fabric of Weimar Foreign Policy.* Princeton: 1973.
Pratt, E. A., *The Rise of Rail Power in War and Conquest, 1833-1914.* New York: 1915.
Ritter, Gerhard, *The Sword and the Scepter: The Problem of Militarism in Germany.* Coral Gables, Fla.: 1969.
—— *The Schlieffen Plan.* New York: 1958.
Robinson, C. W., F. N. Maude, H. H. Verrinder Crowe, C. F. Atkinson, *et al. Wars of the Nineteenth Century.* London: 1914.
Rommel, Erwin, *The Rommel Papers.* Translated by Paul Findlay. New York: 1953.
Ropp, Theodore, *War in the Modern World.* Durham, N.C.: 1959.
Rosinski, Herbert, *The German Army.* Washington: 1944.
Rousset, Leonce, *Histoire General de la Guerre Franco-Allemande.* 2 vols. Paris: 1911.
—— "Scharnhorst to Schleiffen; The Rise and Decline of German Military Thought," *Naval War College Review,* Summer 1976, p. 83.
Sajer, Guy, *The Forgotten Soldier.* New York: 1967.
Savage, Paul L., and Richard A. Gabriel, "Cohesion and Disintegration in the American Army," *Armed Forces and Society,* Vol. 2. No. 3, Spring, 1976.
Schlieffen, Alfred von, *Cannae.* Translated by the U.S. Army Command and General Staff School. Fort Leavenworth: 1931.
—— *Briefe.* Edited by Eberhard Kessel. Göttingen: 1958.
Schmidt-Richberg, Wiegand, *Die Generalstäbe in Deutschland, 1871-1945.* Stuttgart: 1960.
Seeckt, Hans von, *The Future of the German Empire,* New York: 1930.
Senger und Etterlin, Fridolin von, *Neither Fear nor Hope.* New York: 1963.
Shanahan, William O., *Prussian Military Reforms, 1786-1813.* New York: 1945.
Shils, Edward A., and Morris Janowitz, "Cohesion and Disintegration in the Wehrmacht in World War II," *The Public Opinion Quarterly,* Vol. 12, No. 2, Spring, 1948.
Shirer, William L., *The Rise and Fall of the Third Reich.* New York: 1960.
—— *The Collapse of the Third Republic.* New York: 1969.
Speer, Albert, *Inside the Third Reich.* Translated by Richard and Clara Winston. New York: 1970.
Speidel, Hans. *Invasion, 1944.* Chicago: 1950.
Stacy, C. P., "Hitler and the German Generals." *Canadian Army Journal,* April, 1953.
Stamps, T. Dodson, and Vincent Esposito, *et al. A Short Military History of World War I.* West Point: 1950.
—— *A Military History of World War II.* 2 vols. West Point: 1953.

Stockfisch, J. A., *Plowshares into Swords*. New York: 1973.

Stockhorst, Erich, *Fünftausend Köpfe: Wer war Was im 3. Reich*. Velbert: 1967.

Taylor, Telford, *Sword and Swastika*. New York: 1957.

Teske, Hermann, *Die silbernen Spiegel: Generalstabsdienst unter der Lupe*, Heidelberg: 1952.

Tyng, Sewell, *The Campaign of the Marne*. New York: 1935.

U. K. Air Ministry, *Rise and Fall of the German Air Force*. London: 1948.

U. S. Army War College, *March of the German First Army, August 12-24, 1914*. Washington: 1931.

—— *Organization and Administration of the Theater of Operations: The German First Army, 1914*. Washington: 1931.

U.S. Department of the Army. *The German Campaign in Russia: Planning and Operations (1940-1942)*. Washington: 1955.

—— *Military Improvisation During the Russian Campaign*. Washington: 1951.

U.S. Military Academy. *Great Captains Before Napoleon*. West Point: 1949.

—— *Jomini, Clausewitz, and Schlieffen*. West Point, 1951.

—— *Notes for the Course in History of the Military Art*. West Point: 1954.

U.S. National Archives. Various microfilms of German World War II records.

U.S. War Department. *German Tactical Doctrine*. Washington: 1942.

Vagts, Alfred, *A History of Militarism*. New York: 1937.

Waite, Robert G. L., *Vanguard of Nazism*. Cambridge, Mass.: 1952.

Warlimont, Walter, *Inside Hitler's Headquarters, 1939-1945*. New York: 1964.

Wedgwood, C. V., *The Thirty Years War*. New York: 1961.

Westphal, Siegfried, *The Fatal Decisions*. London: 1965.

—— *The German Army in the West*. London: 1951.

Wheeler-Bennett, John W., *The Nemesis of Power*. New York: 1954.

Wilkinson, Spenser, *The Brain of an Army*. London: 1889.

Wilson, Andrew, *The Bomb and the Computer: Wargaming from Ancient Chinese Mapboard to Atomic Computer*. New York: 1969.

Winterbottom, F. W., *The Ultrasecret*. New York: 1975.

Wright, Quincy, *A Study of War*. 2 vols. Chicago: 1942.

Yorck von Wartenburg, *Napoleon as a General*. Translated by Walter H. James. 2 vols. London: c. 1901.

Ziemke, Earl F., *Stalingrad to Berlin: The German Defeat in the East*. U.S. Army Historical Series. Washington: 1968.

—— "Franz Halder at Orsha: The German General Staff Seeks a Consensus." *Military Affairs*, December, 1945, p. 173.

INDEX